B. B. Warfield's Scientifically Constructive Theological Scholarship

The Evangelical Theological Society Monograph Series

David W. Baker, Editor

VOLUME 4
*Did Jesus Teach Salvation By Works?
The Role of Works in Salvation in the Synoptic Gospels*
—Alan P. Stanley

VOLUME 5
*Has God Said? Scripture, the Word of God,
and the Crisis of Theological Authority*
—John Douglas Morrison

VOLUME 6
*The Light of Discovery:
Studies in Honor of Edwin M. Yamauchi*
—John D. Wineland, editor

VOLUME 7
*The Lord Is the Spirit: The Authority of the Holy Spirit
in Contemporary Theology and Church Practice*
—John A. Studebaker

VOLUME 8
The Sinner in Luke
—Dwayne H. Adams

VOLUME 9
*The Contemporary Church and the Early Church:
Case Studies in Ressourcement*
—Paul Hartog, editor

B. B. Warfield's Scientifically Constructive Theological Scholarship

DAVID P. SMITH

edited by June Corduan

With a Foreword by Alan Strange

☙PICKWICK *Publications* · Eugene, Oregon

B. B. Warfield's Scientifically Constructive Theological Scholarship

Evangelical Theological Society Monograph Series 10

Copyright © 2011 David P. Smith. All rights reserved. Except for brief quotations in critical publications or reviews, no part of this book may be reproduced in any manner without prior written permission from the publisher. Write: Permissions, Wipf and Stock Publishers, 199 W. 8th Ave., Suite 3, Eugene, OR 97401.

Pickwick Publications
An Imprint of Wipf and Stock Publishers
199 W. 8th Ave., Suite 3
Eugene, OR 97401

www.wipfandstock.com

ISBN 13: 978-1-61097-185-0

Cataloging-in-Publication data:

Smith, David P.

    B. B. Warfield's scientifically constructive theological scholarship / David P. Smith, edited by June Corduan ; with a foreword by Alan Strange.

Evangelical Theological Society Monograph Series 10

xxii + 320 p. ; 23 cm. Includes bibliographical references and index.

ISBN 13: 978-1-61097-185-0

    1. Warfield, Benjamin Breckinridge, 1851–1921. 2. Theology, Doctrinal. I. Corduan, June. II. Title. III. Series.

BV4490 S4 2011

Manufactured in the U.S.A.

My greatest thanks are due to my wife, Tracy.

You alone have endured all the hardships, all the discouragements, all the disappointments, all the successes—and the clearing of every hurdle. As if the pursuit of a doctoral degree was not enough, you cared lovingly and faithfully for the three children God blessed us with during this process. You endured four moves in eight years. Through it all you have persevered. You have loved me and the children, cancelled out my doubts, done many tasks so that I could read and write, and remained true to the end. Whatever fruit may come from this writing will be greatly the result of your Christ-like perseverance, and so to you I dedicate this work.

Contents

Foreword by Alan D. Strange / *ix*

Acknowledgments / *xi*

Abbreviations / *xiii*

Introduction / 1

1. A Historiographical Review of Old Princeton and Warfield / 15
2. B. B. Warfield: A Biographical Summary / 47
3. Contextual Issues: Biblical Criticism, Theology, and Philosophy in the Nineteenth Century / 63
4. Princeton and Warfield: Responses to Contextual Issues / 88
5. Theology and Epistemology: Science and the Context of Apologetics / 120
6. Systematic Theology's Legitimacy: What Is Christianity? / 156
7. Apologetics in Principle: Establishing the Biblical Gospel / 192
8. Apologetics in Practice: Biblical Doctrines, Morality, Subjectivity, and the Supernatural / 238

Conclusion / 298

Bibliography / 309

Foreword

David Smith is part of a revolution: not a political revolution, but a scholarly one calling for a reexamination of how we understand B.B. Warfield, and others, with respect to their appropriation and use of Scottish Common Sense Realism (SCSR). Thomas Kuhn, renowned Princeton and MIT philosopher and historian of science, spoke of "normal" science as that which works within an established, stable paradigm. As anomalies—data that do not fit the reigning paradigm—accrue, however, they threaten the "normal" operations of science. Those who seek to make sense of such anomalies outside of the regnant paradigm become harbingers of a paradigm shift, part of a revolution to replace one interpretive grid with another.[1] David Smith is no Che Guevara, but he is involved in a revolution in the way in which scholars are viewing the philosophical influences that pertained at Old Princeton Theological Seminary in the nineteenth and early twentieth centuries.

Scholars of American intellectual and church history have, for more than the past half century, viewed Old Princeton (1812–1929; upon which latter date the Seminary was re-organized) as ruled by Scottish Common Sense Realism. David Smith, as part of a growing group of scholars, in this work, challenges the reigning paradigm of SCSR dominance at Old Princeton. Smith does not deny that the professors there imbibed and even promoted SCSR; he does deny, however, that SCSR enjoyed the hegemony with which the reigning paradigm of the last fifty years has credited it. This volume on Warfield is an important part of the revolution that is reassessing evidence and that involves a paradigm shift in which the influence of SCSR is properly relativized and contextualized within the life and history of Old Princeton.

---

1. Thomas Kuhn, *The Structure of Scientific Revolutions,* Second Edition, Enlarged (1962; Chicago; University of Chicago Press, 1970).

Foreword

To be sure, others like Paul Helseth[2] and Fred Zaspel[3] have preceded Smith in this revolutionary undertaking. Helseth, Zaspel, Smith, and others have directly addressed the need for a reassessment of Old Princeton and its relation to SCSR. Other scholars, however, who have worked within the old established paradigm—the one that depicts Old Princeton in the thrall of SCSR—began to soften their stance on this question in more recent years. For instance, E. Brooks Holifield does not take as hard a stance on Princeton-as-captive-to-SCSR as does his mentor, Sydney Ahlstrom, who may, in fact, be said to be one of the architects of the older paradigm. In his volume, *Theology in America: Christian Thought from the Age of the Puritans to the Civil War* (New Haven: Yale UP, 2003), Holifield divided his work into three major parts, the second of which he labeled *The Baconian Style,* under which heading he treated, among others, the Princeton Theology. This means that he views the Princetonians as heirs of Francis Bacon and the Enlightenment scientific methodology that he developed and promoted. Though Holifield's work ends with the U.S. Civil War, what he says about the Princeton theology properly applies to the whole period of Old Princeton and would thus encompass both Charles Hodge (1797–1878) and B. B. Warfield (1851–1921).

Holifield, though a student at Yale of Sydney Ahlstrom, argues a bit more subtly than Ahlstrom did with respect to the Princeton theology (Smith deals at length with Ahlstrom herein). Ahlstrom thought that Princeton's adoption of Scottish Common Sense Realism amounted to a capitulation to rationalistic humanism and involved breaking the link with Hodge's Reformed heritage, sundering his theology from that of John Calvin and John Knox.[4] Holifield does not put things quite that starkly. He acknowledges Hodge's use, for instance, of SCSR, but also writes, "If the Princetonians read scripture through Scottish Realism, however, they read it even more through lenses provided by seventeenth-century theologians and confessions."[5] Here Holifield appears to exceed his mentor Ahlstrom in understanding that whatever use Princeton made

---

2. Paul Helseth, *"Right Reason" and the Princeton Mind: An Unorthodox Proposal* (Philippsburg, NJ: P. & R., 2010).

3. Fred G. Zaspel, *The Theology of B.B. Warfield: A Systematic Summary* (Wheaton, IL: Crossway, 2010).

4. Sydney E. Ahsltrom, "The Scottish Philosophy and American Theology," *Church History* 24.3 (1955), 266.

5. Holifield, *Theology in America*, 381.

Foreword

of SCSR, it did not render them Calvinist defectors. And this is just the point of David Smith in this work.

Holifield's approach is more consonant with the approach of Richard Muller, who has rather decisively demonstrated that "Calvin against the Calvinists" theory (an approach that would pit Calvin against his successors of the later sixteenth and seventeenth centuries) is no longer tenable. It was particularly the Barthianism of Ahlstrom and others that suggested that there was a chasm between Calvin and his followers, with Karl Barth and his followers seeing Calvin's successors as betraying, ossifying, and scholasticizing Calvin's original and fresh vision.

Many of us who were not at all influenced by Barth but by Ralph Danhof, John Vander Stelt, Cornelius Van Til, or other twentieth-century thinkers have believed that Princeton, under Hodge and Warfield particularly, capitulated to the objective, rationalist impulse and erected a theology that Ahlstrom has described as a "complex burden to be borne." In varying measures, significant historians of the American Presbyterian Church, like Mark Noll and George Marsden, also viewed Old Princeton through this lens, and have written about Old Princeton as captive to the Scottish philosophy (particularly when considering Old Princeton's "Enlightenment rationalism" or "modernism" in light of postmodernism). Nonetheless, as David Smith amply demonstrates in this volume, Warfield's appeal was to "right" reason, that ultimately only the regenerate enjoy. The notion that Hodge and Warfield privileged the objective at the expense of the subjective suggests that those who insinuate such need to do more reading in these Princetonians.

I freely confess that as a young Van Tilian (in seminary and beyond), I, too, understood Hodge and Warfield as captive to SCSR and thus as Calvinists who had capitulated to Enlightenment modernism. David Smith, as part of the paradigm shift that does not pit Calvin against the Calvinists, helpfully demonstrates that whatever use that Warfield made of SCSR, he remained chiefly captive to the Scriptures and Confessions. In seminary, we heard about how different Old Amsterdam (Kuyper, Bavinck, et al.) was from Old Princeton. It is the case, in this writer's opinion, that Hodge and Warfield did not understand the antithesis as did Kuyper and then Van Til (who had their own differences) and that the Princetonians might have conceded too much at points to reason. I am not, e.g., convinced of the wisdom of an approach in apologetics that seeks first to prove theism in general and then to demonstrate Christian theism. That Hodge and Warfield took such an approach, however, does not mean that they rejected presuppositional reasoning either, as Smith shows herein.

Van Til's approach is an advance, in my opinion, on the apologetics of Hodge and Warfield (Van Til's approach being one that more self-consciously and consistently employs a transcendental critique and sees the proof of the ontological Trinity and the self-attesting Christ of Scripture, i.e., the Christian worldview, as the impossibility of the contrary). But it is not at every point as radically different as hitherto claimed, albeit Van Til is, I believe, an epistemically more consistent Calvinist than the Princetonians. At the same time, I can appreciate Smith's warning about an over-emphasis on presuppositions, one that fails to examine, and account for, data in historical context. And, frankly, much that professes to be Van Tilian is simply post-modernism hiding under the skirts of Van Til. Certainly Hodge and Warfield were foundationalists, but so was Van Til when that term is rightly understood (what could be more foundational than Van Til's radical approach?).

Since becoming a student of Hodge, in particular, however, I have not found Hodge to be as different from Kuyper and Van Til as I earlier thought. To be sure, Old Amsterdam and Old Princeton have different approaches, the former rejecting apologetics (because of the antithesis) and the latter promoting apologetics (appearing to believe in epistemological common ground). Van Til, of course, cuts the difference, promoting apologetics (there is common grace, after all) while firmly affirming the antithesis. Smith's work, along with fellow-laborers like Paul Helseth, is helping us all to see that the difference between Kuyper, Van Til, and Warfield is not as great as we previously thought and as many of us were taught.

The origin of Scottish Common Sense Realism is somewhat disputed, but it is not disputed that its chief exponents were Francis Hutcheson (1694–1746), who came to the philosophy chair at Glasgow in 1729; Thomas Reid (1710–1796), who taught moral philosophy at Glasgow, and whose *Inquiry into the Human Mind on the Principles of Common Sense* (1764) was considered formative of the movement, particularly as an answer to the skepticism of David Hume; and Dugald Stewart (1753–1828), who succeeded Adam Ferguson in the chair of moral philosophy at Edinburgh in 1785 and was considered the popularizer of the movement because of his impressive rhetorical and oratorical gifts. It was particularly John Witherspoon, however, who imbibed SCSR and brought it

Foreword

with him to the College of New Jersey (later Princeton University) when he came to serve as its sixth president (1768–1794).

What the SCSR movement taught is also not easy to summarize but Smith does a good job of it in this volume. For our purposes here we might note that Reid claimed that our most basic beliefs are intuitive and thus "common sense." This stands over against Hume, who claimed that we know only sensations, not the thing-in-itself. Knowledge, then, for Hume, because solipsistic, reduces to skepticism. Reid utterly rejects this, arguing, as Paul Helm notes, "No one can live as if there is no external world, or as if he had no memory, or as if there is no other person in the universe besides himself. And so the theoretical repudiators of common sense must live a lie."[6] The Princetonians argued this way not infrequently. To be sure, SCSR suffered from epistemological shortcomings (granting the anti-theist a warrant for his common sense beliefs that he ought rather be made to justify), and was not ulitmately the kind of answer that Hume's skepticism needed.

Hodge and Warfield, whatever use they made of SCSR, remained firmly within the Calvinistic sphere, serving as loyal devotees of the Westminster Standards. Hodge, in all his writings, including and perhaps especially in his *Systematic Theology*, defended the system of doctrine contained in Westminster against all comers, particularly taking on all the German rationalists and higher critics of his day who sought to undermine the Word of God and its articulation in the Reformed confessions. Warfield did the same thing in his own day, though more so. Never was there a more thorough or devastating critic of modernism and liberalism than Warfield. As Smith puts it, "Warfield . . . gave a great amount of attention to countering the theological conceptions represented in the Protestant liberal theology of his day. He attempted to demonstrate that this latter theology was not only unfaithful to Scripture, but also failed to give a credible account of all the available data for which the theologian was accountable." This was no mere rationalism or evidentialism on Warfield's part, but a ministerial use of reason to examine the available evidence within a framework of faith. "Warfield," Smith continued, "believed that this liberal theology was indebted to Schleiermacher and Kant, and sought to reconstruct Christianity upon an anthropocentric foundation that manifested itself in rationalism or mysticism" [page numbers not yet available].

---

6. "Scottish Realism," in the *Dictionary of Scottish Church History and Theology*, Nigel Cameron, ed. (Edinburgh: T. & T. Clark, 1993), 759.

Foreword

Far from being a rationalist, then, Warfield, as had Hodge, opposed rationalism, on the one hand, and mysticism, on the other. If rationalism is the Word without the Spirit, then mysticism may be said to be the Spirit without the Word. Old Princeton, as did Calvin, opposed both, insisting that the same Spirit who inspired the Word must illumine it to the hearts and minds of the hearers. It is, in fact, this insistence on the part of Hodge and Warfield on the utter necessity of the work of the Holy Spirit for any real spiritual fruit or understanding that marks them as worthy heirs of Calvin. Warfield denominated Calvin as the "theologian of the Holy Spirit." Calvin was rightly called this by Warfield because of Calvin's more mature doctrine of the Holy Spirit. Before Calvin, the doctrine of the Holy Spirit was underdeveloped in the West. It was Calvin and the Calvinists who developed a mature doctrine of the Holy Spirit.

A bit of reflection on the development of the doctrine of the Holy Spirit might prove useful here because it is a link in the chain binding all Calvinists together. In the ancient church, particularly in the West, the focus of doctrinal development fell primarily on the early loci in the systematic encyclopedia: the doctrine of God, man, and Christ, particularly as developed at the first four ecumenical councils; the doctrine of the Holy Spirit received scant treatment comparatively. Even in the extensive development of the doctrine of Christ, however, the doctrine of the *person* of Christ received most of the attention, leaving underdeveloped the doctrine of the *work* of Christ.

In the middle ages, the doctrine of the work of Christ received attention, particularly in the writings of Anselm, who moved us away from a ransom theory of the atonement to one involving the satisfaction of God's offended honor. This was progress, though not enjoyed by the Eastern church, which remained comparatively underdeveloped in her doctrine of the work of Christ. The Eastern church split in 1054 from the Western and had not experienced then or since much development from the time of the seven councils (occurring from the fourth through the eighth centuries), emphasizing experience (often mystical) more than doctrine.

Though the doctrine of the work of Christ developed in the West in the middle ages, the doctrine of soteriology and pneumatology, the application of the accomplished redemption that is ours in Christ, which is to say, the doctrine of the Holy Spirit, lagged. Both the doctrine of the Spirit and of the church were present in Augustine (Ambrose having translated Basil of Caesarea's work on the Holy Spirit; the East, through

Foreword

the Cappadocians, Athanasius, and other had developed a doctrine of the Spirit, but it tended to be mystical), but the church in the middle ages developed the doctrine of the church, privileging ecclesiology over development of the doctrine of the Spirit. For example, Lombard and Aquinas do not develop pneumatology. Aquinas, in his thirteenth-century *Summa Theologica*, proceeds from the doctrine of God, man, and Christ to the doctrine of the sacraments and the church. A lack of significant development of the doctrine of the Spirit meant that the medieval church, particularly in the High Middle Ages, tended to downplay the divine application of redemption by the third person of the Holy Trinity and to emphasize the role of the sacraments and of the church, tending, in fact, to fold soteriology and pneumatology into ecclesiology. It is little wonder that without a vigorous doctrine of the Holy Spirit that there was an over-developed doctrine of the sacraments and of the church and the adoption of the view that the sacraments were efficacious *ex opere operato*.

It is not until Calvin (1509–1564) that we take up where Augustine (354–430) left off and develop the doctrine of the Holy Spirit. Warfield recognizes this as the genius of the Protestant Reformation: the merits and mediation of God the Son who accomplished our salvation become ours when the Spirit, by the means of grace, applies it to us. In Calvin's *Institutes*, the doctrine of the Holy Spirit is not overleapt after the person and work of Christ are set forth. Rather, Calvin recognizes that as long as Christ remains outside of us, He does us no good. Calvin follows his discussion of the redemptive work of Christ with a vigorous and full treatment of the Holy Spirit's application of such to God's people. Warfield, in writing on Calvin, understood thoroughly what the Reformation brought to the table that had been missed in the medieval church: that we are justified, adopted, sanctified, and glorified, all because of the work of the Holy Spirit to bring Christ home to us and to bring us home to Christ.

The Princetonians were very much theologians of the Holy Spirit, Hodge and Warfield making it plain time and again that without the work of the Spirit there is no real understanding. The Spirit's subjective work, in other words, was necessary for objective knowledge, truly and properly. The Spirit, the Princetonians believed, was needed not only for soteric purposes, but for epistemic ones, as well. In fact, since they believed that knowledge was the first stage of and foundational to faith, one must have right knowledge and reason to enjoy saving faith. The Holy Spirit must work in us to renew us so that we can know the truth and embrace Christ freely offered in the gospel. The Princetonians are not rationalists and cannot be because of their vigorous doctrine of the Holy Spirit.

Old Princeton's doctrine of the Holy Spirit is key to understanding that, whatever use Princeton made of SCSR, the Princeton theologians never left the Reformed ranch. Being a theologian of the Holy Spirit marked Calvin and it marked his followers, the Calvinists, who enjoyed essential continuity with him because of a like commitment to the application of redemption by the Holy Spirit. In fact, Richard Gaffin has argued this as a distinctive feature of the apologetics of Cornelius Van Til: the conviction that only the one in whom the Spirit has worked enjoys both epistemic and soteric renewal. It is only the man who has the Spirit who receives the things of the Spirit and who has the mind of Christ. Only the spiritual man can rightly reason.[7]

The natural man can not rightly reason or properly understand anything. Calvin is saying this. Warfield is saying this. Van Til is saying this. Whatever differences those three have, they have in common a vigorous doctrine of the Holy Spirit. The Princetonians, along with all true Calvinists, affirm the necessity of the work of the Holy Spirit both to illumine the understanding with respect to revelation (both general and special) and to renew the heart. Andrew Hoffecker,[8] David Calhoun,[9] and a few others have understood this. The work of such was not able to dislodge the prevailing paradigm that Princeton was a captive of SCSR. But this work of Smith's, together with that of his fellow revolutionaries, contributes to what appears to be a paradigm shift in which the vigorous Calvinism of Old Princeton is once again appreciated.

Part of the charge against Warfield is that he so stresses the objective and the rational that he voids the faith of vitality. This is a base canard, made only by those who, after the fashion of Schleiermacher, would evacuate the faith of any intellectual content and reduce it to a feeling of dependence (trust without knowledge). A true rationalist, as some claim Warfield to be, would reduce faith to knowledge and assent and strip it of trust. Warfield makes neither of these missteps: he proclaims a fully bibli-

---

7. Richard B. Gaffin Jr., "Some Epistemological Reflections on I Cor. 2:6–16," *Westminster Theological Journal* 57 (1995), 103–24.

8. W. Andrew Hoffecker, *Piety and the Princeton Theologians: Archibald Alexander, Charles Hodge, and Benjamin Warfield* (Phillipsburg, NJ: P. & R., 1981).

9. David B. Calhoun, *Princeton Seminary*, 2 vv. (Carlisle, PA: Banner of Truth Trust, 1996).

cal faith and sets forth a gospel to be believed and a Christ to be trusted. One of Warfield's great articles, in fact, was his masterful "Emotional Life of our Lord." This lengthy article spoke of how this one who was fully God (thus impassible) and fully man had a full-orbed emotional life. This article amply demonstrates that Warfield's theology was not rationalistic or poikilothermic, but as properly pious and warm-blooded as any theology might ever be.

Warfield's doctrine of the Holy Spirit saves him from rationalism and over-objectification. His work on the emotional life of Christ shows him to be no Stoic. His apologetics, while still pre-evangelism (unlike Van Til's), shows him to be warm, pious, and engaged with his hearers, an earnest defender of the Westminster Standards and of the historic Reformed faith, not one who capitulated to SCSR and fatally compromised the faith. Warfield believed in the unitary nature of truth: as a result, he rejected the fact/value dichotomy; affirmed both the objective and subjective in his epistemology; and, sensitive to history and the co-ordination of philosophy and theology, viewed apologetics as a partner of evangelism and integral to Christian discipleship. David Smith's first-rate work is commended to the reading public in the demonstration of these assertions.

Alan Strange

Acknowledgments

At times, written and verbal thanks seem completely inadequate; yet surely they serve as indicators of the deeper gratitude within. I have many people deserving of such thanks. Years of lessons learned at home came back to bear much fruit and have resulted in seeing this project to completion. I give great thanks for my parents, Paul and Barbara Smith.

Dr. J. Render Caines, senior pastor for over twenty years at Covenant Presbyterian church in Chattanooga, Tennessee, deserves thanks for first teaching me Reformed theology and showing me what it means to be a biblical pastor.

During my years (the early 1990s) at Covenant Seminary, St. Louis, Missouri, the professors provided a rich model of the pastor-scholar in the Warfieldian mold. Special thanks go to David Calhoun for introducing me to the Princetonians, and demonstrating what it means to persevere in the midst of suffering during his cancer treatments. Special thanks also goes to Robert W. Yarbrough for sparking and cultivating many interests that have played a prominent role in this project, as well as helping me to better understand various connections between academic work and faithful discipleship to the Lord Jesus.

Thanks is due Rev. Alan Lutz and Dr. Joe Hall for their encouragement and their leadership of the session at Covenant Presbyterian Church, Hammond, Indiana. Covenant's session members Ken Collins, Carl Cross, Mark Eastwood, Ron Junkens, Dave Markley, Andy Norman, Tom Petroskey, Nelson Schoon, and Roy Smith deserve thanks not only for their shepherding care for church members, but for having a view of biblical ministry that goes beyond the immediate pragmatic concerns of the local church. Without their financial support, this volume probably would never have been written. Heartfelt thanks also go to Pat Vitkus for her wit, wisdom, faithful witness, and generous financial support, as well as the ladies in the Hour of Power prayer circle.

Over the years Dave and Angie Weekly and Charles and Karen Clendinen have showered us with personal encouragements, and been

Acknowledgments

shining examples of what faithfulness to the local church looks like. I am deeply grateful for the counsel, friendship, financial support, and constant encouragement of the Rev. Dr. J. Allen Derrick, whose abiding faithfulness as a rural pastor in South Carolina is a bright testimony of fidelity to the Lord Jesus and to the Lord's faithfulness as well.

I am thankful for students and colleagues at Illiana Christian High School and Delaware County Christian School with whom I had the privilege to work during the years of researching and writing of this work. Special thanks go to Jim Favino, Ron Hoch, Vivian McLaughlin, and Chuck Patterson for stimulating conversations.

Joe and Audra Thomas generously and sacrificially opened their home to alleviate my commute miles and time during the first years of doctoral work. I am thankful not only for their hospitality, but also for the many excellent discussions that such times afforded. Several years in the northern Indiana area gave me opportunity for invigorating dialogue with Mid-America Reformed Seminary professors and students, for which I am very grateful. Thanks are also due to the kind and helpful staff at the Princeton Seminary archives.

I am grateful for many recent exchanges with Paul Helseth, who has helped solidify my understanding of many intricate theological and philosophical points, and for Brad Gundlach, who has been a wonderful conversation partner and a faithful writing critic for several years. During "full-time" years at Trinity Evangelical Divinity School I had the immense privilege of learning from D. A. Carson, Scott Manetsch, Doug Sweeney, Willem Van Gemeren, and John Woodbridge. Each shaped this work in significant ways. (Of course, I'll take the blame for all shortcomings.) No one could ever have had a more patient and kind doctoral mentor than I have had. I am deeply grateful for John Woodbridge and his guidance, encouragement, and admonishment.

Abbreviations

BRep	*Biblical Repertory*
CSP	Common Sense Philosophy
CW	*Collected Works (The Works of Benjamin B. Warfield)*, 10 vols.
NASB	New American Standard Bible
OPC	Orthodox Presbyterian Church
PQ	*Presbyterian Quarterly*
PRRD	*Post-Reformation Reformed Dogmatics*, by Richard A. Muller, 4 vols.
PRev	*Princeton Review*
PTR	*Princeton Theological Review*
SCSR	Scottish Common Sense Realism
SSW	*Selected Shorter Writings of Benjamin B. Warfield*, edited by John E. Meeter, 2 vols.
ST	*Systematic Theology*, by Charles Hodge, 3 vols.
WCF	Westminster Confession of Faith
WTJ	*Westminster Theological Journal*

Introduction

🔸 Shortly after Benjamin Breckinridge Warfield died on February 16, 1921, J. Gresham Machen's mother received the following in a letter from her son:

> I am thankful for one last conversation I had with Dr. Warfield some weeks ago. He was quite himself that afternoon. And somehow I cannot believe that the faith which he represented will ever really die. In the course of the conversation I expressed my hope that to end the present intolerable condition there might be a great split in the Church, in order to separate the Christians from the anti-Christian propagandists. "No," he said, "you can't split rotten wood." His expectation seemed to be that the organized Church, dominated by naturalism, would become so cold and dead, that people would come to see that spiritual life could be found only outside of it, and that thus there might be a new beginning.[1]

This conversation reveals one of the things Machen shared with Warfield—participation in a struggle within the church over the nature and presence of philosophical naturalism. Warfield stated: "The chief dangers to Christianity do not come from anti-Christian systems . . . It is corrupt forms of Christianity itself which menace from time to time the life of Christianity."[2] Philosophical naturalism, according to Warfield, was expressed in the epistemology of Immanuel Kant and the theology of Friedrich Schleiermacher, and by those who modified and mediated Kant's and

---

1. Stonehouse, *J. Gresham Machen*, 310.
2. Warfield, "Dogmatic Spirit," in his *Selected Shorter Writings* (hereafter *SSW*) 2:665, 666.

Schleiermacher's beliefs throughout the nineteenth century. Warfield stated that Schleiermacher's view of the inspiration of the Bible was "essentially naturalistic." He believed that Schleiermacher had introduced a "subjectivism" within theology that led to viewing apologetics "with no little scorn" because Christian faith "does not rest on rational grounds, but is an affair of the heart." Warfield further identified Schleiermacher as the "source" of the mysticism that was "disturbing the modern Protestant churches" in the early twentieth century. He felt that this mysticism appeals to "the natural functioning of the religious consciousness" and "is found to gravitate, with pretty general regularity, either toward rationalism or toward pantheism." Common to both mysticism and rationalism is the thought "that they appeal for knowledge of God only to what is internal to man." Thus, mysticism and rationalism are naturalistic *because they find the basis of human knowledge claims* in only that which is within nature.[3]

During Warfield's years as a scholar, he sought to apply the doctrines of the Westminster Confession of Faith (hereafter WCF) and the Larger and Shorter Catechisms to theological debates in both the academy and the church.[4] Upon his inauguration to the Western Seminary Chair of New Testament Literature and Exegesis in 1880, Warfield stated the following concerning his signing of the seminary standards (which affirmed his commitment to the WCF and its catechisms):

> I wish, therefore, to declare, that I sign these standards not as a necessary form which must be submitted to, but gladly and willingly as the expression of a personal and cherished conviction; and, further, that the system taught in these symbols is the system which will be drawn out of the Scriptures in the prosecution of the teaching to which you have called me—not indeed, because commencing with that system the Scriptures can be made to

---

3. Warfield, "Inspiration of the Bible," in *Works of Benjamin B. Warfield* (hereafter *CW*) 1:59–60. For further discussion see Warfield, "Apologetics," *CW* 9:14; and "Mysticism and Christianity," *CW* 9:655–57.

4. Warfield had the Shorter Catechism memorized by age six and the Larger Catechism, along with the Scripture proofs, memorized by sixteen. George Marsden rightly concludes that this was "an arduous and awesome" process (Marsden, *Fundamentalism and American Culture*, 109). An "Assembly of Divines" hammered out the WCF over the years from 1643 through 1647. The assembly continued to work, though, until February 22, 1649. It then acted as a committee for the evaluation of ministerial candidates until March 25, 1652. See Warfield, "Westminster Assembly and Its Work," *CW* 4:1.

teach it, but because commencing with the Scriptures I cannot make them teach anything else.[5]

Yet, even as Warfield uttered those words, that system, which he held as a "personal and cherished conviction," was being called into question. The dissent came not only from European and American Protestant liberals, and from evangelical Arminians opposed to the Confession's Calvinism, but also from some of Warfield's fellow Presbyterians. Already, notable scholars such as Charles Augustus Briggs were declaring that the "Old School" Presbyterian view and the application of the Westminster standards were a relic of the past, the expression of an outmoded view of reality. In 1889, two years after Warfield's arrival at Princeton, Briggs declared:

> But unfortunately there are not a few theologians who have mingled bad science, false philosophy, traditional history, and incorrect exegesis with the genuine truth of the Word of God; they have given forth this mixture of wood, hay, straw and stubble with the fine gold, as the standard of orthodoxy, and have presumed to set it up as a bulwark against the vast and profound discoveries of modern science. We are not surprised that we are hearing shrieks and groans as we see these airy structures disappearing in the flames that have been kindled by the torch of Truth, who is tired of such foolery.[6]

Both Briggs and Warfield claimed that the other's interpretation of the Bible resulted from a philosophy that was antagonistic to the Bible and, by implication, the life of the church. Briggs contended that truth was to be found in modern biblical criticism, the historical-critical method of biblical interpretation. Warfield, of course, launched his own counterattack. He maintained throughout his career that modern biblical criticism not only had failed to dismantle the church's doctrine of verbal inspiration, but had also, unwittingly, supported the doctrine.[7] Rather than arguing that there was no place for "criticism" within biblical interpretation, Warfield believed that a *truly* scientific criticism should be applied. However, he insisted that critics like Briggs did not have an accurate definition of science nor did they apply science correctly. He also maintained that they not only did not have a truly biblical method

---

5. Warfield, "Inspiration and Criticism," *CW* 1:395–96.
6. Briggs, *Whither?*, 15.
7. Warfield, "Inspiration and Criticism," *CW* 1:423–24; and "Christian Evidences: How Affected By Recent Criticisms," *SSW* 2:124–31.

of interpretation, but they did not even have a valid view of Scripture. Warfield contended that the Bible sits in judgment of human beings and their wills, thoughts, and desires—and *also* is the foundational means by which humans could and should define and practice science.

Even in his younger years, Warfield saw no separation between the biblical doctrine of creation and the biblical doctrine of redemption. This Kentucky farmer's son grew up traipsing through the countryside observing and cataloguing all manner of natural resources at the same time as he was training theologically in the WCF and its Larger and Shorter Catechisms. He never separated the two. As a theologian later in life, he did not believe that science could be practiced, in its most perfected and proper form, apart from a saving relationship with Christ. This commitment to the union of epistemology with theology and soteriology has been both misunderstood and distorted. Consequently, a closer consideration of Warfield and his beliefs is definitely warranted.[8]

After Warfield's death, Machen became more immersed in the debate in the Presbyterian Church through both scholarly and ecclesiastical activities. He wrote *The Origin of Paul's Religion* and *Christianity and Liberalism* while simultaneously pressing issues in the Presbyterian Church courts. His involvement in the latter eventually led to his departing Princeton Seminary and in 1929, along with Oswald T. Allis, Robert Dick Wilson, and Cornelius Van Til, Machen became one of the founding professors of Westminster Seminary in Philadelphia.[9] In 1936, he was suspended from the Presbyterian Church (U.S.) and then helped to establish a new denomination, the Orthodox Presbyterian Church.[10] Machen died in 1937, after falling ill on a preaching tour through the Midwest. Nevertheless, there was no shortage of people willing to remain engaged in the debate over theological and ecclesiastical issues similar to those against which he and Warfield had struggled. There were few, if any,

---

8. Noll, *Princeton Theology*, 11.

9. Machen makes broad historical arguments in differing ways in each of these three books: *The Origin of Paul's Religion*, *Christianity and Liberalism*, and *The Virgin Birth of Christ*. These are reflective of points Warfield made throughout numerous essays in his three decades at Princeton (Calhoun, *Princeton Seminary* 2:393–96). See also Warfield, "Right of Systematic Theology," *SSW* 2:219–79; and "Christless Christianity," *CW* 3:313–67.

10. Longfield (*The Presbyterian Controversy*) provides an overview of the conflict within the Presbyterian Church. See also Rian, *Presbyterian Conflict*.

however, who possessed either Machen's or Warfield's intellectual gifts, educational pedigree, or penchant for identifying essential issues.[11]

Eventually what began as a dispute over the nature of Christianity, philosophical naturalism, and the role of modern biblical criticism splintered into sectarian squabbles over doctrinal matters of secondary and tertiary significance. Along the way, the term *fundamentals*, which had been used to describe matters essential to biblical Christianity, led to the use of the term *fundamentalism*. Regrettably, this term was applied to an ideology that significantly distorted the beliefs and aims of those who had initially employed the term *fundamentals*.[12] It was used to pejoratively identify an anti-intellectual, narrow-minded cultural retreat that bore little resemblance to the broad-minded intellectual dispositions of Warfield and Machen.

To be sure, the two did intermittently find common cause with those groups and individuals who willingly identified themselves as fundamentalists. Warfield participated in writing some of the nascent fundamentalist literature. Machen aligned himself with the fundamentalist cause on behalf of the belief that God's written revelation of himself cannot be sufficiently accounted for by just the historical process.[13] However, neither Warfield nor Machen ever willingly threw a full endorsement behind either the theology or strategies of those who were identified as fundamentalists.

The critical issues for both of these men were: 1) that the method and content of biblical revelation was *not* simply a function of historical processes; and 2) that Christianity *cannot* be sufficiently explained by

---

11. Calhoun explains, "By profound study and extensive reading in English, German, French and Dutch, B. B. Warfield, to a degree that has rarely been equaled, excelled in the whole field of theological learning—exegetical, historical and doctrinal. . . . John DeWitt said that he had known intimately the three great Reformed theologians of America in the preceding generation—Charles Hodge, William Shedd and Henry B. Smith—and that he was certain not only that Warfield knew a great deal more than any one of them, but that he knew more than all three of them put together!" (Calhoun, *Princeton Seminary* 2:320; citing Hugh T. Kerr, "Warfield," a paper presented at the Annie Kinkead Warfield Lectures, Princeton Seminary, February 1982. See also Calhoun, *Princeton Seminary* 2:503, endnote 12).

12. For various histories that relate fundamentalism to evangelicalism, see Marsden, *Understanding Fundamentalism* and *Fundamentalism and American Culture*; Sweeney, *Evangelical Story*; Dorrien, *Remaking of Evangelical Theology*; Smith, *American Evangelicalism*; and Noll, *Scandal of the Evangelical Mind*.

13. Chrisope, *Toward a Sure Faith*.

philosophically naturalistic presuppositions.[14] The theological emphases and historical and scientific argumentation of Warfield and Machen found few companions in a fundamentalist movement often identified with a cultural and theological obscurantism.[15] Indeed, many of the theological distinctives that characterized the fundamentalist camp were among those issues that came up against Warfield's polemics.[16]

As the infighting increased, it became apparent to a group of Christian intellectuals in the 1930s and 1940s that an academically viable voice, which was engaging culture, but also biblically sound, needed to be resurrected in America.[17] As a result, the evangelical movement was revived. Although they themselves were not directly involved, Warfield and Machen still have to be seen as central figures in any accurate appraisal of this movement. For this reason alone, they deserve attention, and Machen has attracted it. Warfield is another matter, but that may be changing.

Shortly after Machen's passing, Ned Stonehouse's biographical memoir of Machen was published. This attention to Machen has continued, as evidenced by the periodic publication of books about him and the recent republication of some of his writings by P&R Publishing. Of course, his activity in the Presbyterian Church courts and his role in helping to establish the Orthodox Presbyterian Church have made it more difficult to ignore him.

Warfield, however, lived a rather quiet life as a scholar and, therefore, has been easier to overlook. His legacy, as it were, is largely in the written page. Such pages become less attractive, though, when potential readers think the pages are filled with theological and epistemological views beholden to an outdated Enlightenment philosophy.[18] This neglect is still

---

14. Ibid., 195.

15. Chrisope, "J. Gresham Machen" and *Toward a Sure Faith*; Hart, *Defending the Faith*; and Sweeney, *American Evangelical Story*, 155–78.

16. Warfield, *Perfectionism*, CW 8.

17. Sweeney, *American Evangelical Story*, 170–78. The point here is not to affirm or deny whether this goal was achieved. Rather, it is to simply state that this *was* their goal. See also Henry, *Uneasy Conscience*. The entirety of Henry's book addresses the matters pertaining to the rationale behind the relaunching of the evangelical movement.

18. A detailed look at the criticism of Warfield's theology and epistemology will be provided later, but the Briggs quote (*Whither?*, 15) serves as a representative example of their substance. In short, it was believed by some that Warfield operated with a view of knowledge that was wedded to Scottish Common Sense Realism and a rationalistic view of science that failed to account for the subjective elements in the knowing process. Some,

Introduction

curious, however, given the fact that Machen acknowledged the powerful influence Warfield had upon him and upon his arguments against theological liberalism.[19] Machen wrote upon Warfield's death: "Nearly everything that I have done has been done with the inspiring hope that Dr. Warfield would think well of it. The thought that he at least would read my book has been with me all the time. I feel very blank without him. With all his glaring faults he was the greatest man I have known."[20] Relatively recent dissertations by McClanahan[21] and Riddlebarger,[22] as well as works by Calhoun,[23] Helseth[24] et al., may be a sign of positive change. However, as Calhoun recently observed, this is no *slight* neglect:

> The year 2001 marked the one hundred and fiftieth anniversary of the birth of Benjamin Breckinridge Warfield. That this milestone passed largely unnoticed merely underscores the fact that the most serious omission in the study of American Christianity and theology is the neglect of Princeton Theological Seminary's greatest professor.[25]

One need not be a champion of Warfield's theology to recognize the validity of this assessment. Warfield's literary output alone, both because of its size and scholarly quality, should compel a closer look at him; but there are also a number of other reasons for according him more attention.

Bruce Kuklick argues that the broad epistemological shifts that took place in Western culture are intimately related to the historical-critical method of biblical interpretation. He contends that this method did more

---

in turn, believed his theology was the product of post-Reformation Scholastic rationalism and that it distorted Calvin's true commitments.

19. Chrisope, *Toward a Sure Faith*, 185–97.

20. Stonehouse, *J. Gresham Machen*, 310. Calhoun, *Princeton Seminary*, 2:502 n. 9, speculates on what exactly Machen may have meant by the phrase "all his glaring faults." I believe he is right to state: "Exactly what Machen meant by Warfield's 'glaring faults' is difficult to determine, when his comments about his teacher and colleague are always, as above, so strongly favorable." Although their theological beliefs and scholarly interests were virtually identical, in regard to temperament or personality it seems that Warfield and Machen were quite different, and I think herein may lay the basis for explaining Machen's comments. At this point, though, any explanations are speculative.

21. McClanahan, "Benjamin B. Warfield."
22. Riddlebarger, "Lion of Princeton."
23. Calhoun, *Princeton Seminary*.
24. Helseth, "Moral Character and Moral Certainty."
25. Johnson, *B. B. Warfield*, xi–xii.

to reorder the worldview of twentieth-century thinkers than Darwinism.[26] According to Kuklick, the historical-critical method is indelibly linked to the critical conception of history that now governs the work of most historians in the academy.[27] In turn, Mark Noll notes, "relatively scant historical" work has been done on the Princetonians because of the desire of some to either "exploit" or "blunt" their influence in the twentieth, and now the twenty-first century. One cannot help but note the irony of this assessment. Many who fault the Old Princetonians for being overly polemical would appear to be, according to Noll, guilty of this charge themselves in their own handling of Princeton's theologians.[28] There also seems to be something ironic about Noll criticizing the lack of historical work on the Princetonians at the same time as Kuklick is connecting the ascendancy of biblical criticism in academic and ecclesiastical communities with the rise of a critical conception of history. Warfield, a hundred years earlier, had already responded to the application of biblical criticism to history with blistering censure. Furthermore, this very practice, if not ideology,[29] appears to even have effected the reorganization of Princeton.

Though this debate obviously might draw the attention of those interested in Old Princeton and Warfield, it has much deeper ramifications as well. For as Kuklick argues, there is something quite important about the relationship between people's knowledge claims and their interpretation of the Bible.[30] Therefore, interest in Warfield should not simply be among those in the academy and church who are preoccupied with biblical interpretation, but should also include those who have a keen interest in the history of the West in general, and the history of ideas and the philosophy of science, in particular. Scholars today, both in Christian and non-Christian academic communities, are wrestling in a renewed way with the nature, means, limits, and goals of human knowledge. Noting how one of America's most productive scholars navigated through these matters and answered related questions could be of great benefit to them.

In his 1993 publication *The One, The Three, and The Many: God, Creation and the Culture of Modernity*, Colin Gunton argues that the

26. Kuklick, "Critical History," 54–64.
27. Ibid.
28. Noll, *Princeton Theology*, 11 (emphasis original).
29. See Linnemann, *Historical Criticism of the Bible*.
30. Kuklick, "Critical History," 54–64.

Introduction

quintessential characteristic of modernity can be understood from the perspective of human creatureliness. He asserts that the truly "modern" person thinks of the creational boundaries of time and space primarily as obstacles to overcome, and thus, attempts to either ignore or remove them.[31] The "modern" person, in other words, is one who is not willing to acknowledge and acquiesce to creational realities. Whether Gunton is accurate in his analysis or correct in his conclusions is not our concern at this point. What *is* of interest is that Gunton seeks to define and analyze modernity primarily in terms of a doctrine of creation. Such an approach is similar to Warfield's way of thinking about human beings, science, theology, and apologetics.[32] Warfield, as we will see, derived a doctrine of creation from the Bible that he in turn used as the basis upon which he criticized Protestant liberal theology.

Warfield's views on human knowledge, in general, and theology and apologetics, in particular, find clear confirmation in the conclusions of two contemporary scholars. First, Warfield's views are upheld by the work that Richard A. Muller and others have done regarding post-Reformation Reformed orthodoxy.[33] Second, they are in accord with Robert W. Yarbrough's findings concerning the salvation-historical approach to biblical interpretation, as practiced throughout the nineteenth and twentieth centuries by several European biblical scholars.[34]

Muller is also helpful in clarifying the true nature of the relationship between Calvin and his successors, thus shedding light on the areas of continuity that exist between the medieval, Reformation, and post-Reformation theologians. The latter, Francis Turretin and other successors to Calvin, helped formulate the post-Reformation creeds and confessions. Muller demonstrates that they did *not* distort Calvin's theological distinctives, but instead faithfully built upon them. Thus, his work calls into question the idea that the Old Princeton theologians accommodated their theology and epistemology to a philosophy foreign to Scripture when they relied upon Turretin and other post-Reformation theologians.[35]

31. Gunton, *One, Three, Many*.

32. Rather than arguing for identical approaches, I think I would prefer to use "similar" approaches because it is not clear that either Gunton or Warfield would have endorsed the way the other employed these categories.

33. Muller, *Post-Reformation Reformed Dogmatics* (hereafter *PRRD*); idem, "Problem of Protestant Scholasticism"; Asselt and Dekker, "Introduction." Other scholars reach similar conclusions, including Carl Trueman, Sebastian Rehmann, etc.

34. Yarbrough, *Salvation-Historical Fallacy*.

35. Muller, *PRRD*.

Warfield's view of apologetics as fundamentally prolegomena that is organically united to one's entire system of theology, places him squarely in the post-Reformation orthodox tradition. Yarbrough lists a number of theologians and biblical scholars who *did* accommodate Scripture and Christian theology to a philosophy antagonistic to Scripture, among them: Immanual Kant (1724–1804), Friedrich Schleiermacher (1768–1834), Georg Wilhelm Friedrich Hegel (1770–1831), Ferdinand Christian Baur (1792–1860), William Wrede (1859–1906), and Rudolf Bultmann (1884–1976).[36] Running alongside this series of liberal scholars was another group: Johann Christian Konrad von Hoffmann (1810–1877), Adolf Schlatter (1852–1938), Martin Albertz (1882–1956), Leonard Goppelt (1911–1973), and Oscar Cullmann (1902–1998). The latter group, the Hoffman-Schlatter-Cullman line of scholars, asserts that Protestant liberals were interpreting the Bible as a mere product of historical forces while *simultaneously* denying that human beings had the ability to know of a triune, personal, and supernatural God *in history*.[37] The term *heilsgeschichtliche*, or "salvation-historical," as used by the Hoffmann-Schlatter-Cullmann line, represented the broad belief that the physical material realm of space-time history cannot be rightly interpreted apart from the presence of the supernatural, triune, personal God of the Bible.[38] Interestingly, Warfield made some of these same criticisms.[39]

All of this suggests that the most prevalent view of Warfield as a scholastic, evidentialist, rationalist who was indebted to Scottish Common Sense Realism (hereafter SCSR)[40] may be wide of the mark. It also shows

36. Yarbrough, *Salvation-Historical Fallacy*, 1–7. I have cited the introduction, though this is what the entire book discusses.

37. Ibid., 4; see also 4n12 where Yarbrough quotes Kant's *Streit der Falkutäten*, 62: "For even if God were to speak to man, man could never know that it is God who is speaking to him. It is simply impossible for man to be able to grasp the Infinite One with his senses, to distinguish Him from sense impressions and thereby know him." It is not clear *how* exactly Kant could know this.

38. There has been some elasticity to the use of the term, but the above description fits with all its uses within the Hoffmann-Schlatter-Cullmann line. See Yarbrough, *Salvation-Historical Fallacy*, 5.

39. Ibid. See also Warfield, "Inspiration and Criticism," *CW* 1:395–425; "Rights of Criticism and of the Church," *SSW* 2:595–603; "Christian Evidences: How Affected by Recent Criticism," *SSW* 2:124–131; "Evading the Supernatural," *SSW* 2:680–84; "Divine and Human in the Bible," *SSW* 2:542–48; "Latest Phase of Historical Rationalism," *CW* 9:585–645; and "Ritschlian School," *SSW* 2:448–51.

40. Scottish Common Sense Realism (SCSR) has its origins in the Scottish Enlightenment of the eighteenth century. Its adherents held to the belief that all normally functioning humans have the ability to perceive reality through their five senses and to

that the theological tradition that has accommodated theology and biblical scholarship to a philosophy antagonistic to the Bible is the very one that identifies itself with Protestant liberalism and its related traditions.[41] Gary Dorrien writes as a confessed liberal theologian and affirms their heritage's dependence upon Kant and Schleiermacher and identifies "'Neo-Orthodoxy'" as "a form of liberal theology." If all this is so, then some of the dominant analyses and conclusions regarding the relationships between Old Princeton theology and modern American culture, fundamentalism, and evangelicalism may need significant revision. For Christians in the Reformed and Presbyterian branches of the church, such a reassessment may be of particular interest. This could result in a better understanding of the history of Reformed thought as it relates to a number of issues: church history in general and Warfield in particular, the broad topics of apologetics and systematic theology, and the history of biblical interpretation and New Testament theology. A closer look at Warfield's arguments against Protestant liberal theology would help in a reassessment of all these areas.

Much has been made in recent years concerning the distinction between evidentialist and presuppositionalist approaches to apologetics. Warfield, despite the traditional Van Tilian assessment of him, actually avoids the evidentialist label in important ways.[42] Indeed, Warfield's use of the term "right reason," and the concept he communicates by it, convey that Van Til's analysis of Warfield went awry. Still, Van Til's opinions very likely contributed to others also misevaluating central features of Warfield's epistemology and theology. James Bratt maintains that the Rogers/McKim proposal, which is critical of the Princetonians for their scholastic rationalism and deductive, defensive apologetics, "showed considerable debts to Dutch-Calvinist sources." Muller also criticizes Rogers/McKim for their understanding of the nature of scholasticism,

---

reason about those perceptions so that they are able to acquire knowledge. Thus, the SCSR philosophers argued that there is no reason to doubt that our epistemic faculties are reliable, because those faculties correspond to the objects of our knowledge. Thomas Reid came to be identified as the chief proponent or founder of SCSR because, among other reasons, he probably did more than any of the other Scottish Realist philosophers to persuasively argue for this view of knowledge. Identifying a philosopher as a SCSR, however, does not penetrate very far into their most significant epistemological beliefs, so we must be careful about placing much weight on such an identification. See Ahlstrom, "Scottish Philosophy and American Theology."

41. Dorrien, *Making of American Liberal Theology*, xxi.

42. Of course, one's own definition of an evidentialist will greatly determine whether or not Warfield fits into that category.

as well as their assessment of the relationship between the theological methods and content in medieval, Reformation, and post-Reformation thought.[43] Warfield's view of apologetics shows that he united his apologetics to Christian discipleship and eschatology. If Brad Gundlach[44] and Paul Helseth[45] are largely correct in their findings, a healthy dose of the presuppositional character of thought, frequently credited to Cornelius Van Til or Abraham Kuyper, would seem to have actually been operating widely in the Old Princeton school in at least the early to mid 1800s—reaching its height in Warfield's scholarship.

Although likely of great interest to many Reformed and Presbyterian people, these matters are hardly inconsequential for the whole storyline of American church history, in general, and evangelical history, in particular. Those with concerns related specifically to systematic theology in the life of the church may find Warfield's thoughts to be both illuminating and stimulating for thought. Those who have aligned themselves with Protestant liberalism or Neo-Orthodoxy may find a closer look at Warfield fascinating from the perspective of gaining a better understanding of some of their fiercest opposition. The intensity, intricacies, and importance of these debates regarding the Princetonians may be properly understood in the light of Calhoun's assessment that "Princeton Seminary was one of the centers—in its earlier years, perhaps the center—of American evangelicalism during the nineteenth century."[46] In other words, struggling with the character and future of evangelicalism today forces one to wrestle with its nineteenth-century heritage. Yet it is evidently necessary to state, given the treatment that Warfield and some other Old Princetonians have received since Warfield's death, that in order to understand the Princetonians one must first read their works. The following statement by Martyn Lloyd Jones regarding Warfield's scholarship may provide insight into the nature of the problem:

> No theological writings are so intellectually satisfying and so strengthening to faith as those of Warfield. He shirks no issue and

---

43. Bratt, "Dutch Schools," 122, 123. See also Muller, *PRRD* 1:35, 73, 138, 141n216, 198, 231n33 (for Muller referencing their misreading of Turretin), 285, 372, and 437. For yet another critique of the Rogers/McKim proposal, see Woodbridge, *Biblical Authority*. For the Rogers/McKim proposal, see Rogers and McKim, *Authority and Interpretation*.

44. Gundlach, "Evolution Question at Princeton."

45. Helseth, "Moral Character and Moral Certainty."

46. Calhoun, *Princeton Seminary* 1: xxii. See also Stonehouse, *J. Gresham Machen*, 310.

evades no problems and never stoops to the use of subterfuge. One is impressed by his honesty and integrity as much as by his profound scholarship and learning. The result is that there is a finality and authority about all he wrote. Those who disagreed with him seemed to recognize this. They did so by simply ignoring him. This has continued to be his fate since his death and since the publication of the ten volumes. It is quite amazing to note the way in which this massive theologian is persistently ignored and seems to be unknown. A "conspiracy of silence" is perhaps the only weapon with which to deal with such a protagonist.[47]

One need not agree that there has necessarily been a "conspiracy" to silence Warfield to recognize that a misanalysis of his scholarship could *result* in silencing him. To brand his methodology and conclusions as corrupted by an out-dated philosophy antagonistic to Scripture is certainly not going to endear him to those who are seeking to be faithful to Scripture. There is more than a little irony at this point. Warfield believed that *liberal scholars* reconstructed, or reconceptualized, the Christian faith in their use of biblical criticism. One of his constant refrains was that *they* were the ones beholden to their cultural milieu in their use of naturalistic presuppositions in trying to account for the origin and content of the Bible, and the Christian faith dependent upon it. The gravity of this for evangelicals should increase when they realize that many of those who may be largely responsible for "silencing" Warfield, are working, or have worked, within the evangelical community. Moreover, some of these scholars have analyzed the history of evangelicalism in such a way as to bring current evangelical theology more in line with postmodern currents of thought. If Warfield and the Old Princetonians have been significantly misanalyzed, it not only calls into question a significant amount of evangelical historiography but also, in part, some of the theological direction derived from that historiography. It would seem that Warfield does indeed merit another hearing.

At the center of the historiography about Warfield are assessments of his epistemology and how it relates to his theology. Noting the ways in which Warfield defined apologetics and then used these ideas will serve as a window to a better understanding of his work. This will be the primary question then: How is Warfield's definition of apologetics reflected in the scope and nature of his scholarship? Chapter 1 investigates the secondary literature in order to gain an awareness of all the issues surrounding

47. Lloyd-Jones, "Defender of the Faith," 17. Special thanks to Becky Beardmore at Banner of Truth for her help, and for their permission in using this.

Warfield and the historiography related to him. Chapter 2 provides a brief biographical sketch of Warfield's life in order to gain familiarity with the most seminal influences upon him. Chapter 3 looks at some contextual matters crucial to interpreting Warfield's work as an Old Princetonian. Chapter 4 elucidates the responses to these issues of the Princetonians and Warfield in particular. Chapters 5 and 6 examine Warfield's views on theology and epistemology in more detail. Apologetics will then be viewed from two different angles—apologetics in principle (chapter 7) and apologetics in practice (chapter 8). The conclusion will further assess the historiography highlighted in chapter 1. The entirety clarifies how Warfield thought about apologetics within itself and as part of the system of Christian theology, and then how he put it all into practice.

Throughout his scholarly writings, we find Warfield highlighting the reality that the doctrines of the Christian faith are not only their own defense, but are also a sufficient offense. Yet he believed that the most fundamental matters pertaining to human knowledge and theology had to be addressed in his day because of the confusion regarding these topics. This need still exists today.

1

A Historiographical Review of Old Princeton and Warfield

Throughout the nineteenth century, the Old Princeton faculty[1] was often at the center of controversy. The cause was their conviction that the establishment and advancement of the gospel is related to, if not dependent upon, the church believing and declaring the truth about a variety of key issues. They maintained that the biblical message of the life, death, and resurrection of Jesus Christ is what people need to believe to experience salvation. Therefore, arguments that had an immediate bearing on the veracity of the gospel, such as those about the nature and authority of Scripture, gained most of their attention.

However, the Old Princetonians also believed that the gospel message is ultimately related to every other subject as well. This view is based on a concept they called the "unity of truth."[2] They considered God to be

---

1. Portions of this chapter first appeared in my article "The Scientifically Constructive Scholarship of B. B. Warfield."
"Old Princetonians" refers to the theologians at Princeton Seminary from 1812 to 1921, the year of Warfield's death. For the most part, when scholars refer to "Old Princeton," they have nineteenth-century Princeton in mind. Archibald Alexander was the first professor at Princeton in 1812. Charles Hodge and Samuel Miller were the next two professors. For a history of Princeton Seminary, see Calhoun, *Princeton Seminary*. For histories of its founding and early years, see Loetscher, *Facing the Enlightenment and Pietism*; and Noll, *Princeton and the Republic* and *Princeton Theology*.

2. Gundlach, "Evolution Question at Princeton," 53–72. For the relation of the "unity of truth" to the task of systematic theology, see Warfield, "Task and Method," *CW* 9:95. For the phrase "unity of truth" and post-Reformation, Reformation, and medieval thought, see Muller, *PRRD* 1:85–132. For the use of Francis Turretin's *Institutes of Elenctic Theology* as the primary theological text at Princeton, see Calhoun, *Princeton Seminary* 2:32. See also Turretin, *Institutes of Elenctic Theology*, 3-vol. ed. This reprint edition of the *Institutes*

the creator, sustainer, and redeemer of *all* reality. This meant that knowledge of, and belief in, the gospel are related to the understanding of many things that at first glance might seem *un*related The point here is not to attempt to explain in detail the nature of these interactions. It is to stress the Princetonian emphasis on the relationship between all truth claims and the gospel—they believed *all truth is unified and finds its origin in God*.[3] This belief was integral to the Old Princetonian's view of science, for example, and resulted in their opposition to work that they considered illegitimately labeled as such. In fact, these ideas are central to many of the controversies that still surround Old Princeton today.

Shortly after the close of the apostolic era, the church's theologians began wrestling with, among other doctrines, the influence sin has upon our minds and, thereby, the apprehension of knowledge by reason.[4] The discussion came to a temporary resolution in the fifth century when Augustine's belief in original sin prevailed over Pelagius' belief in an original *propensity* to sin,[5] (although Pelagius' beliefs continued to pop up in various forms). Throughout the Reformation and post-Reformation periods, theologians again worked on clarifying what they believed regarding the effects of sin, not only on human thinking, but also on human affections and choices. They also further developed their views on how these ideas are related to the work of Christ and the life of the church.

---

served as my primary source. Since Archibald Alexander, Princeton's first professor, studied Turretin (in Latin) under his tutor William Graham as early as 1790, we must recognize that whatever influence Turretin may have had with the Princeton theologians, it certainly predates the founding of the seminary. Of course, Alexander, along with other students of Graham, also studied John Owen, Joseph Butler, Thomas Boston, and Jonathan Edwards. Further, prior to studying under Graham, Alexander read copiously in Owen, Boston, Richard Baxter, Joseph Alleine, Thomas Halyburton, Ebenezer Erskine, Philip Doddridge, and George Whitefield, among others. For the diversity of influences on Alexander that centered in Graham, see Calhoun, *Princeton Seminary* 1:43–59. For greater detail into Archibald Alexander's life and insight into the Princetonian view of Christian ministry in relation to true doctrine and preaching, see Garretson, *Princeton and Preaching*.

3. For an example of what this meant for some of the Princetonians with respect to the topic of evolution and how it related to gospel belief, see Gundlach, "Evolution Question at Princeton."

4. Of course, such a discussion is ultimately bound to the broader topics of the nature of humans, of God, and of reality itself. For perhaps the best summary treatment of the development of the church's doctrine in the first six centuries following the apostolic age, see Kelly, *Early Christian Doctrines*.

5. For Warfield's understanding of this debate, see *CW* 4:289–412.

In the Reformation period, both Luther and Calvin emphasized the pervasive nature of sin, which produces an *incapacitation* of the ability of people to turn to Christ for salvation. Calvin, in particular, delineated the need for God to *first* regenerate the sinner. This new birth results in a clearer understanding of Scriptural matters so that the sinner, now, *can* turn to Jesus for salvation. Some scholars, though, believe that Calvin and Luther's post-Reformation successors deviated from these theological distinctives. Such successors, therefore, are at the center of numerous debates—on issues such as the noetic[6] effects of sin and the degree to which Hodge and the rest of the Old Princetonians were faithful to Calvin's emphasis on the total inability of human beings to come to saving faith on their own initiative.

This is why the work of Richard A. Muller, Willem J. van Asselt, and some of the other scholars studying sixteenth- and seventeenth-century post-Reformation theologians is integral to the debate regarding the Old Princeton school and its heritage.[7] Muller's work corroborates that the Princetonians used the phrase "unity of truth" in a way that is consistent with its use in medieval, Reformation, and post-Reformation thought.[8] He also states that the identification of post-Reformation theology as rationalist and dependent on "central dogmas," from which the rest of its doctrine and theology are deduced, does not correspond to either the historical record or the nature of reformed doctrine.[9]

However, Brian Armstrong[10] and Alistair McGrath[11] believe that Calvin's successors distorted his theology by emphasizing particular doctrines, such as predestination. They maintain that those who followed Calvin deduced the doctrine and its importance with the use of the scholastic method. Rather than "scholasticism" being simply a particular method to use in working through theological and philosophical ideas, though, they believe that it automatically delivers a particular philosophy and theology that is rationalistic. Thus, to use the scholastic method is to possess a rationalistic theology. Francis Turretin is one of the post-

---

6. This refers to the mind, to apprehension by reason.

7. Muller, *PRRD* and "Problem of Protestant Scholasticism," 45–64. For further clarification on some of Muller's work, see Asselt and Dekker, *Reformation and Scholasticism*, 11–43. The conclusions of these works substantially conflict with Armstrong, *Calvinism and the Amyraut Heresy*, 31–32; and McGrath, *Reformation Thought*, 129.

8. Muller, *PRRD* 1:85–132.

9. Ibid., 2:32.

10. Armstrong, *Calvinism and the Amyraut Heresy*, 31–32.

11. McGrath, *Reformation Thought*, 129.

Reformation Reformed successors of Calvin that they indict with their analysis.¹² In this, they follow the lead of nineteenth-century Protestant liberal theologians. Muller, van Asselt, and Dekker refute this analysis.

Still others, led by Sydney Ahlstrom, attribute the Old Princetonian's apologetical system to an epistemological dependence on SCSR.¹³ Their arguments are very similar to those of Charles Briggs a hundred years earlier¹⁴—Princetonian theology was rationalistic because it relied upon sources that had been corrupted by philosophies alien to the Bible.

Ahlstrom's Theory: The Scottish Philosophy Thesis

Sydney E. Ahlstrom's thesis is that the Scottish philosophy that was active during the nineteenth century in various American theological traditions held sway over Old Princeton as well. His 1955 article "The Scottish Philosophy and American Theology" set the stage for the way in which many scholars would later approach the historiography of Old Princeton in general, and Warfield in particular. Historians, who as a group have been largely critical of the Old Princetonians, appear to have largely based their assumptions and arguments on Ahlstrom's foundation to varying degrees. This long-range impact makes it important to understand Ahlstrom's theories so that an accurate assessment can be made of the effect of his work on a correct understanding of the debates surrounding Old Princeton and Warfield—as well as the relevance of those debates today.

According to Ahlstrom, Thomas Reid, whom he calls "the archetypical Scottish Philosopher,"¹⁵ propagated a philosophy that can be

---

12. For connecting the use of Turretin at Princeton with rationalism, see Sandeen, *Roots of Fundamentalism*; and Rogers and McKim, *Authority and Interpretation*. For a critique of Sandeen's book as well as Rogers and McKim, see Woodbridge, *Biblical Authority*.

13. Much of the contemporary analyses critical of the Princetonians along these lines is indebted to Sydney Ahlstrom's "Scottish Philosophy and American Theology." Ahlstrom should not be considered as novel, however. For analyses compatible with Ahlstrom's, a short representative reading list would be: Sandeen, *Roots of Fundamentalism*; Rogers and McKim, *Authority and Interpretatio*; Vander Stelt, *Philosophy and Scripture*; Marsden, *Fundamentalism and American Culture*; Dorrien, *Making of American Liberal Theology*; and Grenz, *Revisioning Evangelical Theology*.

14. Briggs, *Whither?*

15. Ahlstrom, "Scottish Philosophy," 260. SCSR is often said to have developed as a result of the Scottish philosopher Thomas Reid's attempts to answer the skeptical arguments of David Hume. However, Ahlstrom did not believe that any *one* man could be called the founder of the philosophy, but that Reid had "carried the work to

summarized in four statements. Ahlstrom maintains that all "or most of them, take central place in the thought of any typical proponent of the 'Scottish Philosophy.'"[16] The four assertions are: 1) the importance of Newtonian physics for the understanding of the mind and its operations; 2) the mind's constitution by which principles "anterior to and independent of experience" are established for knowing;[17] 3) the notion that only an intelligent being can be an efficient cause; and 4) "first principles of morals are self-evident intuitions."[18]

Actually, S. A. Grave shows that there was substantial diversity among those philosophers who actually *did* belong in the SCSR camp.[19] Therefore, to treat SCSR as if it is something that can be easily reduced to an epistemology that simply affirms that we can know truly, does not do it justice. The Princetonians were aware of this diversity among the SCSR philosophers. This can be seen in Hodge's *Systematic Theology* (hereafter *ST*). At times he approvingly cites Thomas Reid[20] on a variety of matters; at other times he disapproves of Reid,[21] and he *blisters* William Hamilton for denying that we can know God[22] (largely echoing Immanuel Kant in this agnosticism).

Still, Ahlstrom maintains that, in America, a variety of men, spearheaded by John Witherspoon at Princeton, David Tappan at Harvard,

---

completion," (260). Other philosophers in the Common Sense tradition are Dugald Stewart (1753–1828), James Beattie (1735–1803), James Oswald (1703–1793), and Sir William Hamilton (1788–1856). Stewart is considered the successor and popularizer of Reid but did not like the term "common sense" and so spoke of "fundamental laws of thought." For a summary of Reid's thought see Van Cleve, "Reid, Thomas"; C. Hodge, *Systematic Theology* (hereafter *ST*) 1:346–65; William P. Alston notes that "what Reid teaches us is that there is no rationally attractive alternative to accepting the testimony of our basic cognitive faculties as (prima facie) correct, and that only if we do this will we ever have any chance to acquire any knowledge whatever" (Alston, "Thomas Reid on Epistemic Principles").

16. Ahlstrom, "Scottish Philosophy," 261.

17. Ibid. Ahlstrom also states here: This "clearly foreshadows the Kantian revolution in philosophy."

18. Ibid.

19. For an introduction to, and the diversity within, the Scottish philosophy, see Grave, "Common Sense," 354–61. Grave contrasts Thomas Reid and Dugald Stewart with James Beattie and James Oswald. He also states that William Hamilton deviated significantly from the other four, had marked affinities with Kant, and was repudiated by the Princetonians.

20. C. Hodge, *ST* 2:83–305; 3:43.

21. Ibid., 2:290.

22. Ibid., 1:304–56.

and Timothy Dwight and Nathaniel Taylor at Yale, drew a great deal of attention to this Scottish philosophy,[23] and that, as a result, its anthropocentrism crept into and corrupted various American theological communities.[24] Mark Noll even states that "this epistemological common sense defined the mainstream of American thought throughout the nineteenth century."[25]

Ahlstrom then zeroes in on Charles Hodge, one of the earliest of the Old Princetonians. Ahlstrom's claim is that, through the influence of Archibald Alexander, Hodge accepted the fundamental tenets "of the Scottish School of 'Natural Realism'"[26] and transmitted this philosophy to his students through his theology. Ahlstrom concludes that this involvement with SCSR led to Hodge's theology becoming separated from that of Knox and Calvin;[27] now standing, instead, in the line of thinking that marks the philosophical commitments of Aristotle, Aquinas, Richard Hooker, John Locke, Francis Bacon, Isaac Newton, the Cambridge Platonists,[28] Lord Shaftesbury, and David Hume.[29] According to Ahlstrom, Hodge got "caught up in the anthropocentrism of Scottish Philosophy," and throughout his life his "confidence in 'philosophical

---

23. Ahlstrom, "Scottish Philosophy," 261–62.

24. Ibid., 261–66.

25. Noll, "Common Sense Traditions," 2.

26. Ahlstrom, "Scottish Philosophy," 259.

27. Ibid., 266. His statement that Charles Hodge deviated from Knox and Calvin is rather brazen given the fact that Hodge (*ST* 1:194), a page after one of Ahlstrom's citations, quotes Calvin in Latin showing that Calvin did indeed believe that all humans possessed an innate knowledge of God. Ahlstrom's final statement in his endnote 51 is: "Actually the influence of rational humanism is diffused throughout the work and is discernible not so much in particular as in the nuances of the whole." How one is to simply accept his analysis based on "the nuances of the whole," when he is not able to differentiate between what Hodge believed versus what Hodge was saying other people believed, is difficult to imagine. This is all evidence of the sort of broad brushstrokes that are used by Ahlstrom throughout the whole article.

28. The Cambridge Platonists were a group of English seventeenth-century theologically trained thinkers. They held that all ancient philosophy, particularly Plato and Plotinus, is relevant to contemporary life. They believed that reason is superior to sense knowledge and emphasized freedom of the will. They were vitally interested in all aspects of the scientific revolution and were involved in formulating practical ethics for Christian conduct. Their most important members were Henry More (1614–1687) and Ralph Cudworth (1617–1689).

29. Ahlstrom, "Scottish Philosophy," 259. For a concise introduction to realism as an epistemology, see Hirst, "Realism."

speculation' seems to have grown."[30] Ahlstrom seems to have overlooked the fact that the section he cites to support his point was Hodge's historical survey of various positions on the topic in the history of the church.[31] In other words, Hodge was not speculating *about* the topic, he was discussing intellectual history in general and historical theology in particular.

Ahlstrom claims that Hodge's confidence in philosophical speculation can be seen in Hodge's *ST*, where the thesis is put forth that "a free act may be inevitably certain as to its occurrence."[32] Actually, again, the section to which Ahlstrom referred is more accurately identified as historical theology and intellectual history. In fact, the very phrase that Ahlstrom quotes is only part of a sentence. The full sentence and the one following read as follows: "All Augustinians maintain that a free act may be inevitably certain as to its occurrence. All anti-Augustinians, whether Pelagians or Semi-Pelagians, or Arminians, and most moral philosophers and metaphysicians, take the opposite ground." If Ahlstrom wanted to communicate that all of this material was Hodge analyzing the philosophical speculation of others then there might be some legitimacy to that. The problem even with that conclusion, though, is that these are matters that are unavoidably a part of various theological systems. Ahlstrom is either mistaken regarding the character of subject matter that he was reading in Hodge, or he is mistaken regarding what Hodge was doing in that section.

Ahlstrom went on to say that this belief suggests that "the foundations of his ethic and his conception of natural theology . . . are Scottish rather than Calvinistic."[33] Furthermore, Ahlstrom asserted that "the influence of Scottish anthropology" upon Hodge can be seen "with special clarity in his interpretation of the doctrine that man's nature not just his acts, but his nature, is 'truly and properly sin.'"[34] It seems that, from

---

30. Ahlstrom, "Scottish Philosophy," 266.

31. C. Hodge, *ST*, 2:296.

32. Ibid.

33. Ibid. Very shortly after beginning *ST* 1:194, Hodge quotes from Cicero, Tertullian, and Calvin to show that the sense in which knowledge of God is innate is that we all have "the general sense of a Being on whom we are dependent, and to whom we are responsible, that the idea is asserted to exist universally, and of necessity, in every human mind." Then Hodge proceeds to present the scriptural evidence for these points. The first place he went was Romans 1. In other words, it is a demonstration that Hodge's belief in these anthropological and epistemological matters was rooted in his exegesis of Scripture and the theology that he saw governing anthropology and epistemology.

34. Ahlstrom, "Scottish Philosophy," 266. For the "truly and properly sin" quote he

Ahlstrom's perspective, Hodge's doctrinal interpretation is actually a *mis*-interpretation because it fails to give proper weight to the noetic effects of sin, the effects that sin has on human thinking and reasoning. This is perhaps the most detrimental criticism leveled at both Hodge and the later Princetonians.

Ahlstrom, then, proceeded to explain why this "diverse philosophical conquest" was able to occur.[35] As he sees it, SCSR was sufficiently apologetical to meet the concerns of American theologians in the Calvinistic tradition, who were suffering from the onslaught of the French Enlightenment within the universities.[36] Moreover, "Hume's skepticism" and "all the major metaphysical heresies" that undermine a Calvinist perspective seemed to be successfully refuted by this Scottish philosophy.[37] The latter's success "lay in its dualism, epistemological, ontological, and cosmological."[38] Ahlstrom asserts that such dualisms mean that "the world which men perceive was in no sense constituted by consciousness." The "firm separation of the Creator and His creation . . . preserves the orthodox notion of God's transcendence, and makes revelation necessary."[39] Finally, according to Ahlstrom, SCSR "made possible a synchronous affirmation of science on one hand, and an identification of the human intellect and the Divine Mind on the other."[40] Thus, the rational basis for a natural theology as well as a "contemplative piety," was established at the same time as there was a move "away from relativism and romantic excesses."[41] However, Ahlstrom *is* of the opinion that a high price was paid for all of this for those within Protestant Orthodoxy, and, in particular, those within the Calvinistic tradition.[42]

> In the seminaries and universities their theology lost its Reformation bearings; "the Augustinian strain of piety" suffered.

---

cites Hodge at a number of places regarding a variety of topics dealing with anthropology. He does not make clear where he got the quote. One would have to comb through almost two hundred pages of material.

35. Ibid., 267.
36. Ibid.
37. Ibid.
38. Ibid.
39. Ibid., 268.
40. Ibid.
41. Ibid.
42. Ahlstrom simply refers to "Orthodoxy" in ibid., 268 and contrasts it with "Unitarians." Those whom he identifies under the label "Orthodoxy" are Protestant and primarily Calvinists.

The belief that Christianity had a proclamation to declare lost its vitality. Park hemmed-in the Scriptures with so many criteria of interpretation that they came to be only an external support to his theological system. And for Hodge doctrine became less a living language of piety than a complex burden to be borne.[43]

Ahlstrom states that there were obviously numerous "forces" that led to these results, but maintains that Scottish philosophy made three definite "contributions." First, "the humanistic orientation of the Hutcheson-Reid tradition" overshadowed the "fervent theocentricity of Calvin which Edwards had striven to reinstate" (in the early eighteenth century).[44] Second, "the adoption of the benign and optimistic anthropology of the Scottish Moderates by American Calvinists veiled the very insights into human nature which were a chief strength of Calvin's theology."[45] Third, "Scottish Realism accelerated the long trend toward rational theology which had developed, especially in England, during and after the long deistic controversy."[46]

It should be noted that perhaps the best way to think about the Old Princeton perspective on what is called the "deistic controversy" is to be aware of what Warfield said about God's providence. Warfield believed that most of our difficulties in Christian living stem from a failure to have our thinking conditioned by the doctrine of God's universal providence. It is "Deistic postulates," said Warfield, "that lead to our theological and religious troubles."[47] According to Old Princeton, as notions of God as a creator not personally active in his creation (deism) began to take hold and shape biblical and theological studies in Europe, Arminianism and rationalistic expressions of Christianity emerged. They viewed these latter expressions of Christianity as undermining the true gospel.

However, for Ahlstrom, the result was that Reformed theology was "emptied of its most dynamic element" and "a kind of rationalistic *rigor mortis* set in" that "made traditional doctrines so lifeless and static that a new theological turn was virtually inevitable."[48] Indeed, according to

43. Ibid., 268. Edward Amasa Park was a nineteenth-century Edwardian theologian.
44. Ibid., 268–69.
45. Ibid., 269.
46. Ibid.
47. Warfield, "God's Providence over All," *SSW* 1:111.
48. Ahlstrom, "Scottish Philosophy and American Theology." This view of Ahlstrom's is quite ironic considering the quote from Machen in my introduction to this book. Machen is talking to Warfield about splitting the church: "'No,' he [Warfield] said, 'you can't split rotten wood.' His expectation seemed to be that the organized Church,

Ahlstrom, "there is no mystery as to why end-of-century theology in America turned with such enthusiasm to evolutionary idealism, the social gospel, and the 'religion of feeling.' It was in search of the relevant and the dynamic."[49]

The Legacy of Ahlstrom's Thesis

As stated previously, Charles A. Briggs[50] makes the general point that a philosophy alien to the Scriptures corrupted the Old Princeton theology. Hence the following:

> Dogmatic Theology in Great Britain and America has been too long *in the bondage of the seventeenth century Scholasticism and the eighteenth century Apologetics*. The time has come for it to burst these bonds and march forward. It ought to run with all its might and march at the head of the column of modern learning. Christ is the king of a kingdom of truth, and his followers ought to be ashamed to drag His banner in the rear. The battle against science, philosophy, exegesis, and history must come to an end. All truth should be welcomed, from whatever source, and built into the structure of Christian doctrine. The attitude of *Traditional Orthodoxy* should be abandoned as real heterodoxy, and the attitude of *Advancing Orthodoxy* assumed as the *true* orthodoxy."

Briggs "called the doctrine of biblical inerrancy 'a ghost of modern evangelicalism to frighten children.'"[51]

Ahlstrom makes the same fundamental accusation regarding Archibald Alexander's *Outlines of Moral Science*, which Charles Hodge used in his teaching, Ahlstrom wrote:

> Any reader unaware that its author was one of the nation's most inflexible champions of Old School Calvinism would assume on reading this book by itself, that it was written, perhaps, by some mild English Latitudinarian bent on mediating the views of *Butler, Reid and Price*. What is important here, though, is that

---

dominated by naturalism, would become so cold and dead, that people would come to see that spiritual life could be found only outside of it, and that thus there might be a new beginning" (Stonehouse, *J. Gresham Machen*, 310).

49. Ahlstrom, " Scottish Philosophy."

50. Briggs, *Whither?*, 18–19.

51. Dorrien, *Making of American Liberal Theology*, 358, quoted from Briggs, *Authority of Holy Scripture*, 35.

these attitudes brought into Hodge's *Systematic Theology* what one Dutch Calvinist critic called the "*stains of humanism.*"[52]

Thus, Ahlstrom argues, Hodge's theology was corrupted by a humanist philosophy antagonistic to Scripture. Ahlstrom further asserts that Hodge's theology, endorsed by Warfield, revealed an anthropology reflective of "*the optimism of the Scottish Renaissance*"[53] and that all of this was rooted in "the father of all common sense philosophies, Aristotle, and his mediaeval champion, St. Thomas, as well as the great Thomistic mediator of the English Reformation, the judicious Richard Hooker."[54] Ahlstrom lists among others in this line of philosophy: John Locke, Francis Bacon, Isaac Newton, and the Cambridge Platonists. Ahlstrom's point then was that a philosophy acquired outside the Bible was used by the Princetonians to interpret the Bible and construct their theology. As stated earlier, Ahlstrom's analysis and conclusions have exerted a powerful influence over the historiography of Old Princeton, and thus Warfield. As Paul Helseth summarizes it, in some scholar's thinking Ahlstrom's thesis has become virtually an unquestioned presupposition.[55]

Gary Dorrien illustrates that the Protestant liberal party line continues, as he echoes the same basic criticisms and arguments used first by Briggs, then Ahlstrom. According to Dorrien, the Old Princeton theologians:

> . . . obscured the differences between Reformationist and post-Reformationist orthodoxy, as well as their own revisions of Reformed orthodoxy. Warfield and Hodges treated post-Reformation scholasticism as fully continuous with Calvin, partly because their own version of Reformed theology owed more to this tradition than to Calvin. Princeton theology as a form of Reformed orthodoxy rarely quoted Calvin.[56] The Princeton theologians were more at home with the systematized neo-Aris-

---

52. Ahlstrom, "Scottish Philosophy," 266 (emphases added).

53. Ibid.

54. Ibid., 259.

55. Helseth, "'*Re*-Imagining' the Princeton Mind," 427.

56. The reader should keep in mind that the entire fifth volume of Warfield's *Collected Works* is devoted to Calvin and Augustine, with hundreds of pages devoted to Calvin, including a one-hundred-page exposition of "Calvin's Doctrine of the Knowledge of God," which Richard A. Muller identifies, along with the rest of the work on Calvin by Warfield, as a sizeable monograph still to be reckoned with in Calvin studies.

totelianism of Protestant scholasticism than with the Augustinian dialectics of Luther and Calvin.[57]

Dorrien's description of the character of Protestant Scholasticism, as well as its relationship to Francis Turretin's work, is at decided odds with Richard A. Muller's analysis and conclusions in his four-volume *Post-Reformation Reformed Dogmatics* (hereafter *PRRD*).[58]

John C. Vander Stelt's 1978 study on Old Princeton and Westminster argues that SCSR was the apologetic tool of choice by Old Princeton, as her professors sought to "retain epistemological certainty" and resist the "new ideas coming from France, England and Germany."[59] More specifically, Vander Stelt believes that Warfield's emphasis on the role of trust in knowledge was consistent "with the thinking of CSP,"[60] so that as a result Warfield "tended to think in terms of objective categories." Vander Stelt cites, as an example, Warfield's belief that regeneration "is something done *to* man, and the testimony of the Spirit is something *for* man."[61] Vander Stelt wrote that in Warfield's concept of revelation from God, "All nonwritten revelations, however, with the exception of the Incarnate Word, are not sufficient for the purpose for which those revelations have been given."[62] However, in assessing Calvin's beliefs regarding God's revelation, Warfield wrote the following:

> [T]he structure and organization of the world, and the things that daily happen out of the ordinary course of nature, that is under the providential government of God, bear witness to God which the dullest ear cannot fail to hear . . . and that the light shines from creation, while it may be smothered, cannot be so extinguished but that some rays of it find their way into the most darkened soul. . . . The sole cause of the failure of the natural revelation is to be found, therefore, in the corruption of the human heart. Two results flow from this fact. First, it is not a question of the extinction of the knowledge of God, but of the corruption of the knowledge of God. And secondly, men are without excuse

---

57. Dorrien, *Remaking of Evangelical Theology*, 19.

58. Ibid., 21–28.

59. Vander Stelt, *Philosophy and Scripture*, 148; see also 48, 57–64.

60. Ibid., 174. CSP is "Common Sense Philosophy" and equivalent to Scottish Common Sense Realism.

61. Ibid. Vander Stelt did not cite anything in Warfield for that point. He relied on Markarian, " The Calvinist Concept of the Biblical Revelation in the Theology of B. B. Warfield." This latter work is cited in Vander Stelt, *Philosophy and Scripture*, 174 n. 183.

62. Vander Stelt, *Philosophy and Scripture*, 174.

for their corruption of the knowledge of God. On both points Calvin is insistent.[63]

Thus, Vander Stelt misrepresented Warfield's belief. Warfield was not saying that non-written revelations were insufficient for the purpose for which they were given. The exact opposite is true: God's revelations all accomplish the purposes for which they were given. Warfield's assertion that man corrupts God's revelation does not mean he affirms that the revelation did not fulfill its purpose. The very fact that he says man is inexcusable for his sin is an affirmation that God's revelation has accomplished its purpose, namely, to condemn all in their sin.

Vander Stelt claims, though, that for Old Princeton in general, and Warfield in particular, the Scottish philosophy provided the fundamental presuppositions by which they understood the infallibility of Scripture. In this, he maintains that they were accepting the "traditional, scholastic, and religiously dualistic distinction between that which is *natural* and that which is *supernatural*."[64] Vander Stelt concludes, therefore, that "Warfield's entire framework of thought in his views on apologetics and Scripture is unmistakably intellectualistic."[65] The result, as far as Vander Stelt is concerned, is that "as far as Scripture was concerned, Christ tended to become an appendage and the Spirit of only relative importance."[66]

Perhaps the most influential propagator of Ahlstrom's thesis has been George Marsden. In *Fundamentalism and American Culture*, Marsden asserts that the Old School Presbyterian lineage, which includes Charles Hodge and Warfield ". . . tended to view truth in its purest form as precisely stated propositions. This applied not only to the *Confession*, but also to the infallible Scriptures that the *Confession* summarized."[67] Moreover, Marsden argued (similarly to Sydney Ahlstrom):

63. Warfield, *CW* 5:44–45.
64. Vander Stelt, *Philosophy and Scripture*, 181.
65. Ibid., 182.
66. Ibid., 182n252.

67. Marsden, *Fundamentalism and American Culture*, 110. Later on 114–15, Marsden identifies Warfield as "the great champion of the Princeton cause, during the critical period of the shipwreck and breaking apart of the Common sense consensus in America, between the Civil War and World War I." Marsden, Noll, and several other historians, following Ahlstrom's lead, believe that SCSR dominated the thought systems most popular at the beginning of the nineteenth century. Their interpretation is that SCSR began to be increasingly called into question, for a variety of reasons, throughout the nineteenth century, and that because the Old Princetonians were committed to SCSR, when the latter went down, so too did Old Princeton.

> This view of truth as an externally stable entity placed tremendous weight on the written word. If truth were the same for all ages, and if truth was apparent primarily in objective facts, then the written word was the surest means permanently and precisely to display this truth. Religious experiences, rituals, traditions, even unrecorded words spoken by God or Jesus, as essential as all these were, were nonetheless transitory. Unassisted, none could guarantee that sure facts would be objectively apprehended in all ages. At Princeton it was an article of faith that God would provide nothing less than the wholly accurate facts, whether large or small. Common Sense philosophy assured that throughout the ages people could discover the same truths in the unchanging storehouse of Scripture.[68]

This was written immediately after Marsden had discussed the work of A. A. Hodge and Warfield in defense of the inerrancy of Scripture. This implies that the doctrine of inerrancy is derived from a view of truth that sees truth as an "externally stable entity . . . not historically relative," in which the subjective element is virtually jettisoned.

The idea of the effective removal of the subjective element in Princeton theology is contradicted by Jaroslav Pelikan.[69] Indeed, if Pelikan is largely correct in *his* analysis regarding the character of the nineteenth-century debates over the infallibility, inspiration, and authority of the Bible, then one has to question the picture Marsden et al. present regarding the character of SCSR and the Princetonians' relation to it, as well as the character of those debates.[70] Pelikan cites Charles Hodge as an example of his point.[71] Hodge states that "'the highest possible evidence' for the authority and inspiration of those Scriptures [was] not some objective criterion (especially, of course, church authority), but 'the testimony of God himself with and by the truth to [one's] own heart.'"[72]

Yet, Marsden claims that a union of Common Sense philosophy and the Scriptures led the Princetonians to what he considered "peculiar views of Scripture and truth" and "heated debates over much narrower issues, such as the inerrancy of Scripture or revision of the *Westminster*

---

68. Ibid., 113.

69. Pelikan, *Christian Tradition* 5:244.

70. Ibid., 244. According to Pelikan, "Instead of the distinction between 'a priori' and 'a posteriori,' the distinction between 'objective' and 'subjective' was probably the one invoked the most often in the discussion of these problems."

71. Ibid.

72. C. Hodge, *ST* 1:153.

Confession of Faith."[73] According to Marsden, this was because of corruptions within the Princetonian's view of truth, which revealed their dependence on SCSR.

> This view that the past could be known directly through reliable testimony meant that Scripture was not regarded as representing the *points of view* of its authors respecting the past, but it was rather an infallible representation of the past itself. This distinction was intimately connected with the demand at Princeton that Scripture be accepted as without error, even in historical detail. Increasingly, modern thought suggested that the point of view of the observer stood between facts and his report of the facts. This would suggest that even the most honest and authoritative accounts of the past would be altered in detail by the observer's point of view. At Princeton, however, the ideal for truth was an objective statement of fact in which the subjective element was eliminated almost completely. In their view, Scripture did just that. Although they did not deny the human element, divine guidance was thought to produce accounts where the warp from point of view had been virtually eliminated.[74]

Thus, the Princetonians, and Warfield particularly, according to Marsden, had based everything on wrong assumptions. Their "view of truth was based on the assumption that truth is known by apprehending directly what is 'out there' in the external world, not a function of human mental activity. The mind discovers objective truth, which is much the same for all people in all ages."[75]

Marsden's own erroneous analysis of Warfield, and the Old Princeton theology and epistemology, led him to articulate a dilemma or scenario present in the nineteenth century that really was not there. He argues that since Warfield believed faith must be grounded in right reason this meant he believed in "the power of unaided reason in demonstrating the truth of Christianity."[76] According to Marsden, this meant that Warfield had to "maintain that intellectually the believer and the non-believer stood on common ground."[77] This led to Marsden assessing Warfield's view of truth and apologetics in the following way:

73. Marsden, *Fundamentalism and American Culture*, 116.
74. Ibid., 113–14.
75. Ibid., 114.
76. Ibid., 115.
77. Ibid.

> This common-ground approach eliminated from Warfield's apologetics the use of a venerable line of explanation for the failures of reason. In the traditions of Augustine, Calvin, and Jonathan Edwards the Fall was often regarded as having so blinded the human intellect that natural knowledge of God had been suppressed and therefore no one could have true understanding without receiving the eyes of faith.[78]

In other words, Warfield, in his approach to apologetics, had failed to condition his view with the basic doctrine of human sin, and, instead, had fallen prey to adopting philosophical tenets antagonistic to Scripture. Such a view is not only an echo of Ahlstrom, whom Marsden studied under, but also very similar to the one held by Cornelius Van Til, another of Marsden's professors.

Van Til, professor of apologetics at Westminster Seminary from 1929 to 1972, has been generally regarded as the doyen of presuppositional thought in the United States.[79] In his comparison of Warfield and the great Dutch theologian and statesman, Abraham Kuyper (1837–1921), Van Til favored Kuyper over Warfield on the issue of the contrast between the non-Christian's reasoning abilities and the Christian's, since, as Van Til stated,

> Having stressed the objective rationality of Christianity, Warfield does not adequately stress the difference between the principles of the natural man and the principles of the Christian. This appears primarily in the fact that he attributes to "right reason" the ability to interpret natural revelation with essential correctness. It is not easy to discover just what Warfield means by "right reason." But clearly it is not the regenerated reason. It is not the reason that has already accepted Christianity. It is . . . the reason that is confronted with Christianity and has some criterion apart from Christianity with which to judge the truth of Christianity.[80]

Those trained in the Van Tillian line have, as a matter of course, been largely skeptical about the benefit of Warfield, and have tended to view him as an "evidentialist" in apologetic methodology.

Adding further support to the SCSR thesis is Mark Noll. Noll's work, though, presents more ambiguity regarding the relationship be-

78. Ibid.

79. The two most thorough treatments of Van Til's life and thought are Bahnsen, *Van Til's Apologetic*; and Frame, *Cornelius Van Til*.

80. Van Til, *Christian Theory of Knowledge*, 167; Bahnsen, *Van Til's Apologetic*, 597–98, 602–12.

tween various manifestations of the Scottish philosophy and the Old Princetonians than Ahlstrom's article communicates.[81] In his early writings, Noll argued that they, and other American theological traditions, were strongly influenced by the Scottish philosophy. He claimed that SCSR led to "scientific system"-building,[82] and that evidentialist apologetics "contributed to the atomistic and mechanical approach to religious life, moral obligation, and the expression of piety which characterizes conservative Protestantism in America."[83] Noll also maintained that this endorsed an ahistorical and atheological approach to the Christian faith.[84] More recently, though, he seems to have qualified his earlier assessment and now distances the Old Princetonians from some of the influences and uses of SCSR, although he still assumes their dependency on it.[85]

Noll discusses those Presbyterian preachers who were part of the heritage leading up to Old Princeton and who participated in the First Great Awakening. They were those who preached a distinctly Augustinian anthropology, stressing the noetic effects of sin, and the human inability to believe in the gospel apart from the regenerating work of God. Noll then claims that though they initially resisted it, they did eventually adopt Scottish philosophy.[86] According to Noll, this resulted when a new voice entered the discussion—John Witherspoon, who came from Scotland to become president of Princeton.[87] According to Noll, he brought Francis Hutcheson's work with him. He goes on to say the Scottish philosophers, in general, appealed to "self-evident truths," or "intuitive truths," and an optimistic anthropology. Noll claims that although these basics came through many (Reid, Hutcheson, Adam Smith (1723–1790), Stewart), Witherspoon relied heavily upon Francis Hutcheson's work, rather than Reid's or others, in advocating a naturalistic and optimistic anthropology. So Noll credits Hutcheson, more so than Reid, with the further increase in naturalistic lines of thought that contributed to forming distinctly "American" theological traditions, although Reid did still play a part.[88]

81. Noll, *America's God*.
82. Noll, "Common Sense Traditions," 19, 25.
83. Ibid., 19.
84. Ibid., 26.
85. Noll, *America's God*, 93–113.
86. Ibid., 102.
87. Ibid., 96–98.
88. Ibid., 109. Noll acknowledges his dependence upon Diamond, "Witherspoon, William Smith."

The fundamental differences between Francis Hutcheson and Thomas Reid can perhaps help us see the breadth of Scottish philosophy, and its inability to adequately explain the origins of many, if not all, of the distinguishing features of Warfield's theology and epistemology. The nineteenth-century Princeton philosopher James McCosh regarded Hutcheson as the "founder" of Scottish philosophy because Hutcheson identified particular "senses" or cognitive powers as part of our "very nature and constitution." This rather broad criterion did not prevent Reid from contradicting much of the substance of what Hutcheson argued or implied.[89] Hutcheson denied the Calvinistic doctrine of the total depravity of humans.[90] Furthermore, Hutcheson's concern was to "dwell on the motive and moral parts of man's nature," not on the "logical and metaphysical subjects," or on the "intellectual powers," as Reid did.[91] Hutcheson seems to have too many aspects to his ethical theory for them to be harmonized, but one of the distinguishing characteristics of his treatment of morals is "the assimilation of morals to aesthetics."[92] What Hutcheson and Reid hold in common, then, is the acquisition of ethical and epistemological theories derived from an analysis of how human beings operate and are constituted.

This is an exceedingly broad characteristic, and is sufficiently broad enough to allow for those who proceed according to this method to contradict each other in their fundamental conclusions, as did many in the Scottish school.[93] Paul Helm has recently argued that Reid denied "that we are entitled to believe that God exists in the absence of argument," and that "he had no conception of some originally natural epistemic endowment now perverted or lost; no conception that those who do not

---

89. McCosh, *Scottish Philosophy*, 69. Alexander Broadie, *History of Scottish Philosophy*, 123, states that Hutcheson appears to have been "well disposed to several of the doctrines" that John Simson (1667–1740) held and which led to the latter's guilty verdict for heresy. Hutcheson received strong opposition from some at Glasgow University when elected to the professoriate, because he was "theologically unreliable," as a result of having prepped under Simson (124).

90. Broadie, *History of Scottish Philosophy*, 140. See his quote from Francis Hutcheson, *Logic, Metaphysics*, 199.

91. McCosh, *Scottish Philosophy*, 75.

92. Copleston, *History of Philosophy* 5:183, see also 179, 181.

93. See the whole of McCosh, *Scottish Philosophy*; Stumpf, *History of Philosophy*; Copleston, *History of Philosophy* 5:179; Hicks, *Philosophy of Charles Hodge*, 26; see the groupings within Scottish philosophy given by Grave, *Scottish Philosophy of Common Sense*.

believe in God are subject to epistemic malfunction."[94] Thus, the Old Princetonians agree with Reid in the sense that they believe arguments are necessary for Christian belief, but since the substance of their claims is theological not philosophical, they are not dependent on him for the substance of either their theology, or epistemology.[95] In fact, it is precisely on this point that Warfield emphasized the noetic affects of sin, the nature of saving faith, and that only God can produce saving faith in the sinner. Warfield recognized the limitations of arguments, but this did not mean that arguments were unnecessary, but rather that while saving faith is the gift of God, it is also not simply rooted in nothing and clinging without reason to its object.[96]

As for Warfield, Noll believes that Charles Hodge placed more emphasis on religious experience than did Warfield, although the latter "occasionally recognized the importance of the subjective predispositions for the faith."[97] In Noll's words, Warfield does not completely jettison "the subjective side of faith, but it plays a less prominent role in his thought than it did for his predecessors."[98] Yet, Noll also says that Warfield's 1911 address "The Religious Life of Theological Students" demonstrates that Warfield "never thought of theology except as liturgical, as well as an intellectual exercise."[99] He also thought that Warfield was guilty of having failed to account for the noetic effects of sin, though he believed that Hodge was innocent of that charge.[100]

One of the things the secondary literature shows is that misinterpretations of Warfield do not simply fall along theologically "liberal" and "conservative" lines. They are found among even the more conservative scholars. Samuel T. Logan Jr. and Kim Riddlebarger are both conserva-

---

94. Helm, "Reid and 'Reformed' Epistemology," 112. While Helm sees similarities between the basic arguments that Reid and Alvin Plantinga offer against radical skepticism proceeding from rationalistic epistemologies, he denies that Reid can be identified "with the most central claim of 'Reformed' epistemology, that theism is rationally acceptable without argument" (105).

95. Warfield, "Review of *De Zekerheid des Geloofs*," *SSW* 2:114–15. See too Warfield, "Apologetics," *CW* 9:16. For the point that for Warfield epistemology is united to his theology, one need only see that saving faith is a kind of knowledge that only God gives. See Warfield, "Biblical Idea of Revelation," *CW* 1:3–34.

96. Warfield, "On Faith in Its Psychological Aspects," *CW* 9:313–42.

97. [AQ?]

98. Noll, *Princeton Theology*, 242. Here the term "side" is perhaps a window into Noll's misanalysis and misrepresentation of Warfield's thought.

99. Ibid., 262.

100. Ibid., 302.

tive Reformed scholars, and many within conservative Reformed circles look to them for guidance on this matter, but they seem to add more confusion than clarity.

Logan Jr., an emeritus Westminster professor of church history, comes from a different perspective than some of the others, but with similar results. He believes that the "downward trend" toward rationalism started when the Cambridge Platonists and Henry More's *Enchiridion Ethicum*,[101] along with a Ramist methodology,[102] sowed rationalism at Christ's College, Cambridge. He maintains that this in turn was largely responsible for "rationalizing" theology at Harvard, Yale, Andover, and of course Princeton.[103] Logan feels that the Ramist methodology of William Perkins and William Ames was the primary impetus for the rationalistic decline and that Henry More then fostered it.[104] Keith L. Sprunger, as well as Muller, criticizes this idea, stating that by crediting a Ramist methodology with conveying rationalism, Logan is confusing methodology with ideology and theology.[105] Logan states, though, that the Ramist methodology of the Puritans at Christ's College had "within it strong intimations of the position at which More arrived in *Enchiridion Ethicum*."[106] Thus, he concludes, "It is no accident that the very institution which was the center of Ramism produced Henry More and the Cambridge Platonism."[107] Although Logan makes *declarations* of a strong connection between Ramism, Christ's College, More, and rationalism, he provides little actual evidence from the historical record—only the following:

> Ramus: "Theology is the doctrine of living well."
>
> Ames: "Theology is the art of living well."

---

101. More, *Enchiridion Ethicum*.

102. Ramist methodology is based largely on the work of Petrus Ramus (1515–1572). It is anti-Aristotelian. It involves working from the general to the particular by means of a series of dichotomies. This resulted in the use of binary charts. Mnemonic recall was seen as unnecessary and dropped in favor of methodologic order.

103. Logan, "Theological Decline in Christian Institutions," 145–63. Other post-Reformation scholars have argued this way as well, namely, Brian Armstrong and Alistair McGrath.

104. Ibid., 156–57.

105. Sprunger, *Learned Doctor William Ames*, 136; Muller, *PRRD* 1:184.

106. Logan, "Theological Decline in Christian Institutions," 156.

107. Ibid., 157.

More: "Ethicks are defined to be the art of living well and happily."[108]

John Frame writes, "the job of theology is to help people understand the Bible better . . . to teach people the truth of God," and theology is "justified by the help it brings to people, by its success in helping people to use the truth."[109] According to Logan's definition, theology that delivers a practical result is rationalistic, and, thus, we would have to identify Frame as a rationalist rather than as faithfully biblical.

Last is the analysis of Kim Riddlebarger.[110] While discussing the debate regarding Warfield's apologetical method and theology, Riddlebarger states, "the name of B. B. Warfield is repeatedly invoked by proponents of both positions, with Warfield's commitment to, and advocacy of, Scottish Common Sense Realism occupying a major role in the debate."[111] Here it appears that Riddlebarger is simply emphasizing the question of Warfield's commitment or non-commitment to SCSR as the central subject in the debate. Yet a couple of pages later, he states that "Warfield's own prolific career as an apologist and theologian is largely indebted to an epistemological foundation which is itself the product of Common Sense Realism expressed in Warfield's own variety of evidential apologetic."[112] Furthermore, quoting Warfield on the idea that apologetic's "deepest grounds is 'the fundamental needs of the human spirit,'"[113] Riddlebarger asserts:

> This emphasis can be directly traced to the epistemology of Scottish Common Sense Realism (SCSR). On Thomas Reid's understanding of human nature and epistemology, necessary and contingent first principles are foundational for all subsequent human knowledge. Warfield's comments echo the beliefs of SCSR regarding these necessary and contingent truths. The capacity for knowledge is by virtue of the *imago Dei*, and the content of that knowledge is the general and special revelation of God, and embodied in the truths of Christianity which apologetics seeks to establish.[114]

---

108. Ibid.
109. Frame, *Doctrine of the Knowledge of God*, 79–80.
110. Riddlebarger, "Lion of Princeton."
111. Ibid., 15.
112. Ibid., 17.
113. Ibid., 90. The Warfield quote is from "Apologetics," *CW* 9:4.
114. Riddlebarger, "Lion of Princeton," 90.

Riddlebarger states that Warfield's emphasis can be "traced to the epistemology of Scottish Common Sense Realism," and further says, "Warfield's comments echo the beliefs of SCSR." The challenge here is in the ambiguity of the language. Is Riddlebarger claiming that Warfield's ideas are similar to those of SCSR or that he derived them from SCSR? If not, from where did he derive them? The confusion is increased when Riddlebarger quotes Warfield to clarify the matter[115] and he states that Warfield's words are an "obvious reference to 1 Peter 3:15."[116] This makes Riddlebarger's position bewildering: Which is more seminal in Warfield's thought—SCSR or Scripture?

Further ambiguity can be seen a few pages later when Riddlebarger analyzes Warfield's statements from his essay "Apologetics" in *The New Schaff-Herzog Encyclopedia*. Riddlebarger quotes Warfield:

> But if theology is the science of God, it deals not with a mass of subjective experiences, nor with a section of the history of thought, but with a body of objective facts; and it is absurd to say that these facts must be assumed and developed unto their utmost implications before we stop and ask whether they are facts. So soon is it agreed that theology is a scientific discipline and has as its subject-matter the knowledge of God, we must recognize that it must begin by establishing the reality as objective facts of the data upon which it is based.[117]

Riddlebarger then states:

> Warfield's allegiance to SCSR is readily apparent in such comments. There is great stress placed upon the historical objectivity of the redemptive events described in Scripture is clearly maintained. [sic] This underlying epistemological structure can be seen throughout Warfield's efforts to develop an effective historical-evidential apologetic.[118]

Like others, because Warfield makes some comments similar to ideas found in SCSR, Riddlebarger makes an unsupported jump to the con-

---

115. Warfield, "Apologetics," *CW* 9:4. "If it is incumbent on the believer to be able to give a reason for the faith that is in him, it is impossible for him to be a believer without a reason for the faith that is in him; and it is the task of apologetics to bring this reason clearly out in his consciousness, and make its validity plain."

116. Ibid. First Peter 3:15 is ". . . but sanctify Christ as Lord in your hearts, always being ready to make a defense to everyone who asks you to give an account for the hope that is in you, yet with gentleness and reverence" (NASB Study Bible).

117. Ibid., 94. The quote is from Warfield, "Apologetics," *CW* 9:7.

118. Riddlebarger, "Lion of Princeton," 94.

clusion that Warfield *took* these ideas from SCSR. Still further, when explaining Warfield's essay "God," stressing Warfield's treatment of the relationship between natural and special revelation, he quotes "'. . . the conviction of the existence of God bears the marks of an intuitive truth in so far as it is the universal and unavoidable belief of men, and is given in the very same act with the idea of self.'"[119] Riddlebarger then concludes: "In words which could have been penned by Thomas Reid, Warfield writes that the existence of God is 'at once dependent and responsible and thus implies one on whom it depends and to whom it is responsible.'"[120] Later on Riddlebarger affirms that "with the epistemological structure of SCSR, natural knowledge of God can be presupposed—those who deny the existence of God can be seen to do so on self-consciously irrational grounds since truth is objective and clear to all rational folk."[121] Moreover, Riddlebarger analyzes Warfield as "following the Scottish dogma" in the latter's affirmation that "'an element of trust underlies all our knowledge.'"[122] At this point, the analysis becomes particularly confusing because the quote is from Warfield's treatment of "Calvin's Doctrine of the Knowledge of God."[123] One is not precisely certain if Riddlebarger means to imply that Calvin's idea regarding an element of trust underlying all our knowledge is something that he acquired from Scottish theologians, whether he simply had it in common with Scottish theologians, or whether Riddlebarger thinks that Warfield's analysis of Calvin is influenced by, or simply correlates with, what Scottish theologians affirmed.

Riddlebarger speaks of Warfield's "allegiance to SCSR," and states that Warfield "has drawn deeply from the well of Scottish Common Sense," that Warfield was "ever faithful to SCSR." His concluding thought on Warfield's essays "The Idea of Systematic Theology" and "The Right of Systematic Theology" is that both reflect Warfield's "reliance upon SCSR." Yet, after making all these statements claiming Warfield is committed to SCSR, Riddlebarger's final deductions leave only confu-

119. Ibid., 102. The Warfield quote is from "God," *SSW* 1:70.

120. Riddlebarger, "Lion of Princeton," 102–3. Those familiar with Calvin's *Institutes* might readily think of the way Calvin begins them as having clear similarities with Warfield's point. The Warfield quote is found in "God," *SSW* 1:70.

121. Riddlebarger, "Lion of Princeton," 104–5, 113.

122. Ibid., 127. The Warfield quote is from "On Faith in Its Psychological Aspects," *CW* 9:329.

123. Riddlebarger, "Lion of Princeton," See also Warfield, "Calvin's Doctrine of the Knowledge of God," *CW* 5:29–130.

sion as to where to place his work within the historiographical literature.[124] In the end, he concludes that much concerning Warfield's apologetics and theological method has been unjustly maligned. He affirms that: 1) Warfield legitimately stands within the historic Reformed tradition; 2) Scottish Presbyterian evidentialists and Reformed Scholastics play a more seminal role in Warfield's theology and apologetics than SCSR; 3) those critical of Warfield actually misanalyze SCSR and its influence on his work, and therefore draw erroneous conclusions about his theology and apologetics; and 4) Warfield's analysis of the relation of faith to reason and the Holy Spirit is "too often ignored or taken out of context, or otherwise misrepresented."[125]

Clear Voices of Opposition to Ahlstrom's Thesis

There is, however, *clear* opposition to those interpreting the Old Princeton theological and epistemological emphases in all of the ways contended for by Ahlstrom et al. In recent years, McClanahan,[126] Calhoun[127] Muller,[128] Gundlach,[129] Helseth,[130] Hicks,[131] Chrisope,[132] and Yarbrough[133] have

---

124. Riddlebarger, "Lion of Princeton," 167, 173, 177, 201.

125. Ibid., 329–31. Part of the misanalysis is a failure to understand that SCSR is not "inherently antithetical to certain Reformed doctrines" (331). This truth, however, is used by some within the Reformed tradition to polemicize for an epistemology *they* believe is faithful to Scripture, yet one they believe is fundamentally at odds with Warfield's. See Plantinga, "Reason and Belief in God," 16–93; Wolterstorff, "Thomas Reid and Rationality"; Vanhoozer, *Is There a Meaning?*, 288–89; Marsden, "Collapse of American Evangelical Academia," 219–64; Terence Penelhum, "Thomas Reid and Contemporary Apologetic," 3–14.

126. McClanahan, "B. B Warfield."

127. Calhoun, *Princeton Seminary*.

128. Muller, *PRRD*.

129. Gundlach, "Evolution Question at Princeton." See also his recent contributions "B Is for Breckinridge" and "'Wicked Caste,'" 13–53, 136–68. Some of the essays in this volume have appeared elsewhere, but together all of the essays provide probably the best introduction to Warfield's life and thought currently available.

130. Helseth, "Moral Character and Moral Certainty"; "B. B. Warfield's Apologetical Appeal," 156–77; "B. B. Warfield on the Apologetical Nature," 89–111; "'Re-Imagining.'"

131. Hicks, *Philosophy of Charles Hodge*.

132. Chrisope, "J. Gresham Machen," 92–109; and *Toward a Sure Faith*.

133. Yarbrough, *Salvation-Historical Fallacy?*

reinforced Hoffecker[134] and Woodbridge[135] and, along with some shorter works, have challenged many of the conclusions that have been standard presuppositions regarding the theological and epistemological emphases of Old Princeton.[136]

Calhoun's two-volume work is not only discerning on most of the crucial issues, but is also the most comprehensive work, by any scholar, regarding Princeton as an institution, as well as its instructors. While utilizing a vast collection of primary and secondary sources, Calhoun weaves a narrative that is comprehensive in scope and yet enjoyable and informative to read. This is the place to begin to gain any proper grounding in the character and concerns of the Princetonians. Though Calhoun sees correlations between aspects of SCSR and some of the Old Princeton theology, he evaluates the latter as both originating in and being faithful to an exegesis of Scripture that is faithful to the WCF.[137]

Chrisope's study of Machen focuses on the latter's struggles with, and response to, modern biblical criticism and the Protestant liberal theology wedded to it. He details Machen's intellectual integrity and spiritual angst in giving modern biblical criticism and Protestant liberal theology a fair hearing, though it resulted in Machen's ultimately criticizing and rejecting them. Chrisope concludes, "if Machen ever had a theological mentor or hero, it was B. B. Warfield."[138] He also finds Machen resisting the fundamentalist template that Marsden forces Machen into, largely because of Marsden's misanalysis of Machen as indebted to SCSR. Chrisope maintains that whatever commitments Machen may have had to SCSR, they were "sufficiently qualified by his Calvinistic theological perspective."[139] Along with Helseth's work, Chrisope helps us see the strong theological, epistemological, and strategic continuity between Warfield and Machen.

---

134. Hoffecker, "Relation between the Objective and Subjective" and *Piety and the Princeton Theologians*.

135. Woodbridge, *Biblical Authority*.

136. Some of the shorter works include D. Clair Davis, "Princeton and Inerrancy"; Fuller/Gardiner, "Reformed Theology at Princeton"; Silva, "Old Princeton, Westminster and Inerrancy"; Wallace, "Foundations of Reformed Biblical Theology"; Anderson, *Benjamin B. Warfield*.

137. Calhoun, *Princeton Seminary*.

138. Chrisope, *Toward a Sure Faith*, 194.

139. Ibid., 231–32, 32 n. 14.

McClanahan's dissertation, while perhaps repetitive and lengthy, nonetheless reveals Warfield's most trenchant concerns and a detailed knowledge of the church's doctrinal history. He correctly identifies Warfield's most vital criticisms of Protestant liberalism when he shows how Warfield addressed the content and historical development of the doctrines of the Christian faith that exposed Protestant liberalism as an innovation and a reformulation. He corroborates the thesis that Warfield saw Christian doctrine as its own defense.

Hoffecker's work, in important ways, serves as a precursor to Helseth's, though the latter was not self-consciously following the former. Still, Hoffecker's study on the stress that the Old Princeton theologians—primarily Archibald Alexander, Charles Hodge, and B. B. Warfield—placed upon Christian piety or holiness helps us see that they saw subjective factors as integral to theological and epistemological enterprises. Hoffecker refutes the idea, as argued by Vander Stelt and Marsden, that Warfield, standing in the Old Princeton tradition, endorsed and operated with an intellectualist and propositionalist approach to truth. Hoffecker rightly identifies the essential subjective element within Warfield's thought and its role within his view of apologetics. He maintains that when some scholars do not accurately represent the "equally strong strand of piety" that accompanied the Princeton men's emphasis on doctrinal objectivity, a "grave injustice" is perpetrated against the Princetonians.[140] Hoffecker sees the Princetonian's emphasis on objectivity as sensing the need to counter the overwhelming and *disproportionate* emphasis on subjectivity present in Protestant liberalism's basic endorsement of Kant's epistemology and Schleiermacher's theology.

Though Muller's work as a whole does not specifically address the Princetonians, it is relevant because of its challenge to the thesis that Turretin and other post-Reformation theologians distorted Calvin, and ended up with a form of rationalism that then affected the Old Princetonians.[141] He does cite Warfield's understanding of Calvin's theology approvingly a number of times.[142] For example, he refers to Warfield's essay on Calvin's doctrine of the Trinity as confirming a variety of posi-

---

140. Hoffecker, *Piety and the Princeton Theologians*, 156.

141. At a number of places, Muller makes reference to Warfield's scholarship. He calls Warfield's study of Calvin's view of the doctrine of God currently "the most extended study," and along with Warfield's study "on Calvin's doctrines of the knowledge of God and of the Trinity, it constitutes a major monographic effort still to be reckoned with" (*PRRD* 3:28).

142. Muller, *PRRD* 3:173, 206, 207, 273, 326, and 542.

tions that Calvin held.¹⁴³ Furthermore, he shows that the fundamental tenets of significant portions of post-Reformation thought are reflected in Warfield's analysis of the relationship between theology, epistemology, and apologetics. Muller also demonstrates that this same heritage is tied to medieval and Reformational thought.¹⁴⁴ While he is not actively attempting to amplify Woodbridge's work, Muller echoes and even advances some of Woodbridge's arguments against Rogers and McKim. The latter duo argues that the doctrine of inerrancy posited by Warfield and A. A. Hodge in their 1881 article on the topic was the creation of the Princetonians only; that it had not been believed throughout the history of the church, and, in particular, had not been the view of the Reformers. They further argued that the WCF did not affirm that only the original documents of Scripture were inerrant.¹⁴⁵

Woodbridge's macrocosmic sweep of the church's entire history regarding biblical authority and the inerrancy of Scripture is a formidable historical defense of the latter doctrine and perhaps deserves reprinting, with the endnotes published as footnotes. Woodbridge responded to Rogers and McKim's thesis that A. A. Hodge and B. B. Warfield contrived the doctrine of inerrancy both as a defensive measure against Protestant liberalism and as an extension of their putative commitment to SCSR. Rogers and McKim argued that the historic position of the church was in line with a generally Neo-orthodox and Protestant liberal understanding of the nature and function of Scripture. Woodbridge's intention was to write a book review, but it developed into an entire book countering the Rogers and McKim thesis, with a staggering amount of historical evidence and critical argumentation. When read along with Muller's four-volume work on *Post-Reformation Reformed Dogmatics*, one is likely to recognize the tendentious and historically inaccurate nature of Rogers and McKim's work.

Gundlach's work maintains that the Princetonians were operating along presuppositional lines of thought in the mid-nineteenth century, long before it became popular in the work of Herman Bavinck

143. Ibid., 4.

144. The work of scholars that demonstrates the continuity of Reformed thinkers with medieval strains of thought is relevant to the discussion of an accurate analysis and assessment of Warfield's thought. For an introduction to that literature, see Leff, *Medieval Thought*; Oberman, *Forerunners of the Reformation* and *Harvest of Medieval Theology*; and Ozment, *Age of Reform*.

145. Rogers and McKim, *Authority and Interpretatio*. For a repetition of this thesis, see Dorrien, *Making of American Liberal Theology*, 364.

and Abraham Kuyper.[146] To recognize the presuppositional nature of Princetonian thought, one has to recognize that theology and philosophy wrestle with concepts and not simply words. This does not mean that words are unimportant, but that their main purpose is to express concepts. Yet a concept can be expressed in multiple ways with a variety of words. To fail to operate according to the latter truth by insisting that a particular concept is only present when a particular word is used or by narrowly restricting the field of words is to commit a word-concept fallacy. The point Gundlach makes is not that the Princetonians of the nineteenth century repeatedly used the *term* presupposition; it is that the Princetonians understood the *concept* that human reasoning operates according to axioms or beliefs that control the content and course of their reasoning. In fact, John Frame asks an interesting question regarding Bahnsen's essay "Machen, Van Til, and the Apologetical Tradition of the OPC."[147] Bahnsen argues that Machen moved in the direction of a Van Tillian presuppositionalism. Frame wants to know, ". . . is it possible that Old Princeton's apologetic was not as far from presuppositionalism as Van Til believed?"[148] It is certainly not unrealistic, therefore, that Gundlach's analysis should call into question the accepted view that identifies Old Princeton apologetics as fundamentally out of step with presuppositional apologetics. In another direction, Gundlach's work also demonstrates that at least some varieties of historical development or process endemic to evolutionary thinking and the discipline of biblical theology were advocated by the Princetonians over the latter half of the nineteenth century. Yet, at the same time, he stresses, they continued to maintain a consistent belief in the supernatural sovereignty of God within the time-space realm of human history.[149]

Paul Kjoss Helseth[150] disputes the interpretation of the Princeton theologians that views them as Scholastic rationalists dependent on an

---

146. Gundlach, "Evolution Question at Princeton," 71 n. 40. Actually, the presuppositional nature of human thought has been understood by philosophers and theologians for centuries.

147. Bahnsen, "Machen, Van Til, and the Apologetical Tradition of the OPC." OPC is the Orthodox Presbyterian Church.

148. Frame, *Cornelius Van Til*, 450.

149. Gundlach, "Evolution Question at Princeton."

150. Helseth, "'*Re*-Imagining' the Princeton Mind." See his *"Right Reason" and the Princeton Mind*. Understanding how the Princetonians used the term "right reason" helps one see how they viewed the objective and subjective aspects of epistemology as organic and united.

Enlightenment view of science. In particular, he argues that Hodge, Warfield, and Machen faithfully maintained a balance between the objective and subjective elements within epistemology. He also asserts that they understood epistemology as inherently moral. Therefore, he argues, to transfer their use of epistemological terms and concepts to an anthropology void of such a moral understanding is to misread and misunderstand their position. His research helps clarify the Princetonian use of the term "science," which is frequently identified as evidence of their capitulation to Enlightenment thinking. An Enlightenment view of science sees human reasoning as the foundation of knowledge, and human rationality as untouched by historically, culturally, and person-specific conditioned presuppositions. Thus, an Enlightenment view of science largely denies the subjective nature of human pursuit and attainment of knowledge. This is what the Old Princetonians are often accused of possessing because they placed a stress on objectivity and facts. Helseth helps us see that when the Old Princetonians—most specifically Hodge and Warfield—referred to theology as a science they did not use "science" in the way an empiricist, rationalist, Enlightenment thinker would use the term. Helseth shows that the Old Princetonians saw human knowing as a moral issue and kept a balance between the objective and subjective elements in human knowing.

Peter Hicks concludes that, according to Hodge, our ability to know truly is the result of who God has made us to be, and who God is as the one who reveals truth. As a result, Hicks concludes that Hodge had a theological epistemology, not a philosophical or, still less, rationalistic one. He affirmed that Hodge and other Old Princeton theologians used the broad range of beliefs held by some of the SCSR philosophers "where suitable, to give philosophical support to a position adopted for other reasons."[151] Those other reasons were theological, and so "there is no indication in" the writings of the Old Princetonians "that they saw Scottish philosophy as in any way binding" for their epistemology.[152] Hicks raises the question as to whether Scottish Realism can actually even function as a useful tool by which to identify and analyze the Old Princeton theology since the former "had never been definitely formulated."[153] As a

---

151. Hicks, *Philosophy of Charles Hodge*, 26, 28, 184–93, 200–219. Hicks, concludes that the case against Hodge rests on "isolated quotations rather than on the general tenor of his thought" (200).

152. Ibid., 26.

153. Ibid.

result, Scottish Realism was not "a well-defined set of doctrines of which people were clearly aware, and deviation from which could be detected and corrected."[154]

Robert W. Yarbrough's book on the history of New Testament theology, *The Salvation-Historical Fallacy?*, helps trace, primarily from the side of German scholarship, the conflict that has existed, and still exists, regarding the use of the historical-critical method of biblical interpretation. The Princetonians understood the nature of the historical-critical method quite well. They were also intensely interested in its uses and were well aware of any developments in it. They even sent some of their own instructors (for example, Hodge, Warfield, and Machen) to Europe to study under its chief proponents. Yarbrough's work is also helpful because it demonstrates the effect that a view of history rooted in Kant's epistemology and putative metaphysical skepticism has had on historical criticism. Such metaphysical skepticism is "putative" because it is not clear why the rejection of a supernatural element in one's metaphysics should result in the rejection of metaphysics in total. Instead, it seems to amount to the rejection of a particular *type* of metaphysics in exchange for one accurately identified as naturalistic.

Conclusion

On one hand it appears that there are two dominant schools of thought regarding interpretation of the Princetonians, and yet, care must be taken in pressing this analysis of the literature too far. It is true that those identifying themselves with the Protestant liberal and Neo-orthodox traditions *generally* follow Ahlstrom's analysis and conclusions, and those in traditionally "conservative" evangelical and Reformed circles *generally* do not. It has been shown, though, that the demarcation of the Princeton historiography into two tidy categories of "liberal" and "conservative" does not accurately reflect the literature. Of course, these two terms are so broad and ambiguous that they rarely provide helpful clarity on any theological issue. That is certainly the case in trying to categorize "schools of thought" regarding Warfield. Perhaps this is best exemplified by the very thesis that Ahlstrom advocated. While the Dutch Reformed heritage out of which Cornelius Van Til came, and which he represented in significant ways as a professor at Westminster Seminary, would generally reject the most seminal aspects of Barthian Neo-orthodoxy and Protestant

154. Ibid.

liberalism,[155] it finds itself keeping company with those traditions when criticizing Warfield for his indebtedness to an Enlightenment view of science and for possessing, at the very least, an implicit rationalism. The issues, therefore, surrounding an interpretation of Warfield's thought are not only varied and conflicting, but also confused within the interpreters themselves, and, at times, more than a little ambiguous.

Of course, one of the plausible reasons for these varied interpretations of Warfield is Warfield himself. Warfield was a formidable intellect and wrote a staggering amount. These two factors alone, I believe, significantly contribute to these varied, conflicting, and at times confusing interpretations of him. To understand the nature of Warfield's scholarship one must appreciate its vast scope, and therefore read widely in it. Though there is undoubtedly some truth to Francis Landey Patton's observation that Warfield was "a dogmatic rather than a systematic theologian, and was less interested in the system of doctrine than in the doctrines of the system," this observation could be dangerously misleading.[156] As one who was thoroughly concerned to highlight the unity of truth, or the circle of the sciences, Warfield's concern for the "doctrines of the system" was the very means through which he communicated his concern for the system, because he believed that all of the doctrines were implicated in each other. Among other things, this means that in order to grasp the significance of his apologetic method and the weight of his arguments, one must not only read widely in his scholarship, but also recognize that his view of theology, science, and apologetics is unitary and organic. When Warfield addresses any one particular doctrine, he will invariably relate it to many other doctrines. Thus, in order for someone to refute what Warfield has said about any one particular doctrine, one will also have to deny virtually everything he has said about the other doctrines to which he related the primary one under observation. Warfield believed that he had knowledge of the whole because he had been grounded in the WCF and its Shorter and Larger Catechism. He, therefore, analyzed and operated with a view of theology, science, and apologetics that was consistent with the doctrines of the Confession. This can be seen by paying attention to what Warfield said about systematic theology as a science and its relation to other sciences, and how all of these matters relate to apologet-

---

155. Van Til, *Christianity and Barthianism* and *Confession of 1967*. For helpful guides through Van Til's thought see Frame, *Cornelius Van Til*; and Bahnsen, *Van Til's Apologetic*.

156. Patton, "Memorial Address Benjamin Breckinridge Warfield," 386.

ics. Warfield *was* systematic in his thinking, and that really ought not to surprise us when we pay attention to the earliest and most profound influences upon that thinking.[157]

---

157. In referring to the doctrines of sin, incarnation, expiation, and regeneration, Patton stated: "These doctrines are the common heritage of the Christians; they constitute the heart of Christianity, and Dr. Warfield held and taught them in their integrity." Patton, "Benjamin Breckinridge Warfield," 378.

2

B. B. Warfield: A Biographical Summary

Although no book-length biography currently exists on Warfield, enough of the details of his life are available to highlight the most significant influences upon his scholarship.[1] These influences are not only apparent in his earliest years, but are also clearly reflected in his scholarly writing, and life decisions. In the Warfield family, love for God, his creation, and his church were united. This unity was expressed in their living out not only the doctrines contained in the WCF and its Larger and Shorter Catechisms, but also the implications of those doctrines.[2] Central among those implications was a love for learning. The categories of thought in the Confession, and the content that fills those categories, were imprinted upon Warfield's mind from the earliest stages of his development, helping to shape his life. Later, in his scholarship, there was a conscious intent to be faithful to the Bible, which, to him, also meant being faithful to the Confession.[3] Of course, whether he was or was not faithful to the Confession is a controversial matter, and whether the Confession is, or is not, a product of scholastic rationalism is also debated. In order to gain resolution regarding the controversies surrounding the assessment and

---

1. Patton, "Benjamin Breckinridge Warfield" (hereafter "Memorial Address"), 369–91; E. Warfield, "Biographical Sketch," *CW* 1:v–ix; Calhoun, *Princeton Seminary* 2:114–19; Gundlach, "B Is for Breckinridge"; McClanahan, "Benjamin B. Warfield"; Riddlebarger, "Lion of Princeton," 5–14; Allis, "Personal Impressions"; Lloyd Jones, "Defender of the Faith."

2. E. Warfield, "Biographical Sketch," *CW* 1:vi; B. Warfield, "Inspiration and Criticism," *CW* 1:395–96.

3. B. Warfield, "Inspiration and Criticism," *CW* 1:395–96.

interpretation of Warfield's scholarship, it is necessary to know what was most influential in Warfield's mature thinking as a scholar. Since his conscious and verbalized intent early in his scholarly career was to be faithful to the WCF, there is a clear link between his expressed adult thinking and one of the significant activities of his youth. Though Warfield was disinclined to speak of himself, there are sufficient observations from others to provide historical evidence to help in tracing the most important influences on his thought.

Warfield's father traced his roots to Richard Warfield, of Puritan descent, who in the mid-1600s settled in Virginia. Forced to leave Virginia because of his refusal to accept the proclamation of Charles II as King, Richard moved his family to a place near Annapolis, Maryland.[4] In other words, Warfield came from a line of highly committed people who were willing to act on their convictions, not just hold them. Benjamin Breckinridge Warfield was born as the first son to William and Mary (Cabell Breckinridge) Warfield near the rolling hills of what would later be called "Grassmere," near Lexington, Kentucky, on November 5, 1851. Warfield's father was a farmer of significant skill, as seen not only in the family's prosperity, but also in his own writings—*The Theory and Practice of Cattle Breeding* and *The History of Short Horn Cattle in America*.[5] Warfield's family heritage was rooted in the church, steeped in education, and committed to church and civil government service.

Benjamin demonstrated early scientific interests. He collected "birds, eggs, butterflies and moths, and geological specimens; studied the fauna and flora of his neighborhood; read Darwin's newly published books with enthusiasm; and counted Audubon's works on American birds and mammals his chief treasure."[6] Some of his father William's ability in writing, as well as those skills used in diagramming and categorizing cattle, were evidently transferred to his eldest son. Later, as a New Testament scholar, Warfield would diagram and categorize New Testament manuscripts in

---

4. The material in this paragraph (with the exception of fn 5) is from E. Warfield, "Biographical Sketch," *CW* 1:iii–vi. Ethelbert Warfield noted that his brother went to private schools in Lexington and received most of his education from Lewis Barbour, who later became a university professor of mathematics, and James K. Patterson, who later became president of the State College of Kentucky.

5. McClanahan, "Benjamin B. Warfield," endnotes 10, 55. We get some insight into the funds available to the family in E. Warfield, "Biographical Sketch," *CW* 1:vi, where he notes that his father "dissuaded" his eldest son from seeking "the fellowship in experimental science" because "he did not need the stipend."

6. E. Warfield, "Biographical Sketch," *CW* 1:vi.

much the same way that his father had applied to cattle, revealing that his childhood interest in analyzing objects of his interest remained strong.[7] His academic and literary skills could already be seen when Warfield graduated from Princeton at the age of nineteen with highest honors. He "won the Thompson prize for the highest rank in the junior year, and was one of the editors of the *Nassau Literary Magazine*."[8]

In addition to an interest in creation, and an acumen in writing and scientific work, William passed on his quiet and gentle spirit to Benjamin, for the latter certainly does not seem to have acquired it from his mother's side of the family, as shown below. B. B. Warfield's reluctance to speak of himself and his quiet disposition were so pronounced that when he announced his plans to enter the Christian ministry "his decision was . . . a surprise to his family and most intimate friends."[9] Part of the surprise was because his greatest interests had always been in the fields of math and science. Indeed, Warfield had obtained "perfect marks" in math and physics while at Princeton College, and was so certain, as a youth, that he would engage in scientific work that he vigorously resisted studying Greek. Everything in his observable life seemed to point in the direction of a career in math and the natural sciences.[10]

There were obviously internal contemplations, however, that eventually led him in another direction. The content and duration of those thoughts, though, will forever remain a mystery due to Warfield's propensity to "keep things close to the vest." The degree to which this marked his personality can be seen in the following account. Charles Barrett, who was one of his closest college friends, a traveling companion, and his seminary roommate, wrote this regarding Warfield's own explanation of why he chose the ministry:

> We were seated together before an open window in Brown Hall. We drew our chairs close together and we sat there in the calm of a September evening. Our souls seemed to draw near together. A close friendship had been established when we were fellow students over in Princeton College, where he led the class. This friendship had been cemented by a year of travel abroad.

---

7. Ibid. The vivid images of his early years can be seen in a letter home in which he compared the look that a student would receive for not having joined one of the literary societies to the look one would give "some stray beast . . . which had wandered into the wrong pasture" (Calhoun, *Princeton Seminary* 2:116).

8. E. Warfield, "Biographical Sketch," *CW* 1:vi.

9. Ibid., 1:vii.

10. The material in this paragraph is from ibid.

> Together we had visited the largest cities. We had wandered through quaint old towns. [And] ... on foot among the Alps—I suppose we wandered for a thousand miles together.... [Now] we sat together there in old Brown Hall, with reminiscences in our hearts. At last I turned to him and said, "What was it that decided you to enter the ministry?" I can see his face, the tender look that came into his face. He was very near to me just at that moment, now forty-three years ago ... I can hear the very tone of his voice. He turned to me and said, "Because I think that in the work of the ministry I can do the most to repay the Lord for what he has done for me."[11]

Warfield's literary inclination was not simply the result of paternal, but also maternal, gifts. Warfield's mother, Mary Cabell Breckinridge, was the daughter of Rev. Robert Jefferson Breckinridge (1800–1871), whose brother John served as a professor of pastoral theology and a part-time fundraiser for Princeton seminary until his death from bronchial consumption on August 4, 1841.[12] John was loved by the seminary community and was a close friend of seminary and college professors, Charles Hodge and James Waddell Alexander.[13] Furthermore, the Breckinridge family also had ties to the political pedigree of the nation. Mary was the granddaughter of Thomas Jefferson's attorney general. In fact, before John Breckinridge taught at Princeton, he had been chaplain to the U.S. Congress (1822–1823).[14] It was Robert Breckinridge, Warfield's maternal grandfather, however, who would leave an indelible mark upon both Princeton and his grandson.

Warfield and Controversy

The Breckinridge family's relationship to Princeton was rather strained by Mary's father. Robert's student years were marked by a serious fight with a fellow classmate from Texas named Furman Morford—which led to suspensions for both. Though both were reinstated, Robert sought and was granted an "honorable dismissal" and subsequently went to Yale, and then completed his studies at Union College. Such pugilistic activity was evidently quite representative of the spirit that ran strong

---

11. Calhoun, *Princeton Seminary* 2:117.

12. E. Warfield, "Biographical Sketch," *CW* 1:v; Calhoun, *Princeton Seminary* 1:209.

13. Gundlach, "B is for Breckinridge," 14. Biographical summaries of Charles Hodge, James Waddel Alexander, and John Breckinridge can be found in Calhoun, *Princeton Seminary* 1:435–46.

14. Calhoun, *Princeton Seminary* 1:435–46.

through the Breckinridge boys, and manifested itself in Robert in sometimes extreme, and violent, ways. Robert eventually curtailed his violence when he was converted to Christ. His aggressive spirit no longer sought opportunities for physical quarrels, but instead sought church service.[15] Breckinridge wrote his own system of theology, "The Knowledge of God Objectively and Subjectively Considered." He also wrote "The Act and Testimony,"[16] as well as fulfilling newspaper editorial duties for the *Spirit of the Nineteenth Century* and the *Danville Review*.[17] Thus, both sides of Warfield's family demonstrated significant scribal tendencies, and there was obviously no shortage of resolve for one's chosen causes.

It would be remiss, however, if attention was not given to the fact that, even from his admirers, Warfield received criticism for his *style* of writing. As A. A. Hodge wrote at the end of a personal letter dated April 5, 1882:

> Please let me make one important fatherly suggestion to you. You are so full of learning—you are so enthusiastic, clear and energetic in your presentation & contentious, your style is so simple, clear & forceful that it is of the utmost importance that your one fault should be corrected & God's truth have in you a faultless champion. The fact is, (& hear [sic] all your Princeton friends agree) you write too eagerly and precipitate hurry—& hence send in your manuscript in a negligent condition—very loose in (1) the matter of the order of clauses. (2) as to the repetition of the same affirmation, in a manner that weakens the emphasis. So as to the "order of clauses" especially you are often very careless. Please forgive my impertinence. I am exceedingly faulty in the same way. In me it is hopeless for I am old & dotish. But you are young & Princely. And the coming King should have no faults.[18]

So, even though verbose and possessing a quick pen, Warfield had to work at perfecting his writing craft.

Regrettably, though his grandfather Breckinridge's commitment and loyalty to the church may have been laudable, at times, it was also

---

15. The material in this paragraph is from Gundlach, "B is for Breckinridge," 17–44. B. B. Warfield would later participate in his own fisticuffs as a first-year college student, after drawing a caricature of a fellow student during a lecture by James McCosh—although the matter did not attract formal disciplinary attention. See Kerr, "Person behind the Theology," 92.

16. Gundlach, "B is for Breckinridge," 23–33; Calhoun, *Princeton Seminary* 1:245.

17. E. Warfield, "Biographical Sketch," *CW* 1:v.

18. B. B. Warfield Papers, box 13, PTS archives.

misplaced, contentious, and even foolish. Apparently void of instruction in the idiosyncrasies of ecclesiastical battles, Robert Breckinridge earned a reputation for contentiousness that no doubt exhausted some, and at times, also made him ineffective. Although he did experience a significant degree of success in some battles—he was voted moderator of the General Assembly in 1841 and helped persuade the 1845 assembly to reject the legitimacy of Catholic baptism—such successes came at a high price. Breckinridge's reputation for conflict and controversy was virtually legendary. One of Breckinridge's friends remarked: "The Rev. Dr. Robt. [sic] J. probably never had peace on any subject, with any person, at any place, during a long and tempestuous life."

During the hotly debated Old School/New School controversy[19] of the early 1830s, Robert Breckinridge wrote "The Act and Testimony," which became the rallying point for nearly 375 ministers. Yet, it also became a point of controversy and disagreement with other Old School advocates, such as Charles Hodge and Samuel Miller, who, though viewing the goal as laudable, saw the means as a strategic mistake. "The Act and Testimony" was written after the conclusion of the 1834 General Assembly of the Presbyterian Church. The purpose of the polemic was to rally Old School pastors to be more stringent in their reforms. Charles Hodge was also an Old School proponent, but he believed that the advocates of "The Act and Testimony" were drawing the theological and ecclesiastical boundary lines too narrowly, and adopting a strategy that was more of a play on emotions than an accurate and constructive theological statement for the benefit of the church. When Hodge published his criticism of "The Act and Testimony" and appealed for caution and chaste dialogue, he was accused of compromising and betraying the Old School. Hodge basically had three criticisms: 1) its test of orthodoxy was illegitimate, 2) it distorted the true condition of the church, and 3) it ac-

---

19. The Old School/New School controversy was a debate that took place in the Presbyterian Church in the United States beginning in the early 1830s. It was over 1) the influence of Arminian strains of thought creeping into the Presbyterian Church through those claiming to be successors to Jonathan Edwards' theology—Nathaniel Taylor and Samuel Hopkins being two of the more prominent; 2) what constituted acceptable and unacceptable interdenominational cooperation [this was one of the chief ways that these Arminian strains of thought had seeped into the Presbyterian Church]; and 3) what constituted legitimate views of subscription to the Westminster Confession of Faith. The Old School, which Princeton Seminary aligned itself with, stood staunchly against Arminian tendencies, was more reluctant to participate in interdenominational cooperation, and did not appreciate what they perceived to be the rather broad view of subscription advocated by their New School counterparts.

complished division, not reform, in the Church because only a minority of men in the Old School could agree with it. Thus, the laudable *goal* was reform, but the actual *effect* was division. Hodge agreed with Breckinridge that reform was definitely needed. He disagreed with him on how to accomplish that reform. Warfield, though related to Breckinridge, was, in temperament and tactics, aligned with Hodge in these kinds of ecclesiastical disputes. In the end, the relationship between Robert Breckinridge and Charles Hodge, who represented Princeton in significant ways, was seriously strained and both sides felt betrayed. Warfield, carrying the Breckinridge lineage but also owing much to Princeton and the tutelage of Hodge, would, in time, be affected.[20]

An episode in his grandfather's combative relationship with Princeton eventually reached out to touch Warfield, whose handling of the situation offers a glimpse into Warfield's manner of handling confrontational situations. An earlier charge of plagiarism was reignited after Robert Breckinridge's death, and this led his son William to defend the honor of his father. William elicited the help of his nephew in this defense. Nephew Benjamin demonstrated what would become a notable trait throughout his scholarly career—a very measured, tactful expression of the truth that shed light without inflammatory rhetoric. By displaying these qualities in this matter, Warfield was not only heeding the counsel of his mother, but also attempting to service the needs of his uncle, while still being faithful to the truth. Warfield's strategy, shown in these words to his uncle, is illuminating: "We want a few words so temperately spoken that they carry conviction with them & the feeling that the writer is standing on such secure ground that he need not be angry over *any* charge." In a letter to Uncle William, Warfield stated that there was a certain ambiguity to the charge of plagiarism—Robert Breckinridge had accounted for borrowing from many sources in a preface, but had failed to cite the sources in the body of the work. In this, Warfield shows his willingness to see the full truth, truth from both sides. Maybe more illuminating, however, are Warfield's words in a draft of this letter. He tells his Uncle that he had "schooled" himself in order to refrain from writing

---

20. The material in this paragraph is from Gundlach, "B is for Breckinridge," 14–44. Some of it can also be found in Calhoun, *Princeton Seminary* 1:245–55. Gundlach observes that the difficulties present for B. B. Warfield can be seen in a letter from his mother dated February 20, 1881, in which she stated regarding the recycled allegation against her father: "Do'nt [sic] you begin to see why I dred to see you my darling—thrown forward as the fighting man of the church? Princeton always stood behind walls—and Pa & men of his stamp did the hard fighting."

anything that did not meet the need at hand. What may be most striking is the fact that he apparently not only "schooled" himself regarding what he wrote in "defense" of his grandfather, but also regarding what he wrote to his uncle, since this admission of disciplined restraint was never sent.

This episode is a clear example of how Warfield operated as a scholar as well—judiciously, graciously, and truthfully, doing his best to avoid causing strife. This does not mean Warfield avoided strife; he obviously did not shirk controversy. He did not, however, seek either to stir it up or to inflame it in tense situations. Indeed, concerning those scholars with whom he had the most stringent disagreements, Warfield also constantly acknowledged what those same scholars did well and those places in which they were correct.[21] A good example of this disposition early on in his scholarly career is his article "Dr. Briggs' Critical Method." Warfield acknowledges that he longed to talk over the various points with the author. He begins by speaking of the approach of any good reader and then moves on into the approach that he himself is taking: ". . . sure of his own good temper, he is sure of that of his author too. This is the spirit in which I purpose to set down here the impression which the critical method set forth in Dr. Brigg's paper has made upon my mind." He ends the brief essay with: "Reverence and dignity are becoming a discussion on such themes, and should be demanded from all. But surely Christian brethren can sit around a common table and inquire of one another concerning the literary phenomena of their common Bible without rancor and with profit."[22]

Warfield and the Westminster Confession of Faith

Family heritage not only influenced Warfield's literary tendencies, but also the content of his theology. He was raised in a devout Presbyterian home where the children memorized the Shorter and Larger Catechisms.[23]

---

21. The material in this paragraph is from Gundlach, "B is for Breckinridge," 48–52. Numerous examples of Warfield speaking well of his opponents could be given, and a quick survey of some of Warfield's most explicitly polemical pieces will reveal his generally irenic approach.

22. B. Warfield, "Dr. Briggs' Critical Method," 1, 4. See also Gary Johnson, "Warfield and C. A. Briggs: Their Polemics and Legacy," in Johnson, *B. B. Warfield*, 195–240. Johnson specifically addresses the differences between how Warfield and Briggs engaged in polemics.

23. Meeter and Nicole, *Bibliography*, iii–iv. It seems rather axiomatic to mention the importance of parental influence and childhood experiences for human growth and

Warfield memorized the Shorter Catechism by the age of six, then the Scripture proofs, and finally the Larger Catechism. George Marsden justly called this an "arduous and awesome" process.[24] This achievement should not be lightly brushed aside. The WCF and the Catechisms were the earliest influence on Warfield's theology and he was steeped in them. The memorization of the Catechisms reveals a family emphasis on the intermingling of learning and the Christian faith from which Warfield never departed.

The Augustinian and Calvinistic perspective expressed in the Confession not only predates the rise of SCSR, but also dominated all of Warfield's developmental years—long prior to any formal academic exposure to the Scottish philosophy. Moreover, the history and content of Warfield's scholarship reveals a *primary* interest in the exegesis of Scripture. He believed that the theological and doctrinal system of the WCF was a direct result of such exegesis. As he stated upon accepting the position at Western:

> . . . the system taught in these symbols is the system which will be drawn out of the Scriptures in the prosecution of the teaching to which you have called me—not indeed, because commencing with that system the Scriptures can be made to teach it, but because commencing with the Scriptures I cannot make them teach anything else.[25]

The epistemology, anthropology, theology, and soteriology in Warfield's writings express the Confession's distinctives, which amounts to echoing and endorsing an Augustinian and Calvinistic understanding of these topics. Indeed, at every turn in the Warfield corpus there is a constant exposition of the doctrines of Scripture contained in the WCF. What is conspicuous by its absence is any reference to SCSR, or an endorsement by Warfield of any formal and codified philosophy of which either the Bible or the Confession of Faith approve. Francis Landey Patton's assessment of Warfield and his scholarship corroborates this fact:

> He was not a philosophical theologian who tried to translate the doctrines of the New Testament into the language of idealistic metaphysics, nor an apologetic theologian who sought to defend the central doctrines of Christianity on the basis of a conceded

---

development. For an example of this point, see Rayburn, "Presbyterian Doctrines," 76–109.

24. Marsden, *Fundamentalism and American Culture*, 109.

25. Warfield, "Inspiration and Criticism," *CW* 1:395–96.

> minimum of historical truth. He was a dogmatic theologian who based the content of his teaching on the plain and obvious meaning of the inspired Word. . . . He believed in the supernatural contents of Scripture, but he believed also in the supernatural structure of Scripture.[26]

According to Patton, what animated Warfield was concern over "how men had dropped the substance of doctrine to grasp its shadow in the stream of idealistic metaphysics."[27]

Thus, a historical treatment of Warfield seems to sanction identifying the WCF and its Catechisms as having a prodigious influence on him, while recognizing that some aspects of SCSR as expressed by some Scottish philosophers[28] have some things in common with the doctrines Warfield espoused. There is a glimpse of the type of pervasive influence the Catechisms were for Warfield, and an expression of his own sentiments, in his essay "Is the Shorter Catechism Worthwhile?"

> How many have had occasion to "thank God for that Catechism!" Did anyone ever know a really devout man who regretted having been taught the Shorter Catechism—even with tears—in his youth? How its forms of sound words come reverberating back into the memory, in moments of trial and suffering, of doubt and temptation, giving direction to religious aspirations, firmness to hesitating thought, guidance to stumbling feet: and adding to our religious meditations an ever-increasing richness and depth. "The older I grow," said Thomas Carlyle in his old age, "and now I stand on the brink of eternity, the more comes back to me the first sentence in the Catechism, which I learned when a child, and the fuller and deeper its meaning becomes:
>
> What is the chief end of man?
> To glorify God and to enjoy him forever."[29]

After persevering through the "arduous and awesome" process of learning the Catechisms, Warfield made a profession of faith and joined the Second Presbyterian Church of Lexington, Kentucky, at the age of sixteen.[30] Joining the church entailed making a credible confession of the

26. Patton, "Memorial Address," 372.
27. Ibid., 378.
28. Ahlstrom, "Scottish Philosophy."
29. B. Warfield, "Is The Shorter Catechism Worthwhile?," *SSW* 1:381–84.
30. The description of the process is from Marsden, *Fundamentalism and American Culture*, 109. See also, Calhoun, *Princeton Seminary* 2:115.

Christian faith, on the basis of comprehension and apprehension of the Shorter and Larger Catechisms. This process reveals an understanding of the intellectual nature of the Christian faith operative in some Reformed and Presbyterian circles. It does not mean that such traditions automatically thought the Christian faith could be reduced to the intellect, and neither did the Princetonians teach that it could be. Their understanding saw human thinking, feeling, and willing as inseparably joined. Having the ability to state truth in a propositional form did not automatically mean, as Marsden has stated, that "Old School Presbyterians tended to view truth in its purest form as precisely stated propositions."[31] Among other things, Warfield makes clear that the term "knowledge" ought to be clarified and that in the Christian view of reality "knowledge" of God "involves the whole man and all his activities."[32] In "St. Paul's Use of the Argument from Experience," Warfield explains Paul's teaching on the relationship between the objective ground of the believer's justification and the believer's subjective experience of the fruit of the Spirit.[33] Warfield states: Knowing God "in the deeper sense is not the act of the mere understanding, nor can theology fulfill its function of making man 'to know God' simply by framing propositions for the logical intellect."[34]

Memorizing the Catechisms meant memorizing the theological content in them. This process imprinted an indelible stamp on Warfield's young mind. The theological content committed to memory at such an early age, and reinforced during Warfield's entire childhood, had a lasting effect upon his thinking. Indeed, the doctrines concerning God, revelation, and human beings expressed in the Confession and Catechisms are what Warfield explicated as he argued against the biblical and theological scholarship that polemicized for the reconceptualization of the Christian faith. Warfield demonstrated that his intent was to bow to the ultimate

---

31. Marsden, *Fundamentalism and American Culture*, 110. This characterization certainly does not correspond to Warfield's view of truth. In "Theology a Science," (*SSW* 2), Warfield criticizes Andrew Dickson White's *History of the Warfare of Science with Theology* for trying to set science against theology. Theology has a practical element to it, just as any science does. Warfield denied a bare propositionalist view of theology, and acknowledged its inherently practical character. For a similar view see Frame, *Doctrine of the Knowledge of God*, 76.

32. B. Warfield, "Theology a Science," *SSW* 2:210. For the vital role of the affective dimensions within the Christian faith see Warfield, "Faith and Life," *SSW* 1:365–68; "Religious Life of the Theological Student," *SSW* 1:411–28; "Authority, Intellect, Heart," *SSW* 2:668–71.

33. B. Warfield, "St. Paul's Use of the Argument from Experience," *SSW* 2:142–51.

34. B. Warfield, "Theology a Science," *SSW* 2:210.

authority of Scripture, recognizing that Scripture warranted his belief in the doctrinal teaching of the Confession. Although SCSR has, in some ways, been correlated to Warfield's views, it has not been, and cannot be, shown to sufficiently account for them. Warfield is not only in correspondence with the Confession, but also heralds the Confession as being in correspondence with Scripture. There is, therefore, good reason to identify the Confession, and the biblical exposition upon which it is based, as a decisive influence on his thoughts and tactics.

Warfield: Learning and Scripture

There is another great influence in Warfield's life that cannot be overlooked: his deep loyalty to his wife. Not long after his marriage to Annie Kinkead, the newlyweds took a trip to Europe.[35] During a hike in the Harz Mountains, they were caught in a thunderstorm that left Annie in a debilitated condition for the rest of her life. Warfield's commitment to caring for her resulted in his living a rather reclusive life. He pretty well confined himself to the town and campus of Princeton. It should not be overlooked here that Warfield believed that the Scriptures taught the sovereignty of the triune God over creation, and, therefore, over human history. Warfield's commitment to his wife would seem to be, in part, the manifestation of a belief that such care was what God had providentially determined for him, as well as for her. One can only speculate regarding the personal pain experienced by Warfield. His reluctance to speak of himself remains a significant obstacle to exploring such matters. Patton observed in his memorial address regarding Warfield, on May 2, 1921, at the First Presbyterian Church in Princeton:

> [T]here was an aloofness and a detachment about him that might easily have been mistaken for a haughty disregard of what other people think. He was habitually objective in his thinking and neither made revelations of his own subjectivities nor cared much apparently for the subjectivities of other people. Few and short were words of praise for other men, and he was silent regarding himself.[36]

It should be emphasized that Patton also commented that it would have been a *mistake* to conclude that Warfield cared little for what other peo-

---

35. Calhoun, *Princeton Seminary* 2:315–16; Allis, "Personal Impressions," 10.

36. Patton, "Memorial Address," 388. Such comments might reveal what is behind Machen's comment that "[W]ith all his glaring faults he was the greatest man I have known" (Stonehouse, *J. Gresham Machen*, 310).

ple thought.[37] The testimony of former students, in addition to Patton's own, along with Warfield's care for his wife, reveal him to have been a man of tenderness and compassion. Furthermore, Warfield's scholarly writings reveal that he understood quite well the idiosyncrasies of subjective impulses in theological analyses and conclusions, as well as in life decisions.

His commitment to caring for his wife did mean that Warfield's life was framed by his scholarly and didactic work. One can easily believe that greater patience and compassion would have been part of the by-products of such a life, but it also afforded him the increased time to read and write that allowed him to have such success.[38] While brief in words about himself and others, Warfield's pen was prolific regarding biblical and theological matters. The sheer mass of his writings places him among the giants in church history. Hugh T. Kerr placed the magnitude of Warfield's writings on the level of "Augustine, Aquinas, Luther, Calvin and Barth."[39] Warfield's scholarly writing, however, is not only staggering in volume, but also impressive in its breadth and depth.[40] Regardless of whether one agrees or disagrees with Warfield, reading his works results in an exposure to virtually an entire seminary curriculum.[41]

B. B. Warfield was taught that the Bible is the only written revelation from the only triune God, and that the WCF and the Shorter and Larger Catechism accurately express the Bible's content. Professionally, Warfield

37. Patton, "Memorial Address," 388.

38. Former students testify to Warfield's admirable personal qualities. See Allis, "Personal Impressions."

39. Riddlebarger, "Lion of Princeton," 8.

40. Calhoun explains, "By profound study and extensive reading in English, German, French and Dutch, B. B. Warfield, to a degree that has rarely been equaled, excelled in the whole field of theological learning—exegetical, historical and doctrinal. . . . John DeWitt said that he had known intimately the three great Reformed theologians of America in the preceding generation—Charles Hodge, William Shedd and Henry B. Smith—and that he was certain not only that Warfield knew a great deal more than any one of them, but that he knew more than all three of them put together!" (Calhoun, *Princeton Seminary* 2:320; citing Hugh T. Kerr, "Person behind the Theology"; see Calhoun, *Princeton Seminary* 2:503 n. 12).

41. Warfield's total number of book reviews was over 780, "of which 318 were 'very substantial critical reviews'" (Riddlebarger, "Lion of Princeton," 8). To give some perspective on this production, volume 10 of the *Collected Works* contains 46 of the reviews (most of which probably fit into the "substantial" category) and consumes 482 pages. Even taking all 46 as substantial, that still leaves 272 not included, which would appear then to be able to fill approximately six more volumes of the same length as volume 10 of the *Collected Works*.

was first and foremost a New Testament scholar. To be certain, he wrote on every topic within the seminary curriculum, and occupied the chair of Polemic and Didactic Theology at Princeton. But Warfield was completely confident that there is no disjuncture between the Scripture's particular details and its unitary nature and message. This commitment to unity is clearly highlighted by his encyclopedic treatment of all theological and biblical matters, while maintaining his interest and skill in biblical exegesis. As previously mentioned, belief in the diversity and unity of the Bible, and the expression of this truth within the doctrinal content and system of the WCF, is not a product of a particular philosophical school or ideology. Moreover, one of Warfield's significant points, throughout the theological controversies of his professional life, was to highlight that the views for which he argued were not essentially new. He recognized that the church's *understanding* of the Scriptures had developed, and would continue to do so, through a historical process providentially governed and illuminated by God. He knew that comprehension of biblical doctrine would become sharper, and in this sense might possibly be labeled as "new," but the "new" will never contradict what God has revealed to the prophets and apostles in what is now the Bible.[42] In addition, the relationship between the text of Scripture, the unity of its message, and the church's progressive understanding and articulation of the doctrinal content of Scripture is reflected in Warfield's career history.

Although he had been offered a position in Old Testament at Western Seminary in Pittsburgh, Pennsylvania, Warfield did not begin his professional career until he was offered a position there as an instructor in New Testament Language and Literature.[43] As Kim Riddlebarger helpfully points out, the first five sizeable published works by Warfield were in the field of New Testament, and these were accompanied by sixty additional works in New Testament from 1880 to 1886.[44] His first volume, *Introduction to the Textual Criticism of the New Testament*, published in England in 1886, was the first book by an American to explain the discipline of textual criticism in biblical studies.[45] Then in 1907, at what

42. B. Warfield, "Latest Phase of Historical Rationalism," *CW* 9:602.
43. E. Warfield, "Biographical Sketch," *CW* 1:vii.
44. Ibid. See also Riddlebarger, "Lion of Princeton," 59.
45. B. Warfield, *Introduction to Textual Criticism*; Calhoun, *Princeton Seminary* 2:113. Warfield's book went through nine editions by 1907. The notable Southern Baptist New Testament scholar A. T. Robertson said, "'No one else outside of [F. J. A.] Hort . . . had so clearly and so fully set forth the principles of textual criticism that the student could readily grasp the science and apply it" (Calhoun, *Princeton Seminary* 2:469 n. 2).

might be considered the height of many of his theological disputes with liberal theologians, Warfield wrote *The Lord of Glory*, which received accolades for its thorough treatment of the New Testament testimony regarding the person and work of Jesus.[46]

He shifted his emphasis to dogmatic and systematic theological endeavors upon receiving the appointment to Princeton as Professor of Polemic and Didactic Theology, but continued to apply exegesis while addressing dogmatic and systematic theological issues. Many of his polemical writings in the early 1900s are against the use of biblical criticism by liberal scholars. Warfield's arguments demonstrate a knowledge not only of the text-critical issues, but also of the history of the canon.[47] He actually did advocate the use of scientific criticism in the study of the Bible. What he objected to was the way in which liberal scholars operated with preconceived biases that ruled out a view of the supernatural that was contrary to their philosophical, naturalistic presuppositions.[48] In the end, Warfield maintained that the liberal scholars were *un*scientific because they could not and would not account for all the available evidence.

Warfield saw no conflict between the role of biblical scholarship, with its commensurate duty of exegesis, and the role of systematic, dogmatic, and historical theology. He saw all of these as a coherent whole, and as mutually dependent and complimentary disciplines. This was another manifestation of the Old Princeton conception of the "unity of truth" as well as the "division of labor."[49] Thus, Warfield did not confine

---

46. B. Warfield, *Lord of Glory*. A certain W. L. L. wrote in *The Southern Presbyterian* 23, 1908: "One stands in amazement at Dr. Warfield's scholarship. This crops out more in the footnotes, eve, [sic] than it does in the main body of the text. He seems to have read every theological and critical work in the English and German languages. I dare say there is not a better furnished man along these lines in America than he." After commending James Orr to the reader he states, "If any one thinks that all the scholarship is on the side of the radical, he is vastly mistaken." B. B. Warfield MSS Scrapbooks, vol. 1 (1900–11), box 53, PTS archives.

47. A sizeable sample of these can be found in *CW* vols. 3 and 10.

48.. B. Warfield, "Inspiration and Criticism," *CW* 1:395–425; "Rights of Criticism and of the Church," *SSW* 2:595–603, "Latest Phase of Historical Rationalism," *CW* 9:585–647, "Evading the Supernatural," *SSW* 2:680–84, "Divine and Human in the Bible," *SSW* 2:542–48, "Heresy and Concession," *SSW* 2:672–79, "Christian Supernaturalism," *CW* 9:25–46; and "Ritschlian School," *SSW* 2:448–51.

49. Gundlach, "Evolution Question at Princeton," 53–72. For the relation of the "unity of truth" to the task of systematic theology, see Warfield, "Task and Method of Systematic Theology," *CW* 9:95. For the phrase "unity of truth" and post-Reformation, Reformation, and medieval thought, see Muller, *PRRD* 1:85–132. For a fuller treatment of "unity of truth," see the first few pages of chapter 1 of this book.

himself to New Testament scholarship or to essays on systematic theology narrowly construed. Instead, he wrote voluminously on historical topics that he saw as joined to the doctrinal matters of the Christian faith. Warfield's *Collected Works*, then, has entire volumes devoted to his essays on Tertullian and Augustine, Calvin and Calvinism, the Reformation and its theology, the Westminster Assembly and its work, the theology of Jonathan Edwards, as well as Warfield's analysis of the Christian perfectionism of Oberlin theology and the Ritschlianism of the late nineteenth and early twentieth centuries.[50] For Warfield, learning and the Christian faith are inextricably intertwined.

What is important to take home from a quick look at Warfield's life circumstances is that he was afforded the opportunity to become conversant with a vast theological literature and that his primary weapon in theological and ecclesiastical conflicts was his pen. His mathematic and scientific proclivities, as well as his training in debate, manifested themselves in meticulous argumentation. He was a Shorter Catechism boy; devoted to the WCF as the system of doctrine giving expression to the content of the Bible. He was given and used an abundant amount of time—to learn the biblical and theological issues of the day, and then to respond to them with clarity and conviction. To further understand Warfield's convictions, more clarity on the biblical and theological issues to which he responded is necessary; which means gaining an understanding of the topics and concerns that colored biblical and theological scholarship during the nineteenth century, and how Warfield thought about them. Benjamin Breckinridge Warfield was a fighter, but he fought with a "running pen."[51]

---

50. B. Warfield, *Studies in Tertullian and Augustine*, *CW* 4; *Calvin and Calvinism*, *CW* 5; *Westminster Assembly and Its Work*, *CW* 6; "Theology of the Reformation," *CW* 9:461–79; "Ninety-Five Theses in Their Theological Significance," *CW* 9:483–511; "Edwards and the New England Theology," *CW* 9:515–38; *Perfectionism*, *CW* 7; and *Perfectionism 2*, *CW* 8.

51. Patton, "Memorial Address," 371.

3

Contextual Issues: Biblical Criticism, Theology, and Philosophy in the Nineteenth Century

WHEN ENGAGING in historical interpretation, the object of interpretation is invariably related to a context. Of course, since human beings are finite, historical interpretations are always in some sense provisional and subject to improvement.[1] However, the very idea of improvement in interpretation presupposes a reality that is what it is, regardless of what one perceives it to be. It also presupposes that an understanding of this reality can achieve degrees of accuracy. In short, it takes for granted an element of *objectivity* in knowledge claims as well as the subjective one.[2] In order

---

1. Evans, *In Defense of History*, 89–110. Evans, on p. 99, rightly criticizes Appleby, Hunt, and Jacobs, *Telling the Truth*, for failing to recognize that "the past does impose its reality through the sources in a basic way," and for asserting that the authority for interpreting the past is grounded in a community of scholars. As Evans mentions "good rules transcend scholarly communities and do not therefore depend on their acceptance by them." From a Christian perspective, Scripture reveals some of the complicated nature of human thought and action, as well as the sovereignty of God over creation. In other words, the biblical doctrines of God and Man ought to cause Christian historians to understand that Scripture does not warrant facile interpretations of past or present human thought and action.

2. One of the hallmark features of Warfield's epistemology is his contention that a biblical view of knowledge, which also corresponds to reality, recognizes a union between the objective and subjective elements. He faulted the rationalism and mysticism present in his day because he believed they were rooted in the work of Kant and Schleiermacher and upset the balance between objective and subjective elements. Thus, in "Inspiration of the Bible," *CW* 1:69, Warfield stated that in the Protestant world during the nineteenth century there were "men still professing historical Christianity, who reason themselves into the conclusion that 'in the nature of the case, no external authority can possibly be absolute in regard to spiritual truth'; just as men have been known to reason themselves into the conclusion that

to have an accurate understanding of the scope and nature of Warfield's scholarship, it is necessary to understand some of the contextual matters with which he worked, and to which he responded. Interestingly enough, concern over how human beings are to understand the relationship between the objective and subjective elements in epistemology is one of the contextual matters that framed Warfield's work.

The Limitations of SCSR

Warfield's epistemology and his apologetic method are theologically based and are wedded to the biblical doctrines expressed in the WCF. The epistemology of SCSR, although it can be correlated in certain ways to Warfield's epistemology, has nothing to say about many of the doctrinal matters that are organically wedded to that epistemology. Indeed, the attempt to identify Warfield and the Old Princeton theological heritage as dependent upon the Scottish philosophy bears a striking resemblance to, and suffers from the same faults inherent in, the idea that post-Reformation Protestant orthodoxy can be adequately explained based on its dependence upon central dogmas.[3]

The "central dogmas" thesis, as it relates to the post-Reformation theologians, is the idea that the theologians who succeeded the first-generation reformers, and sought to be faithful to them, actually rationalized their theology by deducing it from particular doctrinal formulations, or "central dogmas," such as predestination or justification by faith.[4] This hypothesis is significant, among other reasons, because Francis Turretin's work and the WCF are implicated in the "central dogmas" thesis. Thus, any charge of rationalism against the Old Princeton heritage in general, and Warfield in particular, on the basis of the validity of "central dogmas," is already refuted to whatever degree the thesis is refuted. Muller, in his four-volume work, *Post-Reformation Reformed Dogmatics*, concludes that advocates of the "central dogmas" thesis have failed not only to do justice to the historical record regarding what the Protestant Scholastics wrote, but have also failed to accurately and adequately account for the character of Protestant scholastic theology. As he states:

---

the external world has no objective reality and is naught but the projection of their own faculties." Warfield is quoting from Adeney's, "Faith and Criticism," 90. See also Warfield, "Idea of Systematic Theology," *CW* 9:49–87; and "Apologetics," *CW* 9:3–21.

3. Muller, *PRRD* 1:123–32.

4. Ibid.

> It is the hypothesis of a radical discontinuity between Reformation and orthodoxy, of a christocentric Calvin against a "Bezan" predestinarian metaphysic, of a "biblical humanism" against "Aristotelian scholasticism," or of a "dynamic" preaching of reform against a "cold rationalism" that has little scholarly support and even less documentary evidence behind it.[5]

Muller provides significant data demonstrating that the Old Princetonians, who utilized Turretin and the Confession, could not be labeled as rationalistic on that basis. He also shows that the historiography that attempts to label the Princetonians as rationalistic on this basis fails to take into account the historical data available on Turretin and his theological ancestors.

As stated above, this methodology is similar to the methodology that results in scholars concluding that the Old Princeton theologians deduced their theology from the Scottish philosophy. John William Stewart maintains, with regard to the Old Princetonians, "common sense philosophy provided the intellectual foundation for these theologians' hermeneutic."[6] According to Stewart, in Charles Hodge's theology, "traditional Calvinism and the Scots' philosophy were woven together so naturally and intricately that Hodge could scarcely undo either without unraveling the whole garment of the Princeton system." He makes this point even clearer in his treatment of the role he felt Reid's first principles of epistemology exercised in the Old Princeton theology:

> By the time of the Princeton theological endorsement of these "basic beliefs," certain code words were employed to encapsulate them. Such phrases as the "constitution of our nature," the "tribunal of philosophical reasoning," the "common sense of mankind," in the discourses of these Old School theologians were clues to the presence of those "basic beliefs" upon which other beliefs could be indubitably founded.[7]

Ahlstrom, and many of his followers, also inferred that the Old Princetonian's doctrinal emphases were deduced from the Scottish philosophy. Sydney Ahlstrom's thesis regarding the role of SCSR in relation to Old Princeton is part of his larger thesis regarding the dominating influence this philosophy had upon American theological heritage in

---

5. Muller, *PRRD* 4:382.
6. Stewart, "Tethered Theology," 239.
7. Ibid., 249.

general.[8] In his essay on the subject, he gives an overview of the nature and history of the Scottish philosophy, and then proceeds to identify its influence at Harvard, Yale, Andover, and Princeton.[9] In brief, the ubiquitous Scottish philosophy was responsible for sowing rationalistic tares among the biblical or orthodox theological wheat, and one by one, Harvard, Yale, Andover, and Princeton were overrun. Though this narrative has a particular appeal to it, it ultimately claims more than it can sustain. The plan for Princeton, in particular, specifically identified a theological and ecclesiological apologetic rather than a philosophical one. This observation suggests that whatever role philosophy, or philosophical ideas, played within the Princeton theology, it was a subordinate one. For an accurate interpretation of Warfield's scholarship, it is important to understand the diversity and limitations within Scottish philosophy in order to recognize where it does and does not correlate with Warfield's theological and epistemological beliefs.

The Scottish philosophy is often identified with its most significant proponents: Francis Hutcheson (1694–1746), Thomas Reid (1710–1796), Dugald Stewart (1753–1828), James Beattie (1735–1803), James Oswald (1703–93), and Sir William Hamilton (1788–1856). These men are grouped together because of particular similarities regarding their general philosophical beliefs, and in particular, their overall epistemology. But they also had enough diversity that when classified according to the particular *details* of their epistemology, they can be seen to contradict one another. As mentioned previously, S. A. Grave placed Reid and Stewart together and then contrasted them with Beattie and Oswald. He separated Hamilton from all four of these, though, because of Hamilton's close affinities with Kant.[10] Ahlstrom considers the first mediator of Scottish philosophy to Princeton to have been John Witherspoon (1723–94), who became president of the College of New Jersey (later called Princeton).[11]

---

8. Ahlstrom, "Scottish Philosophy," 257–72.

9. Ibid.

10. Grave, *Scottish Philosophy*, 1–6. Introductions on all these men, except for Beattie, can be found in the *Dictionary of Scottish Church History and Theology*. Copleston, in *History of Philosophy* 5:364–83, corroborates Grave and gives a summary of the Scottish philosopher's refutations of Hume.

11. Ahlstrom, "Scottish Philosophy," 261. See also Calhoun, *Princeton Seminary* 1:16–20, 127. Witherspoon was one of the signers of the Declaration of Independence and worked on numerous committees with Thomas Jefferson, Benjamin Franklin, John Adams et al. He may also have been a descendent of John Knox through his mother; see D. F. Kelly, "Witherspoon, John," 880.

Any commonality acknowledged between Princeton theologians and Hutcheson, Reid, or any of the other Scottish philosophers, does not demonstrate that the Princetonians were *dependent* on them for their epistemological beliefs. Nor does it in any way establish that any of the epistemic qualities of Hutcheson's or Reid's beliefs can adequately account for the theologically based and conditioned epistemology that Warfield espoused. This becomes more evident when greater clarity is gained regarding Reid's epistemology.

Reid set forth his epistemic beliefs in three writings: *An Inquiry into the Human Mind on the Principles of Commonsense, Essays on the Intellectual Powers of Man*, and *Essays on the Active Powers of Man*.[12] In *Essays on the Intellectual Powers of Man*, Reid advocates:

> . . . common principles, which are the foundations of all reasoning, and of all science. Such common principles seldom admit of direct proof; nor do they need it. Men need not be taught them; for they are such as all men of common understanding know; or such, at least, as they give a ready assent to, as soon as they are proposed and understood.[13]

Reid called these principles "axioms," and states that "every man of common understanding readily assents to them, and finds it absolutely necessary to conduct his actions and opinions by them, in the ordinary affairs of life."[14] Noah Lemos explains that a commonsense belief according to Reid is:

> . . . one (1) which is universally held by mankind, (2) whose acceptance is reflected in the common structure of all languages, (3) whose contradictory is not merely false, but absurd, and (4) that is irresistible, so that even those who question them are compelled to believe them when engaging in the practical affairs of life.[15]

Those things that fall into these categories are such things as the trusting of our senses, relying upon testimony, belief in a material world outside of ourselves, a cause to everything that has a beginning, and the

---

12. Helm, "Scottish Realism," 759. Riddlebarger, in "Lion of Princeton," 18–34, has a helpful overview of Reid's epistemological views. For further clarification on Reid, see Wolterstorff, "Can Belief in God Be Rational," 135–86; and *Thomas Reid*.
13. Reid, *Essays on the Intellectual Powers of Man*, 31.
14. Ibid., 33.
15. Lemos, "Commonsensism and Critical Cognitivism," 72.

distinction between qualities (attributes) and subjects (objects).[16] It is, according to Reid, these basic "first principles" that form the bedrock of every person's epistemology whether they know it or not. In particular, points 3 and 4 indicate the way in which one can argue for these first principles. One needs to merely point out to the dissenter that he or she, in the very act of denying them, is actually utilizing them, and that it could not be otherwise. The apologetical value of such an epistemology is that it gainsays strident skepticism. It was, in fact, the skepticism of David Hume that was a significant impetus to the emphasis on this realist epistemology. Moreover, it was a rising skepticism in the early years of the American republic that Ahlstrom cites as the reason for Princeton and other institutions utilizing SCSR.[17]

William P. Alston states that fundamental to Reid's epistemology is the belief "that there is no rationally attractive alternative to accepting the testimony of our basic cognitive faculties as (prima facie) correct, and that only if we do this will we ever have any chance to acquire any knowledge whatever."[18] Wolterstorff concurs[19] and explains:

> [M]ost of the time Reid cites certain beliefs as examples of principles of common sense, or "first principles . . . first principles are those immediate beliefs that all properly formed adult human beings hold and which they inescapably presuppose in their ordinary reasoning and living."[20]

In other words, we do not infer from other beliefs that there is someone in front of us; rather, we see and immediately believe what we see. Memory experiences likewise fall into this category.[21] We are justified in believing certain things because of the way we are constituted. This notion that there are beliefs that need no further verification has led Alvin

---

16. Reid, *Essays on the Intellectual Powers of Man*, 34–40.

17. See Copleston, *History of Philosophy* 5:364, for the fact that Reid is responding to Hume. See also Ahlstrom, "Scottish Philosophy," 267; Noll, "Common Sense Tradition"; idem, *America's God*, which gives his current assessment; Marsden, *Fundamentalism and American Culture*; idem, "Collapse of American Evangelical Academia," 219–64; idem, *Understanding Fundamentalism and Evangelicalism*; idem, *Soul of the American University*.

18. Alston, "Thomas Reid on Epistemic Principles."

19. Wolterstorff, *Thomas Reid and the Story of Epistemology*, 216.

20. Wolterstorff, "Thomas Reid and Rationality," 51.

21. Ibid., 47.

Plantinga to defend what he calls "Reformed epistemology," according to which, for the Christian, belief in God is properly basic.[22]

We have already seen previously that Ahlstrom, Noll, and Marsden believe that they have detected conclusions regarding the diverse theologies at American seminaries at the time, of which the theologians who advocated them were unaware. This approach turns out to entail an interesting irony. According to Noll, Common Sense Realism "encouraged participants in theological debate to draw conclusions for their opponents."[23] Noll asserts that *this very ability* is a distinctive feature of a thinker operating according to CSR. Thus, by his own argument, Noll identifies himself, Ahlstrom, and Marsden (not to mention virtually all scholars involved in debates of any kind) as displaying one of the defining features of the Scottish philosophy.

Aspects of the epistemology of SCSR can be correlated with many diverse systems of belief, and it should be obvious that they cannot all be dependent on it. There is a trivial correlation insofar as this epistemology reflects the reality of how people in general propose and defend beliefs. Beyond these basic truisms, however, SCSR philosophy has little relationship to the theologically based beliefs of Warfield and the Old Princetonians.

Introduction to Biblical Criticism

The interpretation of the Bible was of supreme importance to the Princetonians. This emphasis is clearly shown in their concern about, and interest in, the burgeoning discipline of biblical criticism, or the historical-critical method of biblical interpretation. An overview of modern biblical criticism should probably begin with a definition of the practice.[24] Yet, in important ways, that definition represents the whole dispute that

---

22. Plantinga, "Reason and Belief in God," 16–93; and *Warranted Christian Belief*; Vanhoozer, *Is There a Meaning?*, 289; Lehrer, "Reid, Thomas," 427.

23. Noll, "Common Sense Tradition," 28.

24. For various histories of modern biblical criticism or histories of some of the theological positions integral to its theologically Protestant liberal proponents, see Baird, *History of New Testament Research* and "Biblical Criticism: New Testament Criticism," 730; C. Brown, *Jesus in European Protestant Thought*; Harrisville and Sundberg, *Bible in Modern Culture*; McGrath, *Making of Modern German Christology*; Orr, "Criticism of the Bible," 749; Scholder, *Birth of Modern Critical Theology*; Yarbrough, *Salvation-Historical Fallacy?*; Linnemann, *Is There a Synoptic Problem?*; idem, *Historical-Criticism of the Bible*; idem, *Biblical Criticism on Trial*; J. W. Brown, *Rise of Biblical Criticism*.

has energized scholars and non-specialists for centuries. For example, consider the following:

> Historical-critical study of the Bible is a necessary component of responsible theology. To employ historical-critical method is to subject the putatively factual material and literary structure of the bible to independent investigation in order to test their truthfulness and to discern their original historical meaning. This independent investigation assumes that the outcome of research will not be predetermined by a guarantee of the Bible's infallibility. The student of scripture, using historical-critical method, is placed under the imperative of the historian who must seek the facts no matter where they lead.[25]

Another view, though, states:

> Even a cursory glance at the sources of biblical criticism shows why scientific theology began in skepticism rather than science. Of the seven key advocates in biblical criticism at its inception—Hugo Grotius (1583–1645), Immanuel Kant (1724–1804), Hermann Reimarus (1694–1768), Johann Semler (1725–1791), Benedict Spinoza (1632–1677), Matthew Tindal (1656–1733), and John Toland (1670–1722)—only Semler was a theologian. The proportion becomes even more unbalanced when one takes into consideration the names of three other philosophers who doubtless merit inclusion in this list, Francis Bacon (1561–1626), Thomas Hobbes (1588–1679), and David Hume (1711–1776).[26]

While the first of the two accounts above, by Harrisville/Sundberg, begins with a favorable view of, if not polemic for, biblical criticism, the second, by Linnemann, takes us in the opposite direction. These contrasting assessments not only conflict, but also reveal the nature of the conflict. This is brought more clearly to light in Linnemann's additional words regarding the early leaders of biblical criticism:

> Since most of these leaders were philosophers, philosophy furnished the fundamental components for biblical criticism. To a great extent the sacrificial, painstaking labor that scientific theology expends amounts to a working out in intricate detail the philosophical mold into which Scripture must be shaped. Basic philosophical principles, which have been established without

---

25. Harrisville and Sundberg, *Bible in Modern Culture*, 1. See also Frei, *Eclipse of the Biblical Narrative*, 18.

26. Linnemann, *Is There a Synoptic Problem?*, 19.

reference to the Bible, must be harmonized with the actual biblical data.[27]

Present in both of these treatments is a struggle over epistemic authority, and the relationship of the Bible to that authority. Although Harrisville and Sundberg believe that the "historical-critical study of the bible is a necessary component for a responsible theology," this requirement places the student using this method "under the imperative of the historian."[28] For Linnemann, the way in which this has been carried out by numerous scholars has amounted to subversion of the Bible's authority and has resulted in an unbiblical use of Scripture. The purpose here is not to render a verdict on the character and validity of modern biblical criticism for "responsible theology." But it *is* necessary to understand something of its source, nature, and history in order to understand Warfield's response to modern biblical criticism—which he believed reconstructed the Christian faith and ultimately undermined true saving faith in Christ.[29]

Modern Biblical Criticism and it's Cultural Milieu

Biblical scholars have always been influenced by, and have in their own turn influenced, the broader cultures in which they have lived.[30] Contextualization, of course, has limits, and every historian has to choose which historical features to use in contextualizing each particular study. By understanding the fundamental truth claims made by the advocates of modern biblical criticism, it will be possible to identify those contextual features most relevant for understanding its character and development. In order to identify and trace a basic infrastructure, though, it is necessary to begin in the seventeenth century.

Two scholars, Baruch Spinoza (1632–1677) in the Netherlands, and the Roman Catholic scholar Richard Simon (1638–1712) in France, are often credited historically with first practicing what has come to be called, among other things, modern biblical criticism.[31] This piece of in-

---

27. Ibid., 19–20.

28. Recall the discussion in the Introduction to this book on the effects on evangelical historiography.

29. Warfield, "Christian Evidences: How Affected By Recent Criticism," *SSW* 2:124–31; "Rights of Criticism and of the Church," *SSW* 2:595–603.

30. This should be considered a virtual axiom in biblical studies and church history. It seems that most church history or historical theology texts will make this point and usually in a variety of ways. See González, *Story of Christianity*.

31. Harrisville and Sundberg, *Bible in Modern Culture*, 26, 32–48, 50.

formation highlights two important issues in assessing the history of the discipline. First, this criticism is often described as "modern" because the ideas of both of these men were indebted in important ways to the epistemology of Rene Descartes.[32] Descartes, of course, is generally recognized as ushering in the "modern" era with his famous dictum, "Cogito ergo sum," or "I think, therefore I am." The extent to which Descartes should be credited with fathering a modern philosophy could be questioned insofar as his subjective starting point was not novel in the history of philosophy. After all, if Descartes' epistemology is accurately described as enthroning the individual knower as the fundamental arbiter in truth claims, it is difficult to see how the substance of his epistemology is different from the edict of Protagoras in the fifth century BC that "man is the measure of all things."[33] However, in distinction to Protagoras, who was already dismissed by Plato, Descartes set the agenda for a philosophical methodology for centuries to come. Thus, it is important to recognize that in their study of Scripture, both Spinoza and Simon were leaning on Descartes and emphasizing some of the same fundamental presuppositions he articulated. This fact is important, among other reasons, because it helps to identify the philosophical character of the biblical criticism that they exercised.[34]

32. See Copleston, *History of Philosophy* 4:63–132 for an overview of Descartes, and 4:205–63 for an overview of Spinoza. Concerning Spinoza, Copleston states: "It can hardly be denied that Cartesianism exercised an influence on the mind of Spinoza and that it was to some extent at least an instrument in the formation of his philosophy," (4:207). Spinoza is seen by Copleston to be influenced by Descartes (1) "with an ideal of method" (a template) and "with a good deal of his terminology," (2) the content of "certain particular points," such as philosophy inquiring "only into efficient and not final causes," and (3) in helping to "determine the nature of the problems with which he dealt." See also Stumpf, *Socrates to Sartre*, 235–54; Spinoza, *Theologico-Political Treatise*; Allen, *Philosophy for Understanding Theology*, 171–80.

33. Stumpf, *Socrates to Sartre*, 31–33. This also helps to see that whatever differences may be detected between modernism and "post"-modernism, those differences are quite likely not going to be substantive, but rather differences in tendencies, degrees, or emphases. For a very brief, yet helpful summary of some of what characterizes the relationship between modernism and "post"-modernism, see Carson, "Dangers and Delights of Postmodernism," 11–17. For a more detailed analysis of them, with special emphasis on their application within biblical studies see Carson, *Gagging of God*.

34. Spinoza compartmentalized faith and reason, or theology and philosophy, from each other. As Spinoza, in *Theologico-Political Treatise*, 194, states: ". . . theology is not bound to serve reason, nor reason theology, but that each has her own domain. The sphere of reason is, as we have said, truth and wisdom; the sphere of theology is piety and obedience." On p. 197 he says that it is theology that "defines the dogmas of faith . . . only in so far as they may be necessary for obedience, and leaves reason to determine

Secondly, speaking of these two men as the first practitioners of modern biblical criticism accentuates the *specific* way in which they engaged in biblical study and interpretation. It does not mean that they were the first to engage in a study of the Bible that included carefully scrutinizing all the data available in doing informed textual studies. Vigilantly collecting, analyzing, collating, and reading biblical manuscripts in the original Hebrew and Greek languages had been taking place for more than a century prior to Spinoza and Simon.[35] Indeed, an accurate historical judgment regarding their labors can hardly be rendered, if it is *not* recognized that what they received in the way of manuscript evidence and conclusions, as well as linguistic training, was in large measure the fruit of many years of careful study of the Old and New Testament by others prior to them, which can also be rightly labeled as "critical."[36] Consequently, an accurate historical judgment regarding Spinoza and Simon should include the precise manner in which their practice of a critical study of the Bible corresponded to and deviated from their predecessors and contemporaries. Taking this approach of including the philosophical framework of the interpreter, will pave the way for understanding biblical studies before, during, and after the nineteenth century.

Spinoza and Simon did carve out a distinctly different way of engaging in their critical study with their epistemological and metaphysical presuppositions. Yet, these presuppositions also possessed meaningful

---

their precise truth." Finally, on p. 198 he maintains that "philosophy should be separated from theology, and wherein each consists; that neither should be subservient to the other, but that each should keep her unopposed dominion."

35. Luther's role in the Reformation was, in no small part, related to his use of the original languages, and, thereby, he was dependent in significant ways upon the textual work of Erasmus.

36. For a helpful guide in tracing and understanding the critical study of Scripture during the medieval, Reformation, and post-Reformation periods, see Muller, *Holy Scripture*, PRRD vol. 2; Pelikan, *Christian Tradition* 4:306–13. Harrisville and Sundberg, *Bible in Modern Culture*, 14–25, label biblical study prior and up to the post-Reformation Scholastics as "precritical" and then identify the study of the Bible represented by Spinoza as "Rationalist Biblical Criticism." This may obscure the historical record more than it clarifies it, as far as the history of modern biblical criticism is concerned, because it simply equates the term "critical" with the study of the Bible that is in line with the metaphysical presuppositions adopted by Spinoza, Simon et al. If we accept the notion that "critical" is meant to convey a precise and rigorous analysis, then it is difficult to see how one can avoid concluding that a "critical" study of the Bible was going on for centuries prior to Spinoza and Simon, unless, of course, one is simply not aware of a significant portion of church history.

continuity with medieval and Reformation scholars.[37] In part, recognizing this continuity may help avoid attributing types of innovation to them for which they are not responsible, and may also prevent a search for a historical antecedent to their work that is only located in the vicinity of their own time period. Whatever novelty they may have possessed intellectually, it was not in terms of all their metaphysical and epistemological presuppositions.[38] Their contemporaries were no doubt challenged when trying to accurately assess Spinoza and Simon's similarities to Descartes, inasmuch as Descartes was not trying to overthrow Christian belief, but to support it.[39] The concept that they and their contemporaries—Pierre Gassendi (1592–1655), Robert Boyle (1627–91), and Isaac Newton (1642–1727)—may have added to Descartes' thought, was an argument on religiously Christian grounds for a mechanical philosophy, or a mechanistic view of the universe.[40]

Spinoza's philosophy was a philosophical monism that led to a pantheistic theology and a deistic practice. His pantheism can be summed up with his notion that there is only one substance in the universe, which is intrinsically spiritual and manifests itself exclusively in a material mode of existence—therefore, he sought material explanations for the Bible, religion in general, and Christianity in particular.[41] Pantheistic ideas, though, are hardly novel in the history of human thought.[42] In part, this awareness may help in understanding that the story of modern biblical criticism, in both the seventeenth and subsequent centuries, can only be accurately discerned historically when seen in relation to other subjects that inherently impinge upon theology and biblical studies.[43] Thus, we

37. For helpful surveys of the continuity between the medieval, Reformation, and post-Reformation eras in epistemology, theology, and metaphysics see Ozment, *Age of Reform*; Leff, *Medieval Thought*; Obermann, *Harvest of Medieval Theology*; Stumpf, *Socrates to Sartre*, 160–298; Copleston, *History of Philosophy* 4:205–63; Muller, *PRRD*.

38. Copleston, in *History of Philosophy* 4:207–8, makes the point that even though Spinoza's "pantheistic monism" may have been the logical implication of Cartesianism, he may also have been influenced to that position more by Jewish writers than by Descartes. Furthermore, Copleston, later on p. 230, identifies Spinoza's position as quite similar to Plato's theory of knowledge.

39. Ashworth, "Christianity and the Mechanistic Universe," 61–84.

40. Ibid., 73–74. Ashworth clarifies that Gassendi and Descartes differed regarding their understanding of God in relation to the "laws" that could, or could not, be discerned within the universe. See also Copleston, *History of Philosophy* 4:63–66.

41. Copleston, *History of Philosophy* 4:206–7; Stumpf, *Socrates to Sartre*, 250–51.

42. Stumpf, *Socrates to Sartre*, 14, 117–20, 157–59.

43. Scholder, *Birth of Modern Critical Theology*, 3.

should recognize that in the study of modern biblical criticism fine distinctions must be made between related subjects. Otherwise, one ends up with a simplistic, if not erroneous, view of whatever part of history is under investigation. It should also assist in seeing that in any scholarly treatment of modern biblical criticism, Descartes, Spinoza, and Simon should be cited as having significant roles, but that they must be placed within a broader cultural, philosophical, and theological context that is part of the entire history of biblical studies all the way to the present.[44] In light of this fact, it is perhaps important to make two points explicitly clear. First, the substance of what early modern biblical critics believed, that drove their study and interpretation of the Bible, can be found in other sectors of European society during the period in which the discipline developed. Second, due to the ubiquity of these ideas in European culture, identifying the exact sources of any one individual's beliefs regarding these epistemological and metaphysical matters can be very difficult. This truth can be seen more clearly by noting the character of the time in which Descartes, Spinoza, and Simon worked.

As mid-seventeenth-century biblical and philosophical scholars, these were men whose lives helped shape, and in turn were shaped by, tempestuous cultural matters. This was a time marked by ecclesiastical and theological conflicts between Catholics and Protestants. The fruits of scientific discoveries and global exploration challenged long-held assumptions about the very nature of the world and even of reality itself. There was also political strife between Protestant, Catholic, and civil authorities that threatened people's very lives.[45] Modern biblical criticism developed

44. In "The Tethered Theology: Biblical Criticism," John William Stewart's treatment of Princeton's biblical criticism (on contextualizing the subject) moves rather quickly from Simon (1670) to Jean Astruc (1753) and says the following regarding mid-eighteenth-century Old Testament criticism: "Still to come were the infusion of deism's presuppositions and speculations about the probability of divine revelation and miracles, new insights about Hebrew poetry and prophetic literature, and a greater awareness of the variety of Oriental religions" (p. 34). Evidently Stewart was not aware that deism had played a significant role in the work of Spinoza and Simon nearly one hundred years prior to Astruc and that such deism was operative in influencing European thought long prior to Spinoza and Simon. The picture that Stewart presents is not only anachronistic but also fails to do justice to the historical record regarding the true nature of modern biblical criticism. With his having failed to make these rather important and seemingly obvious observations and distinctions about these matters of intellectual history, one is justified in questioning the accuracy of his analysis of the ideas integral to modern biblical criticism in the nineteenth century, as well as the Princetonian's thinking about and response to such matters. See also Hazard, *European Mind*.

45. Cragg, *Freedom and Authority*, 9. In the same book Cragg refers to the seventeenth

during a time when two of the fundamental issues of human society—authority and freedom—were not only questioned and debated, but also provided sufficient cause for people to sacrifice their own lives and those of others. This was the time of reality-changing discoveries and theories by Galileo,[46] Kepler, Newton, Bacon, and La Peyrère. Alongside the work of Descartes, Spinoza, and Simon were the radical theses of Thomas Hobbes, the Dutch Remonstrants, and the English deists. There were also religious controversies between Jansenists and Jesuits, and Calvinists and Arminians, as well as those between Protestants and Catholics.[47] It was the time of the Thirty Years War, the Puritan uprising, the deposing of Charles I, the persecutions by William Laud, the Long Parliament, the Westminster Assembly, the Interregnum, and the exodus of Puritans and others to America. In part, this summation helps bear out the validity of Bruce Kuklick's analysis that modern biblical criticism has been crucial

---

century as "one of the most revolutionary periods in intellectual history," possessing a "confused intellectual heritage" (11, 19). He also wrote *The Church and the Age of Reason*, in which he helps explain some of the details of that "confused intellectual heritage." See also Barzun, *Dawn to Decadence*; C. Brown, *Christianity and Western Thought* vol. 1; Hazard, *European Mind*.

46. Colin Brown acknowledges Pietro Redondi's challenge as to the precise nature of Galileo's trial by the church. Galileo's theory of atoms may have been more of a threat than his heliocentric views because the former challenged the Roman Catholic view of the Eucharist. Concerning the confusing relationship of seventeenth-century Puritan thought to science, see Greaves, "Puritanism and Science," 345–68. He demonstrates the radical and intricate relationship between scientific work, the theories it generated (and from which they were spawned), their effect on theological and philosophical beliefs, and the character of life itself in the seventeenth century. Basil Wiley makes a statement that helps explain part of the relationship between theology and literature: "It is generally agreed that in the seventeenth century a great effort was being made, by representative thinkers, to see things 'as in themselves they really are,' and the ideas of Truth and Fiction which were then evolved seem to have exerted a decisive influence upon the poetic and religious beliefs of succeeding times. . . . Both, at any rate, seem to have been similarly affected by the 'philosophic' spirit, and those who are interested in the fate of either can hardly avoid feeling some concern for that of the other." Wiley classifies the seventeenth century, along with the period of Greek philosophy, as one of two time periods in which separating "the 'true' from the 'false,' the 'real' from the 'illusory'" seemed "to have been carried on much more actively and consciously" than at any other times in history. Wiley, *Seventeenth Century Background*, vii, 1.

47. Stumpf, *Socrates to Sartre*, 216–74; Gonzalez, *Story of Christianity* 2:70–134; Scholder, *Birth of Modern Critical Theology*, 82–87. Scholder, on pp. 88–89, makes the point that though very different in their subject areas, La Peyrère's intent was the same as the Socinians, and *their* intentions were in turn the same as virtually everyone else sorting through the matters endemic to modern biblical criticism: to reconcile Christian faith with natural reason. See also Colie, "Spinoza and the Early English Deists," 23–46; Woodbridge, *Biblical Authority*.

in producing a revolutionary epistemological shift in the West. He also asserts that it was more influential than Darwinism, or anything else, in nurturing the shift in biblical criticism during the nineteenth century.[48] If for no other reason, Kuklick's thesis is important because it accurately reflects the fact that modern biblical criticism is not only integral to other ideas and events promoting change in Western culture, but is also part of a long history that predates Darwin and his evolutionary theory by over two hundred years. The broad and foundational matters, then, regarding the definition, sources, and methods of human knowledge coalesce in any analysis of modern biblical criticism.

A View of History and Modern Biblical Criticism

One of the ways that the union between modern biblical criticism and the broader concerns of human knowledge becomes apparent is that it came to be defined by, and used according to, a particular view of history.[49] This view of history, which has come to be called "critical," is so united to modern biblical criticism that the discipline is often referred to, as previously mentioned, the "historical-critical method."[50] As we have already seen from Harrisville and Sundberg, this approach places the interpreter "under the imperative of the historian who must seek the facts no matter where they lead."[51] It was the German Gotthold Ephraim Lessing (1729–81) who articulated a problematic idea, one that percolated in the minds of many modern biblical critics, an idea derived from this particular view of history and indelibly connected as well to a particular epistemology. As Lessing expressed it: "If no historical truth can be demonstrated, then nothing can be demonstrated by means of historical truths. That is: accidental truths of history can never become the proof

---

48. Kuklick, "Critical History," 54–64, esp. 57.

49. For the contemporary restatement and endorsement of the view of history that informs modern biblical criticism, see Harvey, *Historian and Believer*. For a critique of Harvey's position see C. S. Evans, "Empiricism, Rationalism," 134–60. For histories of modern biblical criticism that bring out the relationship between its practitioner's view of history and their biblical scholarship, see C. Brown, *Jesus in European Protestant Thought*; McGrath, *Making of Modern German Christology*; Yarbrough, *Salvation-Historical Fallacy?*; Frei, *Eclipse of the Biblical Narrative*.

50. Maier, *Biblical Hermeneutics*, 209–306.

51. Harrisville and Sundberg, *Bible in Modern Culture*, 1. Ironically, the Old Princeton theologians' stress on "facts" gained them, and continues to gain them, a considerable amount of criticism by many who would give hearty approval to this agenda.

of necessary truths of reason."[52] Lessing was embracing the Cartesian and Spinoza position "that only clear and distinct ideas may serve as the basis of a system of thought."[53] Furthermore, in keeping with this view, he anticipated Kant's view of morality in the sense that he affirmed a "belief in morality that superseded the sanctions of religion."[54] Finally, his view of history in relation to the Christian faith led him to endorse the "implication" that "the whole fabric of orthodox Christology was without historical basis."[55] Yet, it is important to recognize that over one hundred years *prior* to Lessing, Isaac de la Peyrère, in 1655, had questioned the biblical account of history in his book *Pre-Adamites*.[56] The spirit of modern biblical criticism, then, operates from a particular view of history, but the same spirit was operating prior to the work of Spinoza and Simon, though the exact formalization of that spirit, consistent with the Cartesian epistemology of Spinoza and Simon, seems to crystallize, at least in the eighteenth century, with Lessing.[57]

Lessing's "broad ugly ditch," that attempts to challenge the biblical scholar on putatively historical grounds, presupposes a particular epistemology and metaphysic that has definite correlations to Descartes and Spinoza. Moreover, to the degree that deistic and pantheistic strains of thought can be identified in Spinoza, it seems it must be acknowledged that the view of history intrinsic to modern biblical criticism, or the historical-critical method, as it has been practiced since the eighteenth

52. C. Brown, *Jesus in European Protestant Thought*, 19.

53. "For the same basic point see Frei, *Eclipse of the Biblical Narrative*, 44, quoting from Spinoza, *Works*, 61: "Scripture does not explain things by their secondary causes, but only narrates them in the order and the style which has most power to move men, and especially uneducated men, to devotion; and therefore it speaks inaccurately of God and of events, seeing that its object is not to convince the reason, but to attract and lay hold of the imagination." Further: "The truth of a historical narrative, however assured, cannot give us knowledge nor consequently the love of God, for love of God springs from knowledge of Him, and knowledge of Him should be derived from general ideas, in themselves certain and known, so that the truth of a historical narrative is very far from being requisite for our attaining our highest good."

54. C. Brown, *Jesus in European Protestant Thought*, 25.

55. Ibid., 27.

56. Scholder, *Birth of Modern Critical Theology*, 82–83.

57. Harvey, *Historian and Believer*, 249. He states this as the position of the "historical critic": "The real issue, then, is not whether faith is independent of all historical criticism but whether Christian faith requires certain specific historical assertions that, in the nature of the case, are dubious or not fully justified."

century, was already present in Europe during the early seventeenth century, and present in a less codified form even before then.⁵⁸ As Colin Brown observes:

> If we look at Reimarus's work against the background of late seventeenth-century and early eighteenth-century thought, it no longer appears, as it did to Albert Schweitzer, as something new, revolutionary and epoch-making. It was an expression of a development that was already considerably well advanced. It was merely one, and not a particularly original one at that, of the many sides of the movement known as the Enlightenment. Wilhelm Dilthey saw the characteristic features of the Enlightenment to be everywhere the same: "the autonomy of reason, the solidarity of intellectual culture, confidence in its unimpeded progress and the aristocracy of the spirit." Ernst Troeltsch believed that the unifying factor in Enlightenment thinking was the rejection of supernaturalism and that Deism was the religious philosophy of the Enlightenment. R. G. Collingwood saw the Enlightenment characterized by the endeavor "to secularize every department of human life and thought. It was a revolt not only against the power of institutional religion but against religion as such."⁵⁹

According to Brown, though, ". . . the definitions of Troeltsch and Collingwood would exclude from the Enlightenment thinkers who belonged to the Age of Enlightenment."⁶⁰ Still, it *was* characteristic of the work of Lessing, Reimarus, and the deists to try and "desupernaturalize and secularize religion in general."⁶¹ Such work was buttressed by Spinoza's deistic strains of thought that rejected "the Christian theistic view of a personal God whose interaction with the world culminated

---

58. Colie, "Spinoza and the Early English Deists."

59. C. Brown, *Jesus in European Protestant Thought*, 50. Hermann Reimarus (1694–1768) was a German biblical critic who in significant ways embodied the conflicts of the eighteenth century regarding matters endemic to modern biblical criticism. His most famous work *Apology*, was published after his death and revealed more specifically Reimarus's antipathy to seeing the Bible as revelation from a personal and trinitarian God. Reimarus excoriated the Old Testament, denied the bodily resurrection of Jesus, and assigned the Church's belief in the latter (and the view of the Bible integral to it) to the corruption of the apostles. See also Harrisville and Sundberg, *Bible in Modern Culture*, 49–65.

60. C. Brown, *Jesus in European Protestant Thought*, 50.

61. Ibid. On p. 50 Brown questions whether Sir Leslie Stephen's distinction between "Constructive" and "Critical" deism "can be sustained." Brown states that the only substantive difference between Stephen's "constructive" deists and his "critical" deists is that the former are less specific.

in the incarnation."[62] This means that modern biblical criticism, or the historical-critical method, operated with a view of both history and knowledge that rejected the authority of an epistemology that saw God as personally operative in history, governing it by his personal presence. Thus, the agenda of many Enlightenment figures in the eighteenth century coalesced with the historical-critical method in the attempts of both to reconfigure the way people thought about knowledge claims, history, and the Bible.[63]

The integrated nature of these disciplines demonstrates that historical analysis of any one of them cannot achieve much depth and accuracy without recognizing some of the significant relationships that unite the disciplines. Furthermore, it is really only within the context of an interdisciplinary study that the subjects can be effectively distinguished from each other. In the history of modern biblical criticism, not only views of knowledge and history are central, but also the views of rationality and rationalism held by a number of other disciplines.[64] Among other things, this means that beliefs about history are inextricably linked to views about God, illustrating that historiography is inherently theological in character.[65] Moreover, because all these interdisciplinary matters coalesce with *any* interpretive method for biblical study, it should begin to be apparent why it is difficult to identify the precise sources and lines of influence for various individuals' beliefs and practices regarding knowledge, rationality, God, and the very nature of reality.[66] What certainly can

62. Ibid., 51.

63. Gay, *Enlightenment*.

64. For the distinction between rationality and rationalism, see Curley, "Rationalism," 411–15; Cohen, "Rationality," 415–20. Curley's opening line is illuminating: "'rationalism' is a multiply ambiguous term whose meaning varies greatly according to the context." He goes on to state, on p. 411: "The common thread running through its various uses seems to be that the philosopher classified as a rationalist gives undue weight to reason at the expense of something else: in politics, tradition; in morals, feelings or sentiment; in epistemology, experience, etc. This apparent commonality is deceptive, however, since 'reason' tends to bear different meanings in the different contexts, referring to a faculty of a priori knowledge in epistemology, but being construed much more broadly in religion, morals, or politics." Cohen, on p. 415, mentions *nine* forms of "rationality," which further accentuates the need for clarification in these matters.

65. Herrera, *Reasons for Our Rhymes*. Recall Barth's and C. Hodges' point that philosophy and theology are enmeshed and that philosophers and theologians overlap in their disciplines. For a discussion on the theological character of historiography, see Frame, "Defense of Something Close," 26–91; Wells, "Being Framed," 293–300; Muller, "Historiography," 301–10.

66. For an example of this point, as well as some of the complicated nature of

be seen from historical records are the more overt attempts, throughout the seventeenth to twentieth centuries, to define and explain knowledge in a way that contradicts or conflicts with a theistic epistemology that is based on, and conditioned by, a belief in the Bible as a revelation from the only triune God, who created, sustains, and guides history.[67] The biblical criticism practiced by Spinoza and Simon was the expression of deistic and pantheistic presuppositions, and correlates with the general epistemological crisis that can be seen, not simply in biblical scholars of the period, but also among scientists, philosophers, and Catholic and Protestant disputants.[68] Furthermore, the integrated nature of these subject areas resulted in the work among scientists, philosophers, and biblical scholars in the sixteenth and seventeenth century affecting each other's labors, a trend which has continued up to the present.[69]

Kant, Schleiermacher, and Modern Protestant Liberalism

In the eighteenth century, the issues central to biblical criticism became enmeshed in the philosophical work of David Hume (1711–1796) and Immanual Kant (1724–1804).[70] In a sense, those two philosophers brought about a turning point in the conflict over the historical criticism of the Bible. Hume's radical skepticism and Kant's revolutionary response helped set the stage for the conflicts in biblical interpretation that would

---

identifying the character and locating the sources of the Cambridge Platonist's thought that Logan (in "Theological Decline in Christian Institutions") cites as instrumental in the rationalism at Princeton, see Gabbey, "Cudworth, More," (see 122 n. 8); Colie, *Light and Enlightenment*; Jordan, *Development of Religious Toleration in England* 2:319–22; Levine, "Latitudinarians, Neoplatonists"; Cassirer, *Platonic Renaissance in England*; Copleston, *History of Philosophy* 5:60; Tulloch, *Rational Theology and Christian Philosophy* 1:170. Logan's analysis fails to give proper weight to the complexities in the subject matters.

67. Woodbridge, *Biblical Authority*; Harrisville and Sundberg, *Bible in Modern Culture*; Linnemann, *Is There a Synoptic Problem?*; Scholder, *Birth of Modern Critical Theology*, 9–142; Yarbrough, *Salvation-Historical Fallacy*?

68. C. Brown, *Jesus in European Protestant Thought*, 31; Popkin, *History of Skepticism*.

69. Lindberg and Numbers, *When Science & Christianity Meet*; Woodbridge, *Biblical Authority*; Wilkens and Padgett, *Christianity and Western Thought* 2 (entitled *Faith and Reason in the 19th Century)*; Gundlach, "The Evolution Question at Princeton."

70. Lindberg and Numbers, *When Science & Christianity Meet*; Woodbridge, *Biblical Authority*. For summaries of Hume's thought see Copleston, *History of Philosophy* 5:258–353; Stumpf, *Socrates to Sartre*, 280–89. For summaries of Kant's thought see Copleston, *History of Philosophy* 6:180–392; Stumpf, *Socrates to Sartre*, 299–324.

occur in the nineteenth century.[71] When one realizes the radical French *philosophes* such as Voltaire (1694–1778), Montesquieu (1689–1755), Diderot (1713–1784), Condorcet (1743–94), and Holbach (1723–89) were their contemporaries, the serious assault that would be made on traditional Christian belief in the nineteenth century becomes clear.[72] Of course not only Hume and Kant affected biblical interpretation during the eighteenth century; men such as Reimarus, Jean Astruc, Johann Semler, Johann David Michaelis, Johann Jakob Griesbach, and Lessing all contributed in their own way to reconfiguring the idea of revelation and the method of interpreting the biblical text.[73]

However, it is Kant's revolutionary work that became foundational for nineteenth-century biblical criticism and theology. In short, Kant's turn toward the subjective and his assignment of controlling authority in knowledge claims to the human knower became the impetus for Schleiermacher's theology, in which the "religious consciousness" of the believer is considered "the proper subject of theology."[74] With this concept, Schleiermacher not only reconfigured theology and the Christian faith along Kantian lines, but also aligned himself with modern biblical criticism, which had embraced the same fundamental anthropocentricity.[75] As Colin Brown concludes, "What was given for Schleiermacher

71. Padgett and Wilkens, *Christianity and Western Thought*, 13–21.

72. Stumpf, *Socrates to Sartre*, 290; Gay, *Enlightenment*.

73. Harrisville and Sundberg, *Bible in Modern Culture*, 53–68; C. Brown, *Jesus in European Protestant Thought*, 1–28. Brown, on p. 31, helpfully distinguishes between the heresies of Servetus and the Socinians and the more radical beliefs of Reimarus and Lessing and captures the character of these matters: "The questions of Servetus and the Socinians were posed within the framework of a revealed theology based on Holy Scripture. The questions of Reimarus and Lessing were questions which attacked the very idea of revelation. To appreciate them in their broader context would require a comprehensive analysis of the Enlightenment and the changing attitudes to science, history and philosophy together with their impact on theology."

74. Dorrien, *The Making of American Liberal Theology*, xvi. See also Colin Brown, *Jesus in European Protestant Thought*, 131–32; Wilkens and Padgett, *Christianity and Western Thought*, 13–21.

75. Dorrien, *Making of American Liberal Theology*, xvi; C. Brown, *Jesus in European Protestant Thought*, 131. See Gerrish, "Natural and Revealed Religion," 662, for Schleiermacher, "religion is not correct belief, nor correct behaviour [sic] either, but the poetic expression of lively feeling." Further, on p. 663, 'The essence of religion is an elemental 'feeling' or 'intuition,' and our access to it is by observing the structure of consciousness—in the final analysis, our own consciousness." For general biographical details on Schleiermacher, see the entry in *The Oxford Dictionary of the Christian Church*, 1243–44. Here it is stated that his influence on Protestant thought through the nineteenth century was "enormous," but this influence was later "diminished" by Karl Barth and

was Christian experience, and this together with its implications had to be understood and interpreted in a way which was compatible with a modern scientific world view."[76] Among other things, this means that whether Jesus' resurrection actually took place is not an essential aspect of Christian theology or the Christian life.[77] As Schleiermacher concludes regarding this very issue: "We can therefore regard this whole matter as one of no importance and consider the details without prejudice and without any definite interest in proving one hypothesis or the other."[78] For Schleiermacher, whatever was considered "historical" and "scientific" in the Christian faith bore little continuity with the physical time and space realm of a person's present circumstances and condition, or with what marked the past in any physical, material way either.[79] In this indifference, if not disparagement, of "time/space" history, Schleiermacher is aligned with Spinoza. In Schleiermacher's theology, there is very little in

Emil Brunner. It is certainly a live question as to what degree Barth and Brunner directed theology along a course substantively different from that of Schleiermacher's predecessors. Dorrien, in *Making of American Liberal Theology*, xxi, regards Barth and what came to be called "Neo-orthodoxy" as "a form of liberal theology." In *History of Christian Thought*, 388–400, Tillich argues that when Schleiermacher stated that Christianity is a "feeling of absolute dependence," he did not mean that it was a subjective emotion. Tillich faults Hegel et al. for misreading Schleiermacher. It is difficult, however, to conceive that Tillich's analysis gives us a substantively different read on Schleiermacher, other than the one that still attributes to him the grounding of Christianity on an unbiblical anthropological foundation.

76. C. Brown, *Jesus in European Protestant Thought*, 131. See also Dorrien, *The Making of American Liberal Theology*, xxiii. Dorrien agrees with Hutchison, *The Modernist Impulse in American Protestantism*, on this point.

77. Colin Brown, *Jesus in European Protestant Thought*, 113, 123, 131. Brown, on p. 131, mentions Hegel's rather scathing criticism of Schleiermacher's emphasis on *Gefühl*, by quoting on p. 313n154, Hegel's introduction to Hermann Hinrichs, *Die Religion in ihrem Verhältnis zur Wissenschaft*: "'If the feeling of absolute dependence is the essence of religion and of the Christian faith, the dog would be the best Christian, for he bears this the strongest in himself and lives predominantly in this feeling. The dog has even feelings of release [Erlösungegefühle], if satisfaction is brought to his hunger by a bone. Only the free spirit has religion and can have religion.'"

78. Colin Brown, *Jesus in European Protestant Thought*, 129.

79. Harrisville and Sundberg, *Bible in Modern Culture*, 82–88. They argue for the interpretation that Schleiermacher's famous *Christmas Eve* play demonstrates that he "did not abandon historical faith to subjectivity," and that Schleiermacher's "'feeling of absolute dependence' takes its origin, its occasion and its content from Jesus of Nazareth" (p. 87). Though there is material to argue this thesis, their treatment demonstrates that at best the matter is ambiguous and there are plenty of those with more than a little sympathy for the liberal tradition, such as Strauss and Barth, who argue against such a conclusion.

the way of a union between the spiritual and physical. Not only does it not matter whether there was a bodily resurrection for Jesus, it is also of little importance whether Jesus even actually physically died. According to Schleiermacher, "once the act of dying had taken place in its spiritual significance, whether the physical part of death had been completed or not seems to me to be of no importance whatever."[80] Schleiermacher's theology, then, gives little emphasis to physical and historical matters, but casts theology upon an understanding of the spiritual that places the focus upon that which is internal to human beings and bears little correspondence to that which is outside of the individual.[81] Thus, Colin Brown maintains that "Schleiermacher's mature thought stood in sharp contrast with the monistic pantheism of Absolute Idealism."[82] Still, in the words of H. R. Mackintosh, Schleiermacher '"expounded as the Christian view of salvation what too often is but the attenuated creed of idealistic Monism.'"[83] As Colin Brown further analyzes it: "the attempt to penetrate outer forms and express the essence of the Christian faith in a manner relevant to the modern mind was the dominating characteristic of Schleiermacher's theology."[84]

Though subsequent nineteenth-century Protestant liberal theologians did not simply duplicate, or rubber-stamp Schleiermacher's beliefs, they nonetheless did accept his most fundamental postulates. They turned theology inward and thereby justified the allegation that their theology was really anthropology.[85] It is this trajectory of thought, running from Spinoza and Simon, through the eighteenth-century proponents of the historical-critical method (operating with a Kantian epistemology and expressed by Schleiermacher's theology), upon which a series of nineteenth-century theologians and biblical scholars in Europe and America formulated their varieties of Old and New Testament theology, and based their view of the Christian faith.[86] If nineteenth-century American biblical and theological scholarship is to be rightly understood then it must

80. C. Brown, *Jesus in European Protestant Thought*, 130.

81. Ibid., 131. Brown states that Schleiermacher possessed "an empirical approach to religion" in that he recognized "the importance of religious awareness as the basic datum of theological reflection."

82. Ibid., 131.

83. Ibid., 132. Brown is quoting H. R. Mackintosh, *Types of Modern Theology*.

84. Ibid., 107.

85. Ibid., 133.

86. Yarbrough, *Salvation-Historical Fallacy?*; Dorrien, *Making of American Liberal Theology*, xiii–xxv.

be seen, in part, within the midst of the radical recasting of Christian theology—and the general skepticism associated with this—that took place through the seminal influence of a Cartesian line of thought.[87]

The Other Side of the Coin

While modern biblical criticism was developing within Western culture, there were still plenty of Christians at the highest levels of academia, as well as those whose lives were preoccupied with concerns not immediately related to the academic arena, who operated with full confidence in the veracity of Scripture.[88] Such people continued to think and live in a way that corresponded to the belief that the Bible is the word of the triune God, who providentially governs his creation for his glory, and who incarnated himself in Jesus of Nazareth, as reported in the four Gospels. Indeed, we would operate with a skewed understanding of the developments of modern biblical criticism throughout the seventeenth and eighteenth century if we failed to recognize the resistance there was to the revolutionary nature of its pronouncements. There was still a preponderance of those who believed in the full trustworthiness of the Bible.[89] Therefore, during the years of the rise and development of modern biblical criticism, there were still intellectually credible and practically relevant arguments being espoused for an interpretation of Scripture that bore continuity with devout Christians throughout the history of the church.[90]

---

87. Dorrien, *Making of American Liberal Theology*, xiv. He states: "As modernists of a distinctive kind, the founders of American theological liberalism were always concerned to find a progressive way between the religious conservatism that they discarded and the rationalistic radicalism they dreaded." Dorrien, however, rightly contends for the controlling influence of Schleiermacher and Kant in American liberal theology, and in doing so aligns the latter with an anthropocentric line of thought that is the heart and soul of any rationalistic radicalism. It is questionable, then, to what degree there is any fundamental or essential difference between rationalistic radicalism and American liberal theology. Dorrien, on p. xvi, seems to recognize the Cartesian heritage in his acknowledgement that theological liberalism has made its appeal "to the authority of critical rationality and religious experience" and that it "derives historically from eighteenth-century Continental rationalism." Still further, the appeal to an internal authority can be seen, according to Dorrien (on p. xxiii), in that "[L]iberal theology seeks to reinterpret the symbols of traditional Christianity in a way that creates a progressive religious alternative to atheistic rationalism and to theologies based on external authority."

88. Woodbridge, *Biblical Authority*; Muller, *PRRD*; Sweeney, *American Evangelical Story*.

89. Woodbridge, *Biblical Authority*; Muller, *PRRD*; Sweeney, *American Evangelical Story*.

90. Woodbridge, *Biblical Authority*; Muller, *PRRD*; Sweeney, *American Evangelical*

It is important to bear this in mind both to understand what the advocates of modern biblical criticism considered themselves as rejecting and to accurately recognize the differences between these conflicting beliefs concerning the Bible. In order to understand the character of heretical thought one has to accurately understand the character of truly Christian thought. The latter thinking is not simply "'the product of choice, or of the will,'" but is that which conforms to "'the divine Word.'"[91] Indeed, commitment to the word of God for the true Christian means that God's word functions as the foundational authority for all knowledge claims.[92] This is not to say that other authorities or sources of knowledge are not accepted, but rather that the ultimate authority to which all other sources have to bow is the word of God.[93]

Problems do arise, though, because "Christianity is immersed in the world," and therefore, it comes into conflict in various ways with the "modes of thought" and "teachings" which are "products" of the world.[94] Unfortunately, it is not only conflict that can mark the relationship between truly Christian thinking and the thinking of the world, but also, to some degree, correspondence and concord.[95] In the case of modern biblical criticism, there *was* conflict over what constituted true criticism, which became just another way of debating what was and was not true science. This debate related to the Scriptures fundamentally in two ways: first, the Scriptures became an object of investigation to which "scientific method" was being applied; second, the Scriptures were under consideration as a source of authority to which a definition of science could correspond or by which a definition might even be determined. Thus, the whole matter addressed the issue of one's ultimate authority for knowledge claims and an accurate estimate of what the Bible was and was not. It highlighted the convergence of theology with philosophy—epistemology and metaphysics, in particular.[96]

Story. See also J. N. D. Kelly, *Early Christian Doctrines*; Davidson and Leff, *Medieval Thought*.

91. Warfield, "Heresy and Concession," *SSW* 2:672; quoting Fisher, *History of Christian Doctrine* (no page citation). Thus, Warfield uses "Christian" thinking as a synonym for "biblical" thinking.

92. Warfield, "Heresy and Concession," *SSW* 2:674.

93. Ibid.

94. Ibid.

95. Ibid.

96. Warfield, "Real Problem of Inspiration," *CW* 1:174–75.

Fundamental to understanding the substance of Kant's position and Warfield's response to it is a recognition that the former did not merely articulate a precise relationship between the subject who knows and the object that is known. That had been done for centuries. Kant's "revolution" consisted in giving *controlling authority* for what constitutes knowledge to the subject who knows. Kant believed that "objects must be viewed as conforming to human thought, not human thought to the independently real."[97] Though it is incorrect to identify Kant's expressed beliefs as solipsistic, there seems to be little preventing the logical consequences of his epistemological theory from resulting in metaphysical skepticism and epistemological relativism.[98] Schleiermacher's theology adopts this epistemology in his reconfiguring of theology and the Christian life. The key to understanding the difference between Kant's epistemology, Schleiermacher's theology, and Warfield's theology and epistemology is to distinguish the precise way in which they all thought of the metaphysical status of the object known and its relationship to the knowing subject.

Warfield had a clear conception of the relationship between philosophy and theology. He was well aware of all that had taken place leading up to the nineteenth century, and of how this overlap was manifesting itself in philosophies and theologies with which he differed. Identifying and explaining the relationship they had to each other ultimately formed the substance of his own work.

---

97. Copleston, *History of Philosophy* 6:211–76; Stumpf, *Socrates to Sartre*, 302–11. For the appeal of Kantian and neo-Kantian thought in some mid-nineteenth-century German theological circles, see Yarbrough, *Salvation-Historical Fallacy?*, 73–75. Yarbrough, on p. 75, mentions that the German liberal New Testament scholar William Wrede spoke of "'the quintessence of historical understanding' as 'being able to take control of [bemächtigen] the phenomena.'" Further, he states that this follows from "Kant's dictum that 'objects must be viewed as conforming to human thought, not human thought to the independently real.'"

98. Frame, *Doctrine of God*, 214.

4

Princeton and Warfield: Responses to Contextual Issues

IN ASSESSING the work of the church's past members, it is vital that we give significant weight to the expressed intentions that they themselves had for their work. As Warfield wrote, when analyzing the formidable biblical scholarship of the nineteenth century, "fierce controversies can rage only where strong convictions burn."[1] Strong convictions generally reveal that people perceive that something of crucial importance is at stake, and such convictions and controversies alert us to the possibility that historians will present a picture that corresponds to their own convictions.[2] This reality, of course, highlights why it is essential to remain in dialogue with historians who draw conclusions differing from one's own. Sometimes, even assured ways of interpreting a person, event, institution, or movement need to be reassessed simply on principle. Presuppositions and paradigms through which interpretive explanations are generated need to be re-explored, re-questioned, and possibly challenged.[3] Understanding what Princeton Seminary originally stood for

---

1. Warfield, "Century's Progress in Religious Knowledge," *SSW* 2:13. Certainly, both the fallen human condition and our finitude ought to serve as a check against a wholesale acceptance of any person's intentions, but such human frailties are no less operative in the historian than they were in the men and women the historian investigates.

2. One is reminded of Colin Brown's comment regarding Hegel: ". . . like other thinkers of the previous half-century, Hegel had no qualms about philosophizing about the inner meaning of history without subjecting himself to the arduous discipline of historical research. It was sufficient merely to supply from history illustrations for a thesis that owed its origin to other sources" (*Jesus in European Protestant Thought*, 93). I recognize that I, too, possess biases that affect my perceptions and conclusions.

3. Stout and Taylor, "Studies of Religion in American Society"; C. Smith, "Introduction." Christian Smith's work, in particular, highlights the point that the dominant thesis governing secularization suffers from a number of "defects." He lists seven: (1) far too much abstraction; (2) a lack of human agency; (3) a sense of over-

and against (as well as the relationship between the two) is integral to an assessment of Warfield. Moreover, it will be necessary, while wrestling with the contextual matters that are central to an accurate interpretation of Warfield, to also interact with those interpretations of him and the Old Princeton school that are inaccurate because those same contextual matters have been mishandled.

Princeton Seminary: A Theological and Ecclesiological Apologetic

As has already been seen, many scholars interpret the Old Princeton heritage as significantly influenced by SCSR, claiming that they used this philosophy for apologetic purposes. Though the founders of Princeton Seminary were self-consciously apologetic in their establishment of the school, their apologetic bent led them to employ a self-consciously *theological* approach that *pre*dates SCSR. Furthermore, their theological approach in its origin, character, and purpose was substantively different from the Scottish philosophy, or any other human philosophy. While philosophical ideas are related to the Princetonian's theological beliefs, and the Scottish philosophy can be correlated with some of those beliefs, no philosophy or philosophical epistemology can adequately account either for the strategy of the seminary founders in establishing Princeton, or for Warfield's theology and apologetic method. Recognizing the broader theological matters that formed Princeton's framework, will not only help in seeing what energized the Old Princeton school, but will also shed light on how the various manifestations of Scottish philosophy lacked the capacity to accomplish Princeton's apologetic purposes. Moreover, by paying attention to the theological and ecclesiological concerns of the seminary founders, it will become more apparent that the primary context needed to interpret Warfield's theology and apologetic method is a theological one.

---

deterministic inevitability; (4) an orientation (primarily among historians) of idealist intellectual history; (5) an over-romanticization of the religious past; (6) an over-emphasis on religious self-destruction; and (7) an under-specification of the causal mechanisms of secularization. Numbers 2–7, in particular, characterize historicist approaches to historiography that exclude the biblical idea that the trinitarian God acts within his creation, yet is not dependent upon his creation. Smith's work is not only a reminder of the importance of being willing to take a fresh look at dominant theses, but is also a reminder that knowledge claims of any kind are related to sociological matters. More specifically, he shows that any scholarship that operates with a fact-value split is itself a manifestation of a particular ideology that is hardly neutral, or to be viewed as inherently superior to scholarship that does not operate according to that split, unless, of course, one simply wishes to beg the relevant questions regarding these matters.

The Founding of Princeton Seminary

The stated goal of Princeton Seminary was to "form men for the Gospel ministry" who would administer the word of God in a way that was consistent with "the Confession of Faith, Catechisms and Plan of Government and Discipline of the Presbyterian Church; and thus to perpetuate and extend the influence of true evangelical piety, and Gospel order."[4] The developing of these men meant, among other things, that each "must have read and digested the principal arguments and writings relative to what has been called the deistical controversy—Thus will he be qualified to become a defender of the Christian faith."[5] Princeton Seminary's founders desired to equip ministers who would be pastorally polemical, or polemically pastoral, and they sought to achieve this goal by grounding them in the WCF and its Catechisms, as well as the Plan of Government and Discipline of the Presbyterian Church. In other words, Ahlstrom correctly recognized the apologetic bent of Princeton, but missed the mark on how they intended to accomplish their goal. It was not Scottish philosophy that was either the foundation or the primary tool that the founders of Princeton Seminary thought necessary for combating false ideas inimical to the gospel. Instead, the apologetic tool of choice for the Princeton founders was the WCF and its accompaniments. The seminary founders believed not only that particular theological beliefs were essential to their apologetic purpose, but also that a specific ecclesiology, and actions commensurate with it, were vital to accomplishing this purpose as well.

Their goal was supported by another theological tool—Francis Turretin's *Institutes of Elenctic Theology*.[6] James Waddell Alexander (1804–

---

4. Calhoun, *Princeton Seminary* 1:416.

5. Ibid., 1:423–24.

6. Turretin, *Institutes of Elenctic Theology*. The current reprint edition of Turretin's work includes a helpful summary at the end of volume 3 by Dennison Jr., the editor of "The Life and Career of Francis Turretin." Turretin was born October 17, 1623, to a third-generation Protestant and wealthy Italian family that traced its knowledge of the faith to Peter Martyr Vermigli's evangelical work in the north central Italian city of Lucca. After completing his studies at the Genevan Academy, Turretin embarked on an ambitious educational journey that allowed him to sit under the teaching of the leading Reformed theologians in Leiden, Utrecht, Paris, and Saumur. By 1647 he had become well acquainted with the diversity of thought in the Reformed community—a community that not only was marked by internal squabbles, but also engaged in polemics with other religious communities of varying theological positions. For a helpful summary of the years of Turretin's theological work, see Cragg, *Church and the Age of*

1854), professor of Ecclesiastical History and Church Government at Princeton from 1849 to 1851, believed that Turretin was just what was needed to counter the theological malaise sweeping over the minds and hearts of many in their time.[7] He based this conviction on the fact that it had "long been admitted that Francis Turrettin [sic] was the best expounder of the doctrine of the Reformed Church, as matured into completeness of form in the period following the Synod of Dort."[8] The nature and depth of the theological discontent they intended to battle is expressed in the following:

> It has now for years been apparent to the public, what kind of theology was generated by the methods of those schools which hoodwinked their pupils in regard to the giants of Protestant theology, under the pretext of having no text-book but the Bible; who carried the pedigree of theologians no further back than a century; whose whole library contained no Latin volume; and whose model names were only such as Bellamy, Hopkins and Emmons. Men of education in all our churches were demanding a more generous and a more masculine preparation in their religious teachers. Knowing as they did that theology is a science, and that in all sciences the history of opinion, in its gradual development, is an indispensable aid in the prosecution of truth, they detected the meagerness of a training which deliberately cut off the young theologian from all acquaintance with the monuments of reformation theology, and which condemned whole libraries of pious learning under the name of Scholastic rubbish.[9]

Joseph Bellamy, Samuel Hopkins, and Nathaniel Emmons, who considered themselves faithful to the legacy of Jonathan Edwards (1703–1755), were chief among the theological agitators of the time.[10] As part of the

---

Reason. For a thorough treatment of the content and antecedents of post-Reformation Reformed theology, see Muller, *PRRD*.

7. For details of J. W. Alexander's life as a Princetonian, see Calhoun, *Princeton Seminary* 1:114–15, 286–87, 312–13, 338, 354, 369–71, 378–79, 489–90, 490 n. 53. Alexander had a great concern for pastoral ministry, and was particularly touched by the needs of the poor, neglected, and marginalized people of society. Though a Princeton professor at one point, the bulk of his work was as a church pastor.

8. J. W. Alexander, "Institutio Theologiae Elencticae," 452.

9. Ibid.

10. For a helpful introduction to how the Old Princeton school responded to these controversies, see *Princeton versus the New Divinity*—the author is listed as the *Princeton Review* and most of the articles appear to be written by Archibald Alexander and Charles Hodge. For an introduction to the scholarly discussion regarding Edwards' legacy, see

"New Divinity," these men, from the perspective of the Princetonians, were helping sow theological seeds that would produce the wrong crop. Alexander explains:

> There can be no better field for sowing the tares of new divinity, than the minds of novices, uncatechized in childhood, untouched by logical discipline in youth, prejudiced against the schemes of truth which they could not understand, and gaping for the latitudinary definitions and dogmas of a narrow, inelegant, mediocre and neological metaphysic.[11]

It was felt that Turretin's *Institutes* would help remedy the conditions that made it easy for the theological errors of the New Divinity to take root—as well as those of other doctrinal and theological systems. According to Alexander, Turretin's *Institutes* revealed to students "that a large part of the objections urged against the doctrines of grace by the new divinity, are the identical objections which were far more ably urged by Pelagius and Celestius, or by Estius and Episcopius, or by the Jesuits and Molinists."[12] Theological illness required theological medicine, and Old Princeton theologians thought that the system of doctrine taught in the WCF and its accompaniments was the right remedy.[13] The Princetonian's systematic theology was wedded to their practical and polemical theology.

Doctrine and Life; Beliefs and Actions

Princeton's primary concern was what was proclaimed and practiced in the church. This emphasis highlights the union they believed existed between doctrine and life, beliefs and practices—in other words, a union of intellect with actions and affections. They believed that theology and the

---

Sweeney and Guelzo, *New England Theology*; Sweeney, *Nathaniel Taylor*; Hart, Lucas and Nichols, *Legacy of Jonathan Edwards*; Lee and Guelzo, *Edwards in Our Time*.

11. J. W. Alexander, "Insitutio Theologiae Elenticae," 452–53.

12. Ibid., 453.

13. Warfield thought of truth and systematic theology as an organism and likened incorrect theology and doctrinal systems to a virus. Consider the following: "There is no difficulty in stating evangelical religion so as to exclude pure Pelagianism. The problem is how to state it so as to exclude those dangerous compromise schemes in which the deadly virus is hidden ever more and more subtly. Were it not for these it might be enough to say, Trust in God, not in yourself. In the presence of these, it is necessary to define ever more and more closely, as the virus of dependence on self hides itself ever more and more subtly. And in this fact lies the need of the close definitions of our present propositions: and in this fact is betrayed their importance." Warfield, "Revision and the Third Chapter."

practical realities of life existed in an organic union.[14] To possess eternal life and have God-glorifying behavior, one had to, at least to some degree, think biblically, or in a way that was consistent with the theology warranted by Scripture.[15] This was not to reduce salvation to a mere assent to particular theological propositions, but rather to affirm that those who had eternal life would affirm particular theological propositions as true, and thus, these affirmations were the fruit, not the ultimate cause, of their salvation.

From the Old Princeton perspective, the chief barrier to receiving the gospel is ideas and beliefs that do not correspond to what Scripture reveals as true. This is why, as part of his opening address of the fall term at Princeton Seminary on September 20, 1912, J. Gresham Machen affirmed:

> False ideas are the greatest obstacles to the reception of the gospel. We may preach with all the fervour of a reformer and yet succeed only in winning a straggler here and there, if we permit the whole collective thought of the nation or of the world to be controlled by ideas which, by the resistless force of logic, prevent Christianity from being regarded as anything more than a harmless delusion.[16]

This was vintage Princeton, but it would be a serious misread of church history to think that it was only the Princeton view. The entire history of God's people, dating back to the Old Testament era, testifies that the Scriptures affirm the union between doctrine and life, beliefs and actions.

---

14. Warfield, in "Authority, Intellect, Heart," *SSW* 2:671, is illuminating: "The revelations of the Scripture do not terminate upon the intellect. They were not given to merely enlighten the mind. They were given through the intellect to beautify the life. They terminate on the heart. Again, they do not in affecting the heart, leave the intellect untouched. They cannot be fully understood by the intellect, acting alone. The natural man cannot receive the things of the Spirit of God. They must first convert the soul before they are fully comprehended by the intellect. Only as they are lived are they understood. Hence the phrase, 'Believe that you may understand,' has its fullest validity. No man can intellectually grasp the full meaning of the revelations of authority, save as the result of an experience of their power in life." This union of doctrine and life; thinking and living, does not have its origin in, nor depend upon, Greek philosophy. See Holifield, *Theology in America*, 8, for this line of argumentation.

15. For an explicit description of the connections between doctrine and life, see chapter 6 in this book.

16. Machen, *What Is Christianity?*, 162.

The reality of this union was believed by countless Christians throughout the history of the church prior to the nineteenth century.[17]

Moreover, it needs to be recognized that it was not simply the reality of a union between doctrine and life that was emphasized by Old Princeton and Warfield. Those opposing the Old Princeton beliefs and practices also affirmed a union between doctrine and life.[18] The substantive questions were: (1) What is the precise way that each group understood and described the nature of this union? (2) What was the basis or ground for their claims?

The centrality of these questions regarding doctrine and life highlights the importance of the historical character of the Christian faith. The essential conflict in beliefs between Warfield and his theological opponents was not that one of them taught that Christianity had a historical character to it that conditioned it, while the other did not. Both sides taught that Christianity had a historical character, because both recognized a union between beliefs and human actions.[19] Thus, the historical situation in which humans lived was inextricably united to their beliefs, and was understood to condition those beliefs in particular ways. The actual questions regarding history that both sides in the debate had to answer, and which became the seminal matters regarding modern biblical criticism, were: (1) What is the nature or character of history? (2) In what ways does history condition the Bible and the Christianity derived from it?[20] Obviously, these questions are joined to numerous other subjects as well, and so the matters that energized Warfield, and the theological opponents with whom he differed, involved them in critical and expansive

---

17. J. N. D. Kelly, *Early Christian Doctrines*; Williams, *Retrieving the Tradition* and *Evangelicals and Tradition*; Leff, *Medieval Thought*; Ozment, *Age of Reform*; Muller, *PRRD*; Pelikan, *Christian Traditio*; González, *Story of Christianity*.

18. See Dorrien, *Making of American Liberal Theology*.

19. Warfield, "Latest Phase of Historical Rationalism," *CW* 9:585–645; and "Right of Systematic Theology," *SSW* 2:219–79. This latter essay will be the subject of detailed scrutiny in a later chapter.

20. This question is central to the identity and development of modern biblical criticism or the historical-critical method of biblical interpretation. See Baird, *History of New Testament Research* vos. 1 (*From Deism to Tubingen*) and 2 (*From Jonathan Edwards to Rudolf Bultmann*); idem "Biblical Criticism: New Testament Criticism," 1:730; C. Brown, *Jesus in European Protestant Thought*; Harrisville and Sundberg, *Bible in Modern Culture*; McGrath, *Making of Modern German Christology*; Orr, "Criticism of the Bible," 2:749; Scholder, *Birth of Modern Critical Theology*; Yarbrough, *Salvation-Historical Fallacy?*; and Linnemann, *Is There a Synoptic Problem?*; *Historical-Criticism of the Bible*; and *Biblical Criticism on Trial*.

questions regarding human knowledge, and led them to address multiple subject disciplines.[21] Intimately joined to the rise and development of modern biblical criticism, then, has been the broader questions and issues related to epistemology that have influenced Western culture for centuries.[22]

Scottish Common Sense Realism

While one can certainly correlate some manifestations of SCSR epistemology with these matters, and even with Warfield's convictions concerning them, the Scottish philosophy *cannot* account for his theological beliefs, his view of history, or his apologetic approach. Since his epistemology is integrally wedded to his theology and doctrinal beliefs, its source is first and foremost Scripture, not nature (or his contemplation of nature apart from biblical presuppositions), and its character is first and foremost theological, not philosophical.

Warfield's epistemology and apologetic method are wedded to the biblical doctrines expressed in the WCF, but the epistemology of SCSR simply has nothing to say about many of the doctrinal matters that are organically united to the Confession. Before Warfield, Archibald Alexander demonstrated clear knowledge of some of the tenets of Scottish Realism, and Charles Hodge analyzed and critiqued Hamilton's beliefs regarding knowledge of God and rejected them.[23] Alexander affirmed "that we are so constituted that we are under the necessity of believing many propositions."[24] Therefore, there are *some* of Alexander's, Hodge's, and Warfield's epistemological beliefs that agree with *some* of the Scottish philosophers. If there is a worthy distinction to be made between Reid's realist thought and Hutcheson's sentimentalist thought, then we should identify the Princeton theologians' epistemology as more accurately correlated with Reid's than Hutcheson's.[25] Reid's epistemological beliefs

21. This appears to be the reason why Karl Barth considered philosophers to be theologians and gave them a prominent place in his history of nineteenth-century theology. See Barth, *Protestant Theology in the Nineteenth Century*, xvi–xvii. Charles Hodge made a similar insight when he acknowledged that in some sense every theology is connected to a particular philosophy. See Hodge, "What Is Christianity?," 121.

22. Hazard, *European Mind*; Scholder, *Birth of Modern Critical Theology*; Cragg, *Church and the Age of Reason* and *Freedom and Authority*.

23. Archibald Alexander, "Nature and Evidence of Truth." Alexander titled this: "Theological Lectures, Nature and Evidence of Truth." See also Hodge, *ST* 1:346–65.

24. Archibald Alexander, "Nature and Evidence of Truth," 63.

25. Noll, *America's God*, 109.

center on the idea that human beings know things by virtue of the way they are constituted. Due to the very nature of reality, it overlaps with the theologically based epistemology of the Princetonians. The WCF affirms that human beings were created male and female, in the image of God, with knowledge, righteousness, and holiness, and with dominion over the creatures.[26] This insight shares characteristics with the idea in SCSR that humans are so constituted that they automatically possess knowledge within the reality that they occupy. Overlap and correlation, however, do not constitute dependence.

Consequently, it can appear that Archibald Alexander and the other Princeton men found common cause with Reid's first principles and some of the fundamental tenets of SCSR. Yet, Ahlstrom argues that scholars at Harvard, Yale, and Andover—whose theological convictions were not the same as the Princetonians'—did as well. If the Scottish philosophy was generative for the Princeton theology, one is left questioning how the same philosophical principles could be so significant in producing not only Old School Presbyterian Calvinism, but varieties of the Edwardsean New Divinity, Unitarianism, an anti-traditionalist and anti-creedal theological orientation, the Mercersburg theology, late nineteenth-century confessional Lutheranism, the Dutch Reformed tradition of the twentieth century, and an ahistorical and atheological approach to the Christian faith as well.[27] Though these theologies certainly have some things in common, they also stand in direct contradiction with one another on significant doctrinal points. It is hardly evident how SCSR could produce such varying doctrinal emphases, or even any one of them.

When Charles Hodge returned from studying in Germany in 1829, he organized the *Princeton Review* (*Biblical Repertory*) to better combat Protestant liberal theology and other theological traditions that he believed were unfaithful in varying ways to Scripture. As stated previously, Noll highlights this activity as evidence that CSR "encouraged participants in theological debate to draw conclusions for their opponents."[28] Hodge's activities with the *Princeton Review* actually accentuate the point that the Old Princeton theologians had an explicitly theological

---

26. WCF, IV, 2; SC Q. & A. 10; LC Q. & A. 17.

27. Ahlstrom, "Scottish Philosophy," 261; Noll, "Common Sense Tradition," 4, 19, 25, 26, 28. As we have seen, though, Noll's more recent work presents a more nuanced understanding of these matters that does not correspond in every way with Ahlstrom's thesis.

28. Noll, *America's God*, 299–300.

purpose in their work, and whatever common cause they may have had with philosophical ideas was done with (1) the full consciousness of not compromising their theological beliefs and (2) the specific purpose accomplished in any use of those philosophical ideas.

Though some of the characteristics of the varieties of the Scottish philosophy were employed by numerous theological traditions within early nineteenth-century America, the analyses by Ahlstrom, Marsden, and to some degree Noll, regarding the uses of the Scottish philosophy within these diverse theological traditions, and with the Old Princeton school in particular, contain important flaws. While Noll's analysis is a bit more complex, this complexity actually leads to virtual contradictions that leave one wondering just exactly what he means to conclude regarding the nineteenth-century Princeton theologians and Scottish philosophy, or even regarding SCSR's role in the development of theology in nineteenth-century America.[29] *All* of the analyses result in significant inaccuracies in the historiography regarding Old Princeton and Warfield.[30] These analyses fail to identify precisely how the Scottish philosophy is an adequate explanatory device to account for theological and doctrinal beliefs that the Scottish philosophy does not address, other than affirming that one can truly know objective reality based on how human beings are constituted. In other words, how the Scottish philosophy accounts for doctrines of justification, the eternal decrees of God, the church, revelation, or any of the other doctrines in the Confession is not spelled out. The distinctive emphases of the Old Princeton confessionalism are written off as "lifeless and static," by Ahlstrom, and even implicated in

---

29. Ibid., 301, refers to the 1820s and 30s and states: "The conservative Presbyterianism of Hodge and like-minded colleagues was influential in the era and later because it was learned, because it had a clear vision of God-centered Christian faith, and because it always kept the larger national picture in view." Then, two sentences later, on p. 302, we are told: "For Hodge, the interests of church, country and Christianity more generally were always interwoven. When he and his Princeton allies entered the lists, they brought a conservative counterweight into the unfolding of Reformed theological history, but that counterweight shared almost as much with the era's American ideology as the most self-consciously methodical revivalist or the most deliberate New England reviser of Jonathan Edwards." How he can then affirm that Hodge "always kept the larger national picture in view" is not clear. Moreover, it is a rather alarming analysis to identify the Princeton theologians as so clouded and confused that they could not detect how their beliefs were quite in line with the New Divinity proponents against whom they so thoroughly polemicized.

30. See chapter 1 of this book for a discussion of some of the influence that Ahlstrom in particular has had upon numerous historians' accounts of the Old Princeton school and Warfield.

the demise of the Scottish philosophy itself.³¹ *If* the two were joined, one would expect a more detailed analysis of the nature of that relationship beyond the simple assertion or inference that a realist epistemology can be correlated with the Confession's view of human beings. As it is, a relationship of correlation is illegitimately passed off as a relationship of dependency.

Second, their analyses fail to take Princeton's avowed goal seriously—that their primary and fundamental apologetic tool was the WCF, supported by the Government and Discipline of the Presbyterian Church and Turretin's *Institutes*. These theological and ecclesiological documents predate any mature presentation of SCSR. When the WCF is located historically in relation to the Scottish philosophy, it soon becomes apparent that the Confession predates the latter by at least eighty years, using Hutcheson's scholarship as a benchmark, and by over one hundred years if Reid's is used. The Westminster Divines could not have been under the influence of Hutcheson and Reid when they wrote the WCF, although it is certain that the two Scots were quite familiar with the Confession. It is the Catechisms that Warfield memorized, and that the Old Princeton school intentionally employed for apologetic purposes. Whatever use the Princetonians in general, and Warfield in particular, may have made of SCSR, it would have been in terms of correlations they saw with at least some of the doctrines expressed in the Confession. As has already been mentioned, affirming that human beings know things by virtue of how they are constituted corresponds with the doctrine that human beings are creatures created in the image of God, who thereby possess knowledge. The true nature and thrust of the Princeton apologetic, and of Warfield's specifically, is missed when one ignores the *historical* testimony that it was the WCF and the Government and Discipline of the Presbyterian church that was meant to be used for accomplishing Princeton's apologetic goals.³² The primary issue that concerned the founders of Princeton was any theology that they deemed unbiblical.

---

31. Ahlstrom, "Scottish Philosophy," 269.

32. I refer to this historical testimony as "ignored" because it is too obvious a piece of historical data to be missed. One possible explanation for why it is ignored is offered by Seeman, "Evangelical Historiography beyond the 'Outward Clash.'" Seeman criticizes Marsden, Noll, and Harry Stout for adopting an "alternation" approach in which they alternate between what they affirm as academic historians, who play by the philosophically naturalistic rules of the academy, and what they affirm as believing Christians for the church. Their approach fully embraces a fact/value split that Warfield, as we will see, denied was true and denied was able to be adopted by Christians for apologetic purposes.

Princeton and Biblical Criticism

According to Charles Hodge, the way to avoid error in biblical interpretation is not by applying a spiritualized exegesis that thinks that the study of the original languages, textual issues, and historical questions is unnecessary. It is attained by entering into a thorough study of those very things.[33] In keeping with his conviction, Hodge prevailed upon his seminary colleagues Archibald Alexander and Samuel Miller—as well as the seminary board of directors—to allow him to study in Europe with some of the German scholars who advocated the biblical criticism associated with Kant and Schleiermacher, so that he might be better equipped to accomplish his task as a professor.[34] Shortly after his return in 1825, Hodge assumed responsibility for the periodical *Biblical Repertory* (*BRep*), which he then managed for over forty years.[35] The *BRep*, and its devotion to articles on biblical literature and interpretation, reveals the seminary's concern over German higher criticism and other theological matters impinging upon the church.[36] *BRep* articles not only addressed the issues raised by higher criticism, but identified the source of that criticism as seventeenth-century English deism.[37] As stated previously, Princeton Seminary was established for the purpose of supplying the Presbyterian Church in America with pastors who were well-informed regarding "the

---

Indeed, Warfield faulted Kuyper and Bavinck for acquiescing in some ways to this type of thinking. See chapter 7 in this book.

33. Calhoun, *Princeton Seminary* 1:117.

34. Ibid.

35. Noll, "*Princeton Review*," 285–86.

36. Ibid., 116. The contents of the *BRep*'s first two articles, "Translation of Beckii Monogrammata Hermeneutices N. T." and "Translation of Tittmann on Historical Interpretation," are representative testimony of the concern for accuracy in biblical interpretation and an awareness of the developments in biblical scholarship that had been, according to the Princetonians, undermining it. For a general history and analysis of the *Biblical Repertory* see Noll, "*Princeton Review*"; and Calhoun, *Princeton Seminary* 2:83. The *Biblical Repertory* underwent a number of name changes and purposes throughout its history. In 1837 it became the *Biblical Repertory and Princeton Review* until, in 1871, it merged with the *American Presbyterian Quarterly* and became the *Presbyterian Quarterly and Princeton Review*. It became *The Princeton Review* in 1878 and focused primarily on "philosophy, science and literature" (Calhoun, 2:83). It became the *New Princeton Review* in 1886. It was the creation of the *Presbyterian Review* in 1880 under the joint leadership of A. A. Hodge and Charles Augustus Briggs that took up the theological matters central to the Presbyterian Church. It was in this latter journal that Hodge's and Warfield's joint article on "Inspiration" appeared.

37. See "Translation of an Extract from Staeudlin's *Geschicte der Theologischen Wissenchaften*."

deistical controversy."[38] The Princetonians' awareness of the presuppositional nature of thinking and its relationship to biblical interpretation is seen in Charles Hodge's editorial remarks in the initial *BRep* issue. There he mentions that the warnings in the articles were addressed to those who:

> ... introduce the speculations of Philosophy into the study of Theology, and who avowedly or unconsciously interpret the Sacred Volume in accordance with the opinions previously formed, and resting upon some other foundation than the revelation of God.[39]

Moreover, in his retrospect of the journal, Hodge testified to the theological concerns that animated the Princetonians in preserving particular theological doctrines. This article includes his much quoted statement: "Whether it be a ground of reproach or of approbation, it is believed to be true, that an original idea in theology is not to be found on the pages of the *Biblical Repertory and Princeton Review* from the beginning until now. The phrase "Princeton Theology," therefore, is without distinctive meaning."[40] What is important to recognize is that Hodge and the other Princetonians, in keeping with the founders of the seminary, sought to be faithful to the WCF. They were concerned with theological

38. Calhoun, *Princeton Seminary* 1:416.

39. *BR* 1.1 (1825) iv.

40. C. Hodge, "Retrospect." It is uncertain to what kind of novelty Hodge is referring. Warfield affirmed that, at least with the doctrine of imputation, there had been four views of imputation held among Congregationalists and Presbyterians in the nineteenth century, and thus he distinguished between Hodge's "Federalistic" view and the "mediate imputation" view of the New School Presbyterians, and the "Realistic" view of Henry B. Smith. See Warfield, "Imputation," *CW* 9:301–9. This appeared in the 1909 edition of *The New Schaff-Herzog Encyclopedia of Religious Knowledge*. It may well be that Hodge's point was that in terms of novelty of substance or essential matters there is no "new" theology, and thus all that the Princetonians affirmed was the substance of what was affirmed in the Reformed creeds and, in particular, the WCF. In such an interpretation it would be denied that Hodge was saying that there was complete unanimity among the Princetonians on all theological matters that were related to the whole doctrinal system of the Confession. At any rate, Warfield certainly disagreed with A. A. Hodge on Hodge's conception of the *Ordo Salutis* (Order of Salvation). According to Warfield, A. A. Hodge reversed the order and placed justification before faith and regeneration. He faulted A. A. Hodge for pressing God's condemnation of the sinner into the extreme, and for failing to recognize that even while under condemnation God "shows us favor." He accused Hodge of having a position that is a) anti-confessional (WCF ch. 11; SC Q30), b) a confusing scheme, and c) anti-Scriptural (Rom 8:29). See Warfield, Systematic Theology Lecture Notes, "Faith," 58, B. B. Warfield Papers, box 49, PTS archives. The latter disagreement occurred long after Charles Hodge had died.

matters and were quite well aware of the relationship that existed between the disciplines of theology and philosophy.

Warfield, Biblical Criticism, and Philosophy

As we have already seen, Warfield's earliest years of seminary teaching were in New Testament studies, and he demonstrated an up to date knowledge of the critical issues in biblical scholarship. Warfield was not only immersed in text critical matters, but also understood how particular theological affirmations were inseparable from the methodological concerns raised by the practice of modern biblical criticism. The theological and ecclesiological apologetic of Old Princeton, and Warfield, highlights the impact of biblical criticism on nineteenth and early twentieth-century biblical and theological scholarship, as well as Friedrich Schleiermacher's (1768–1834) influence upon that scholarship.[41] To the degree that Schleiermacher followed Immanuel Kant's epistemological lead, the latter can also be identified as a concern for Warfield. Warfield's philosophical concerns were subordinated to theology in two primary ways: (1) his areas of primary interest and (2) his theological apologetic method. Warfield's concern was over doctrinal and theological Protestant liberalism that he believed reconceptualized or reconstructed the Christian faith on naturalistic lines of thought. He identified Kant's philosophy as the primary philosophical impetus to the Protestant liberal project, but his weapon to combat this was twofold: (1) explaining the theological system of doctrine that he believed to be faithful to the Bible (i.e., WCF), and (2) criticizing liberal scholarship on the basis of the truthfulness of the Confession's theological doctrinal system. Warfield not only believed that the WCF is faithful to the Scriptures, he also believed that it corresponds to reality in general. One of Warfield's most significant claims is his insistence that those who sought to reconstruct the Christian faith along theologically liberal lines did not handle all the available evidence. In so doing, Warfield accentuates the relationship between the objective and subjective elements in epistemology.

Warfield was quite aware that interpretive methodology is simultaneously a theological and a philosophical matter that is part of every branch of learning or science. In 1883, while still at Western and after his work with A. A. Hodge on their famous article on inspiration, Warfield

---

41. For a concise introduction to Schleiermacher, see Gerrish, *Prince of the Church*. The first American scholar to use some of the methods of the German higher critics was Moses Stuart. For a concise summary of his life and work see Giltner, *Moses Stuart*.

wrote an essay entitled, "Dr. Briggs' Critical Method."[42] Here Warfield not only reveals that he advocates a true and rigorous criticism of the Scriptures, as he does in "Inspiration and Criticism," but also demonstrates his belief that Briggs' method falls short of even satisfying the higher critics themselves.[43]

In his response, Warfield conveys his thoughts about the foundational matters that ought to inform a proper methodology for biblical interpretation. He first establishes an irenic tone, which he carries throughout the article, by commending Briggs for his "large learning" and "abounding strength." He also acknowledges that Briggs' "critical position" is evangelical and "in harmony with the confessional theology of our own church."[44] Warfield's inherent cordiality can be seen when he calls it, "a great pleasure to read and criticise [sic] a paper like this," and that the reader ". . . feels proud of himself when he agrees with it and his disagreements are purely of the genial kind."[45] He makes it plain that his desire is ". . . not acrid controversy, but frank and brotherly, if eager, discussion."[46] Warfield further explains his own intentions by saying: "[H]e longs to talk over the various points with the author. . . . sure of his own good temper, he is sure of that of his author too. This is the spirit in which I purpose to set down here the impression which the critical method set forth in Dr. Briggs' paper has made upon my mind."[47] This expressed collegiality, however, did not mean that he refrained from subjecting Briggs' method to rigorous criticism.

---

42. A. A. Hodge and Warfield, "Inspiration"; Warfield, "Dr. Briggs' Critical Method." In the Meeter and Nicole bibliography of Warfield's work, this was erroneously listed as appearing in 1882, although it is correctly placed under the date 1883. In the margin of the archive copy is the date February 15, 1883, which may be the date that Warfield received his copy.

43. Letis, "B. B. Warfield." Unfortunately, he relies upon Ahlstrom's SCSP thesis and the historiography dependent upon it. As a result, he fails to understand that Warfield's view of science calls into question the putative science of the higher critics.

44. Warfield, "Dr. Briggs' Critical Method," 1. Still, within the confines of the denomination's theology, Briggs' position eventually, of course, brought him to the point of a heresy trial and he was removed from the Presbyterian Church. Warfield, though, at the time he wrote this article, acknowledged Briggs as his "brother" in the Christian faith by the following words: "I trust it will be remembered that it is the weak places in a fellow-soldier's harness which alone call for the attention of his companions."

45. Ibid.
46. Ibid.
47. Ibid.

Though critical of Briggs' *method*, Warfield regarded the paper that Briggs had written on the matter to be of significant apologetic value.[48] As Warfield states, "It seems to me to demonstrate that the theories of destructive criticism are not the necessary or even the natural outgrowth of the facts on which they found themselves."[49] Instead, when the facts are viewed correctly "the divine origin of this wonderful legislation becomes especially apparent."[50]

Warfield's primary field of expertise was the New Testament and Briggs' was the Old Testament, but Warfield clarifies that the issue is not simply a matter of biblical interpretation. Instead, it has to do with questions regarding a method of interpreting any piece of literature. Or, as Warfield states, it is a matter for "the purview of every lover of polite letters."[51] In other words, biblical interpretation is not a *sui generis* discipline with its own set of private rules, but a discipline unavoidably related to the methods of interpretation of any written document. This assertion by Warfield demonstrates the characteristic Princetonian emphasis on the "unity of truth."[52] By doing so, Warfield establishes that the questions regarding modern biblical criticism actually centere around the soundness of method, regardless of subject matter. Is the method truly critical and scientific? As he saw it, neither the unbelieving higher critics nor Briggs were employing a "sound critical method."[53]

Warfield makes certain that he does justice to Briggs' method by quoting Briggs himself on the topic. Brigg's declares that one should: "(1) Inquire what the Scriptures teach about themselves, and separate this divine authority from all other authority; (2) apply the principles of the *Higher Criticism* to decide questions not decided by divine authority; (3) use *tradition*, in order to determine as far as possible questions not settled by the previous methods."[54] Warfield, however, believed that such a method would not satisfy "either wing of the great critical army," and he explains why by using a hunting analogy.[55]

---

48. Ibid.
49. Ibid.
50. Ibid.
51. Ibid.
52. Gundlach, "Evolution Question at Princeton," 53–72.
53. Warfield, "Dr. Briggs' Critical Method," 1.
54. Ibid.
55. Ibid.

> Advanced critics will justly demand by what right a preserve is fenced off to begin with, within which Higher Criticism is forbidden to hunt. Traditionalists will as justly refuse to hunt at all behind dogs whose scent seems confessedly untrustworthy outside the leash. The former will insist that it is impossible to arrive at truth, if that precious quarry has just at its side an impenetrable hedge of traditional authority behind which it can always step. The latter will equally strenuously insist that dogs which have to be held well in to prevent their running heedlessly across the trail of truth, probably do not run very closely on that trail at any time. Both alike will point out that this scheme of procedure begins by discrediting the Higher Criticism, proceeds by depending on it and discrediting Tradition, and ends by assigning conclusive authority to doubly discredited Tradition.[56]

Briggs' methodology renders immaterial any questions pertaining to what authority either the higher critics *or* the traditionalists utilize—and therefore seems confused about the fact that both parties had to bow to common reality; a common reality that meant that the pursuits of science were *not* contrary or inimical to Christian faith. As Warfield puts it, "I am free to confess that every particle of scientific spirit in me and every particle of faith, alike, protests against such a scheme."[57] As Warfield saw it, the Bible was a fact of creation, making it a part of everyone's reality, Christian or not. Whatever the Bible is or is not, it must correspond to a reality that is, in some sense, common to all people. Whatever Christian faith is, as well, it certainly cannot be at fundamental odds with a reality that is common to everyone. Warfield, therefore, reasons:

> An inspired statement which cannot stand the test of criticism is not foundation enough to build faith on. A criticism which cannot be trusted to accord independently with inspired statements, cannot be trusted where we have no such divine authority to check its vagaries. Faith asks exactly what science demands; that the Bible be treated like any other book. No statement of even our Divine Master himself, be it never so direct and never so clear, concerning the composition of the Pentateuch, can be, to ought but weakness, a rule of procedure; to strength it would be but a blessed assurance of result.[58]

---

56. Ibid.
57. Ibid.
58. Ibid., 1–2.

Warfield was not willing to allow those practicing what he calls "negative" criticism to simply ignore the question of what authority they were using to determine what constitutes science. Warfield's perspective entailed a creator who determined what all things are. If "critical" means rigorously seeking correspondence to reality in order to determine truth, then Warfield would not concede that negative critics are either "scientific" or "critical." He was secure in his belief that true criticism of the Bible would reveal it for what it was; true science and true Christian faith were not enemies but compatriots. As Warfield writes:

> A true science and a sturdy faith alike would read it, *not* "You must not let criticism destroy the Mosaic origin of the Pentateuch," *but*, "A sound criticism *will not* destroy it." In the name of both, then, let it be insisted that the leash be cut, the dogs of criticism be let loose, and all men be allowed to observe at once whether a Scripture statement is sound testimony, and whether the prevalent criticism is proceeding on sound lines. Least of all need we who know that no word of Scripture can ever be broken, fear to lay it on the anvil or cast it into the furnace. Hammers may break but not it—be the furnace never so hot, gold is but refined.[59]

Warfield also postulates that Briggs himself seems a bit divided regarding the methodology. Warfield's analysis highlights his own view of the unitary nature of knowledge. As Warfield expresses it:

> The bounding off of a field within which, and within which alone each kind of evidence will be allowed to speak, has naturally two chief effects. It tends towards an unjust narrowing of the field assigned to one kind of evidence so as to afford room for another. And by excluding all opposing presumptions from other sources in each field, it tends to an overestimation of the decisiveness of each kind of evidence within its own domain. Dr. Briggs appears to have fallen into both snares. He narrows unjustly the field of external evidence in order to clear the ground for internal criticism. And he accords decisive weight to internal considerations of a kind to raise only the weakest presumption in one direction, through failure to note the opposition to it of a field of stronger presumption in the same field.[60]

According to Warfield, the above procedure can be seen in Briggs' "tendency, doubtlessly followed unconsciously, to minimize, for instance, the

---

59. Ibid., 2.
60. Ibid.

Scripture testimony to the origin of the Pentateuch."[61] Warfield is quick to point out, however, that this tendency was not the result of a lack of "loyalty" to Scripture on Briggs' part, but simply the result of the methodology he was employing.[62] That methodology, says Warfield, does not bow to the authority of Scripture, but rather asserts its own authority over Scripture. Warfield articulates it this way:

> The inquiry as to the evidence from the New Testament, for example, from the very nature of the case, does not take the form of, What presumption as to the origin and authorship of the Pentateuch arises from the New Testament notices? but rather, Within how narrow bounds do the New Testament notices confine the investigations and conclusions of the Higher Criticism? Necessarily, therefore, it is asked, in interpreting each New Testament passage, *not*, Exactly what does this passage probably mean? b*ut*, What is the sense less than which this passage cannot mean? It is clear that one effect of this is to gain just what Dr. Briggs' scheme of criticism demanded, an exact knowledge of the line beyond which the conclusions of criticism cannot pass without flying full in the face of the authority of the New Testament.[63]

Thus, the issue is one of competing authorities, as well as that of coming to grips with *all* the evidence relevant to the matter. Does the New Testament have any authority to speak to the questions regarding the Pentateuch? It is certainly a piece of evidence that needs to be considered, and denying that it is evidence impairs any investigation into the Pentateuch before it is even begun. According to Warfield, in this case, the result of this faulty methodology is:

> (1) The exact truth as to the New Testament witness is not obtained, and therefore the exact weight of the presumption arising from it, for the Mosaic authorship of the Pentateuch, is not estimated; and (2) The presumptions that arise from the internal criticism of the Pentateuch are left with the appearance of standing as the only witnesses in the case, and therefore as rendering a conclusion in their direction probable; whereas it may well be that presumptions stronger in the opposite direction may lie from

---

61. Ibid.
62. Ibid.
63. Ibid.

other sources across this path. The exact truth as to the origin of the Pentateuch is, therefore, not obtained.⁶⁴

Having critiqued Briggs' methodology, Warfield proceeds to clarify his own ideas on the correct approach. Though doubtlessly the following statement could be further explicated, the substance of Warfield's view of a truly critical methodology for biblical interpretation can be seen.

> The sound method of procedure would rather be to note with anxious care the force of the presumption which arises from the external evidence, including the natural (not minimum) sense of the Scripture statements, on the one side, and the force of the presumption which arises from the critical examinations of the Pentateuch, on the other; and then, if they be found to conflict, to determine by the use of the finest critical scales their relative weights. The two classes of presumptions are of the same kind (both being chiefly exegetical in their final analysis), and hence, in this case, their comparison is easy. But, whether easy or difficult, the exact truth cannot be obtained by any other method.⁶⁵

Warfield's stress on handling *all* the available evidence manifests itself in criticism of Briggs' thinking "poorly of all external evidence."⁶⁶ While Warfield conceded that the external evidence for the Pentateuch was "not as strong as could be desired," it was not, in his estimation, legitimate to present it as anything less than "constant" and "unconflicting."⁶⁷ Ultimately, though, whatever one might think of the value of any particular external evidence, one could not simply ignore it, or force it "to be silenced."⁶⁸ Warfield drives home the point by giving an example of how one should proceed in attempting to determine the author of "The Whole Duty of Man," and then relates this to the questions surrounding biblical criticism.⁶⁹ According to Warfield, one should:

> . . . seek to discover (1) exactly what the external evidence proved, rendered probable or rendered plausible; (2) what the work itself

---

64. Ibid.
65. Ibid., 3.
66. Ibid.
67. Ibid.
68. Ibid. About five years later, Warfield wrote concerning the negative critics: "with a truly Herod-like indifference they have murdered a host of innocent facts which stood in the way of their purposes, and yet the reconstruction still always fails" ("Christian Evidences: How Affected by Recent Criticisms," *SSW* 2:130).
69. Warfield, "Dr. Briggs' Critical Method," 3.

asserted, or implied concerning itself; and (3) what the more subtle internal phenomena of the writing suggested. Then, but only then, after the whole evidence was in, would he examine the natural relations and relative weights of all the various presumptions thus obtained, and so reach his certain, or probable, or plausible conclusion, according to the complication of the case or the weight or conflict of the evidences. This is the natural order of procedure; perhaps the only trustworthy order. It is not, however, Dr. Briggs' order, and still less is it the order of those who would exclude appeal to the New Testament passages altogether, as if, forsooth, their inspiration made them less trustworthy than the communications of a Josephus or an Esdras. Let them by no means be used to stifle internal criticism; but let them by all means be used along side of internal criticism.[70]

As a result, Warfield finds Briggs' conclusions regarding the Pentateuch less than compelling, since they were "from the observation of numerous minute and slight literary indications."[71] Warfield's assessment, then, is that the negative critic's "theory" of the "facts" is faulty and should not be confused with an established fact.[72] Therefore, neither should it be confused with true criticism.[73] In other words, Warfield's line of argumentation is that there is a reality that is common to all people, and our theories to account for any single aspect of that reality can and should be evaluated based on particular epistemic responsibilities that everyone has, precisely because of the nature of that reality, and our relationship to it. Theories regarding factual data can and should be evaluated because data cannot simply be explained by whatever theory one individual, or group of individuals, deems plausible. Warfield believed that this did not contradict the noetic affects of sin in any way. The latter doctrine explains how or why some people do not affirm a particular conclusion regarding particular physical evidence, but it does not allow contradictory explana-

70. Ibid.

71. Ibid.

72. Ibid.

73. This is a point Warfield made repeatedly. See his "Inspiration and Criticism," *CW* 1:395–425; and "Christian Evidences: How Affected by Recent Criticisms," *SSW* 2:124–31. True criticism is the "careful scrutiny of the facts, and is good or bad in proportion to the accuracy and completeness with which the facts are apprehended and collected, and the skill and soundness with which they are marshaled and their meaning read. Deny the criticism of the Bible! Nobody dreams of it. Abate the practice of it! At our soul's peril, we dare not" ("Rights of Criticism and the Church," *SSW* 2:596).

tions of the same factual data to claim equal status as truth, knowledge, or science.

Warfield, Philosophy, and Science

In his analysis of Briggs' critical method, Warfield's thought demonstrates both a distinction and a union between external data (the facts) and the theories that are employed to explain the data. When the data is the Bible itself, then theories for explaining it invariably reveal the union between philosophy and theology, and highlight the issue of epistemic authority. As Charles Hodge wrote, many years prior to Warfield's birth, to remain true to the principle of sola Scriptura one must be on guard against the introduction of "the speculations of Philosophy into the study of Theology," and "unconsciously" interpreting "the Sacred Volume in accordance with the opinions previously formed, and resting upon some other foundation than the revelation of God."[74] What formed the fabric of Warfield's career was his concern for illuminating the ways in which various theological positions were dependent upon philosophies antagonistic to Scripture. This is highlighted in his assessments of modern "negative" criticism, Schleiermacher's theology in its relationship to Kantian thought, and the Protestant liberal theology that sought to reconstruct the Christian faith along the lines set forth by Kant and Schleiermacher. The broader context of an interpretation of Warfield should be governed, then, by the developments within these areas, which, as has already been demonstrated, became united to the substance of modern biblical criticism.[75]

74. C. Hodge, *BR* 1.1 (1825) iv.

75. That Warfield eventually recognized that Briggs had not only come out in full support for form of criticism, but had totally aligned himself with it can be seen, among other places in Warfield, "Real Problem of Inspiration," *CW* 1:171: "Dr. Briggs is more blunt and more explicit in his description of the changes which he thinks have been wrought. 'I will tell you what criticism has destroyed,' he says in an article published a couple of years ago. 'It has destroyed many false theories about the Bible; it has destroyed the doctrine of verbal inspiration; it has destroyed the theory of inerrancy; it has destroyed the false doctrine that makes the inspiration depend upon its attachment to a holy man.' And he goes on to remark further 'that Biblical criticism is at the bottom' of the 'reconstruction that is going on throughout the Church'—'the demand for revision of creeds and change in methods of worship and Christian work.'" Dorrien, in *The Making of American Liberal Theology*, tells the story of American liberal Protestant theology by setting the story within the context of Kant's and Schleiermacher's beliefs and influence. He quotes William Robertson Smith, who was the Scottish Old Testament scholar at Aberdeen's Free Church College and who stimulated the crisis over biblical criticism within the United States: "'the fundamental principle of the higher criticism lies in the conception of the organic unity of all history.'" Dorrien, on pp. 346–47, discusses the

Warfield stated in 1888, "Historical criticism has been as busy and as radical as philosophical and scientific."[76] He continued by pointing out that the philosophical and scientific character of historical criticism meant an increased activity in apologetic arguments that resulted in "a series of entirely new systematic natural theologies, based on the teachings of our current philosophies."[77] Warfield used as an example an anonymously published book, *Faith and Conduct*, that sought to establish "a new apologetic . . . in philosophical skepticism," and then postulated that more attempts like it "may be expected from the adherents of the newer trends of thought every year."[78] Because of the character of the "nature and claims" of these varying ways of explaining the factual data, "every criticism creates against itself . . . a new order of apologetic."[79] Indeed, Warfield considered "the richness of the new apologetic . . . beaten out by the controversies of the last half-century" to be "almost incredible."[80] He also felt that the "scientific attack on the supernatural" had triggered a backlash that had resulted in "a new conviction of divine power and presence" that threatened "permanently to banish deistic conceptions from the minds of men."[81] The attempts to overthrow people's confidence in the Bible had actually provided new evidence for *strengthening* the Christian's faith. He states:

> So the efforts of the naturalistic school of historical criticism, to bring into doubt the genuineness and unity of the books of the Bible, with a view to rearranging their material in an order for which a plausible plea for natural development might be put in, has not only called forth a mass of direct evidence for the authenticity of the books, such as was undreamed of before, but has also given birth to a whole library of more indirect argumentation of a

---

union between biblical criticism and metaphysical presuppositions regarding history: "Any 'historical' account that violates the continuity of history and conditions of life as we know it must be untrue." On 347, he rightly calls this the "unflinching principle of modern historiography."

76. Warfield, "Christian Evidences: How Affected by Recent Criticisms," *SSW* 2:125.

77. Ibid., 126.

78. Ibid.

79. Ibid.

80. Ibid.

81. Ibid., 126–27.

nature and amount sufficient almost to revolutionize the science of "the evidences."[82]

Still further, he notes, "the effort to reconstruct Old Testament history in the same naturalistic interest bids fair to perform a similar service for it."[83] Thus, it was Warfield's belief that the very criticism that was meant to undermine faith in the veracity of Scripture actually bolstered it. He concludes:

> Criticism has proved the best friend to apologetics a science ever had. It is as if it had walked with her around her battlements and, lending her its keen eyes, pointed out an insufficient guarded place here and an unbuttressed approach there; and then, taking playfully the part of the aggressor, made feint after feint towards capturing the citadel, and thus both persuaded and enabled and even compelled her to develop her resources, throw up new defenses, abandon all indefensible positions, and refurbish her weapons, until she now stands armed *cap-a pie*, impregnable to every enemy. The case is briefly this: recent criticism has had a very deep effect upon the Christian evidences in modernizing them and so developing and perfecting them that they stand now easily victor against all modern assaults.[84]

Warfield believed that a thorough knowledge of the philosophical ideas that are used by various scholars to challenge the truthfulness of Scripture, or to reconstruct the Christian faith along philosophical lines of thought, contrary to the doctrinal system of the Confession, will strengthen one's faith in the traditional interpretation of the Bible (that was in keeping, broadly speaking, with the Confession).[85] As an apologist Warfield, therefore, made it one of his chief concerns to learn of such philosophies

---

82. Ibid., 127.

83. Ibid. He says further, on pp. 127–28: "It is in opposition to the reconstruction of the Old Testament by the presently prevailing negative criticism that appeal is being ever made sharper and sharper to the authority of the God-man when testifying to the origin and meaning of the Scriptures which he himself revealed and inspired."

84. Ibid., 131.

85. Warfield was certainly broad-minded in spirit, and believed that someone could be a genuine Christian while not confessing to believe all that was expressed in the WCF. Yet, at the same time, he believed that one might fail to believe a particular point of doctrine that the Confession expresses by simply being inconsistent in one's thinking. In other words, Warfield made a distinction between possessing genuine saving faith and the accuracy of one's understanding of what constituted that faith. See Warfield, "Biblical Doctrine of Faith," *CW* 2:501–4.

and the arguments that their proponents marshaled to reconceptualize the Christian faith.

In his essay "Heresy and Concession," Warfield begins by quoting from G. P. Fisher's *History of Christian Doctrine*:[86]

> When Christianity is brought into contact with modes of thought and tenets originating elsewhere, either of two effects may follow. It may assimilate them, discarding whatever is at variance with the gospel, or the tables may be turned and the foreign elements may prevail. In the latter case there ensues a perversion of Christianity, an amalgamation with it of ideas discordant with its nature. The product then is heresy. But to fill out the conception, it seems necessary that error should be aggressive and should give rise to an effort to build up a party, and thus to divide the Church. In the Apostles' use of the term, "heresy" contains a factious element.[87]

Warfield notes that one need not be all that knowledgeable regarding "the history of religious thought" to recognize the validity of Fisher's statement.[88] To illustrate that statement, Warfield then does a brief analysis of Gnostic strains of thought and the Pelagian controversy that centered on the character of sin.[89]

After that analysis, Warfield draws an analogy between the practice of idolatry and the heretical thinking of his day, and leaves no doubt as to whose philosophy he believes to be at the root of this heretical thinking:

> And just as the pagan considers his idol as his property, and requires of it the services which he asks of it—beating it when it fails to give according to his desires, and destroying it when it no longer fulfils his expectations—so modern "thinkers," still considering themselves Christians, look upon their God as the product of their intellection, keep him strictly to the activities for which they have invented him, and require at his hands all that they have made him for . . . and so our new Kantians acknowl-

---

86. Warfield, "Heresy and Concession," *SSW* 2:672. Fisher was a nineteenth-century church and doctrinal historian. For the idea that some were attempting to reconstruct or "recast" the Christian faith along philosophical lines antagonistic to the Bible, see Warfield, "Century's Progress in Biblical Knowledge," *SSW* 2:3–13. In this latter essay Warfield referred to "'Biblical Theology' . . . wrapped in the swaddling-clothes of rationalism, and it was rocked in the cradle of the Hegelian recasting of Christianity" (12).

87. Warfield, "Heresy and Concession," *SSW* 2:672.

88. Ibid.

89. Ibid., 672–73.

edge God only so far as they have need of him to harmonize their intellectual difficulties or solve their moral doubts.[90]

The true Christian, according to Warfield, is open to truth from any source, and such a one had, in the Bible, the "means by which he can thread his way through the labyrinths of the world's thought."[91] As a result, "The condition of right thinking—or 'orthodoxy'—is, therefore, that the Christian man should look out upon the seething thought of the world from the safe standpoint of the sure Word of God."[92] He contrasts this with the heretical person who "is often found looking at the teachings of God's Word from the standpoint of the world's speculations."

Warfield then turns to an explanation of how one might be pulled into adopting heresy. First, the world communicates an air of superiority with its knowledge claims. As Warfield phrases it, "the world is very confident of its own conclusions," quite "sure of the infallibility of its own methods of research," does not refer to its "tenets" with words like " 'opinions,' 'views,' 'conjectures,'" but rather dresses them up with "the abstract names of 'philosophy,' 'science,' 'learning,' [and] 'scholarship.'"[93] Second, the Christian's concern for evangelizing the world in the midst of its sin can actually become a snare. This genuine interest in people's salvation can easily result in accommodation to the world's "methods" or "conclusions."[94] After all, the Christian might be apt to inquire, ". . . what is the use of flinging into the face of an unbelieving world as truth that which the consensus of scholarship or of scientific investigation proclaims impossible?"[95] Third, the world has possessed some powerful intellectual weapons that have been so powerful that some in the history of the church have speculated that there is "an evil inspiration to account for the brilliancy of the world's attack on the religion of Christ."[96]

Regardless of the reasons that some confessing Christians compromise with the world's thought, giving it ultimate authority over Scripture, the fact remains that such accommodation is the essential characteristic of heresy. Moreover, according to Warfield, it was also the "the ruling

90. Ibid., 673.
91. Ibid.
92. Ibid., 674–75.
93. Ibid., 675.
94. Ibid.
95. Ibid. This seems to be the very question and pitfall to which the "Alternation Approach" practiced by Noll and Marsden falls prey.
96. Ibid., 676.

spirit" of his time.⁹⁷ He describes what he believes had been going on, and was still going on, in the reconstruction of the Christian faith. He makes his awareness of the union between philosophy and theology clear, as well as the crucial necessity of distinguishing between them in order to possess salvation, and to assist others in avoiding the dangers of deceitful forms of unbelief:

> "Modern discovery" and "modern thought" are erected into the norm of truth, and we are told that the whole sphere of theological teaching must be conformed to it. This is the principle of that reconstruction of religious thinking which we are now constantly told is going on resistlessly about us and which is to transform all theology. What is demanded of us is just to adjust our religious views to the latest pronouncements of philosophy or science or criticism. And this demanded with entire unconsciousness of the fundamental fact of Christianity—that we have a firmer ground of confidence for our religious views than any science or philosophy or criticism can provide for their pronouncements. It is very plain that he who modifies the teachings of the Word of God in the smallest particular at the dictation of any "man-made opinion" has already deserted the Christian ground, and is already, in principle, a "heretic." The very essence of "heresy" is that the modes of thought and tenets originating elsewhere than in the Scriptures of God are given decisive weight when they clash with the teachings of God's Word, and those are followed to the neglect or modification or rejection of these.[98]

Furthermore, it was some of the "recent apologetics" that had "played into the hands of this 'concessive' habit" by seeking to only defend a "minimum" of what was necessary to believe to be a Christian.[99] Warfield's belief, however, was that when people begin to believe that all that *can* be defended is the "minimum," it can easily nurture the idea that the only thing *worth* defending is the "minimum" and, as a result, the "maximum" becomes "undervalued."[100] Warfield's idea of the unitary nature of truth can be seen in his analysis of what he called the defended minimum. He believed that when trying to defend the "minimum" of Christianity, then one would inevitably feel a need to effect its "completeness, with scraps borrowed from tenets originating elsewhere than in the Word of God;

---

97. Ibid.
98. Ibid., 676–77.
99. Ibid., 677.
100. Ibid., 678.

and so 'a perversion of Christianity' arises, an amalgamation with it of ideas discordant with its nature."[101] Moreover, it is in the unity of truth that the power for thought and life inheres. Warfield writes:

> He who only defends the *minimum* renounces the strongest and best of all the evidences of Christianity. That great demonstration of the truth of Christianity which springs at once from an apprehension of it as a whole, as a perfect and perfectly consistent system of truth: the evidence of the gospel itself as the grandest scheme of thought ever propounded to the world, is entirely lost.[102]

There was another detrimental consequence of failing to attend to all the truth—forfeiture of the Holy Spirit's testimony. As Warfield articulates it:

> Finally and above all else, there may easily enter into the habit of defending a minimum of the gospel alone a certain unfaithfulness to the truth committed to us, which may go far to forfeit the testimony of the Holy Spirit, which needs to attend all defense of the gospel if it is to prevail with men. After all, God wishes a large trust in him and in his power, and will honor those who are not afraid to make great drafts upon him. In this sphere, too, it may well prove that he who speaks boldly in God's name all the truth that has been entrusted to him will have cause to admire God's power.[103]

Warfield concludes by once again emphasizing the unitary nature of truth by affirming that God "is able to defend and give due force to the whole circle of revealed truth."[104] He also states that "the most outstanding conflicts of our age" are over whether "all the conjectural explanations of phenomena by men" in "science, philosophy, and criticism" will be deemed ultimately more authoritative than the "declaration of God."[105] Warfield believed that the core of the issues before him and others, who confess saving faith in the Lord Jesus and who seek to stand upon the Bible as the written word of God, is whether ideas hostile to the Bible will be given ultimate authority in all spheres of human knowledge. Central

---

101. Ibid.

102. Ibid.

103. Ibid. Some might see in these words some of what energized J. Gresham Machen.

104. Ibid., 679.

105. Ibid.

to a defense of the Christian faith, as he understood it, is recognition of the lines of demarcation between the prevailing philosophies of one's time and the system of truth revealed in the Old and New Testament. For Warfield, that meant having a clear understanding of the substance of Kant's philosophy and Schleiermacher's theology.[106] Some of this is discussed in summary fashion in Warfield's treatment of the doctrine of revelation.[107]

While acknowledging that "most types of modern theology explicitly allow that all knowledge of God rests on revelation," Warfield adds that the real question of the day, or any day in which revelation is debated, has to do with one's *conception* of revelation.[108] During the eighteenth century the issue revolved around deism and "its one-sided emphasis upon the divine transcendence, and with the several compromising schemes which grew up in the course of the conflict, such as pure rationalism and dogmatistic [*sic*] rationalism."[109] The situation in the nineteenth century revolved around Kant's critique of rationalism and the modifications of his views. As Warfield expresses it:

> Kant's criticism struck a twofold blow at rationalism. On the negative side his treatment of the theistic proofs discredited the basis of natural (general) revelation, in which the rationalist placed his whole confidence. Thus the way was prepared for philosophical agnosticism and for that Christian agnosticism which is exemplified in the school of Ritschl. On the positive side he prepared the way for the idealistic philosophy, whose fundamentally pantheistic presuppositions introduced a radical change in the form of the controversy concerning the reality of a special revelation without in any way altering its essence. Instead of denying the supernatural with the deists, this new mode of thought formally denied the natural. All thought was conceived as the immanent work of God.[110]

The question now arose as to "whether there is any special revelation of God possible, actual, extant, whether man has received any other knowledge of God than what is excogitable by the normal action of his

---

106. Warfield, "Apologetics," *CW* 9:14–15. There will be a detailed look at this essay in a later chapter of this book.
107. Warfield, "Idea of Revelation and Theories of Revelation," *CW* 1:37–48.
108. Ibid, 38.
109. Ibid.
110. Ibid.

own unaided faculties."[111] In other words, "the natural was accordingly labeled supernatural."[112] This was not merely a belief that there is a radical union between the two spheres—the natural and the supernatural. Rather, it is an affirmation that there is only one realm of reality. Thus, the issues for the nineteenth century, as Warfield saw it, were:

> . . . no longer chiefly with the one-sided emphasis upon the transcendence of the deist, but with the equally one-sided emphasis upon the immanence of God of the pantheist, and with the various compromising schemes which have grown up in the course of the conflict, through efforts to mediate between pantheism and a truly Christian theism.[113]

This meant that the content of a defense of the biblical view of revelation had changed. One now needed to:

> . . . distinguish between God's general and God's special revelations, to prove the possibility and actuality of the latter alongside of the former, and to vindicate for it a supernaturalness of a more immediate order than that which is freely attributed to all the thought of man concerning divine things.[114]

Warfield elaborates further: "in order to defend the idea of a distinctively supernatural revelation" it would be necessary to "emphasize the supernatural in the mode of knowledge and not merely in its source."[115] As he explains, "when stress was laid upon the source only without taking into account the mode of knowledge, the way lies open to those who postulate immanent deity in all human thought to confound the categories of reason and revelation."[116] When this was done, a truly supernatural revelation was done away with in people's minds. What now needed to be clarified to people was not simply that God was the source of supernatural knowledge, but in order to classify such knowledge as truly supernatural, they needed to understand that such knowledge only "becomes the property of men by a supernatural agency," and "that it

---

111. Ibid., 38–39.
112. Ibid., 39.
113. Ibid
114. Ibid.
115. Ibid.
116. Ibid.

does not emerge into human consciousness as an acquisition of human faculties, pure and simple."[117]

It can be seen from this that Warfield had a clear conception of the union between philosophy and theology. He also had a clear picture of the attempts to discriminate and distinguish between them that had taken place leading up to the nineteenth century and how their relationship was now manifesting itself in philosophies and theologies with which he differed. Identifying and explaining the relationships they had to each other formed the substance of his own work.

A recognition that these debates within the church address the union of theology with philosophy and science leads to understanding that they involved the broad epistemic matters of the knowing subject to the objects known. This, in turn, means that these epistemic matters must also be understood in relation to what is revealed in Scripture—and, for Warfield, this meant what was expressly set forth in the doctrinal system of the Westminster Confession of Faith.[118]

Subsequent to Kant, Schleiermacher and others gave controlling authority in knowledge claims to the human subject who knows. In doing so, they gave the knower the power to determine the metaphysical status of the object known. Warfield, on the other hand, believed not only that there is a bond between the subjective and objective elements in epistemology, but also that when that relationship is correctly understood, one recognizes that the objects of knowledge are themselves subjective in nature because they are an extension and revelation of God.[119]

---

117. Ibid., 40.

118. Warfield, "Inspiration and Criticism," *CW* 1:395–96.

119. Warfield, "Idea of Systematic Theology," *CW* 9: 49–87. Warfield's point, in other words, is that the empirical phenomena that humans attempt to subsume under various methods of explanation are not rightly thought of as simply having objective status, but that they are, ipso facto, subjective in nature because they reveal God. As a result, God is imposing himself upon us in the empirical data that we seek to know and which we correlate and explain in various ways. This seems to have direct parallels with Charles Peirce's notion of an "outward clash." See Seeman, "Evangelical Historiography beyond the 'Outward Clash,'" 114–24. As mentioned previously, it also corresponds to Richard Evans' point in *In Defense of History*, 67 n. 1, 99. The parallels can be seen, among other ways, in Seeman's assessment of Peirce's fundamental point: "Knowledge of external reality comes not primarily from efforts to set aside one's history or subjectivity, but rather through the shock of resistance met when encountering an external reality (the physical presence of the traces and the constraint they place on interpretation) forces its way through their prejudices to communicate itself" (117). Or, as Seeman also notes on p. 116: "There are stubborn traces historians cannot rightly ignore and to which historians may appeal in challenging another's story. And so, there will be a very small,

Consequently, Warfield not only explicated human science and theology by relating the subjective and objective elements present in both, but also considered God as the source, means, and goal of all knowledge. Moreover, by acknowledging that God is present in the empirical data of human sense experience, affirming God's authority is not only done by accentuating the authority of the Bible, but also by emphasizing the authority of the empirical data that impinges on one's interpretation or explanation of the Bible. In his theological epistemology, Warfield also identified knowledge and theology in organic terms that revealed their personal, or living character. Moreover, because his was a theological epistemology, his epistemological beliefs were correlated to the other doctrines of the Christian faith, with which theology is united. Since he believed that these matters were central to what constitutes true biblical Christianity, they formed the warp and woof of his apologetic against views of the Christian faith that were, in various ways, either explicit representations of Schleiermacher's theology, or unknowingly represented the substance of Kant's epistemology. Warfield has been shown to have been keenly aware of the philosophical and theological issues of his day and the union between theology and philosophy.[120] This will become even clearer by studying more of his essays.

---

very important locus of recalcitrance in the study of history—the physical encounter with traces that all historians must face as they give their accounts of history."

120. McClanahan, "Benjamin B. Warfield," stands as abundant evidence of Warfield's knowledge of the history of theology and the ideas that were either compatible or incompatible with the WCF's system of doctrine—to say nothing of *CW* vols. 4–5, in which we find essays on Tertullian, Augustine, and Calvin.

5

Theology and Epistemology: Science and the Context of Apologetics

WE HAVE already seen that Warfield was immersed in the content and categories of the Westminster Confession of Faith from his earliest years. The doctrines of God were the heart and sinew of Warfield's expositions of science, theology as a whole, and systematic theology and apologetics in particular—the doctrines of God as creator, as providential superintendent of all creation, and as predestinating redeemer, of his revelation (written and made flesh)—who created Man, male and female, in his image, in knowledge, righteousness, and holiness, with dominion over the creatures. The use of an organic description is apt because Warfield's view of truth, to which his view of apologetics is inextricably bound, is that God himself—Father, Son, and Holy Spirit—*is* truth. Thus, truth is a Person, who is living and active, producing his life in anyone who believes in him. God is able to be known by humans, but he is not able to be controlled or *fully* comprehended by them.[1] God's revelation, given

---

1. Warfield, "Incarnate Truth," *SSW* 2:455–67. In "Latest Phase of Historical Rationalism," *CW* 9:585, Warfield calls truth "the greatest power on earth." In "Supernatural Birth of Jesus," *CW* 3:457–58, written for the *American Journal of Theology* 10 (1906) at the request of the editors in answer to the question, "Is the doctrine of the supernatural birth of Jesus essential to Christianity?," he teaches that "faith is the instrument by which salvation is laid hold upon; the instrument by which the prerequisites of the salvation laid hold of by faith are investigated is the intellect. As it is certain that the only Jesus, faith in whom can save, is the Jesus who was conceived by the Holy Ghost, born of the virgin Mary, according to the Scriptures, it is equally certain that the act of faith by which he is savingly apprehended involves these presuppositions were its implicates soundly developed. But our logical capacity can scarcely be made the condition of our salvation. The Scriptures do not encourage us to believe that only the wise are called. They even graciously assure us that blasphemy itself against the Son may be forgiven. It would surely be unfortunate if weakness of intellect were more fatal than wickedness of heart. On the

to the prophets and apostles, is a revelation of God himself, which takes place progressively throughout history.[2] God's truth can be described as not only advancing progressively on the macro level of all of human history—with God's redeemed people as its locus—but also on the micro level with each individual believer.[3] According to Warfield not only is proclaiming the truth fundamental, but also defending it—reasoning in accordance with it—because these are the weapons by which the truth advances and conquers.[4] By having his revelation written by the prophets and apostles, and by illuminating his people through the Holy Spirit, God has not only brought about salvation, but has also provided the means by which his people are, and have been, progressively guided throughout history. This revelation points to correlations of the truths that constitute the entire system of doctrine that God's people are to believe.[5] In other words, truth is organic and unified.[6] All human knowledge claims are connected, so that any particular claim is related to all truth. This is not only seen in Warfield's view of the relationships between theology, apologetics, and science, but also in his apologetic methodology. The latter is seen in his explication of various doctrines, as he demonstrates the correlated nature of the entire system of biblical doctrine.[7] The result is that Warfield's unified view of theology, apologetics, and science requires that those who wish to refute Warfield must deal with his rather massive

---

whole, we may congratulate ourselves that it was more imperative that Jesus, by whom the salvation has been wrought, should know what it behooved him to be and to do that he might save us, than it is that we should fully understand it. But, on the other hand, it will scarcely do to represent ignorance or error as advantageous to salvation."

2. Warfield, "Biblical Idea of Revelation," *CW* 1:3–34; "Idea of Revelation and Theories of Revelation," *CW* 1:37–48; and "Century's Progress in Biblical Knowledge," *SSW* 2:3–13.

3. Warfield, "Biblical Idea of Revelation," *CW* 1:3–34; and "Idea of Revelation and Theories of Revelation," *CW* 1:37–48.

4. Warfield, "Christianity the Truth," *SSW* 2:213–18; and "Apologetics," *CW* 9:8–9, 15.

5. Warfield, "Biblical Idea of Revelation," *CW* 1:3–34; "Idea of Revelation and Theories of Revelation," *CW* 1:37–48; and "Century's Progress in Biblical Knowledge," *SSW* 2:3–13.

6. This is another way of expressing the Old Princeton distinctive of "the unity of truth and the division of labor." See Gundlach, "Evolution Question at Princeton," 54. Gundlach, states: "the Princeton understanding was that science was divided into many subfields according to the nature of the object of study and the evidence appropriate to it." See also Warfield, "Apologetics," *CW* 9:4, where he makes reference to "the circle of the sciences."

7. See chapter 7 of this book, which is on apologetics in practice.

systematic correlation of *all* the biblical doctrines and relate these to their *own* view of science, as well as handling all the available evidence relevant to their own knowledge claims.

Theology, Apologetics, and Science: Building the Temple of God's Truth

Warfield's view of apologetics is clarified in his article on the subject, which first appeared in *The New Schaff-Herzog Encyclopedia of Religious Knowledge*.[8] Warfield's beliefs regarding the unitary nature of truth, or knowledge, and how theology in general, and apologetics in particular, fit with science, are explained in a series of essays on systematic theology which were written during the late 1890s and early 1900s. An understanding of his apologetics can also be acquired by looking at a number of the essays on systematic theology, which preceded the *Schaff-Herzog* article on apologetics.[9] In "The Idea of Systematic Theology," "The Right of Systematic Theology," "The Indispensableness of Systematic Theology to the Preacher," all of which were prior to his article on apologetics, and "The Task and Method of Systematic Theology," increasing clarity can be seen in Warfield's ideas of how human knowledge in general is related to Christian theology as a whole, and apologetics in particular.[10] Furthermore, since Warfield kept a keen eye on the theological and philosophical scholarship of his day, his assessment of, and concern for, the increasing subjectivism and rationalism that he saw around him can

---

8. Warfield, "Apologetics," *New Schaff-Herzog Encyclopedia of Religious Knowledge*, 232–38, reprinted in *CW* 9:3–21.

9. The concern here is not to try and capture the historical progression or development of Warfield's views in order to know precisely when all of his views regarding apologetics expressed in the "Apologetics" article actually crystallized in his thinking. But there is nothing in the essays on systematic theology that differs from what is expressed in the "Apologetics" article. Kim Riddlebarger is correct when he states that when investigating and discerning Warfield's apologetical method a "chronological approach . . . is not fruitful since Warfield's apologetic efforts do not change substantially over the course of his career." See Kim Riddlebarger, "Lion of Princeton," 87.

10. Warfield, "Idea of Systematic Theology," *CW* 9:49–87 (hereafter IST). This was the revised and expanded form of "Idea of Systematic Theology Considered as a Science," his inaugural address as Professor of Didactic and Polemic Theology at Princeton (May 8, 1888. See also "Right of Systematic Theology," *SSW* 2:219–79; "Indispensableness of Systematic Theology to the Preacher," *SSW* 2:280–89; and "Task and Method of Systematic Theology," *CW* 9:91–105. These are listed in chronological order. He divided theology into four categories in addition to apologetics: exegetical, systematic, historical, and practical. He arranged biblical theology under the heading of exegetical (IST, 64–72).

be traced through these articles. He believed these two "isms" were not only reconceptualizing Christian theology and the Christian faith in the church, but also eroding the awareness of the need for apologetics. He also believed that Jesus is the Truth and at work through his Holy Spirit in building his kingdom through his people. He had faith that as he explored and explained the basis for the knowledge of God that is the hope of every true Christian, he would assist in establishing, through the enabling grace of the Holy Spirit, the same knowledge of God in other people. As Warfield expresses it:

> . . . apologetics does not derive its contents or take its form or borrow its value from the prevailing opposition; but preserves through all varying circumstances its essential character as a positive and constructive science which has to do with opposition only—like any other constructive science—as the refutation of opposing views become from time to time incident to construction.[11]

Still further:

> It is, in other words, the function of apologetics to investigate, explicate and establish the grounds on which a theology—a science, or systematized knowledge of God—is possible; and on the basis of which every science which has God for its object must rest, if it be a true science with claims to a circle of the sciences.[12]

Warfield considered apologetics to be scientific and constructive, and an aid to advancing the gospel; therefore, his perceptions of his own work should be thought of along those lines.

As previously mentioned, and as the above quote indicates, Warfield, standing in the Old Princeton tradition, believed in "the unity of truth" or the "circle of the sciences." All truth originates and is unified in God, since God is the creator, providential sustainer, and redeemer of all reality. Therefore, any knowledge claim in any sphere of human knowledge is related to all other knowledge claims. Knowing that truth is unified does not ensure knowledge of all the relationships inherent in that unity, but it certainly has numerous and profound implications for a *study* of truth. Possibly foremost among these is the knowledge that truth can, and should be systematized. In Warfield's eyes, apologetics has a large role

---

11. Warfield, "Apologetics," *CW* 9:4.
12. Ibid.

to play in the growth of Christians in their ability to understand God's truth and to give a clear and accurate expression of it.

Apologetics will be the focus in a close look at Warfield's essay "Apologetics," his "Introduction to Francis R. Beattie's *Apologetics*," and his review of Herman Bavinck's 1901, *De Zekerheid des Geloofs*.[13] First, however, it is important to grasp his understanding of the larger context of which apologetics is a part by looking at his essays on systematic theology. These will show that Warfield believed that there is an intensely practical result that follows from right or correct thinking, or reasoning, and right verbal and written communication of the doctrines of Scripture. There are eternally significant practical benefits to be pursued and possessed, and practical consequences to be avoided, through correct theology.[14] These ideas energized Warfield in expressing what Scripture teaches; so that he could build up "the temple of God's truth"[15] for the strengthening of the church, and thus engage in a constructive and scientific work. It should be understood, as well, that Warfield's belief that *true* theology is an organic reality is integral to his view of the constructive nature of theology as a scientific work.

Avoiding a "Mutilated Gospel" and "Mutilated Lives"[16]

According to Warfield, the indispensability of systematic theology for the preacher is based on the belief:

> . . . that it is through the truth that souls are saved, that it is accordingly the prime business of the preacher to present this truth to men, and that it is consequently his fundamental duty to become himself possessed of this truth, that he may present it to men and so save their souls.[17]

---

13. Ibid., *CW* 9:3–14; "Introduction to Francis R. Beattie's *Apologetics*," *SSW* 2:93–105 (Beattie's book was published in 1903); and "Review of Herman Bavinck's *De Zekerheid des Geloofs*," *SSW* 2:106–23 (Bavinck's book was published in 1901).

14. Warfield's view of the inherently practical work of theology is in line with the post-Reformation theologians, who defined theology in such a way as to include this component. See Muller, *PRRD* 1:112–13.

15. IST, 77.

16. Warfield, "Indispensableness of Systematic Theology to the Preacher" (hereafter "Indispensableness"), *SSW* 2:287.

17. Ibid., 2:280. Warfield expressed the same reality in a very pointed way in a Sunday Afternoon Conference address "Summation of the Gospel," 173, 174–75: "Mark, then, first of all, the function which the Ascended Jesus assigns to his witnessing servants. It is summed up in a single term—it is 'to open men's eyes.' Now, of course, the eye of the

Indeed, Warfield stated that "Systematic Theology is nothing other than the saving truth of God presented in systematic form."[18] He believed that the real issue that was being pressed upon the life of the church during his day was whether Christian truth lay at the basis of Christian hope and life. It was being argued that the preacher's responsibility was to make Christians, not theologians. Therefore, the argument continued, a "thorough systematic knowledge of the whole circle of what is called Christian doctrine" could be set aside in favor of a "firm faith in Jesus Christ as Savior and a warm love toward him as Lord."[19] Warfield was attempting to counter the argument that it is the heart, or one's affections, that is of chief, if not sole importance, and that, therefore, these should be emphasized, not learning and the exercising of one's intellectual faculties. The head and the heart were being set against each other. For Warfield, this was profoundly flawed, and any conception of the Christian faith rooted in such thinking was bound to have deleterious practical consequences.

Warfield made it clear that the issue, as it was being presented and argued, contained a false either/or. He did affirm that, if faced with *choosing* between a "chilly intellectualistic" approach to Christian ministry or a "warmly evangelistic" one, the latter was to be preferred over the former.[20] He illustrates his point in this way:

---

heart can be opened only by the Spirit of God; and it is not this unperformable duty which Christ lays on his servants. But the eyes of the mind are opened, in a lower sense, by the presentation of the truth and it is this that the Lord requires of His servants. . . . We must not fail to mark the honour which is thus put by the Ascended Jesus on what we have learned to call by way of eminence, the Truth—or the Gospel message. Everything is made to turn on that. It lies at the root of all. The Apostle's duty is to open men's eyes. Whatever of salvation may come to men comes subsequently to that and as an outgrowth of this root, 'Truth is in order to godliness'—that is a true formula. But it must not be read—should we wish to remain in harmony with the Ascended Christ—as a depreciation of 'truth' and 'knowledge' (its subjective form), but as an enhancement of their importance. Truth exists only to produce godliness; that is true and needs to be kept constantly in mind. But no truth, no godliness—that too is true and that, too, needs to be kept fully in mind. The only instrument in your hands or my hands for producing godliness is the truth; we are not primarily anything else but witnesses to truth; and the truth of God is the one lever by which we can pry at the hearts of men. Preach the Word; that is our one commission. And it is no more true that the Word cannot be preached without a preacher, than that the preacher cannot preach without a Word. Men are in darkness, they need light, and we are sent to give it to them."

18. Warfield, "Indispensableness," *SSW* 2:281.

19. Ibid.

20. Ibid.

> A high capacity and love for mathematics may live in a sadly unpractical brain, and, for aught I know, the world may be full of pure mathematicians who are absolutely useless to it; but it does not follow that the practical worker in applied mathematics can get on just as well without any mathematics at all.[21]

Warfield felt that those who wanted to jettison systematic theology's importance for the preacher are bereft of an accurate understanding of human psychology, and that human experience is evidence of this, since actions are ultimately rooted in beliefs.[22] In step with the Old Princeton heritage, Warfield emphasized that correct understanding and reasoning[23] about doctrine is also organically related to both ardent feelings and holy conduct. This is not only taught in Scripture, but is the testimony of human experience as well. To set intellectual study and comprehension against spiritual feelings and actions is detrimental to the message of Scripture and misconstrues human beings and their experience.[24] Warfield acknowledged that in his own life he could "testify from experience to the power of the Westminster Confession to quicken religious emotion, and to form and guide a deeply devotional life."[25] The matter is much graver, though, than simply a correct assessment of his or others'

---

21. Ibid., 282.

22. Ibid., 283.

23. A more extensive treatment of Warfield's view of "right reason" will be explored later. For Warfield, "right reason" was the reasoning of the *regenerated* sinner whose reasoning had been "righted" (my term) by the Holy Spirit so that the sinner could reason rightly about Jesus to the degree that he or she placed faith in the Lord Jesus for salvation. He did not use the term to refer to a "neutral" standard of reasoning that all people could agree to so that apologetics could take place with the non-Christian. For the best treatment in the secondary literature regarding how Warfield used "right reason," see all works by Helseth listed in the bibliography. In *The Defense of the Faith*, 264, Van Til states that Warfield "attributes to 'right reason' the ability to interpret natural revelation with essential correctness. It is not easy to discover just what Warfield means by 'right reason.' But clearly it is not the regenerated reason. It is not the reason that has already accepted Christianity. It is . . . the reason that is confronted with Christianity and has some criterion apart from Christianity with which to judge the truth of Christianity." See also Van Til, *Christian Theory of Knowledge*, 244. Regarding how Warfield used the term "right reason," the statement is completely incorrect. Why Van Til had such difficulty understanding Warfield on this point remains a mystery to me. The idea that Warfield wanted to operate in "neutral territory" with the non-Christian (Van Til, *Defense of the Faith*, 265) is also false.

24. Warfield, "Indispensableness," *SSW* 2:282.

25. Ibid., 286.

experience. It is a matter of the quality of people's lives on earth and even their eternal destinies.

In Warfield's words "A mutilated gospel produces mutilated lives, and mutilated lives are positive evils."[26] He believed that not only is a true theology an organic thing, but a false theology is as well. For him, false theology is like a "virus."[27] Moreover, people do not really get to *choose* whether they are going to operate with a systematic theology or not, only whether the one they possess is in accordance with Scripture. If the preacher fails to communicate the systematic theology directed by Scripture, then parishioners will inevitably construct their own and the results will be predictably catastrophic. Warfield states:

> We cannot preach at all without preaching doctrine; and the type of religious life which grows up under our preaching will be determined by the nature of the doctrines which we preach. We deceive ourselves if we fancy that because we scout the doctrines of the creeds and assume an attitude of studied indifference to the chief tenets of Christianity we escape teaching a system of belief. Even the extremest doctrinal indifferentism, when it ascends the pulpit, becomes necessarily a scheme of faith.[28]

Furthermore, those catastrophic results can occur without the preacher even being conscious of them. Given the unitary nature of truth, the possibility exists that "a neglected or discredited" truth that is, in fact, part of the "whole system of Christianity" could lead to someone abandoning Christianity entirely.[29] Whether the preacher recognizes it or not, his preaching forms lives; it has practical consequences. The preacher is accountable for those "marred or ruined" lives that ensue because of his neglect of systematic theology, or his deficiencies in it, and therefore, he should be diligent and not neglect so vital a discipline.[30]

---

26. Ibid., 287 (emphasis added). Warfield would later make clear in IST that everyone systematizes. The human mind is not content with a "bare cognition of facts" (p. 54) that remain disconnected in our thinking.

27. While making the point that precise propositional statements in theological creeds and confessions are important matters, Warfield used the example of the difference between a Pelagian and Augustinian theology and referred to Pelagianism as a "deadly virus" or a "virus of dependence on self." See Warfield, "Revision and the Third Chapter."

28. Warfield, "Indispensableness," *SSW* 2:286.

29. Ibid., 287.

30. Ibid. It should be noted that Warfield is acknowledging that people left to their own thinking and interpretation go sinfully astray.

According to Warfield, then, the issue of systematic theology in relation to the preacher is no mere intellectual exercise, no mere debate among scholars without real practical application to the lives of real people. Warfield's beliefs on this issue provide a glimpse of how he viewed his own work. Although as a professor he was not a preacher with a particular local congregation, his duty was to train others who would be. What applied to them also applied to him in principle. He admits that systematic theology can be done "in a cold and unloving spirit,"[31] but maintains:

> In that case it may be for the preacher an unfruitful occupation. But so undertaken it has also lost its true character. It exists not for these ends, but to "make one wise unto salvation." And when undertaken as the means of acquiring a thorough and precise knowledge of those truths which are fitted to "make one wise unto salvation," it will assuredly bear its fruit in the preacher's own heart in a fine skill in rightly dividing the word of truth, and in the lives of the hearers as a power within them working a right attitude before God and building them up into the fullness of the stature of symmetrical manhood in Christ.[32]

In Warfield's assessment, then, the preacher's task is to be fruitful and constructive, to build up those in his charge. One does not accomplish this by some innocuous commitment to affirming others, but by believing and acting upon God's truth as incomparably set forth in the Scriptures of the Old and New Testament. Such truth is a unified whole that can and should be understood in a systematized way, because God is one and human beings were created in God's image so they could know God. The Scriptures are meant to be systematized so that they will place an increasingly greater weight upon a person's thinking and living. Warfield speaks of the truth bearing "its fruit" and "as a power within them [Christians] working a right attitude before God and building them up."[33] For Warfield, then, there were intense and unavoidably practical issues involved in the discussion regarding the systematizing of one's knowledge claims concerning God and Man. This belief helps explain the detail and fervor with which he addressed issues in this field.

---

31. Ibid., 288.
32. Warfield, "Indispensableness," *SSW* 2:288.
33. Ibid.

Systematic Theology: The Science of God

In "The Idea of Systematic Theology,"[34] Warfield begins by analyzing theology in general and then moves on to systematic theology specifically. Among other things, he defines what he means by a science, discusses how theology can be considered a science—and how it relates to other sciences—and then highlights systematic theology's practical nature. Warfield correlates theology, epistemology, and metaphysics, with theology holding the central position, uniting all the other branches of knowledge. He explains that the name "systematic theology" does not imply that the other theological disciplines are unsystematic, but neither is it a mere tautology.[35] Rather, it is so called not only because its material is presented in a systematic form, but also because its practitioners must, therefore, employ a systematic—*philosophical* or *scientific*—method.[36] In order to clarify the nature and role of systematic theology, Warfield, therefore, first sought to clarify how one should think about science.

Though Warfield acknowledged that the terms *philosophical, systematic,* and *scientific* might be treated as synonyms, he clarified that they are "*practically* synonyms."[37] He felt, in fact, that there is a slight difference. A philosophy should be thought of as referring to a broader scope of work than a science. As Warfield expressed it: "A science reduces a section of our knowledge to order and harmony: philosophy reduces the sciences to order and harmony."[38] Warfield's analysis, then, maintains that there can be many sciences, but only one philosophy. Still further, when addressing systematic theology as "Philosophical Theology," Warfield states: ". . . we should be conceiving it as a science among the sciences and should have our eye upon its place in the universal sum of knowledge."[39] But when identifying systematic theology as "Scientific Theology," he continues: "our mind should be occupied with it in itself, as it were in isolation, and with the proper mode of dealing with its material."[40] He contrasts this way of thinking with thinking of theology with a historical method, which though legitimate in its own right, is simply another way of engaging in a theological task. Systematic theology is a discipline that "deals

---

34. Reprinted in *CW* 9:49–87.
35. Ibid., 49.
36. Ibid.
37. Ibid., 50 (emphasis added).
38. Ibid.
39. Ibid., 51.
40. Ibid.

with its material as an organizable system of knowledge."[41] Warfield then draws out the implications of this assessment.

First, by referring to systematic theology as a science, Warfield is stating "that it seeks to discover, not what has been or is held to be true, but what is ideally true; in other words, it is to declare that it deals with absolute truth and aims at organizing into a concatenated system all the truth in its sphere."[42] Further, whatever label one attaches to a particular science requires that there not be another science by that very same name. Thus, there is one science of geology, not two or more sciences called "geology" that, furthermore, conflict in their basic pronouncements, organization, and aims.[43] This very point became the center of his argument against Andrew Dickson White's *History of the Warfare of Science with Theology*.[44] In his criticisms of White, we can see how Warfield applied his principle concerning science and, thereby, gain a better understanding of his points regarding the inherent nature of theology and epistemology.

Theology versus Science: Both or Neither—Intellect and heart
Warfield describes White's view as follows:

> . . . there is often apparent a low view of theology which denies to it, in principle, all scientific character, and sets it, indeed, over against Science as its very antipodes. A specially gross form of this misconception may be found in Dr. Andrew D. White's *History of the Warfare of Science with Theology*, the very truth of which sets aside without a word of justification all claim of theology to be itself a science . . . it is just as absurd to talk of "Science having evidently conquered Dogmatic Theology," as Dr. White does, as to talk of "Science having evidently conquered Biology or Physics."[45]

Following this assertion, in his criticism of White's treatment of the relationship between science and theology, Warfield contends that the term *knowledge* needs to be clarified, and that in the Christian view of reality, knowledge of God "involves the whole man and all his activities."[46] He then makes an analysis of science similar to the one expressed in his

41. Ibid.
42. Ibid.
43. Ibid., 51–52.
44. Warfield, "Theology a Science," *SSW* 2:207–12.
45. Ibid., 208.
46. Ibid., 210.

works on systematic theology.⁴⁷ In addition, he asserts that knowing God "in the deeper sense is not the act of the mere understanding, nor can theology fulfil [*sic*] its function of making man 'to know God' simply by framing propositions for the logical intellect."⁴⁸ As Warfield further clarifies, theology is not simply about the intellect narrowly conceived, or about framing propositions that need to be comprehended. Rather, it is concerned with that knowledge of God that highlights the religious nature of man, or the practical obedience of man in relation to God. Warfield's standard way of thinking of theology and religion was to recognize their organic union:

> Religion is the name we give to religious life; theology is the name we give to the systematized body of religious thought. Neither is the product of the other, but both are products of religious truth, operative in the two spheres of life and thought. Neither can exist without the other. No one but a religious man can be a true theologian. No one can live religiously who is innocent of all theological conceptions. Man is a unit; and the religious truth which impinges upon him must affect him in all his activities, or in none.⁴⁹

Thus, for Warfield, knowledge and theology are thoroughly subjective enterprises.⁵⁰ This subjective nature spoke to Warfield's organic way of conceiving theology, knowledge, and human beings. Another glimpse of this perspective can be caught in the conclusion to his essay "Theology a Science":

> It follows, still further, that there is much that passes current as "Theology" that is not Theology at all. All that does not naturally take its place in the general scheme of investigation which tends

---

47. Ibid., 208. Defining terms, of course, is basic to philosophical or theological debate. James McCosh reflects this fact in his analysis of Kant's philosophy, "Recent Works on Kant," 425–40. He praises Kant for thorough consistency in his logic, saying that if you accept his beginning premises you have to take the whole system. McCosh called for a challenge to Kant's most basic premises, and thereby called for a presuppositional offensive against Kant's philosophy. See especially his endorsement of Kählin's argument that "'I have no right or power to say a thing is if I am in entire ignorance how or what it is.'" And further, "'The real existence of things outside of us, and independently of our consciousness of them, is an assumption, without which Kant could not have found even a beginning for his philosophy; and he himself gives it as his opinion that, apart from this presupposition, thought would do nothing but revolve round itself as a centre'" (437).

48. Warfield, "Theology a Science," *SSW* 2:210.

49. Warfield, "Authority, Intellect, Heart," *SSW* 2:668.

50. Warfield, "Theology A Science," 211.

to produce a true and vital knowledge of God—a truly *religious* knowledge of God—lies outside of the limits of "Theology."[51]

Still further:

> Theology, therefore, not only may remain a science while yet "practical" in aim; it cannot even exist without this "practical" aim. As long as we remain in the region of the pure intellect we remain out of the proper region of Theology. Theology is the product of, appeals to, and impinges on the religious elements in man's nature, and nothing is "Theology" which does not move in this sphere.[52]

Warfield was opposed to anything that led to a conclusion that science and theology are antagonistic to each other. Positively speaking, he identified true science with true theology, and, by virtue of this relationship, as being inherently characterized by a subjective element in the knowing process that includes one's affections and actions. This is shown more precisely in his analysis of all sciences, as he lays it out in "The Idea of Systematic Theology."

Science Further Defined

Warfield believed that for a science to be present:

> . . . three things are presupposed: (1) the reality of its subject-matter; (2) the capacity of the human mind to apprehend, receive into itself, and rationalize this subject matter; and (3) some medium of communication by which the subject matter is brought before the mind and presented to it for apprehension.[53]

---

51. Ibid.

52. Ibid., 212. Warfield considered it impossible to traffic "in the region of the pure intellect" alone, or for human thought to be disconnected from any practical implications or applications. His reference to "remaining in the region of the pure intellect," is properly interpreted, I believe, to be the acknowledgement of what others may have believed or the logical consequences of particular theories that they did believe (i.e., Idealism). Consider the following: "It is thus impossible to give maxims to guide the life without implying in them a system of truth on which the practical teaching is based. According to the system of faith that lies in the depths of our hearts will be, therefore, the maxims by which we practically live; and out of the maxims of any man we can readily extract his faith" ("Bible's 'Summum Bonum,'" *SSW* 1:131).

53. IST, 53. What Warfield affirms here is very similar to what Thomas Reid believed was necessary in order to have a science. Still, this is a rather broad statement, and commonality on simply these points tells us nothing regarding the source of either of their beliefs, or to what else these beliefs are, by necessity, related. Warfield makes it explicit that the triune God of Scripture is at the heart of human knowing. Reid analyzes

In this definition, Warfield treats these three issues as related, yet distinct. He does not conflate them into one another so that the human mind simply knows itself, revolves around itself, and terminates upon itself. Because he treats them as related, yet distinct, and states that all three must be presupposed for something to be termed a science, he essentially denies the status of science to any view that does not correspond to his analysis. Therefore, any view that tries to dismiss these three presuppositions cannot claim for itself the name "science."

Warfield further depicts these three ideas as follows. First, every science has a subject matter that has a distinct metaphysical reality outside the human mind.[54] That reality can be recognized by at least some human minds, and indeed, can only be spoken of as having distinct metaphysical reality if it actually can be and is comprehended by some human minds.[55]

Second, in order for a reality that has independent status outside one's mind to actually be known, there must be some means by which one can comprehend it, or reason about it. If a person cannot make intellectual or rational sense of a reality, then that person cannot speak of possessing knowledge of that reality.[56]

Third, in order to communicate any subject matter to the human mind, the medium of communication must also have some kind of metaphysical status distinguishable from, but correlated to, both the subject matter and the mind. Warfield maintains that even before the human knower is involved in the unavoidably subjective process of reasoning about data, that there is another element in the process that is rightly characterized as subjective—the communication of the data to the mind.

---

the process of human knowing by analyzing the operation of the human epistemic faculties. Warfield does not share Reid's concerns on this point. It is therefore illegitimate to conclude any one of the following at this point: (a) that Reid is the source of Warfield's belief on this matter; (b) that Reid and Warfield could not have independently arrived at similar conclusions; (c) that these could not be implied from the Old and New Testament; and (d) that these could not be arrived at by either a Christian or non-Christian simply by reflecting upon one's place in the physical material universe.

54. Psychology, as a distinct and formal discipline, was just beginning to develop in the late nineteenth century. Distinguishing between the brain and the mind was at its nascent stage based on the state of medicine and physiology at that time. Since the Old Princetonian's anthropology affirmed that humans were body and soul, they did not reduce the "mind" to simply physiological processes. So they would not have simply equated the mind with the brain in a facile way.

55. See note 43 above for Kahlin's argument.

56. See Hodge, *ST* 1:49.

Then the human mind must interpret the sensory data brought before it, if true knowledge is to be attained. These features continue to be seen in Warfield's epistemology when he discusses the contours of systematic theology.[57]

What is, of course, of great interest to many is how Warfield perceived the interplay between the metaphysical reality of the subject matter of a science and the human mind's apprehension and comprehension of that subject matter. It is Warfield's thoughts concerning the process of combining the facts of a science into a rational correlated system that are at the heart of many of the controversies regarding his epistemology and theology. In his analysis of theology as a science, Warfield discusses his conception of the dynamic between a person and God. Understanding what he says about the relationship between the knowing subject and the object that is known is central to understanding what he says about this relationship when the object known is God, who is Himself a subject.

Human Knowledge and Systematic Theology

Warfield maintained that in the knowing process all people systematize.[58] He believed that as human beings we are so constituted that we do not simply collect facts, but we put all the matters of our sense experience into a correlated system that makes sense to us, in short, that seems reasonable to us.[59] As Warfield stated, "Subjectively speaking, sense perception is the essential basis of all science of external things; self-consciousness of inter-

---

57. IST, 53. Warfield uses astronomy as the illustration of his analysis of science. If there were no heavenly bodies, there could be no science of astronomy. If there were no human minds to perceive the heavenly bodies, we certainly could not speak of a science of astronomy, and moreover, apart from a rational comprehension of the heavenly bodies as expressed in how the bodies are "combined into a correlated system" there could be no science of astronomy.

58. Ibid., 53–54.

59. This will be seen to be conceptually identical to the idea of a "worldview," when one affirms the validity of the following definition: "A conceptual scheme in which we consciously or unconsciously place or fit everything we believe and by which we interpret and judge reality" (Nash, *Faith and Reason: Searching for a Rational Faith*, 24). Old Princeton operated with the concepts or features that inhere in the worldview concept before the term itself became popular (see Gundlach, "Evolution Question at Princeton"). This is, in part, why it is misleading to tell the story of the worldview concept and a presuppositional approach to apologetics from the perspective that James Orr and Abraham Kuyper introduced it to America and were its primary facilitators (Naugle, *Worldview*, 5).

nal things."⁶⁰ Yet, because there must be some "media by which the facts should be brought before and communicated to the mind," it should be acknowledged that "subjective and objective conditions of communication must unite, before the facts that constitute the material of a science can be placed before the mind that gives it its form."⁶¹ For Warfield, then, every science was inherently both objective and subjective. It would simply be incoherent to speak of any science as being only subjective or only objective. No area of human knowledge, according to Warfield, is strictly objective or strictly subjective. There has to be a union of objective and subjective elements in knowledge:

> Facts do not make a science; even facts as apprehended do not make a science; they must be not only apprehended, but also so far comprehended as to be rationalized and thus combined into a correlated system. The mind brings to every science somewhat which, though included in the facts, is not derived from the facts considered in themselves alone, as isolated data, or even as data perceived in some sort of relation to one another. Though they be thus known, science is not yet; and is not born save through the efforts of the mind in subsuming the facts under its own intuitions and forms of thought.⁶²

Warfield gives a prominent place, then, to what each person brings to epistemic endeavors in terms of the reasoning process. Each person has "intuitions" or "forms of thought" that are "included in the facts" but are "not derived from the facts considered in themselves alone, as isolated data, or even as data perceived in some sort of relation to one another." Though not using the term *presupposition* to describe the specific things that the mind brings to the data, Warfield, nonetheless, embraced the concept that the term normally represents. In other words, he avowed that every person operates with presuppositions by which he or she reasons about the data in order to bring the data into some type of "correlated system."

Speaking of theology as a science, then, "presupposes the affirmation that God is, and that he has a relation to His creatures."⁶³ It also means

---

60. IST, 54.

61. Ibid. Notice that Warfield said they *unite*. They do not dissolve into each other and become indistinguishable.

62. Ibid., 53. For a similar view of the relation of facts to science, see Hodge, *ST*, 1–60.

63. IST, 55.

that "the whole body of philosophical apologetics is, therefore, presupposed in and underlies the structure of scientific theology."[64] Moreover, to affirm that theology is a science:

> . . . presupposes the affirmation that man has a religious nature, that is, a nature capable of understanding not only that God is, but also, to some extent what He is; not only that He stands in relations with His creatures, but also what those relations are. . . . that there are media of communication by which God and divine things are brought before the minds of men, that they may perceive them and, in perceiving, understand them.[65]

It should be noted, then, that Warfield analyzed the relationship of theology to science by emphasizing the presuppositions that one has to hold in order to affirm that theology is a science. His analysis attends to both the objective and subjective nature of all human knowing, and unites these in an inseparable union. Moreover, all of this is inextricably wedded to his anthropology, which included the affects of sin on the knowing process, and, at the same time, gave him the ability to speak of sin in objective terms, an objective perspective that was the grounds upon which all people could actually be held accountable for their allegedly scientific enterprises.

Schleiermacher and the Confusion of the Objective and Subjective in Theology

According to Warfield, it was necessary to clarify the objective and subjective in theology because Schleiermacher and others, following the lead of Kant, had confused the issue.[66] As Warfield explains, theology and religion should be thought of as "parallel products of the same body of facts in diverse spheres."[67] Theology belongs "in the sphere of thought" and religion "in the sphere of life."[68] He states that Schleiermacher confused "the two distinct disciplines, theology, the subject-matter of which is objective, and the science of religion, the subject-matter of which is

---

64. Ibid.

65. Ibid., 55–56.

66. Ibid., 56. See also, Warfield, "Mysticism and Christianity," *CW* 9:649–66; and "Apologetics," *CW* 9:14.

67. IST, 57.

68. Ibid. This seems to have been Warfield's regular use of these terms.

subjective."[69] Schleiermacher's move resulted in "lowering the data of theology to the level of the aspirations and imaginings of man's own heart."[70] Warfield's pronouncement that the subject matter of theology is objective meant that he was affirming that the primary subject matter from which theology derives its name, method, and aims is God and God is who God is. That is, God has an ontological status distinct from us and the rest of creation and he is who he is, apart from our individual perceptions of him. There is, of course, a correct understanding of God present in the world, because God has revealed himself in creation, in the Scriptures of the Old and New Testament, and in his Son, the Second Person of the Trinity, the Lord Jesus Christ. Warfield's belief was that some just have a more accurate perception of God than others.[71] Thus, the next topic Warfield addresses in this essay on the idea of systematic theology is revelation.

For Warfield, revelation is the best term to use to describe our knowledge of God because God is a person, and thus, he can only be known insofar as he reveals himself.[72] Reflecting the theology of Calvin, the Westminster standards, and Francis Turretin, Warfield asserts that all of our thoughts and inferences about God are only possible because God has chosen "to make Himself intelligible to us, to speak to us through work or word, to reveal himself."[73] The disciplines of systematic theology in general, and apologetics in particular, should be analyzed according to, and practiced in a manner that corresponds with, what Scripture reveals, because Scripture alone is the supreme authority for Christians,' and indeed all people's, thinking and living.[74]

69. Ibid.

70. Ibid.

71. For corroboration of these points, see the following: Warfield, "Christianity and Revelation," *SSW* 1:23–30; "God of Israel," *SSW* 1:82–87; "Biblical Idea of Revelation," *CW* 1:3–34; "Authority and Inspiration of the Scriptures," *SSW* 2:537–41; "Biblical Doctrine of the Trinity," *CW* 2:133–72; and "Person of Christ," *CW* 2:17–209.

72. IST, 58.

73. Ibid. Warfield followed the accepted practice of classifying revelation into two categories, but he labeled these two categories in three different ways. One could think of revelation as: (1) general and special, (2) natural and supernatural, or (3) creational and soteriological ("Biblical Idea of Revelation," *CW* 1:6). This is simply a reiteration of Calvin's emphases and was also taught by Turretin. See Calvin, *Institutes* 1:vi–vii; Turretin, *Institutes of Elenctic Theology*, 1:55–59; Warfield, "Calvin's Doctrine of the Knowledge of God," *CW* 5:29–130.

74. According to Warfield, the church did not establish the authority of the Bible for her faith and life, but received the Scriptures as authoritative on the basis of the authority

Still, saying that God's revelation of himself is the "sole source of theology" does not clarify the various ways in which God has revealed himself. There are, Warfield adds, various "methods" of revelation that God has used.[75] Thus, he continues, "nature, providence, and Christian experience" along with the Scriptures of the Old and New Testament, and consummately, Jesus, are all methods of revelation by which God, through the Holy Spirit, makes himself known.[76] Furthermore, to acknowledge these "divers manners" of revelation is to acknowledge that they possess varying messages, with varying degrees of importance and clarity.[77] In particular, Warfield states, in typical *sola Scriptura* fashion, it is the Scriptures of the Old and New Testament that are

> . . . easily shown to not only be incomparably superior to all other manifestations of Him in the fullness, richness, and clearness of its communications, but also to contain the sole discovery of much that it is most important for the soul to know as to its state and destiny, and of much that is most precious in our whole body of theological knowledge. The superior lucidity of this revelation makes it the norm of interpretation for what is revealed so much more darkly through the other methods of manifestation. The glorious character of the discoveries made in

---

of the apostles through their relationship to Jesus. He stated in 1889 in "Authority and Inspiration of the Scripture," *SSW* 2:538–39, "That the apostles thus gave the Church the whole Old Testament, which they had themselves received from their fathers as God's word written, admits of no doubt, and is not doubted. That they gradually added to this body of old law an additional body of new law is equally patent. In part this is determined directly by their own extant testimony. Thus Peter places Paul's Epistles beside the Scriptures of the Old Testament as equally law to Christians (2 Peter 3:16); and thus Paul places Luke's Gospel alongside of Deuteronomy (1 Tim. 5:18)." Since the Bible was authoritative for thinking and living, it did not bow to human reasoning but rather human reasoning had to come into subjection to it ("Heresy and Concession," *SSW* 2:674). Warfield was endorsing the same thing expressed by Hodge, which, in part, explains why one critic of Charles Hodge stated, "It is enough for Dr. Hodge to believe a thing to be true that he finds it in the Bible!" (Calhoun, *Princeton Seminary* 2:34). See Hodge, *ST* 1:48, for the belief that the Bible is received by faith based on its authority. Hodge affirmed that the Christian's "duty, privilege, and security are in believing, not in knowing; in trusting God, and not our own understanding." Further, Warfield denied that the authority of the Scripture rested on a previous proof of their inspiration ("Authority and Inspiration of the Scripture," *SSW* 2:540). This was a repetition of what he had affirmed in "Inspiration and Criticism," *CW* 1:395–425. In other words, Warfield, as well as Hodge, considered the Bible to be the ultimate, or foremost presupposition upon which the thinking and living of the Christian is based.

75. IST, 58.
76. Ibid., 58–59.
77. Ibid., 60. "Divers manners" is from Hebrews 1:1.

it throws all other manifestation into comparative shadow. The amazing fullness of its disclosure renders what they can tell us of little relative value.[78]

Thus, it is a sign of a "decadent theology" and a "decaying faith" to rely upon one of the "lesser sources of theological truth" from which to "draw our knowledge of divine things."[79] Prominent among these lesser lights is the inner world of the person. Warfield believed that there were two ways of depending primarily, if not exclusively, on one's inner world for knowledge of divine things that were active in his day. One could either rest on one's own reasoning to interpret natural revelation, or on the subjective feelings of the Christian heart. In the former case the result is despair, while the latter is a "refuge of lies in which there is neither truth nor safety."[80]

Scripture: "The Only Sufficing Source of Theology"

Though Warfield[81] maintained that, in the act of making someone a Christian, God revives the human soul, giving the new Christian the capability to be able to reason rightly about God and many other things, he also denied that this work resulted in the eradication of sin from the person.[82] Thus, God's regenerating work does not allow the Christian to have an infallible or inerrant ability to reason and acquire knowledge. Warfield's view was that of the WCF, namely, that sin affects the whole person, affects all the faculties of the soul. The Christian's *sanctification* renews them "in the whole man after the image of God," so that the Christian is "enabled more and more to die unto sin, and live unto righteousness."[83] Thus, sanctification, the production in the sinner of a character like Jesus' is progressive. Its full completion, known as glorification, will not take place until the sinner dies physically and, eventually, on the last day, is raised with a new body united to the Christian's soul.

---

78. Ibid., 60–61.
79. Ibid., 61.
80. Ibid., 62.
81. Ibid., 63 is the referent for the section title quotation.
82. WCF SC 31, 35; LC 67, 75. See too, Harkness's Systematic Theology lecture notes from Warfield's class, in which Warfield expounds on the doctrines of regeneration and sanctification (Warfield Papers). See also Warfield, "Biblical Idea of Revelation," *CW* 1:3–34.
83. WCF, SC 35; LC 75.

Since Warfield had memorized the Larger Catechism by the time he was sixteen, he would have had the following committed to memory:

> The imperfection of sanctification in believers ariseth from the remnants of sin abiding in every part of them, and the perpetual lustings of the flesh against the spirit; whereby they are often foiled with temptations, and fall into many sins, are hindered in all their spiritual services, and their best works are imperfect and defiled in the sight of God.[84]

It is this Larger Catechism perspective that is reflected in Warfield's cautions concerning both unregenerate, rebellious human reason *and* human reason improved by the Holy Spirit's work, but still stained by sin's pollution and power.[85] As Warfield summarizes it:

> . . . we know in part and feel in part; it is only when that which is perfect shall appear that we shall know or experience all that Christ has in store for us. With the fullest acceptance, therefore, of the data of the theology of the feelings, no less than of natural theology, when their results are validly obtained and sufficiently authenticated as trustworthy, as divinely revealed facts which must be wrought into our system, it remains nevertheless true that we should be confined to a meager and doubtful theology were these data not confirmed, reinforced, and supplemented by the surer and fuller revelations of Scripture; and that the Holy Scriptures are the source of theology in not only a degree, but also a sense in which nothing else is.[86]

Apologetics, Theology, and Other Sciences

Warfield next addresses the place that systematic theology has among the other sciences and among the other theological disciplines. He divides theology into four branches: exegetical, historical, systematic, and practical.[87] Warfield's conception of apologetics is expressed in terms of prolegomena. It is apologetical theology that establishes the "necessary

---

84. WCF, LC 75.

85. "Pollution" and "power" apparently were Warfield's chosen terms to summarize the consequences of sin. See Harkness's Systematic Theology lecture notes (Warfield Papers).

86. IST, 62–63. See also Warfield, "Authority, Intellect and Heart," *SSW* 2:668–71 for the union of the intellect, the heart, and the will working as one in a person in order to produce "a vital religion" (671).

87. IST, 64.

presuppositions without which no theology is possible."⁸⁸ Doing this "places the Scriptures in our hands for investigation and study."⁸⁹ The way Warfield expresses this is likely to seem problematic to those presuppositionalists who want to argue that the Bible is the ultimate presupposition by which we interpret everything. After all, Warfield's statement seems to communicate the idea that we can only receive the Bible on philosophical grounds acquired apart from the Bible. The question then is: Is Warfield *denying* that the Bible is our ultimate presupposition and has final authority for all our knowledge claims? The short answer is: No. This answer, though, warrants a more detailed explanation which can be gained by paying attention to how Warfield understood theology as a discipline within itself and how this is unavoidably connected to the practical element within theology.⁹⁰

Practical Realities: Human Beings as Sinful Creatures in Time and Space

For Warfield, theology is a human endeavor having a practical goal. Consequently, creation had great significance for Warfield, and he understood it in light of God's revelation in Scripture, yet, he also understood the Scriptures in light of creation.⁹¹ Warfield sought to give full weight to the practical goal of theology, which was "to save and sanctify the soul,"⁹² and to understand the relationship between theology's practical and conceptual aspects. The practical element in theology and apologetics highlights the fact that humans are creatures created in the image of God, who are fallen sinners in need of redemption. Thus, Warfield's understanding of the practical element must be understood in light of his beliefs regarding the correlation of the doctrines of creation and redemption.

On one hand, a surface reading of how Warfield construed the different branches of theology makes it all seem rather simple. When one looks at Warfield's chart of apologetics in relation to God, religion, Christianity, the Bible, and then the four theological disciplines, one might get the impression that his conception was not just simple but

88. Ibid.

89. Ibid.

90. Ibid.,79.

91. Warfield, "Biblical Idea of Revelation," *CW* 1:3–34; and "Idea of Revelation and Theories of Revelation," *CW* 1:37–50.

92. IST, 9.

simplistic, even possibly naïve.[93] This is a copy of the chart as it appears in a footnote of IST on page 74. He offered the chart because "It *may be useful* to seek to give a *rough* graphic representation of the relations of Systematic Theology as thus far outlined."[94]

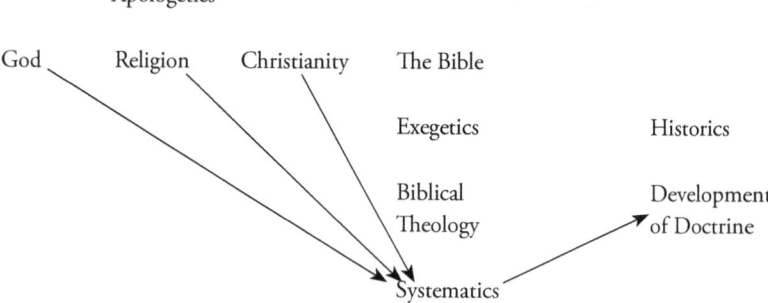

Upon closer examination, however, one discovers that Warfield understands quite well the complexity and intricacies of these relationships. Though he presents a chart that looks more like a taxonomy mimicking his work in the physical sciences, his conception of the theological disciplines in their relationships to each other, and of theology in relationship to the other sciences, was also categorized by him as a circle.[95] Warfield had an organic view of theology, for he thought of it as "a constituent member of the closely interrelated and mutually interacting organism of the sciences"[96] Or, as he would later describe it in another essay:

> But "Systematic Theology" does not exist by itself or for itself. It is a member of an organism, and it exists for the organism of which it is a part and in which it plays its part for the benefit of the whole. And the action of the whole culminates in, and all the functioning of the parts press on toward, the vital effect made operative in "Practical Theology." The scientific character

---

93. Ibid., 74.

94. Ibid. Emphasis added.

95. Ibid., 68. Here Warfield uses the phrase "the circle of the sciences." See also Warfield, "Task and Method of Systematic Theology," *CW* 9:97.

96. IST, 68.

of Theology, so far from clashing with its practical issue, therefore, is one of the elements working toward this practical issue.[97]

Warfield believes that, although thinking of systematic theology in and of itself is legitimate, it does not do full justice to how one ought to think about it, since there is a practical purpose toward which all its parts work. Moreover, the relationship of systematic theology to the greater whole, of which *it* is part, has to be understood if one is to accurately know systematic theology. Theology, according to Warfield, "enters into the structure of every other science."[98] In asserting this he was, in principal, acknowledging that every knowledge claim in any sphere is ipso facto theological.

But for Warfield, there was no true theology apart from Scripture. It was the "deluded" person who neglected Scripture and relied upon the "faint gleams of a dying or even a slowly reviving light" for knowledge of theology, and, ultimately, knowledge of anything.[99] In saying this, though, Warfield was stressing that the human beings who engage in the theological task are, historically, time and space bound creatures. Humans and all their activities can only be rightly understood when related to the categories and realities of time and space—creational realities. Human "theologizing" takes place in creation and it relates creational realities to human beings and to God. Thus:

> . . . the affirmation that theology is a science presupposes the affirmation that man has a religious nature, that is, a nature capable of understanding not only that God is, but also, to some extent what He is; not only that He stands in relations with His creatures, but also what those relations are.[100]

According to Warfield at least two things should be kept in mind when considering apologetics from a practical perspective: (1) the goal of theology is "to save and sanctify the soul," and (2) this representative list of necessary presuppositions which Warfield mentions as being established by apologetics: "the existence and essential nature of God,

---

97. Warfield, "Theology a Science," *SSW* 2:210.

98. IST, 69.

99. Ibid., 62–63. Warfield states, "The natural result of resting on the revelations of nature is despair; while the inevitable end of making our appeal to even the Christian heart is to make for ourselves refuges of lies in which there is neither truth nor safety." Warfield went on to explain that only through God's written word do we have the means by which we can begin to approach an accurate interpretation of our experiences.

100. Ibid., 55.

the religious nature of man which enables him to receive a revelation from God, the possibility of a revelation and its actual revelation in the Scriptures."[101] These are all necessary for saving and sanctifying the soul, which is to say that they are not divorced from Scripture itself. Put another way, one does not leave apologetics behind when engaging in the theological task that is meant to save and sanctify the soul. One could, according to Warfield, think of apologetics (1) in itself or in principle, (2) in practice, with respect to its accomplishing a particular goal, or (3) in terms of the relationship between the former and the latter.[102]

Theology and Science: United, Circular, Organic

Warfield states that it is apologetics that "prepares the way for all theology" and "places the Scriptures in our hands for investigation and study."[103] This is not only true because of the practical goal of apologetics, but also because of the systematic unity which reflects reality—which it is the business of apologetics to reveal to people. As Warfield saw it, apologetics was for the purpose of investigating, explicating, and establishing:

> . . . the grounds on which a theology—a science, or systematized knowledge of God—is possible; and on the basis of which every science which has God for its object must rest, if it be a true science with claims to a place within the *circle of the sciences*.[104]

Thus, there is a circularity to knowledge, of which theology and apologetics is a part, and this circularity directs how one ought to think about science, theology, and apologetics. Indeed, each discipline feeds, and in turn is fed by, the others. Therefore, theology as a whole, and even science in general, cannot be regarded so narrowly that the relationships between the disciplines are assessed in a one-dimensional manner.[105] Ever ready to

101. Ibid., 64.

102. This is simply a correlate of what Warfield states directly in the essay "Authority, Intellect, Heart," *SSW* 2:662, 662 n. 45. Man's religious life and theological thoughts are united, but they are not the same reality. They possess an "intimate relation" that "is not always perceived." Therefore, it is also the direct contradiction of a rationalist view of theology and religion.

103. IST, 64.

104. Warfield, "Apologetics," *CW* 9:4.

105. IST, 63–68. At the end of this section, he addresses what characterizes the relationship of the theological disciplines with respect to their content. Warfield viewed the relationship between systematic theology, in general, and apologetics in particular, to the other theological disciplines from three different angles in this section: nature, sources, and contents. One can see why those who are not used to careful, disciplined

emphasize the characteristic Princetonian view of the circularity of truth and knowledge, Warfield continues by stating that systematic theology claims for itself a high place "within the circle of the sciences:"[106]

> The place that theology, as the scientific presentation of all the facts that are known concerning God and his relations [meaning, therefore, Systematic Theology], claims for itself within the circle of the sciences is an equally high one with that which it claims among the theological disciplines. Whether we consider the topics which it treats, in their dignity, their excellence, their grandeur; or the certainty with which its data is determined; or the completeness with which its principles have been ascertained and its details classified; or the usefulness and importance of its discoveries: it is as far out of all comparison above all other sciences as the eternal health and destiny of the soul are of more value than this fleeting life in this world.[107]

Obviously, for Warfield, the whole matter was so richly complex that even his verbosity had difficulty doing justice to the reality of what characterizes systematic theology and its place within the sciences as a whole. Central to an explanation of this important truth is an emphasis on the reality that all the sciences are an interrelated whole and systematic theology holds an integral and "high" place among them.

All Knowledge Is Theological

Warfield's emphasis on the circular and integrated character of human knowledge gives systematic theology a central role, so that all human knowledge claims possess a theological character. Speaking of the sciences in relation to systematic theology, he declares:

> There is no one of them all which is not, in some measure, touched and affected by it, or which is not in some measure included in it. As all nature, whether mental or material, may be conceived of as only the mode in which God manifests Himself, every science which investigates nature and ascertains its laws is occupied with the discovery of the modes of the divine action, and as such might be considered a branch of theology. And, on the other hand, as all nature, whether mental or material, owes its existence to God, every science which investigates nature and ascertains its

---

reading, or who may, in fact, not be spending enough time, for whatever reason, might have difficulty in following these various distinctions.

106. IST, 68.
107. Ibid.

> laws, depends for its foundation upon that science which would make known what God is and what the relations are in which He stands to the work of His hands and in which they stand to Him; and must borrow from it those conceptions through which alone the material with which it deals can find its explanation or receive its proper significance. Theology, thus, enters into the structure of every other science.[108]

For Warfield, then, knowledge, or science, is an inherently theological endeavor, because all the objects of human knowledge are derived from God and are the means by which God reveals himself. Thus, every branch of knowledge must borrow from systematic theology in order to explain its material and find its practical significance or meaning.[109] In Warfield's conception, one cannot separate the knowledge claims of any subject sphere from theology and ethics. The latter is the practical application of knowledge and theology, which exist as a unit. Again, the objective realities of what science is, who God is, what human knowledge claims are, what theology is, and how all these issues are subjectively conceived and practiced by people are seen as an indissoluble union, while being distinct at the same time. This unified vision also provides insight into why Warfield and other Princetonians believed that there were issues of grave importance that need to be addressed in the intellectual realm—they knew there are unavoidable practical consequences that mark people's lives when they think out of line with Scripture.[110]

Warfield acknowledges that there is a sense in which one can speak of the "existence" of a "natural ethics" that is independent of theological conceptions," but, he adds, this "would be a meager thing indeed," and "has always been an incomplete ethics."[111] At this point, Warfield quotes from W. S. Bruce, "The Ethics of the Old Testament,"[112] which highlights the contrast between a natural ethic and the one revealed in the

---

108. Ibid., 68–69.

109. The idea, then, of setting forth the antithesis between Christian and non-Christian scholarship as a matter of the former being religious and of faith, while the latter is not, would be decidedly at odds with what Warfield is claiming. From Warfield's perspective, everyone is religious, of faith, and making theological claims, whether they know it or not. This is all central to Warfield's disagreement with Kuyper and all those who endorsed the latter's idea of their being two kinds of people with two kinds of science, not simply in "perfection of performance" but "difference in *kind*." See "Introduction to Francis R. Beattie's *Apologetics*," *SSW* 2:93–105, esp. 100–101.

110. IST, 69–70.

111. Ibid., 69.

112. Ibid., 69–70.

Scriptures, and also strikes at the evolutionary notion, prevalent in some quarters of biblical studies, both at that time and even today, that the ethics taught in Scripture are simply the product of a naturalistic process. This notion would, in essence, conflate theology and ethics and envisage the matter in a materialistic or philosophically naturalistic way. This method, of course, is precisely the way that many regarded the matter in Warfield's day, but it is, according to Warfield, not only unscientific, but also unbiblical.[113] It is unscientific because it completely disperses the objective reality of the object known into the subjective comprehension and apprehension of the human knower. Materialistic or philosophically naturalistic science results in an eradication of the distinct ontological reality of the subject matter known. The distinct reality of the subject matter known is, according to Warfield, a necessary part of true science.[114] What is allegedly "known" in a philosophically naturalistic conception of science is, in fact, not a reality that is, ontologically speaking, distinct from the human knower, but is only an extension or product of the knower.[115]

All Knowledge Is Subordinate to the Doctrine of God in Scripture and the Confession

Warfield affirms that, "All science without God is mutilated science, and no account of a single branch of knowledge can ever be complete until it

---

113. Ibid., 70.

114. Ibid., 55.

115. The term "distinct" is very important here. Warfield constantly made fine distinctions in which he would distinguish between two or more realities and then identify the exact relationships that exist between the realities. Here the point is to understand how he can speak of two things as distinct from each other, yet unavoidably related to each other—that there can be similarities between two things without convergence. At issue here is simply the age-old discussion regarding the problem of the one and the many or unity and diversity. A problem that is, to say the least, at the forefront of many scholarly debates across a wide spectrum of human knowledge claims. For a concise summary of the philosophical issues inherent in this debate, see Stumpf, *Socrates to Sartre*, 13–18. For a treatment of this issue as it pertains to the doctrine of the Trinity, see Gunton, *One, Three, Many*. In Charles Hodge's *ST* 1:442–43, Hodge states: "It is a great mistake to regard that doctrine [the Trinity] as a mere speculative or abstract truth, concerning the constitution of the Godhead, with which we have no practical concern, or which we are required to believe simply because it is revealed. On the contrary it underlies the whole plan of salvation, and determines the character of the religion (in the subjective sense of the word) of all true Christians."

is pushed back to find its completion and ground in Him."[116] Quoting from E. B. Pusey, Warfield clarifies:

> God alone *is* in Himself, and is the Cause and Upholder of everything to which He has given being. Every faculty of the mind is some reflection of His; every truth has its being from Him; every law of nature has the impress of His hand; everything beautiful has caught its light from His eternal beauty; every principle of goodness has its foundation in His attributes. . . . Without Him, in the region of thought everything is dead; as without Him everything which is, would at once cease to be. All things must speak of God, refer to God, or they are atheistic. History, without God, is a chaos without design, or end, or aim.[117]

He then concludes, in his own words:

> It is thus true of sciences as it is of creatures, that in Him they all live and move and have their being. The science of Him and His relations is the necessary ground of all science. All speculation takes us back to Him; all inquiry presupposes Him; and every phase of science consciously or unconsciously rests at every step on the science that makes Him known. Theology, thus, as the science which treats of God, lies at the root of all sciences.[118]

It should be noted that in this quote Warfield identifies sciences as possessing "being." Furthermore, true science is only possible by operating with an interpretive framework that requires one to possess an accurate understanding of Scripture, because, Warfield believed, the word of God is "the instrument which so far increases the possibilities of the science as to revolutionize it and to place it upon a height from which it can never descend."[119] And, of course, for Warfield, that true understanding is most clearly articulated in the WCF—Scripture, rightly interpreted, is the fundamental presupposition for all human knowledge.

Having set forth the place and prominence of theology, thereby establishing the correct conception of God in all human knowledge, Warfield goes on to explain that theology as a science has a particular

---

116. IST, 70–71. He quotes Pusey, "Collegiate and Professorial Teaching and Discipline," 215–16. Pusey (1800–1882) was Regius Professor of Hebrew and Canon at Christ Church, Cambridge. For more information on Pusey, see "Pusey, Edward Bouverie," in *Oxford Dictionary of the Christian Church*, 1147.

117. IST, 70–71.

118. Ibid., 71.

119. Ibid., 63.

advantage over the other sciences "inasmuch as it is a more inductive study of facts conveyed in a written revelation, than an inductive study of facts as conveyed in life."[120] As a result, theology has attained a level of completeness not attained by the other sciences; yet, this does not mean that there is no further progress to be made in theology. Still, by saying that theology or any science is progressive, Warfield recognized it was necessary for him to clarify what he meant by progress.

Progress in scientific work does not mean simply storing up the raw material of a science. With respect to theology it means that we should not expect new revelations; the canon is closed, and has been for nearly two thousand years. Progress in theology means theology "had a history—and a history which can be and should be genetically traced and presented."[121] Warfield briefly describes the organic nature of theology's progress by accentuating those things that were determining factors in theological progress—the need, intrinsic to Christianity, for Christians to comprehend "the nature and modes" of God's existence and "the person of its divine Redeemer."[122] As a result, Warfield expected that this history and growth of this progress would continue past his own day. Moreover, the essential character of theology's progress can be identified.[123]

Theology: Scientific and Constructive

According to Warfield, progress and construction are synonyms in the realm of science. Because *theology* is a science, it, too, is marked by progress, or construction. That is, over time, the church has grown in its knowledge and understanding of truth, and this means that it has also grown in the knowledge and understanding of falsehood.[124] It is foolish to think that progress can be made in theology, or any science, by jettisoning previously established truth. Certainly there have been and are errors that need to be corrected, but to attempt "to overturn the established basal truths of theology" in the name of construction is, in Warfield's estimate, "utter folly."[125] Warfield acknowledges that there are disputes about particular matters. Yet, just because there are disputes over specific issues

120. Ibid., 74.
121. Ibid., 75.
122. Ibid.
123. Ibid., 76.
124. Ibid.
125. Ibid., 77. People who do such things are compared by Warfield to those who "are striving to prove that the earth is flat and occupies the center of our [solar] system."

does not mean that there is no truth to be known at all. Such a position is incompatible with the very idea that God himself is truth and that he has revealed himself, and will continue to do so.[126] With the use of a building metaphor, Warfield admonishes his readers that if progress is going to be made in building "the temple of God's truth . . . we must not spend our efforts in digging at the foundations which have been securely laid in the distant past."[127] He then depicts the work of every Christian as helping to construct the edifice of God's truth, and even highlights some of the particular contributions that different ethnic groups and nations have had in that construction.[128] Therefore, it is legitimate to speak of the history of theology as a "progressive orthodoxy," as long as the phrase is clarified.[129]

Warfield declared that it was fine to be progressively orthodox but that this label should not be confused with "retrogressive heterodoxy."[130] Orthodoxy means believing truth, and modifying it with "progressive" means that there is growth occurring toward greater and greater knowledge of that truth. In Warfield's estimation, to be progressively orthodox means that one is growing in a more accurate understanding of the truth, and participating in the construction of "the temple of God's truth."[131]

Progressive, Therefore Historical

Warfield clearly had a deeply historical view of the Christian faith and theology. The Christian is part of a historical process. A Christian's understanding and knowledge is significantly shaped by what has preceded him or her. No one can simply engage in theology, or at least do it well, without a well-developed awareness and knowledge of history. God has brought this history into existence, providentially governs it for the express purpose of revealing himself, and will bring it to its final consummation.[132] The very warp and woof of Warfield's scholarship is rooted

---

126. Ibid.

127. Ibid.

128. Ibid. On pp. 77–78 Warfield says: "The Greeks laid the foundations, the law-loving Romans raised high walls, and all the perspicuity of France and ideality of Germany and systematization of Holland and deep sobriety of Britain have been expended in perfecting the structure; and so it grows."

129. Ibid., 78.

130. Ibid.

131. Ibid., 77.

132. See Warfield, "Predestination," *CW* 2:3–67.

in and reflected by a view of history that, as expressed in the words of Calvin, all creation is "the theater of God's glory."[133]

Each branch of human knowledge must operate within the reality of "the history of the advance of every science."[134] This fact culminates in a recognition that:

> In any progressive science, the amount of departure from accepted truth which is possible to the sound thinker becomes thus ever less and less, in proportion as investigation and study result in the progressive establishment of an ever increasing number of facts.[135]

Thus, even though an increase in theological knowledge, as in other branches of knowledge, may bring with it increased blessings, it is also true that it increases the limits within which an orthodox person can operate. Hence, "the progressively orthodox man is he who is quick to perceive, admit, and condition all his reasoning by all the truth down to the latest, which has been established as true."[136] There was still one implication that required expounding. To speak of progress is to speak of a goal to be achieved; therefore, Warfield next explains the character of theology's goal, and its impact on anyone who recognizes it.

The Goal of Theology

According to Warfield, speaking of progress denotes a goal that is evident; that is, the "completeness and perfecting as a science—as a department of knowledge—is naturally the proximate goal towards which every science tends."[137] Beyond this, though, theology has a specific and practical purpose. Indeed, theology "is an eminently practical science" whose purpose "is to save and sanctify the soul."[138] Warfield's elaboration on this idea provides a glimpse of how he viewed his own life and scholarship:

> And the discovery, study and systematization of the truth is in order that, firmly grasping it and thoroughly comprehending it in all its reciprocal relations, we may be able to make the most efficient use of it for its holy purpose. Well worth our most la-

---

133. See vols. 20 and 21 of Calvin's *Institutes*. For an extensive treatment of this topic and evidence of its pervasiveness in Calvin's thought, see Schreiner, *Theater of His Glory*.
134. IST, 78.
135. Ibid.
136. Ibid., 79.
137. Ibid.
138. Ibid.

> borious study, then, as it is, for its own sake as mere truth, it becomes not only absorbingly interesting, but inexpressibly precious to us when we bear in mind that the truth with which we thus deal constitutes, as a whole, the engrafted Word that is able to save our souls. The task of thoroughly exploring the pages of revelation, soundly gathering from them their treasures of theological teaching, and carefully fitting these into their due places in a system whereby they may be preserved from misunderstanding, perversion and misuse, and given a new power to convince the understanding, move the heart, and quicken the will, becomes thus a holy duty to our own and our brothers' souls as well as an eager pleasure of our intellectual nature.[139]

Thus, Warfield gives, not only an explanation of the practical nature of theology, but also a description of his own endeavors. Although he does not explicitly state that he is describing his own scholarly work, the description fits what he sought to accomplish in his scholarly endeavors. It clearly expresses his thoughts on the nature and purpose of theology as a practical science.

Systematic Theology: An Eminently Practical Science

For Warfield, knowledge of the truth was not some abstract, dry, impersonal, and rationalized proposition terminating with the intellect, disconnected from any spiritual or religious affections or actions. As he states:

> It is not a matter of indifference, then how we apprehend, and systematize this truth. On the contrary, if we misconceive it in it parts or in its relations, not only do our views of truth become confused and erroneous, but also our religious lives become dwarfed or contorted.[140]

As a result, "the character of our religion" is determined by "the character of our theology."[141] For Warfield, "theology" is synonymous with one's thought life, while "religion" is synonymous with one's affections and actions—and these two realities are forever joined.[142] Theology has an intensely and unavoidably practical and experiential dimension to it.

---

139. Ibid., 79–80.
140. Ibid., 80.
141. Ibid.
142. Warfield, "Religious Life of a Theological Student" and "Religious Elements in the Preparation for the Ministry," 48–58.

Theology and Epistemology: Science and the Context of Apologetics

The Christian, then, is not going to benefit by trying to *make* theology practical (a human activity to create a reality), but rather by recognizing theology's already practical character (a human activity in discerning what already *is*).[143]

Consequently, because theology is practical, advances in it as a science, according to Warfield, have always been made "in response to a practical demand," and "made in a distinctly practical interest."[144] Warfield states:

> We wholly misconceive the facts if we imagine that the development of systematic theology has been the work of cold, scholastic recluses, intent only upon intellectual subtleties. It has been the work of the best heart of the whole Church driving on and utilizing in its practical interests, the best brain.[145]

Addressing the contention that a systematic knowledge of biblical truth has little value for the religious life, Warfield clarifies some of what he believed characterizes the relationship between human thinking, willing, and feeling. At least some of what Warfield believed regarding human beings as the image of God (and their place in the unified created order) is reflected in his assessment of the indissoluble union between theology and anthropology, and this, in turn, is reflected in the practical character of theology. As Warfield expresses it:

> We do not possess the separate truths of religion in the abstract: we possess them only in their relations, and we do not properly know any one of them—nor can it have its full effect on our life—except as we know it in its relations to other truths, that is, as systematized. What we do not know, in this sense, systematically we rob of half its power on our conduct; unless, indeed we are prepared to argue that a truth has effect on us in proportion as it is unknown, rather than in proportion as it is known. To which may be added, that when we do not know a doctrine systematically, we are sure to misconceive the nature of more or fewer of its separate elements; and to fancy, in the words of Dr. Charles Hodge, "that it is true which a more systematic knowledge would

---

143. Notice the fundamental difference between the two activities. The first is the very nature of a "modernist impulse." See Hutchison, *Modernist Impulse in American Protestantism*. The second is viewing theology from a perspective that denies the truthfulness of the modernistic mindset, or denies that what the modernist believes actually corresponds to what is; to what is real; to what God created and superintends.

144. IST, 81.

145. Ibid. See also Briggs, *Whither?*, 18–19.

show us to be false," so that "our religious belief and therefore our religious life would become deformed and misshapen."[146]

Thus, in Warfield's conception of the Christian faith, Christian doctrine in general, and a systematic knowledge of it in particular, is not only related to all branches of human knowledge, or all other science, but is also indispensable for Christian living. Neither doctrine nor systematics is tangential to Christian living, nor are they an optional matter that can be left to the dictates of each individual Christian. In Warfield's estimation, the ultimate work of the systematic theologian is gospel preaching, not simply the arrangement of truths in a logical manner according to doctrine. The systematic theologian's work is:

> . . . the moving of men, through their power, to love God with all their hearts and their neighbors as themselves; to choose their portion with the Saviour of their souls; to find and hold Him precious; and to recognize and yield to the sweet influences of the Holy Spirit whom He has sent. With such truths as this he will not dare to deal in a cold and merely scientific spirit, but will justly and necessarily permit its preciousness and its practical destination to determine the spirit in which he handles it, and to awaken the reverential love with which alone he should investigate its reciprocal relations. For this he needs to be suffused at all times with a sense of the unspeakable worth of the revelation which lies before him as the source of his material, and with the personal bearings of its separate truths on his own heart and life; he needs to have had and be having a full, rich and deep religious experience of the great doctrines with which he deals; he needs to be living close to his God, to be resting always on the bosom of his Redeemer, to be filled at all times with the manifest influences of the Holy Spirit. The student of systematic theology needs a very sensitive religious nature, a most thoroughly consecrated heart, and an outpouring of the Holy Ghost upon him, such as will fill him with that spiritual discernment, without which all native intellect is in vain. He needs to be not merely a student, not merely a thinker, not merely a systematizer, not merely a teacher—he needs to be like the beloved disciple himself in the highest, truest and holiest sense, a divine.[147]

Systematic theology is not simply an idea to be exposited, but is central to what God created human beings to be and the purpose for which he created them. To call into question the legitimacy of system-

---

146. IST, 83.
147. Ibid., 86.

atic theology is, in Warfield's assessment, not only out of accord with Scripture, but also questions its validity and purpose, namely, the saving of souls.[148] Attacking, or even belittling, systematic theology as a legitimate Christian pursuit, as was done by Briggs and other modern Protestant liberals, showed that they failed to understand the relationship between systematic theology, Scripture, and the Christian faith. This, then, raises the question of a deficiency in one's understanding and handling of Scripture, as well as one's conception of the Christian faith.[149] Thus, it was necessary not only to address the idea of systematic theology, but also its very right to exist and to be pursued.

Conclusion

Warfield had an organic and unitary view of science (or knowledge), theology, and apologetics. He saw the three as united, and explained them in relationship to each other. Human involvement in these activities highlights their practical and historical character, because human beings engage in them as creatures created in God's image. Because all reality originates and has its fulfillment in God, theology is central to all human knowledge. This means that there is an unbreakable union of the objective and subjective elements within epistemology, and that the pursuit of systematic theology not only corresponds to the realities of human experience, but also is central to human redemption, since humans were created to know God. Warfield, therefore, saw science and theology as unitary, organic, and historical because they involved the person in a knowing process with created realities in time and space.

Still, there were many in Warfield's day that disagreed with Warfield's views and sought to reconceptualize the Christian faith along other lines. Warfield responded with his understanding of the systematic nature of the knowledge of God and his belief that all things not only correspond to what Scripture reveals but also provide the only coherent way of thinking about the matters under question.

---

148. See Warfield, "Biblical Idea of Revelation," *CW* 1:12. For a contemporary stating of this same fundamental view and its biblical support see Ridderbos, *Redemptive History and The New Testament Scriptures*.

149. It also raises questions regarding the *person*. As Warfield states regarding systematic theology, "Only the atheist or the agnostic on the one side, the idiot or lunatic on the other can be without such a theology" ("Task and Method of Systematic Theology," *CW* 9:95).

6

Systematic Theology's Legitimacy: What Is Christianity?

According to Warfield, questioning the right of systematic theology to exist raises all the significant questions of apologetics.[1] Of course, European and American liberal theologians had been doing just that in their efforts to reconceptualize the Christian faith throughout the nineteenth century (and would continue to do so on into the twentieth). As Warfield analyzed it, however, the liberal reconceptualization was not only lacking in biblical support, but was also incoherent in its most fundamental pronouncements. Continuing to claim the name "Christian" for it was especially pernicious and rendered biblical Christianity worthless. Warfield believed that, "the chief dangers to Christianity do not come from the anti-Christian systems."[2] Instead, it is "corrupt forms of Christianity itself which menace from time to time the life of Christianity."[3] Princeton's Polemicist did not remain idle as this assault was inflicted upon the church under the guise of faithfulness to her Lord. Warfield not only clarified the true character of this assault, but also called into question the character of some of the men perpetrating it.

In his essay "The Right of Systematic Theology," Warfield addresses his remarks to those "professing to be Christians." The essay centers on the challenge to systematic theology that, according to Warfield, was the reflection of "the impatience which is exhibited on every hand with the effort to define truth and to state with precision the doctrinal presuppositions and contents of Christianity."[4] It was not only seen in the Presbyterian Church in the United States with those, such as Charles

---

1. Warfield, "Right of Systematic Theology" (hereafter ROST), *SSW* 2:219.
2. Warfield, "Dogmatic Spirit," *SSW* 2:665.
3. Ibid., 666.
4. ROST, 221.

Augustus Briggs, who were voicing displeasure with the alleged scholasticism of the Princetonians, but also in Europe with some of those who were championing the use of higher criticism to question the veracity and character of Scripture. Warfield identified this way of thinking as "latitudinarian indifferentism," and this indifference to doctrine, which produced an attack on the validity of systematic theology, was actually an indifference to Christianity itself.[5] Indeed, according to Warfield, if some of the arguments against systematic theology were ever to truly take hold, then Christianity as a whole would be rendered "nugatory."[6] So, in discussing the right of systematic theology to exist, the question was actually: What is Christianity?[7]

In his methodical and precise way, Warfield answered the question in relation to the assertions and accusations of those whose conception of the Christian faith centered and terminated on feelings and the personal experience of the individual. Although he was methodical and precise, he was also stern and relentless. Warfield believed the very identity of Christianity was at stake. Therefore, he was quite clear about what he believed was occurring, and he maintained that the ubiquitous and re-

---

5. Ibid.

6. Ibid., 220.

7. David F. Wells, though acknowledging that Warfield "was not addressing the question of theological method directly," nonetheless criticizes him for the "innocence of his conception" regarding the theological task. Wells states "What he [Warfield] seems to assume is that if the Bible is treated as divinely inspired, as it should be, it will naturally and without difficulty deliver its doctrinal cargo. Once the matter of inspiration is settled, the question of what doctrine the Bible teaches will resolve itself more or less automatically." Wells was correct to recognize that Warfield was not addressing the theological task directly. Indeed, the only way in which Warfield addressed theological methodology in this essay at all was at its most foundational level, or its very core in terms of the character of the relationship between theology and actions and feelings. Wells' conclusion appears to be the result of an ahistorical and generally inaccurate reading of the essay. Warfield was addressing the liberal theological idea that in Christianity the metaphysical and epistemic order was actions and feelings before beliefs or doctrine. Thus, Warfield was arguing against a particular conception of Christianity as a whole that he saw as the renouncing of Christianity. Wells' criticism of Warfield is also linked to a praising of Kuyper for his recognition of the subjective character of the theological task. As we have already seen and will continue to see, Warfield abundantly accounted for the noetic affects of sin and the subjective element in epistemology. Wells, "Theologian's Craft," 184–85. There is a certain irony here. The very thing that Warfield is arguing against—a conception of Christianity that minimizes an emphasis on doctrine, if not removing it altogether from the worship and life of the church—Wells himself has so perceptively and devastatingly criticized in his five volumes addressing the state of contemporary evangelical theology. See the monographs by Wells listed in the bibliography.

lentless nature of theological indifference would not allow him to avoid this fight.[8] Still, this particular attack on Christianity was marshaled by those professing an indifference to doctrine, and this very indifference made it difficult for them to see Warfield's points. After all, Warfield's points were doctrinal. Those whom Warfield was criticizing were at the very least, by their own admission, minimizing the centrality of doctrine for the Christian faith, if not championing the removal of it completely. This made arguing against them difficult in the extreme.

Despite their professed indifference to doctrine, Warfield believed it was still necessary to employ *reductio ad absurdum* arguments. As he saw it, the issue was not simply whether the current adherents of theological indifference were affected by his arguments, but whether the *propagation* of such indifferentism could be slowed or stopped. Though those who were theologically indifferent were seemingly impervious to being attacked doctrinally, they certainly were not indifferent to lobbying their own attacks against a self-consciously doctrinal Christianity. They were quite intent on propagating their own beliefs. From Warfield's perspective two things stood out quite clearly: (1) theological indifferentism was actually the substitution of one set of doctrines for another, and (2) there was a certain kind of disingenuousness about those propagating theological indifferentism. However, since this propagation was ubiquitous and relentless, the fight could not be avoided. One either had to fight or succumb to the reconceptualized Christianity.[9]

Warfield maintained that, carried to its logical outcome, embracing the doctrinal indifferentism of his day would "banish Christianity from the earth."[10] He was not proposing that Christianity was truly capable of being banished from the earth. Warfield believed that God's purpose to save his people would be realized. He was asserting that *the idea that doctrine and systematic theology were of no importance was the rejection of Christianity*. Propagating this way of thinking was, in reality, an open attack on Christianity. The fact that others might not see it that way was not the issue. Warfield was operating from the belief that there is an organic and unbreakable union between the objective and subjective realms in epistemology. To refrain from pressing the issues because others did

---

8. ROST, 221. It might be legitimate to say that the "Breckinridge" tendencies emerged a bit more in this essay than in some others.

9. Ibid., 221–22.

10. Ibid., 224.

not see things his way was to simply concede that Kant, Schleiermacher, and all those following their lead were correct.

This massive assault, from Warfield's perspective, was bad enough, but that was not the end of the matter. It was not merely that Christianity was attacked; it was the way it was attacked that deserved attention. To identify Christianity as the fruit of a nebulous and ill-defined religious sentiment was to "cut-up Christianity . . . by the roots."[11] Warfield also believed that the problem goes even deeper—that such an indifference to doctrine is simply incoherent; a flagrant contradiction. It is incoherent because the act of reconceptualizing Christianity in this way is actually just polemicizing for a *different doctrine*. Therefore, the stance of the allegedly doctrinally indifferent is, in reality, just an argument for another *type* of doctrine.[12]

Warfield acknowledged that there most certainly could be discussion within Christianity regarding essential and non-essential doctrines, but he maintained that the acknowledgement of *any* essential doctrine makes the practice of calling doctrine itself into question moot. The very idea of useful or important doctrines implies not an indifference to doctrine, but a question of which doctrines are the useful and necessary ones. In addition, acknowledging the existence of any such doctrines also acknowledges the need for understanding those doctrines—which reinforces Warfield's whole point regarding the need for and the role of systematic theology.[13] Indifference to the idea of doctrine will always be incoherent.

Moreover, recognition of these points is, ipso facto, an acknowledgement of the circular nature of truth. The Old Princeton conception of truth's unitary nature implies that one cannot distinguish between two things unless they first have something in common. Thus, distinguishing between an essential truth and a non-essential one is predicated on being able to ascertain properties of each that are distinctive and yet are, in some sense, defined by the relationship of the essential and non-essential truths to each other. Warfield explains how this ends up creating "a pretty complete Systematic Theology":

> Let us say that only the "essential" doctrines are to be included: but surely, in a systematic treatment of these, we cannot exclude the statement and development of those other truths which,

11. Ibid., 226.
12. Ibid., 227.
13. Ibid.

> while not "essential" in and of themselves, are yet necessary to the integrity and stability of these "essential" doctrines, and so are, in a secondary and derived sense, themselves "essential." And so on in the tertiary and quarternary rank. Thus the body of doctrine will grow until it will be hard if we do not find ourselves at last in possession of a pretty complete Systematic Theology.[14]

Further, in the process of expanding one's knowledge, more of the features inherent in "the circle of truths" must be apprehended and comprehended. For Warfield, the way that our sensory data and reasoning relate to each other in one "concatenated" whole is a distinctive characteristic of human knowledge.[15] It was these foundational epistemic matters that Warfield addressed.

If the question within the church was framed as: What are the essential and non-essential doctrines?, then the right of systematic theology to exist was already conceded. If such an attack were pursued on the basis of serving Christ, one could do so only on the grounds of attacking Christianity in the name of Christianity. Given the incoherency of the stated position of the theologically indifferent, Warfield surmised that, in the end, they would not be able to establish their views based on a putative hostility to systematic theology. Instead, they would have to operate on the basis of other grounds. He was right. It was direct *hostility* to doctrine that was the actual ground from which the theological indifferentists operated. It was this hostility to doctrine that taught that Jesus did not teach doctrine, but instituted a lifestyle, that became increasingly popular throughout the late nineteenth century.[16] To be part of their "Christianity" one had to confess that the "elaborate theological constructions of the dogmatists," i.e., the post-Reformation Scholastics, had warped and distorted Christ and his work.[17] Such a view harbored a "violent hostility to doctrine—or to 'dogma.'"[18] Warfield left little doubt where he stood on this issue and what he thought of those who attacked Christianity by using its own name.

---

14. Ibid., 228.

15. This view is elucidated by Warfield in "Idea of Systematic Theology." (*CW* 9) "Concatenated" seems to be one of Warfield's favorite terms.

16. ROST, 228–29.

17. Ibid., 229. For an accurate assessment of some of the more significant post-Reformation theologians and their work, see Muller, "Calvin and the 'Calvinists,'" Part I, 345–75, and Part II, 125–60, as well as his "Problem of Protestant Scholasticism." For further clarification on some of Muller's work, see Asselt and Dekker, "Introduction."

18. ROST, 229.

An Attack from Within: Seeds of Christianity and Liberalism [19]

Warfield had a strong response to James Anthony Froude's quip that "'Truth itself becomes distasteful to me when it comes in the shape of a proposition. Half the life is struck out of it, in the process.'"[20] Warfield's response reveals what he believed was at stake. His argument is quite intriguing, especially given the belief in some scholarly guilds that Warfield did not account for the noetic affects of sin very well. Consider the following:

> There are many theologians to whom truth in propositional form is in like manner distasteful, and half, or all, its life seems dissipated, for the same reason—because *they* too are *afflicted with a "lamentable and constitutional inaccuracy."* No wonder that upon such minds exact statement seems to act like an irritant, and theology appears to be an enemy of religion. *Men like these must be classified as deficient*; and we can no more yield the right of theology in obedience to their outcries than the physicist can consent to refuse all discussion of color to please the color-blind, or the musician all study of harmony lest he should bore those who have no ear for music. *Men who have no faculty for truth* will always consider an appeal to truth an evil. But the assault upon doctrinal Christianity is far from being confined to those whom *we must believe to possess reason*, indeed, *for they too are men*, but who seem very chary of using it. *On the contrary*, it is being carried on today by the very leaders of Christian thought—by men whose shining intellectual gifts are equaled only by their trained dialectical skill and the profundity of their theological learning.

---

19. Machen, *Christianity and Liberalism*, written in 1923, two years after Warfield died. I am not trying to draw a definitive conclusion regarding the relationship between ROST and Machen's *Christianity and Liberalism*. The similarities, though, are striking. Both address the idea of treating and identifying Christianity as a life and not a doctrine, and exposing the presuppositions behind this and their logical outcome. Machen develops this argumentation a bit differently than Warfield did in ROST, but they are identical in their *basic* topic, thesis, argumentation, and conclusions.

20. ROST, 229. As we have already seen, Warfield specifically rejected the idea that theology terminates with the intellect and that truth finds its fullest manifestation in a proposition. This rejection did not cause him to reject the reality that truth could be, had been, and would continue to be stated in propositions. See "Theology a Science," *SSW* 2:210. Consider the following from "Authority, Intellect, Heart," *SSW* 2:671: "The revelations of the Scriptures do not terminate on the intellect. They were not given merely to enlighten the mind. They were given through the intellect to beautify the life. They terminate on the heart. Again, they do not in affecting the heart, leave the intellect untouched. They cannot be fully understood by the intellect acting alone. The natural man cannot receive the things of the Spirit of God."

> "Theology is killing religion" is *not merely the wail of those who are incapable of theology* and would nevertheless fain preserve their religion. It is *the reasoned assertion of masters of theological science whose professed object is to preserve Christianity in its purity* and save it from the dangers which encompass it in this weak and erring world.[21]

There are a number of things worth noting in this statement. First, there is a significant subjective quality to Warfield's argument. He asserts that particular men simply have an aversion to truth stated propositionally. The problem with these men rests with their personality and character and is, in essence, an epistemic problem, for they have "no faculty for truth" and "are incapable of theology." Second, it is *not these types of men*, in particular, who are the primary problem. The church was under attack from her own leaders in Christian thought, those whose professed intentions were not to jettison Christianity, but to preserve it. Third, these two points draw attention to a distinction that Warfield would continue to make, namely, the distinction between what particular men believed or argued for in their theology versus their personal confession regarding their true status before God. One of the places that Warfield does this, among others, is with respect to Albrecht Ritschl. Ritschl promoted the idea that we cannot really say we believe in God, but rather that God is "a useful postulate for the validating of our practical ends." [22] Warfield lauded the fact that along the way Ritschlites affirmed the deity of Christ, yet emphasized that "we are not here concerned with Ritschl's personal convictions, nor with the indications in his followers of a not unnatural recoil from the full rigor of his teaching: but with the logical implications of that teaching itself."[23] This leads to a fourth observation. Warfield believed that one could not just stop using truth and reason to combat the leaders of Christian thought since that would just concede the whole matter. This was no minor quibbling over a particular doctrine, or exegetical point. According to Warfield, this was about the very character and existence of Christianity. It was about people's eternal destinies. A sense of urgency definitely marks Warfield's words and argumentation.

21. ROST, 230 (emphasis added). The identification of being a human being and possessing reason is reflective of Warfield's anthropology, expressed in the WCF and the Bible. He considers Man to be originally created in the image of God, male and female, possessing knowledge, righteousness and holiness, with dominion over the creatures.

22. ROST, 248.

23. Ibid. In this Warfield demonstrated his gentlemanly spirit. His concern was over ideas—not personal conflict or status as a genuine Christian.

Systematic Theology's Legitimacy: What Is Christianity?

It would appear that after having written copiously, intricately, and judiciously for approximately twenty years on the issues that were animating and nurturing modern Protestant liberalism, Warfield [24]felt it was time to call people out for who they were and were not, what they were either knowingly or unknowingly doing, and what the consequences of their formulations would be.[25] Therefore, in detailed and forthright fashion, Warfield exposed the indifferent, irrational, incoherent, and unchristian

---

24. It is, therefore, inaccurate to assess that Warfield has a "markedly cynical, if not sarcastic tone" in this essay (Riddlebarger, "Lion of Princeton," 166). To interpret Warfield as cynical and sarcastic would seem to ignore some of the most significant historical realities that marked the life of the church in the United States and Europe during Warfield's time as a professor at Western and Princeton. Of course, if one believes Warfield is simply indebted to Scottish philosophy for his epistemology and apologetic approach, an interpretation of him as cynical and sarcastic seems more plausible. After all, if one of the chief features of SCSR is thought to be the idea that facts just speak for themselves apart from a human interpretation of them, then a certain kind of incredulity would set in with the one indebted to SCSR, when others did not share one's conclusions. As we have seen, though, the historical realities of Warfield's life do not allow us to conclude that he subordinated his epistemology or apologetic approach to SCSR. Warfield uses the *reductio ad absurdum* argument repeatedly in this essay. In his pointing out the absurdity of the absurd it is understandable how one might conceive him to be sarcastic. Even still, sarcasm generally has a greater purpose to serve in communication. Warfield was not "flying off at the handle." Warfield's writings portray a very calculating approach to not only *what* he said but also *how* he said it. Interestingly, Riddlebarger's comment seems to indicate that sarcasm is lower on the scale of accepted speech than cynicism. Sarcasm, however, is a legitimate rhetorical device, and Warfield was not beyond using it. See "Dr. Duffield's Proposition to the Presbytery," *The Presbyterian*, September 12, 1900, Warfield Papers, box 53, PTS archives. Warfield was responding to a truly ridiculous and absurd proposal by Duffield. Duffield meant for it to be taken seriously. Warfield would not allow the charade to continue. To accuse Warfield of cynicism, however, is historically inappropriate. Cynicism communicates a pejorative negativity and imbalance in understanding historical realities, the nature of people, and their motives that cannot be attached to Warfield simply from his words in this essay.

25. It would seem that this type of thinking was disturbing Warfield during this time as can be seen in his "Review of Dr. Wildeboer's treatise on *The Literature of the Old Testament in its Chronological Sequence*," *Presbyterian Quarterly and Reformed Review* 6.23 (1895) 537: "When open materialists like Ernst Haeckel, as in his recently published *brochure* called *Monism*, still talk of their belief in God, the soul, immortality, and pose as the conservators of religion—only, a purified religion, a religion without God, soul or immortality—we can scarcely wonder that theologians like Prof. Wildeboer should still claim to believe in the existence of a revelation after they have gored its sole vehicle to power. What is needed above everything in these days of confusion is some electric spark to flash through the world of thought and crystallize parties on their lines of real cleavage. Above everything, the world needs to know now on which side men are standing, and we need not doubt that there are many who need to have their real position revealed even to themselves." I am indebted to Bradley Gundlach for calling my attention to this quote.

beliefs of those who would discard true Christianity in the name of their own brand of "Christianity."

Aversion to Clear Thinking

Warfield's counter assault begins in a way that accentuates his adherence to the subjective element in epistemology. After all, he identified and faulted Froude, and others, for being *"afflicted with a 'lamentable and constitutional inaccuracy,'"* saying such men are to be "classified as *deficient*;"[26] they are men who have an *"innate antipathy to clear thinking,"* exhibiting the expression *"of a not very rare incapacity for truth."*[27] Warfield made it clear, when asserting that these men had a subjective problem in the apprehension and comprehension of truth, that such men were not brute beasts; they were not arational. Rather, with respect to reason, they were men who seemed "very chary of using it."[28] The argument Warfield presents in the remainder of the essay is couched in the context of a full recognition of the subjective nature of the knowing process. Those who would call into question whether Warfield held to or emphasized the noetic affects of sin, or the subjective nature of truth, certainly cannot make their argument from this passage, for it is here in strident boldness that Warfield affirms that there is something wrong with these people, and in particular, their epistemological apparatus. Their aversion for truth in propositional form makes them *defective epistemically*. Warfield's statements on this point are intense,[29] which emphasizes all the more the sobriety of the matter. According to Warfield, the gravity of the situation can be understood when one recognizes that those who have a constitu-

26. ROST, 229.

27. Ibid.

28. Ibid., 230.

29. This is an example of Warfield affirming a particular concept in a way that is not often done in our day. It is elementary that theologians work with concepts, and use a multitude of words to do so. When one keeps this in mind, then one may be less likely to identify or fault Warfield et al. for having failed to communicate a concept in a particular way. It ought to go without saying, but evidently must be said, that there are many ways to communicate one particular concept. Given Warfield's educational background, intellectual capabilities, life-long development of his gifts, and prodigious facility in multiple languages we ought not to be surprised that he would have expressed one concept in a variety of ways. Those who honestly think that Warfield did not accentuate the noetic affects of sin either have not read or comprehended much of Warfield or have committed, in a rather flagrant way, a word-concept fallacy. The latter are like those who would complain about a man who never rides in a car because he rides in a variety of luxury cars instead of confining himself to one single compact.

tional problem with the truth are buttressed in their folly by the leaders of the Christian church. These leaders, though, are not afflicted with the inability to handle truth in propositional form, and they profess to actually be attempting to argue *for* Christianity, but they have succumbed to a pattern of thought inimical to truth. As Warfield phrased it:

> It is the reasoned assertion of masters of theological science whose professed object is to preserve Christianity in its purity and save it from the dangers which encompass it in this weak and erring world. It is a position, therefore, which deserves our most respectful consideration, and if we still feel bound to refuse it, we owe it to ourselves to give a reason for the faith that is in us.[30]

Thus, Warfield sets out to "exegete" the position of those who deny the right of doctrinal Christianity.

Facts and Dogma, Life and Doctrine

Warfield stated that there were two fundamental conceptions of Christianity that were used to assault doctrinal Christianity.[31] People were told that either Christianity consists of facts, not dogma, or that it consists of life, not doctrine. In the end, for the Princeton Polemicist, both approaches were inherently flawed and, therefore, could not do justice to Scripture. So, by addressing both, Warfield sought to expose their flaws and give a more faithful account of the character and content of Scripture and the Christianity rooted in it. In doing this, he sought to demonstrate which conception of Christianity meets people's existential needs.

Warfield begins by addressing the view that Christianity consists of facts, not dogmas. This issue brings out into full view the biblical doctrine of revelation and its relationship to the whole doctrine of salvation. A Christianity of facts and not dogma considers dogma to be simply an intellectual construct that an individual finds desirable, but that is not basic to Christianity. They maintain that dogma is really just a theory

---

30. ROST, 230. It should be noted that the last phrase of the sentence is taken from 1 Peter 3:15. Note too, that Warfield doesn't say that "we owe it to *them*," that is those who would jettison the doctrinal element from Christianity. Instead, he wrote, we owe it to *ourselves*. There may be two primary reasons for this: First, it corresponds perfectly with his view that apologetics is necessary for saving faith—it is the very nature of saving faith that it must also have reasons. Second, from the standpoint of intellectual integrity, it is necessary to know what one is refuting before one refutes it.

31. ROST, 230. Warfield made reference to these in terms of their "modes of *conceiving* Christianity."

of God's acts in human history. It is God's acts in human history upon which Christianity is founded; Christianity is not any particular theory about those acts. As a result, there is no need to ground one's salvation on a particular theory about God's acts. No particular theory of the atonement is necessary; the fact that Jesus lived and died is all that matters. Thus, theologians need not meddle in the realm of theories *about* facts. They just need to establish what the facts are.[32]

According to Warfield, this conception not only reveals a particular conception of revelation, but also a view of saving faith and human beings that he considered contrary to Scripture and reality. The view is contrary to Scripture because it does not correspond to the biblical concept of revelation that consists of both God's acts and his words.[33] For Warfield, both are necessary in order for people to know the correct interpretation of God's acts. It is God's word written that, at the very least, explains God's acts. Apart from God's word, there is no sure and certain interpretation of these acts, which brings up the second point. It is contrary to reality because the human mind cannot apprehend or comprehend just a fact—apart from an explanation of that fact. Speaking of facts without any explanatory theory is incoherent. Warfield argues that what are called "facts" automatically include, ipso facto, a theory that corresponds to them.[34]

32. Ibid., 231.

33. Warfield expressed these, and other matters regarding the biblical doctrine of revelation, more fully in "Biblical Idea of Revelation," *CW* 1:3–4.

34. ROST, 232. This is simply another way of saying: "There are no brute facts." Warfield's entire argument at this point is that facts require an interpretation, and that a fact not interpreted is unintelligible to the human mind. It also affirms that God's revelation in propositional form warrants a particular belief about the character of the reality that God created. If one wishes to argue, as George Marsden does, that an indebtedness to Scottish Common Sense Realism can be seen in Machen's belief that facts have no need for interpretation, because they speak for themselves, then one's argument simply cannot hold. Marsden cites Machen, *What is Faith*, 249. Yet the broader context of the Machen quote that Marsden uses in *Understanding Fundamentalism and Evangelicalism* (191) is Machen explaining that apart from the subjective awareness or recognition of "the hollowness and hopelessness" of one's life apart from Christ one will not "discern the facts" (248). Machen makes very clear that it is sin that prevents a person from recognizing the "cogency" of "the proofs of the Christian religion" (248). As Machen states, 248, "And when that recognition comes, the proofs of the Christian religion suddenly obtain for them a new cogency; everything in the Christian system falls for them into its proper place; and they believe." Shortly thereafter, Machen took up an emphasis characteristic of Warfield's thought (see "Apologetics," *CW* 9:14–15). Machen says: "It is one of the root errors of the present day to suppose that because the philosophical and historical foundations of our religion are insufficient to produce

Disconnecting facts from theories as the higher critics were doing is, in Warfield's thinking, tantamount to saying that Christianity has flourished best in darkness rather than light, and that the Christian matures in the midst of, indeed because of, ignorance. This does not mean that God, first and foremost, requires a sinner to understand him exhaustively before believing him; the rejection of that idea was part of the Old Princeton heritage.[35] Nonetheless, Warfield states that the Scriptures teach that God created human beings with knowledge as an inherent part of their constitution, and that saving faith corresponds to our personhood. Again, it bears repeating that Warfield's belief in the human

---

faith, they are therefore unnecessary. The truth is that their insufficiency is due not at all to any weakness of their own but only to a weakness in our minds." After calling upon the Christian to avoid pragmatism, Machen, 249, wrote what Marsden identified as reflecting Common Sense philosophy: "The facts of the Christian religion remain facts no matter whether we cherish them or not: they are facts for God; they are facts for angels and for demons; they are facts now and they will remain facts beyond the end of time." Yet, Marsden omits the two sentences that follow: "But, as we have observed in an earlier part of our discussion, the facts are one thing, and the recognition of the facts is another. And it is the recognition of the facts that depends for us upon the sense of need." Put another way, a person will not recognize the resurrection as a fact at all unless there is for that person a subjective encounter or experience that enables that person to cognitively affirm that the resurrection is true. Integral to this is the awareness of one's sin that makes the life, death, and resurrection of Jesus necessary for one's salvation. Apart from that subjective experience, which Machen believed had to be the work of the Holy Spirit, the person's thoughts about the resurrection of Jesus could aptly be described in the terms used by Warfield: "like a rock in the sky." What Machen was highlighting in the entire discussion was the same thing that Warfield accentuated, namely that there is an objective realm outside of the individual that does not come into objective reality or existence because it is perceived. Machen believed, like Warfield, that facts comprehended are facts interpreted.

35. The position of both Hodge and Warfield was that God first and foremost requires the sinner to believe him. Because humans are created, male and female, in the image of God in knowledge, righteousness, and holiness, with dominion over the creatures, humans already possess, ipso facto, a critical mass of understanding of God that allows all humans to be held accountable for their sin (Romans 1), while needing the regenerating work of the Holy Spirit to provide enough knowledge of God to cause the sinner to understand Jesus to be the sole sufficient remedy for sin, causing the sinner to believe in Jesus for salvation. This belief in Jesus for salvation, by necessity, entails knowledge of, or the ability to explain, particular truths, i.e. doctrines, and, in turn, will bring about an increasing understanding of those doctrines as the sinner lives in obedience to God's word, or more precisely, the knowledge of God's word that he or she already possesses through the power of the Holy Spirit. This was the position of Turretin as well. See Turretin, *Institutes of Elenctic Theology* 1:23–43 for Turretin's teachings on the relationship of faith and reason. Turretin explicitly denies that the word of God can be subordinated to human reason, and clearly affirms the noetic affects of sin. See also Hodge, *ST* 1:34–54 and 3:83.

possession of knowledge as a result of how they are constituted was not due to belief in SCSR, but was due to his belief in the Scriptures and the faithfulness that the WCF exhibits in expressing the Scripture's content, as well as its categories and system of theology. In this understanding, faith and knowledge are not mutually exclusive realities, but mutually dependent ones. To set facts off against doctrines or dogma is, in Warfield's estimation, to misconstrue the nature of saving faith and the nature of human beings, to contradict Scripture, to misunderstand the relationship between facts and the interpretation of facts, and thereby, to function contrary to reality. Warfield links these beliefs to other biblical doctrines throughout numerous essays and books through the remainder of his career. His correlations clarify what human beings are, that they possess true knowledge, and that how they know is dependent upon God and conveyed as part of the process of his revealing himself. Thus, Warfield's correlations reveal not only where he acquired his idea that human beings possess knowledge, but also how his understanding of human knowledge was part of the entire system of doctrine that he believed. Since, SCSR simply correlates with only a few aspects of Warfield's epistemology; it provides an insufficient basis upon which to understand and explain his epistemology.[36]

Warfield, therefore, clarified what truly characterizes the relationship between facts and dogma. In short, Christian doctrine consists of a particular interpretation of the facts as given in God's word.[37] Warfield states:

---

36. At this point, Riddlebarger, "Lion of Princeton," 177, again approaches the correct analysis but then takes a wrong turn. He recognizes the inaccuracies of Marsden et al. in their failure to recognize that Warfield and the Old Princetonians did account for the noetic affects of sin and the subjective element in epistemology, and also explained the knowledge of facts in terms of the presuppositions one brings to the facts, but then he identifies this as demonstrating Warfield's faithfulness to SCSR. SCSR is not Warfield's source for these beliefs. Instead, it is his belief in the doctrines of God, creation, Man, and sin revealed in Scripture and expressed in the WCF. It is not denied here that particular features of SCSR can be correlated with the aforementioned doctrines. Indeed they can, but the question here has to do with the *source* of Warfield's beliefs on these matters. See chapter 8 of this book.

37. ROST, 234–56. Those who want to conclude that Warfield or the other Old Princeton theologians embraced a fact/value split are rebuffed by what Warfield wrote in this essay alone. A particularly disappointing treatment, which completely contradicts this point, is Pearcey, *Total Truth*, ch. 11. Her footnotes through this section reveal that she is heavily, if not exclusively, indebted to the Dutch Reformed and Neo-orthodox scholars who have erroneously analyzed Warfield and Old Princeton on this and several other points.

Systematic Theology's Legitimacy: What Is Christianity?

> No one would contend that Christianity consists in doctrines as distinguished from facts, far less that it consists in doctrines wholly unrelated to facts. But neither ought anyone contend that it consists in facts as distinguished from doctrines, and far less that it consists in facts as separated from doctrines. What Christianity consists in is facts that are doctrines, and doctrines that are facts. Just because it is a true religion, which offers to man a real redemption that was really wrought out in history, its facts and doctrines entirely coalesce. All its facts are doctrines and all its doctrines are facts.[38]

Therefore, those who advocate the idea that the Christian faith embraces the *fact* of the incarnation but reject an *interpretation* of the incarnation have wholly misconstrued the Christian faith, and the very way in which human thinking and living are related. If Warfield was correct, then such a construal and the utterances used to formulate it really amount to babble.

Facts without Theories: Rocks in the Sky

As Warfield clarified, facts can only truly be understood within their context, their interpretation. This definitely shows that any analysis of Warfield that states that he operated as a Common Sense Realist is quite flawed. The SCSR approach Warfield allegedly used construes the relationship between facts and the human mind as the human mind being void of theories about the facts, or the facts as "not a matter of interpretation."[39] Whatever relationship may have existed between the thoughts and conclusions of Charles Hodge, Warfield, and Machen on epistemology, one thing is certainly true; SCSR is not a viable explanation for accurately assessing that relationship. Warfield flatly denied that view. Indeed, his whole argument against the liberal theologians at this point is that the facts cannot be intelligible to the human mind apart from an interpretation or explanation of them. The explanation of the facts that concerned the biblical writers was the church's doctrine. Setting doctrines against facts results in facts that are simply not understood.[40]

---

38. ROST, 234.

39. Marsden, *Understanding Fundamentalism and Evangelicalism*, 193.

40. ROST, 235. Warfield's point here reflects his presuppositional understanding of human thinking. For Warfield, however, presuppositions were unavoidably dependent upon an objective realm that allowed presuppositions to be evaluated and judged. One recalls a description of rationalism by Adolf Schlatter: "There is admittedly plenty of evidence to show that academic work is always tempted toward rationalism, toward a

To support his point, and to further illuminate his antipathy to what he considered a metaphysical mirage, Warfield quotes James Denny:

> A fact of which there is absolutely no theory is a fact which stands out of relation to everything in the universe, a fact which has no connection with any part of our experience; it is a blank intelligibility, a rock in the sky, a mere irrelevance in the mind of man. There is no such thing conceivable as a fact of which there is no theory; such a thing could not enter *our* world at all; if there could be such a thing, it would be so far from having the virtue in it to redeem us from sin that it would have no interest for us and no effect upon us at all.[41]

This is a reaffirmation of the position that Charles Hodge taught regarding human reasoning and the Christian concept of revelation:

> . . . reason is necessarily presupposed in every revelation. Revelation is the communication of truth to the mind. But the communication of truth supposes the capacity to receive it. Revelations cannot be made to brutes or idiots. Truths, to be re-

---

pride of judgment that expects to get the whole of reality into its own intellectual grasp and so reduces it to its own field of vision. But these cheap thrills are not overcome by ignoring and despising the task of obtaining a coherent understanding. . . . a construction that has cut loose from observation is the enemy not only of the New Testament, but also of the aims and rules of academic work. It may be that a tendency toward rationalistic conjectures that are far away from the facts clings to all academic work. But we must be continually aware that this conflicts with science as well as the New Testament; it is irrational as well as impious. When our object is driven out by a theory that denies the real and puts our imaginings in its place, we oppose not only the past, but at the same time the ground and law of our own thinking activity, and so our own existence. In opposing the object we are also opposing the subject. The borders between dreaming and thinking, between scientific and rationalistic explanation, are established by the laws that govern our thinking. These demand evidence in support of judgments, which means that we are here dependent upon sight and hearing that give material and basis for such judgment. Where judgment cuts loose from the perception that is indispensable to it, where the intellect's productive power tries to be in command and play the creator so that what we produce is no longer connected with a prior receiving, where thought circles around one's own self, as though this could create from itself the material from which knowledge comes and the rules by which it is to be judged, there we have rationalism. It stands in irreconcilable hostility to the very basis of the New Testament, because acknowledging God is the direct opposite of rationalism. But this rationalism is at the same time the road to dreamland and the death of intellectual integrity." See Schlatter in Neur, *Adolf Schlatter*, "Appendix C," 196–97.

41. ROST, 235–36. Interestingly, Warfield cites a work by Woodrow Wilson regarding historians and their work. Wilson affirms that facts by themselves do not comprise the truth, but rather, it is the facts arranged and ordered in a particular way that give us meaning.

ceived as objects of faith, must be intellectually apprehended. A proposition, to which we attach no meaning, however important the truth it may contain, cannot be an object of faith. . . . unless we know the meaning of the words nothing is communicated to the mind, and the mind can affirm or deny nothing on the subject. In other words knowledge is essential to faith. In believing, we affirm the truth of the proposition believed. But we can affirm nothing of that of which we know nothing. The first and indispensable office of reason, therefore, in matters of faith, is the cognition, or intelligent apprehension of the truths proposed for our reception.[42]

Warfield believed in the inseparable union, or continuity, between the physical material realm that is accessed through the senses and the intellectual realm that is the locus of apprehension, comprehension, and meaning. These cannot be disconnected from each other, nor can they be collapsed into one, as in a radical metaphysical monism. Together they provide continuity, a united spiritual reality.[43] Far from embracing a radical discontinuity between the natural and supernatural, the physical and the spiritual, Warfield, as an Old Princetonian, embraced a *radical continuity* between them, but it is a continuity that, by the very nature of the case, can only be understood because there are *real* distinctions, in an ontological or metaphysical sense, between the object or subject known and the knower. These distinctions are the only basis, context, or presuppositions upon which human beings can speak of knowledge

---

42. Hodge, *ST* 1:9. Further, in volume three, Hodge affirms that exercising saving faith is reasonable and not ever irrational (83). This is what Hodge means when he speaks of reason *judging* revelation. He does not mean that human reason decides or determines God's revelation. That would amount to an obvious and crass form of rationalism. Rather, he is simply saying that humans are not animals. We speak and communicate in intelligible language that is the warp and woof of reason. Human reason, thus, is the instrument created by God in humans that is the means by which God brings revelation to them.

43. The criticism that Kenneth Cauthen, in *The Impact of American Religious Liberalism*, 1–22, and others sympathetic to the liberal tradition, attempt to lobby against the Protestant orthodox position, at least as it is expressed by Warfield, shows a total misunderstanding of Warfield's point. Of course, it is in some sense not surprising that Cauthen would miss the argument given his historical sketch of the nineteenth century context in which the polemics between the liberals and classic Protestants took place. To simply speak of Edwards and his successors and completely omit mentioning the Princetonians is to be ignorant of the most significant aspects of the whole matter. It was in large measure, according to the Princetonians, some of Edwards' successors who were contributing significantly to the erosion of biblical authority and relocating it in the individual's powers and experience.

in an intelligible way. There are only two fundamental ways of thinking that can conclude that there is no such reality. One could posit a radical disconnection between known and knower so that there is no discernible intersect of any kind. Or, one could conceive that the two were not really two distinct realities at all, but simply one reality, not simply in the sense that they are united, but rather that a radical metaphysical monism characterizes reality. The latter, simply collapses any substantive distinctions of any kind in a metaphysical sense. If either were true, then according to the Princetonians, we simply could not account for human knowing at all. That is, ultimately, one would not even have categories with which to work and, therefore, speak about knowledge.[44]

Christianity: A Particular Meaning of the Facts

So, for Warfield, there was an unbreakable union between facts and ideas, not an unbridgeable chasm or a dissolution of one into the other. It is the "chasm" view that holds Warfield's attention at this point in his essay on "The Right of Systematic Theology." In the course of his arguments against this view, he clarifies the character of Christianity in relation to facts and their meaning. Christianity, according to Warfield, can be defined, *inter alia*, in terms of a particular understanding, or interpretation of particular facts. Furthermore, this particular understanding comes through particular men, who were given the authority to grant this interpretation or understanding of those facts. It is not up to individuals to gather whichever facts they so choose and then to give their chosen facts whatever understanding or interpretation they wish.[45]

---

44. One might counter with the notion that the liberals did speak intelligibly about knowledge. But this misses the point. The question was (and still is): Did they speak of this knowledge on the ultimate basis of the presuppositions that they said were true, or on the basis of presuppositions that they actually denied? If it was the latter, then they were simply guilty of contradicting themselves, and not knowing it. This is part of what makes Warfield's opening salvo against them so strategic and enlightening. In essence he was saying: "Some of them are incapable of seeing the point. Some of them simply cannot see that they are contradicting themselves. It is why they contradict themselves." Still, just because they contradicted themselves, and could not see that they did, does not mean that Warfield was not going to press the arguments against them. There were other things of eternal significance at stake besides the salvation of those whom Warfield was criticizing. For the Princeton distinction between knowing and understanding see Hodge, *ST* 1:50. For how one of Warfield's contemporaries demonstrated how Albrecht Ritschl's theology did not allow for these necessary distinctions and resulted in agnosticism see Galloway, "Theology of Albrecht Ritschl."

45. ROST, 237.

Christianity, according to Warfield, is nothing less than a particular meaning of the facts, and both the facts and their meaning are inextricably related to the way God has created humans. In other words, he gives weight to the presuppositional nature of human thinking and knowing. Though Warfield does not use the term *presupposition* here, he *is* using the concept. The point then is to investigate the one interpretation of the facts that constitutes Christianity. This also forces recognition of the doctrinal authority that is central to Christianity, which is only found in Christ, mediated through his chosen apostles. Furthermore, acknowledging this is acknowledging the role and authority of systematic theology as a Christian discipline.[46]

Thus, Warfield highlights the organic unity between knowledge of God, Christology, canon, doctrine, and apostolic authority. Moreover, when we understand the inherent union or continuity between all of these matters, the fatal flaw of trying to conceive of the Christianity that is taught in Scripture as operating with a dichotomy, or antagonism, between facts and dogma, and doctrine and life, becomes very clear. In other words, Warfield postulated that the very Scriptures his opponents were using to support their conception of Christianity actually testifies against it. Scripture is written to particular people regarding particular historical facts and their meaning and this testifies to the reality of this unbreakable and harmonious relationship between facts and doctrine, or dogma. So, for an exegesis of Scripture to result in the conclusion that facts and doctrine can be disconnected can only occur by doing violence to the text. In a word, Warfield was accusing them of an unscientific exegesis. He again quotes James Denny to make his point:

> A mere exegete is sometimes tempted to read New Testament sentences as if they had no context but that which stands before him in black and white; they had from the very beginning, and have still, another context in the minds of Christian readers which it is impossible to disregard. They are not addressed to minds in the condition of a *tabula rasa*; if they were, they could hardly be understood at all; they were addressed to minds that had been delivered—as Paul says to the Romans: a church, remember, to which he was personally a stranger—to a type or mold of teaching; such minds have in this a criterion and a clew [*sic*] to the

---

46. Ibid., 238–39. For an identical thesis and understanding of Christianity, the canon, Christology, and apostolic authority as expressed in Warfield's words, see Ridderbos, *Redemptive History*.

> intention of a Christian writer; they can take a hint, and read into brief words the fullness of the Christian truth.[47]

The question, therefore, was: How can one make the Scriptures teach the absence of a fact/dogma union, when the very reality of the document and its historical cultural setting presupposes that union?[48] We should note here that this argument is rooted in the very nature of the biblical text. This, of course, can be correlated with some of the affirmations of the Scottish Common Sense Realists, but the argument is not dependent on SCSR. It is rooted in a particular understanding of Scripture that stresses its literary and historical character and the Christian faith's dependence upon it.

Although having made the point that facts and their interpretation form an inseparable union within Christianity and are inherent in its doctrinal authority, Warfield recognized that there were those who would allow for the necessity of *interpretation*, but deny the presence of an external doctrinal authority. Those who denied an external authority in Scripture took refuge in an individual's subjective experience, which they considered to be outside the authority of Scripture to interpret. Thus, they promoted the view that the most important element of Christianity is that God speaks to us, and then this was set against the doctrinal authority of Scripture.[49] After quoting M. Henri Bois' argument for this position, Warfield reflects on the weight of Bois' argument:

> We could scarcely have a neater or completer refutation by the method of reduction to absurdity. The pity is that everybody does not see that the reduction is to absurdity. For the absurd position to which M. Bois would thus drive M. Rivier—that very position

---

47. ROST, 240–41.

48. It should be noted here that this whole argument rests completely on a historical and cultural awareness of the biblical writers and their audience. The idea that Warfield did not operate with an "historical" view of the bible or its interpretation, simply cannot be sustained from Warfield's writings, unless, of course, one simply wants to beg the question regarding what constitutes "historical." For those who seem to be unaware of Warfield taking the "historical" element in the Bible's interpretation seriously and how that element related to the nature of truth and the Christian conception of Revelation see "God's Providence over All," in *SSW* 1:110–15. This is erroneously listed in the table of contents as beginning on p. 111. See also "Christianity and Revelation," *SSW* 1:23–30; and "Divine and Human in the Bible," *SSW* 2:542–48. See also Cauthen, *Impact of American Religious Liberalism*, 21, who believes that the historical and social conditioning of the biblical writers was largely unknown to the orthodox divines, or at least was not recognized as being of significance for theology.

49. ROST, 242–43.

is voluntarily assumed by others. Would M. Bois show that by parity of reasoning with that by which M. Rivier would refuse to be bound by the doctrines of the Bible, the facts, too, may be refused? Undoubtedly, replies, for example, Mr. G. Frommel: religion cannot consist of or rest upon external facts any more than upon external doctrines.[50]

Thus, Warfield again emphasizes the subjective nature of truth claims ("everybody does not see that the reduction is to absurdity") and, by implication, the knowing process, and he then highlights the fact that this argument simply drove some people to "another class who equally refuse to allow the validity of Christian doctrine—those whose cry is that Christianity consists in life, not doctrine."[51] In an analysis of Warfield, his emphasis on the subjective nature of knowing should be highlighted as well as the fact that he believed that at a certain point it becomes necessary to draw attention to the personal deficiencies of one's opponents in their reasoning, or ultimately, in their comprehension and apprehension of truth.

In the second part of this essay, Warfield addresses the idea that doctrine and life can be radically juxtaposed in one's conception of Christianity, but first he considered it necessary to address the views of Albrecht Ritschl, whom he saw as a representative of an "extreme form" of the fact/doctrine dichotomy.[52] As Warfield saw it, the Ritschlian conception abandoned any metaphysical element of Christianity, relegating it to a religious character divorced from metaphysics. It also attacked the "facts" of Christianity so that the only "great fact" of Christianity left was Jesus Christ.[53] Though Warfield commended Ritschl for focusing on Jesus, he nonetheless faulted him for drawing a "sharp discrimination" "between religious and metaphysical knowledge."[54] On the basis of this discrimination, Ritschl was guilty of abandoning "the whole body of Christian doctrine."[55] Warfield concluded that in an "essentially positivist" age, Ritschl's anti-metaphysical move would play well, and yet, while

50. Ibid., 243–44.
51. Ibid., 244.
52. Ibid., 244–45. For the condition of the Protestant churches in Germany and Scandinavia leading up to and following Ritschl's scholarship, one that does not paint a very favorable picture of Ritschlian theology for church life see, Hope, *German and Scandinavian Protestantism*.
53. ROST, 246.
54. Ibid., 247.
55. Ibid.

it appeared anti-metaphysical in its following of Kant's lead, it was, in reality, simply substituting Kant's own metaphysic for the Bible's and interpreting Christianity in terms amenable to *that* metaphysic. As Warfield saw it, speaking of God and religion is, ipso facto, speaking of metaphysics. Setting them against one another is contradictory or incoherent.[56]

A sharp separation of God, religion, and metaphysics reflects thinking that also harbors a radical disunion between nature, history, and the Christian faith. As part of his criticism of Ritschlianism, Warfield cites James Denny's summary of Rischl's ideas, as well as the German theologian Wilhelm Hermann, who was a proponent of ideas similar to Ritschl's.[57] These ideas include the division of knowledge into two classes with no crossover—one scientific and the other religious. This division has become a virtual canon in certain sectors of biblical and historiographical scholarship since Warfield's time.[58]

> "God, in other words"—as Mr. Denny brings out Ritschl's idea—"is a necessary assumption of the Christian's view of man's chief end; but, scientifically—in its bearing on the interpretation of nature and history, for example—it may be left an open question whether there be a God or not." In a similar fashion, Hermann teaches that for "the maintaining of the impulse of religious faith," "it does not matter whether our conception of the world is theistic, pantheistic or materialistic."[59]

This class division results in the historian being unable to make any judgment concerning the miraculous element within Christianity since this question lies in the domain of religious knowledge, not scientific or historical. Warfield also quotes the German theologian Adolph von Harnack's endorsement of the notion that the historian is unable to deal with a miracle in its traditional sense because the only investigative

---

56. Ibid., 247–48.

57. Stonehouse, *J. Gresham Machen*, 105–12. The German theologian Wilhelm Hermann would later make a deep impression on Machen.

58. For probably the best contemporary restatement of this position see Harvey, *Historian and Believer*. For a concise critique of Harvey's position, see Evans, "Critical Historical Judgment and Biblical Faith." For a detailed history of the developments of matters inherent to this debate, as it impinges on New Testament scholarship, see Yarbrough, *Salvation-Historical Fallacy?*

59. ROST, 248–49, 249n28. Warfield quoted and agreed with James Orr's assessment that this "'practically amounts to a resuscitation of the old doctrine of a 'double truth'—the one religious, the other philosophical; and it is not held necessary that even where the two overlap they should always be found in agreement.'"

method available to the historian rules out the possibility of miracles. Miracles, in the traditional sense, are in the domain of religion and ethics, while history belongs in the domain of science.[60] This means that the "historical Jesus" or the "historical Christ" that the liberal theologians were appealing to could not be the exalted Christ of the virgin birth, who suffered for the sins of his people, died on the third day, rose bodily from the grave, and then eventually ascended into heaven. Instead, it had to be, according to Warfield, "the Christ of critical history: of whom we can say but this—he lived and died and left behind him the aroma of a life of faith."[61] In Warfield's estimation, this extreme bifurcation between religion on one hand and history and science on the other results in the "evaporation of the whole essence of Christianity."[62] It was also to the very same principle, Warfield maintained, that Abraham Kuyper capitulated when he relegated apologetics to the periphery of Christian theology, and which was endorsed in Kuyper's postulate of two kinds of men with two kinds of science.[63] Though Kuyper's view of apologetics and science amounted to a tacit approval of this radical dualism, the liberal theologians embraced it and reconstructed all of Christian theology around it. To Warfield, it was blatantly contradictory, truly absurd, and had to be shown as such.

---

60. Ibid., 249–50. For a critique of Harnack's position from one of his contemporaries, and a one-time colleague at Marburg, see Schlatter, "The Theology of the New Testament and Dogmatics." Despite their disagreement over these crucial matters, Schlatter and Harnack maintained a good relationship in which they intellectually challenged and benefited one another.

61. ROST, 251.

62. Ibid., 252–53.

63. Warfield, "Introduction to Beattie's *Apologetics*," *SSW* 2:93–105; and "Review of *De Zekerheid Geloofs*," *SSW* 2:106–23. Abraham Kuyper (1837–1921) was a Dutch Reformed theologian and statesman, who helped establish the Free University of Amsterdam and was prime minister of the Netherlands in the very early 1900s. It was Kuyper's formulation of the antithesis that exists between the epistemic abilities of the Christian and the non-Christian that Van Til sided with over and against Warfield. Though Warfield disagreed with Kuyper, believing that Kuyper had regarded the difference between the Christian and non-Christian in too absolute a way, he nonetheless appreciated Kuyper's work. It was Warfield who was largely responsible for having Kuyper's work on systematic theology, *Encyclopedia of Sacred Theology*, translated into English and for bringing Kuyper over for the Stone Lectures on Calvinism at Princeton in 1898.

Actually Absurd

Warfield states that this division of knowledge "passes beyond the apparent absurdity of paradox into the actually absurd," and "brings us to nihilism in the matter of religion."[64] The weight and nature of this criticism should not be swept over too quickly. It not only corroborates Warfield's unreserved endorsement of a radical union or continuity between metaphysics and religious faith, history, and Christianity, but also reveals what he thought regarding the nature of the modernist impulse that was at work in the theological reconstructions of modern Protestant liberalism.[65] According to Warfield, all that was left of Christianity under their construal was sentiment, and, therefore, his conclusions regarding the rights of systematic theology and the contradictory nature of the liberal reconceptualization simply could not be avoided. After all, the moment one decides that there is something besides mere sentiment, the question regarding dogma is back on the table. In that case, the question is no longer *if* there is dogma in Christianity, but "*what* 'dogmas' may be rightly recognized as holding that position."[66] Furthermore, Warfield was not hesitant about identifying exactly what he thought the liberals were asking their "fellow" Christians to do. If indeed Jesus Christ embodies Christianity, and yet his true identity and work is in question, then the unavoidable question becomes:

> What Jesus Christ? The Jesus of the Gospels? Or the Jesus of Strauss? The Logos Jesus of John's Gospels? The heavenly Jesus of the Apocalypse? Or the purely earthly Jesus of Pfleiderer and Renan? Or even perchance the entirely imaginary Jesus of Pierson and Naber and Loman? It is an insult to our intelligence to tell us that it makes no difference to Christianity how these queries be answered. But the first beginnings of an answer to them introduce the dogmatic element. From which it follows at once

---

64. ROST, 253, 254.

65. Ibid. The difference that holds virtually across the board with theologians and historians is whether the beliefs of Protestant liberalism are a viable way in which to construe our place in the world, and to think about both human knowledge and Christianity. See Averill, *American Theology*; Cauthen, *Impact of American Religious Liberalism* (see n142); C. Brown, *Jesus in European Protestant Thought*; Dorrien, *Making of American Liberal Theology*; Hutchison, *Modernist Impulse*; McGrath, *Making of Modern German Christology*; Schleiermacher, *On Religion*; Sloan, *Faith and Knowledge*.

66. ROST, 254.

that Christianity cannot exist without the dogma which it is the business of Systematic Theology to investigate and state.[67]

For Warfield, there simply is no way to separate faith *in* Jesus from historical matters *about* Jesus, as well as the metaphysical issues that are intrinsic to such matters, and this brings the authority of the apostles and their teachings to the forefront of the debate. Yet in their bifurcation of metaphysics and theology, the liberal theologians were operating with a belief that, in order for their writings to have religious significance for people in subsequent eras of history, the Bible could not be conditioned in any way by the historical realities of the its authors' time and place. Warfield, on the other hand, viewed this as contrary to the biblical view of God, human beings, and salvation.

Remember that what drove Warfield's beliefs on these matters was his belief that the Bible teaches that God is the creator and providential sustainer of all reality, revealed in and through creation. Since God created the world, he also created the time and the space that human beings occupy as creatures. Human history, then, was begun by God, is directed by him, is filled with his presence, is interpreted by him, and will be brought to the goal he decreed for it (before he even began creation). In Warfield's conception, then, the biblical doctrines of God, revelation, Christ, and salvation are part of a perfectly correlated whole that can only be truly understood when their relationships to each other are understood. Moreover, the Scriptures of the Old and New Testament reveal truths about the relationship between these doctrines that answer the very questions that the liberal reconstruction of the Christian faith raised.[68] In particular, the historical realities of the Greek and Roman cultures, which were being alleged to be the stuff of metaphysics, cannot be set against the contents of Scripture, but are to be understood as under the providential control of God and thus as *intended* to be an intrinsic part of each New Testament writer's thought and life. In other words, even if these are metaphysical elements, they are still part of what God determined would enter into the biblical revelation. So, for Warfield et al., these elements that seemed distasteful to the liberal theologians were "of the essence of

---

67. Ibid.

68. The following are places to gain a grasp of the pervasive nature of the doctrine of God in Warfield's conception of history and salvation: "Predestination," *CW* 2:3–67; "Biblical Idea of Revelation," *CW* 1:3–34; "Idea of Revelation and Theories of Revelation," *CW* 1:37–48; and "Inspiration of the Bible," *CW* 1:51–112.

Christianity," precisely because Christianity encompasses the whole of reality, not simply an aspect of it fractured from the whole.[69]

In Warfield's estimation, it is illegitimate to think of the origin of Christianity, or the character of the Bible as a whole, in such a way that they are antiseptically removed from the other realities going on in creation during their formation. Warfield understood the God spoken of in Scripture to be the God of everything—the source, sustainer, interpreter, guide, and redeemer. Warfield thought of these matters first and foremost from the perspective of God not only having been revealed, but also being active, in the details of creation *and* history, and of Christianity being an integral part of the whole. Liberal theologians were setting history against religious faith, metaphysics against dogma, Greek thinking against the apostolic testimony in Scripture. In the process, they were, in principle, postulating a radical discontinuity, but were actually collapsing these pairs into singular realities. Warfield understood these pairs in relationship to each other, as existing in an organic union. These doctrines, in all their details, are only discernible and distinct when seen in relation to each other, and are unable to be set against one another. Doing so results in irreparable violence to the Scripture's message and the Christian faith. Further evidence of Warfield's thinking on these matters is seen in his criticism of the liberal project for setting doctrine against life.

Christianity a Life, Not Doctrine? Who Is Operating with a Fact/Value Split?

The corollary of the creed that "Christianity is facts, not dogmas" was "Christianity is a life, not doctrine." Warfield briefly explains the position:

> According to its mode of thinking, the sole immediate purpose of the Bible is to quicken life, not to satisfy curiosity, and we divert it from its proper use when we go to it as anything else than the living and abiding word through which we are begotten again—than the implanted word which is able to save our souls. When it has performed this function its immediate employment is at an end: its dogmas and its facts may alike be passed by in indifference when we possess the life—that Christ-life which, being once formed in us, surely renders us superior to all extraneous aid. And for the inception of this life we cannot be dependent on any book

---

69. ROST, 254–56.

or on any dogmas or facts whatever, laid hold of by the intellect and embraced in knowledge.[70]

In his response to this position, Warfield readily admitted that there is some validity to this construal of the Christian faith, but maintained that the idea was in need of qualification and correction. In his characteristic fashion, he stated that the things liberals had juxtaposed and expressed in a discontinuous relationship, actually possess a continuous and harmonious relationship, indeed, they can only be defined by and understood within their relationship to one another. For Warfield, the very nature of the problem with the liberal reconception of the Christian faith was that it *appeared* to be holding on to the details of the Christian faith but was, in reality, relating these details to each other in such a way that it actually abandoned the true Christian faith. In fact the liberals had really only traded one systematic theology for another, and all in the name of rejecting systematic theology. Warfield realized that the only way to make people aware of what was happening was to accentuate the logical and true resting point of this reconstruction. In the name of jettisoning systematic theology, these liberal theologians were still actually relating the details of the Christian faith to each other—they were systematizing!—yet, everything they were doing was denuding the Christian faith of its defining features. Warfield felt that by showing this inconsistency, their view would appear ridiculous and foolish because it really *was* ridiculous and foolish. Moreover, the first sign that a person is actually grounded in *reality* is a *recognition* that this reconceptualization is ridiculous and foolish. In other words, Warfield consistently employed a *reductio ad absurdum* argument. Still, it is important to recognize that Warfield did not accomplish his purpose with literary and verbal rancor. He did it through argumentation. Yet, in the end, if Christian doctrine and life really do go together in a correlated whole, as Warfield claimed, then the liberal idea of a conflict between doctrine and life truly is foolish or absurd. Yet, this foolishness can only be comprehended and apprehended when a sufficient number of the details of the correlated nature of the whole are brought before people's minds. *This* is what Warfield attempted to do.

Life and Doctrine Together, Not Separated

Warfield acknowledged that the liberal theologians were at least wrestling with the right issues. It would be silly to think that Jesus lived, died, and

70. Ibid., 256–57.

rose again simply to "insert so many marvelous facts into the dull course of natural history."⁷¹ Christ's purpose was to save sinners from sin "that they might have life and have it abundantly."⁷² Integral to this Christian life, though, is Christian doctrine. Warfield qualifies this by clarifying that the noetic effects of sin are overcome by the Holy Spirit, so that the sinner is able to have knowledge of the truth to such an extent that it saves from sin and unto life:

> And no single Christian doctrine has been revealed to men merely as a tenet in philosophy, to make them wise; each and every one is sent to them as a piece of glad tidings that they may be wise unto salvation. Yet though all Christian knowledge is thus only in order to life and terminates on life, it is not in the power of all knowledge to give life. We live by the power of the Son of God, by virtue of a vital relation of our souls to him: and it is only because of the indwelling of the Spirit of God in our hearts that our ears are open to the truth or that our souls are amenable to its discipline. This Christian life that we live is not the creation of the doctrines or of the facts: it is the working of the Spirit of God, who, abiding within us becomes to us a second and higher self.⁷³

Christian doctrine by itself cannot make one a Christian. Only the Holy Spirit regenerating the sinner's heart can cause the sinner's ears to be opened to truth. Still, the Holy Spirit's regeneration *is* for the purpose of the sinner receiving truth. Warfield's point is that we need to recognize the exact relationship between Christian life and Christian doctrine. Warfield was glad for the emphasis on Christianity as a life, and for the mystical element present in this conception. Still, he concluded that the Ritschlian conception of Christianity could not do justice to the biblical text, the history of the Church, nor the reality of human thinking and living. In order to make this point, he criticized the articulation of the "Christianity is a life, not a doctrine" dogma, as it was expressed by Auguste Sabatier.⁷⁴

71. Ibid., 258.
72. Ibid.
73. Ibid.
74. Ibid., 260. Auguste Sabatier was a French Reformed theologian of the late nineteenth century. For treatments of Sabatier contemporaneous with his work, see Stevens, "Auguste Sabatier and the Paris School of Theology." He called Sabatier's views (on page 554) "French Ritschlianism." See also Ménégoz, "Theology of Auguste Sabatier of Paris." See Sabatier, *Outlines of a Philosophy of Religion*, for how he took his lead from Kant and Schleiermacher, and continually

Systematic Theology's Legitimacy: What Is Christianity?

Heraclitus Redux

Warfield quotes Sabatier: ". . . feeling comes first in time as well as in value: ideas come only afterwards and ideas cannot produce feeling, or if they can produce it, this happens so imperfectly and so rarely that we need not take account of this in the role of ideas."[75] Sabatier did not stop there, but related his conception of the Christian faith to the theory of evolution—we should think of Christianity as simply one manifestation of the religious growth of human beings that is inevitably pressing on towards a more perfect development. Warfield states that this is thinking of Christianity as merely one stop on the evolutionary train of progress, which is, in essence, the rejection of Christianity. For Sabatier, everything is in flux and he adopted this principle of change as an absolute. Christianity, therefore, cannot be thought of as an exception to this law of change. Warfield surmised that this means that Christianity will eventually be surpassed by a religious conception superior to it. It is also apparent from this conception that Jesus cannot be considered the supreme revelation of God.[76]

Anyone familiar with the teachings of the Greek philosopher Heraclitus will recognize the similarities Sabatier's position has to them. Sabatier's restatement of the essential position of Heraclitus, is exemplified by his use of Heraclitus' illustration of a river. "The river of the spiritual life flows on continuously," and though the sons use the same words as their fathers, the sons understand the words differently than their fathers

---

set science off against religion, and historical data off against Christian faith. For example, on 311–12: "Truths of the religious and moral order are known by a subjective act of what Pascal calls *the heart*. Science can know nothing about them, for they are not in its order." Further, in Stevens, on 555, "'All the ideas which the religious consciousness forms and organically combines, from the first metaphor which religious feeling begets, to the most abstract concept of theological speculation, are unavoidably inadequate to their object, and can never avail for its completely equivalent expression, as is the case in the exact sciences." See also Ménégoz, 30. Stevens, on 563, acknowledged that Sabatier believed that Protestantism exchanged the "infallible Church" for the "infallible book." Thus, at least Sabatier, contra Rogers and McKim, recognized what the historic position of the Protestant church had been, though Sabatier considered it faulty. The substance of Sabatier's emphasis on life before doctrine has been re-expressed in Grenz, *Revisioning Evangelical Theology*.

75. ROST, 260.
76. Ibid., 261–62.

because "the river flows on forever."⁷⁷ For Warfield, it strained credulity that one could conceive of faithfulness to Christianity by defining it by, subordinating it to, and ultimately dissolving it by means of an evolutionary philosophy alien to it. It strained credulity simply because the evolutionary philosophy by which Sabatier defined Christianity led him, according to Warfield, to commit a "flagrant" contradiction. For even though Sabatier et al. adopted an evolutionary mode of conceiving reality and the Christian faith, they simultaneously wanted to announce Jesus as the perfect embodiment of love and the founder of the perfect religion. In other words, everything is constantly changing, yet Jesus established the changeless religion nearly two thousand years ago.⁷⁸

Reveling in Doctrinal Contradiction

If similarities to Heraclitus and blatant contradictions were not enough evidence of the inadequacies of Sabatier's construal of the Christian faith, Warfield elaborated further on the latter's denigration of both the doctrinal element and the role of the human intellect in Christianity. Sabatier did not merely minimize the doctrinal element, he saw the moral unity that Jesus and his followers had as thriving in the midst, or even because of, contradictory conceptions regarding God. Rather than seeing contradictions regarding the doctrine of God as a problem to overcome, Sabatier saw the coexistence of these contradictions as the fulfillment of Jesus' prayer for Christian unity. He maintained that pietistic feelings provide a unity that the doctrine of "God" cannot.⁷⁹

Once again, Warfield uses the *reductio ad absurdum* argument, showing how the presuppositions on which Sabatier based his arguments

---

77. Ibid., 263. Warfield does not specifically identify Heraclitus as someone on whom Sabatier is dependent, or to whom his ideas can be traced. He simply identifies evolutionary thought as the lens through which Sabatier is thinking about Christianity. Heraclitus developed his philosophy at the beginning of the sixth century BC, and was essentially a pantheist, who believed that fire was the perfect example of how to understand reality. The world is a living "fire." For Heraclitus, God is Reason, not a person, and in this way is the immanent universal law in all things, and therefore all people share in the common universal Reason that is God. It is this strain of thought that has strong affinities with natural law theory as it is expressed by both non-Christian and Christian thinkers. The similarities with Hegel and Absolute Idealism are also prominent, though Hegel was obviously responding to Kant's legacy and formulating matters in a more specific way. Ritschl's view of the Holy Spirit also bears striking similarities to it. See Stumpf, *Socrates to Sartre*, 13–16, 325–41; Galloway, "Theology of Albrecht Ritschl," 202.

78. ROST, 265.

79. Ibid., 267–68.

contradict his conclusion. Furthermore, Warfield contended that only the claims of Christian doctrine can account for the claims of a Christian life. It seems that Sabatier, in other words, was living on "borrowed capital." Sabatier's indifferentism was only able to stay afloat, argued Warfield, because it allowed some legitimacy to Christian doctrine rather than rejecting it and resting only on the putative philosophical basis of religious evolution.[80] Warfield explains it this way:

> Indifferentism, we will remember, does not precisely condemn Christian doctrine; it only neglects it. And, true to his indifferentist results, M. Sabatier does not deny the possibility or the right or even the necessity of Christian doctrines, or even of Christian dogmatics. He confesses that a living religion must needs express itself in appropriate religious thinking and in doctrines which embody this thinking. For him this is only a special case under the general rule that faith without works is dead. No faith is a living faith which does not produce doctrine. It is not then against the possibility or the right of Christian doctrine that he protests: it is only its usefulness that he denies . . . Life does not, therefore, fluctuate, and the nature of faith change, according to doctrine: but doctrine fluctuates according to the life-movements of which it is only a reflection.[81]

Warfield, therefore, acknowledges that Sabatier's position was not one of antagonism to doctrine, but it was, rather, an indifference to its importance that results in neglecting it in the Church's life. Moreover, doctrine was not only neglected by Sabatier, but volatility in doctrinal difficulties was seen as a sign of true health and vitality.[82] According to Warfield, this principle not only meant there can be no fixed creedal forms in the church, but also that a variety of conflicting doctrinal expressions should be encouraged. This view roots Christianity in mere religious sentiment, and means there is nothing that sets Christianity apart from any other religion in any meaningful way.[83] Furthermore, there was no assurance that later in time there might not be another religion that supersedes Christianity because of its fuller expression of human religious sentiment.[84]

80. Ibid., 269.
81. Ibid, 269–70.
82. Ibid., 270.
83. For a contemporary treatment of apologetics that bears a resemblance to this, see Stackhouse, *Humble Apologetics*.
84. ROST, 271–72.

Warfield did not deny that Christianity entails sentiments or feelings. Instead, he denied that such human sentiment is Christianity's energizing source, the hub around which it rotates and from which it draws its defining principle. The true Christian conception does not see doctrine as subordinate to or created by our feelings. Rather, for Warfield, the Christian conception is that Christian feelings are created by Christian doctrine, under the nascent operation of the Holy Spirit.[85] Furthermore, it is the distinctive doctrines of the Christian faith that not only set it apart from all the other religions of humanity, but that also produce a distinctively different religious sentiment than the other religions.[86] To deny this, and to conceive of Christianity as religious sentiment that is indifferent to doctrine is, in the end, to deny Christianity. It simply places the label "Christianity" on the constitutive religious affections of all people. In the end, this simply turns Christianity into whatever one wants it to be.

The True Sense in Which Life Precedes Doctrine; Blind and Meaningless Feelings

Warfield was quick to point out, however, that there is a sense "in which it is true that life precedes doctrine."[87] It is here that Warfield really emphasizes the noetic affects of sin. He quotes the Apostle Paul from 1 Corinthians 2:14, stating that life precedes doctrine in a qualified sense because the natural man does not receive the spiritual things of God. The sinner must be regenerated by the Holy Spirit, and thus, in this sense, God must resurrect the deadened sinner, giving new life, so that Christian doctrine can be understood. Warfield points out that this was not only the teaching of the Apostle Paul, but also that of the Reformers,

---

85. Ibid., 272–73. There is really no mystery as to what the Old Princeton tradition taught regarding religious affections and whole-person psychology. The writings by the Old Princetonians in general, and Warfield in particular, are quite replete with explanations on these points, and yet this continues to be one of the most distorted points in the secondary literature. I am not affirming that all of the Princetonians were in complete agreement on every single matter; they were, however, in general agreement, and abundantly testified to the noetic affects of sin, and the subjective religious affections and how they relate to doctrine. See A. Alexander, *Thoughts on Religious Experience*; and Hodge, *ST* 1:1–103, 191–203; 2:192–204, 255–309; 3:3–93. Hodge called the denial of the immediate imputation of Adam's sin to the human race a novelty that only gained ascendancy with the rise of Arminianism (*ST* 2:204). See also Warfield, "Authority, Intellect and the Heart," *SSW* 2:668–71; and "Religious Element."

86. ROST, 272–73.

87. Ibid., 273.

the Schoolmen, "the greatest of the Fathers," and that it was even to some degree embraced by Aristotle.[88] So, if one is willing to affirm that life precedes doctrine in the sense that God must give life to the dead sinner before that sinner will understand and believe Christian doctrine, then Warfield could affirm the statement. Additionally, the recognition that the Spirit of God must regenerate the sinner before he will understand and believe Christian doctrine also testifies to the inertness of bare doctrine. Christian doctrine by itself, said Warfield, cannot create life. It is only God the Holy Spirit who gives spiritual life. This was not, however, the sense in which Sabatier and others were using the statement, "life precedes doctrine." So, while Warfield was willing to acknowledge his theological opponents knew *some* of the truth, he maintained that they had distorted it in such a way that it contradicted and assaulted the Christian faith.[89]

Warfield was not content, though, to leave the matter there, but rather sought to elaborate the vacuous notion of feelings disconnected from thinking. Again he marshals Henri Bois as his ally, who states, "To make religion a feeling without precedent knowledge is to make it an illusion or a disease." Or, as Warfield phrases it, "feeling without a known object is blind and meaningless to us."[90] For Warfield, this articulation of the union of anthropology with soteriology, and the apologetical approach commensurate with it, was not grounded in any particular manifestation of SCSR, but rather in Scripture, as can be seen, not simply from the content of Scripture, but also from its very structure. Warfield states:

> It will add greatly to the confidence with which we recognize this fundamental place of Christian truth with reference to Christian life, to remind ourselves that such was evidently the conception of the founders of the Christian religion concerning the relations of doctrine and life. This fact is written large over the epistles of Paul, for example, by the very distribution he makes of his matter: it is ever first the doctrine and then the life with him. The transition at the opening of the twelfth chapter of the Epistle to the Romans is a typical example of his practice in this regard. Eleven chapters of doctrinal exposition had preceded; five chapters of precepts are to succeed: and he passes from the one to the

---

88. Ibid., 273–74 (see n53). In the footnote he quotes from Hilary of Poitiers, *De Trinitate*, and Augustine, *Sermones de verb. Dom.*
89. ROST, 274. He called such thinking "a blow at distinctive Christianity itself."
90. Ibid., 275.

> other with what has been called his "tremendous therefore": "I beseech you *therefore* brethren—"therefore" because all this is so. In these "tremendous therefores" is revealed Paul's conception of the relation between truth and life. The same conception, it need scarcely be said, was that of his Master before him. How much Jesus makes of the Father's Word which had been given to him and which he had given to his followers, that they might know the truth and have eternal life, and that his joy might be fulfilled in them! His prayer for them was that they might be sanctified by the truth which God's word was."[91]

In addition, none of this contradicts in any way the truth that Christian obedience is the avenue to greater understanding of the truth, or that the good soil of a good heart is the only fit condition in which Christian fruit can be produced. This is true, but these were not the precise points under consideration. Instead, the point under consideration was whether the apostles ever taught that the good seed and its sowing were superfluous to the harvest. Warfield strongly denied that this is taught in Scripture and, furthermore, denied that it had ever been the "fundamental conception" of Christianity among those who professed it, since Jesus' day.[92]

The Appeal to Reason—Distinctively Christian or Scottish Common Sense?

Since doctrine is at the foundation of Christianity, there are inevitable and organic consequences to this reality. Chiefly, this means that Christianity makes its appeal, first and foremost, to people's reason. Citing James Macgregor's book *The Apology of the Christian Religion*, Warfield corroborates Macgregor's point that the attempt to *reason* the world out of its worldliness into godliness is distinctively Christian. According to Warfield, then, the very nature of the Christian faith means that the appeal that Christianity makes is "primarily to the intellect."[93] It is essential to note that Warfield affirms this in the midst of his explication of (1) the character of the Christian faith, (2) the relation of human thinking to feeling, (3) the relation of doctrine to life, and (4) the relation of liberal

---

91. Ibid., 2:276.

92. Ibid., 276–77.

93. Ibid., 277 n. 56. In the footnote, Warfield quotes James Orr as affirming that Christianity is distinguished from other religions by being a religion of knowledge that is "only attainable under moral conditions." This corroborates Helseth's thesis that for the Old Princetonians in general, and Warfield in particular, knowledge was inherently moral. See Helseth, "Moral Character and Moral Certainty."

conceptions of the Christian faith to his own and that of others. Never once does he cite SCSR philosophers, and not once does he *fail* to show that his beliefs were rooted in an exposition of Scripture and the history of the church, and were still prevalent among other theologians and biblical exegetes of his day. This suggests that the only way one could explain Warfield being indebted to SCSR for these affirmations, both in terms of their particular details and the general macrostructure of his thought, would be to show through a detailed correlation of these subject to SCSR that the latter is truly their source, and that Warfield was simply unaware of this latter body of knowledge. None of this has been done. Though it appears that there was an increasing rapprochement with philosophical naturalism among some of the Scottish philosophers at the beginning of the eighteenth century, Warfield clearly aligns himself with the church's heritage, which depicts human reason as fallen and fallible and in need of a special supernatural intervention by God to attain the understanding that results in salvation.[94] Natural reason, apart from Scripture and the Holy Spirit's regenerating work, allows human beings to have a very limited amount of true knowledge, but it is not this knowledge that results in salvation. Warfield wrote elsewhere that Adam's sin did not cause Adam to become something other than a human being. Sin did not create a brand new metaphysical entity in either human beings or the creation as a whole. Instead, it corrupted and distorted the reality in which God had created humans to live. This means that there is a basis or means by which Christians can reason with non-Christians, but that only by the supernatural work of the Holy Spirit can people reason rightly about reality in a way that will result in salvation.

It is on this note, emphasizing the doctrinal character of the Christian faith by an exposition of Scripture and discussing its several implications, that Warfield concludes his essay. As he does, he imparts a grim warning to those who contradict the conception of the Christian faith that he exposits and for which he argues:

94. For the movements among Scottish theologians and philosophers from the mid seventeenth century to the late eighteenth century, see Emerson, "Science and Moral Philosophy." Emerson makes clear that men such as Robert Leighton (1611–1684), Samuel Rutherford (1600–1661), James Wodrow (1637–1705), and Thomas Halyburton (1674–712) operated with a view that natural reason is subordinate to, and in need of, supernatural revelation and grace in order to know God for salvation. Still, they understood God's special revelation and grace as working in harmony with the basic reliability of human senses and reason not in contradistinction to them or by circumventing them. It is within this tradition that Warfield is aligned. This does not mean that Warfield agreed with all of the aforementioned men on all points of their beliefs regarding Christian doctrine.

> In insisting, therefore, on the primacy of Christian doctrine, and on the consequent right and duty to ascertain and accurately to state this doctrine—which is the task of Systematic Theology—we have the consciousness of being imitators of Paul even as he was of Christ. How much the apostle made, not merely of the value of doctrine as the condition of life, but of the importance of sound doctrine! His boast, we will remember, is that he is not of the many who corrupt the truth, but that he, at least, has preached the whole counsel of God. He is not content that Jesus Christ should be preached, but insists on a special doctrine of Christ—Jesus Christ and him as crucified. He even pronounces those that preach any other gospel than that he preached accursed: we should carefully note that this curse falls not on teachers of other religions, but on preachers of what we might speak of today as different forms of Christianity. In a word, in all his teaching and in all his practice alike, Paul impresses upon us the duty and the supreme importance of preserving that purity of doctrine which it is the aim of Systematic Theology in its investigation into Christian truth to secure.[95]

Conclusion

The correct conception of Warfield's scholarship is one that affirms that he is self-consciously seeking to be faithful to the Scriptures in both the content that he expresses and the methodology that he uses to present it. For Warfield, God's written truth, the Scriptures of the Old and New Testament, are a unified whole from which the church has formulated her numerous doctrines, which are all related to one another. One can only speak meaningfully about anything at all because of the radical unity of all reality. Human knowledge includes, ipso facto, truth about the correlations inherent in all reality. Still, the unitary nature of reality and truth is not where Warfield stopped, and the substance of his arguments against Protestant liberal theology can only be understood through comprehension of what he says characterizes this unity. With respect to the Bible, its doctrines, and the Christian faith, it is systematic theology as a discipline whose task it is to discover the ways in which the biblical doctrines are related to one another and how they form one systematic whole. When done in accordance with what Scripture reveals, one is able to discern the truth about the unitary nature of truth.

---

95. ROST, 279.

By the very nature of the case, systematic theology is a project that corresponds to what God created humans to be within the whole creation, and it is integral to human salvation. So, according to Warfield, systematic theology has a tremendously practical benefit—increasing knowledge concerning the union that exists between the character and fulfillment of human beings, Christian doctrine, and the nature of reality. To deny the right of systematic theology to exist, one has to actually affirm thoughts that contradict reality, that deny the true nature of human beings, and that are contrary to Scripture's content and character. Such a denial means that one is embracing beliefs that cannot claim for themselves the adjectives "scientific," "constructive," "Christian," or "biblical" and are ultimately incoherent. By recognizing the epistemological relevance of the coherent model for knowledge that Warfield lays out, and how the biblical exposition that he presents meets the exigencies of human beings, one can recognize the legitimacy of identifying Warfield's scholarship as "scientific," "constructive" and "biblical." There are some, though, who are defective in their ability to see or understand these matters. Warfield does not hesitate to call them men with "a 'lamentable and constitutional inaccuracy'" and men who are "deficient."[96] He states that some have "no faculty for truth."[97] Such a blatantly subjective mode of argumentation, however, did not mean that Warfield would be content to discontinue reasoning and simply yield the field to those whose conceptions of reality and the Christian faith were distorted. The pragmatic goal of converting those with a 'constitutional inaccuracy' was neither the only, nor even the primary, purpose for reasoning with such people. To understand more clearly Warfield's thoughts on why these people should still be reasoned with, one has to understand some of his seminal beliefs regarding God, human beings, and salvation. These issues are discussed more thoroughly in his article "Apologetics" in the *New Schaff-Herzog Encyclopedia of Religious Knowledge*, and other shorter writings that address apologetics in a pointed fashion. These writings reveal Warfield's understanding of how apologetics relates to God, human beings, and salvation. As he affirms the distinctive doctrines expressed in the Westminster Confession, it can be seen that he emphasizes both the objective and subjective character of human knowing and how these relate to God, sin, and salvation. In the process he emphasizes not only the unitary nature of truth, but also discusses the precise details of that unity.

96. Ibid., 230.
97. Ibid.

7

Apologetics in Principle: Establishing the Biblical Gospel

HAVING DEFINED, diagramed, and described theology in all its branches in "The Idea of Systematic Theology,"[1] Warfield had occasion in the early 1900s to clarify his perspective on apologetics even further. His most explicit delineation is his article "Apologetics," in *The New Schaff-Herzog Encyclopedia of Religious Knowledge*.[2] It is difficult to determine exactly when this perspective crystallized in Warfield's mind. It does not appear that the distinctive emphases in his view differed greatly, if at all, from the theological emphases of his Princeton predecessors.[3] Obviously, some of the matters to which he refers in the *Schaff-Herzog* article, such as the manifestations of rationalism in Ritschl's theology, were not discussed by his predecessors simply because some of the issues to which Warfield was referring were only contemporary to his own situation.[4] The following analysis emphasizes the *content* of his beliefs on apologetics rather than a strict temporal progression. The *Schaff-Herzog* article will be examined first, followed by an exploration of the application of these thoughts to two important works that directly touch upon

---

1. As in chapter 5, hereafter this essay will be referred to in the notes as IST.

2. Reprinted as Warfield, "Apologetics," *CW* 9:3–21.

3. See Aiken, "Variable and the Constant in Christian Apology." Aiken denied that any "true exhibition of the nature of Christianity can be purely defensive" (12). Thus, "a negative conviction of innocence must . . . be followed by a persuasion of the absolute excellence of the arraigned religion" (12–13). "Christianity must be the sole occupant of the shrine" (13). Still further, "the self-justification of Christianity is of course the refutation of all opposing claims" (14). Thus, Christian apologetics was seen as an enterprise that was offensive and defensive simultaneously.

4. Warfield, "Apologetics," *CW* 9:14–15. This is not to say rationalism was not present previously, but rather that Ritschl and the distinct expression he gave to rationalism was not part of the lives of those who lived prior to him.

his perspective. The first is his review of Herman Bavinck's book *De Zekerheid des Geloofs*, and the second is his introduction to Francis R. Beattie's book *Apologetics*.[5] In the former, Warfield criticizes Bavinck and Abraham Kuyper, along with what came to be known as the Amsterdam School. In his introduction to Beattie's book, Warfield addresses the topic of an "Apologetical *minimum*,"[6] which he briefly touches upon in the *Schaff-Herzog* article, but does not deal with at all in the Bavinck review.

Admittedly, the order is not the order in which these writings were published. The reason for this approach is that the precise time at which Warfield's perspective on apologetics formalized in his thinking is not known; therefore, a chronological approach is of little benefit. Instead, a thematic approach has been adopted. Hopefully, this way of organizing the description of his thoughts, and seeing his ideas demonstrated in practice, will aid in significantly clarifying Warfield's view of apologetics.

Defining, Describing, and Defending Apologetics

After noting that the work of Planck and Schleiermacher helped apologetics become an "accepted name of one of the theological disciplines or departments of theological science," Warfield addresses the term "apologetics" itself.[7] He distinguishes between "apologies," which "are defenses of Christianity," and "apologetics," which "undertakes not the defense, not even the vindication, but the establishment, not, strictly speaking, of Christianity, but rather of that knowledge of God which Christianity professes to embody."[8] Thus, from the beginning, Warfield emphasizes the constructive nature of apologetics. As he clarifies, "apologetics does not derive its contents or take its form or borrow its value from the prevailing opposition; but preserves through all varying circumstances its essential character as a positive and constructive science."[9] He also states,

---

5. Warfield, "Review of *De Zekerheid des Geloofs*," *SSW* 2:106–23 (hereafter "R. *Zekerheid*"). The Dutch title translates to "The Certainty of Faith." It was published in 1901, while Beattie's book was published in 1903. Warfield's review of Bavinck's book, though, first appeared in the *Princeton Theological Review* (January 1903) 138–48. There is significant overlap in the two works, even, at certain points, nearly verbatim wording. But each possesses some particular emphases that make them valuable for understanding Warfield's perspective. Warfield, "Introduction to Francis R. Beattie's *Apologetics*," *SSW* 2:93–105. (hereafter "Beattie's *Apologetics*").

6. Warfield, "Beattie's *Apologetics*," *SSW* 2:104.

7. Warfield, "Apologetics," *CW* 9:3.

8. Ibid.

9. Ibid., 4.

"so little is defense or vindication of the essence of apologetics that there would be the same reason for its existence and the same necessity for its work, were there no opposition in the world to be encountered and no contradiction to be overcome."[10] According to Warfield, the need for apologetics correlates with its essential nature, and has to do with the "fundamental needs of the human spirit."[11]

As he saw it, it is "incumbent" upon the Christian "to give a reason for the faith that is in him," and this means that it is "impossible to be a believer without a reason" for one's faith.[12] This, in turn, delineates the work of apologetics, which is "to bring this reason clearly out in his consciousness and make its validity plain."[13] Consequently, Warfield states:

> It is, in other words, the function of apologetics to investigate, explicate, and establish the grounds on which a theology—a science, or systematized knowledge of God—is possible; and on the basis of which every science which has God for its object must rest, if it be a true science with claims to a place within the circle of the sciences.[14]

Here we see the characteristic Princetonian emphasis on the unity of truth, the union of theology, epistemology, and metaphysics, the theocentric nature and ground of human knowledge, and the ability of the human mind to apprehend, comprehend, and rationally articulate knowledge. As a result, Warfield placed apologetics "at the head of the departments of theological science," or as prolegomena to the several branches of theology.[15]

In the article's second section, Warfield continues by expanding his discussion of the place of apologetics within theology.[16] He notes that "considerable confusion has reigned with respect to the conception and function of apologetics, and its place among the theological disciplines."[17] He then observes that writers have defined and described the work of apologetics in their own idiosyncratic ways, and he identifies the confus-

---

10. Ibid.
11. Ibid.
12. Ibid., 4. Warfield's language here reflects 1 Pet 3:15.
13. Ibid.
14. Ibid.
15. Ibid., 4–5.
16. Warfield, "Apologetics," *CW* 9:5. There are a total of eleven sections in the article.
17. Ibid.

ing of *apologetics* with *apologies* as driving these different treatments.[18] He proceeds to briefly explain some of the differing ways in which apologetics was being perceived in his day. Chief among these was to present apologetics as either (1) "the theory of apology" or (2) "the systematically organized vindication of Christianity in all its elements and details."[19] If the former is used, then apologetic's "function is to teach men how to defend Christianity," and it should be seen as part of the department of practical theology.[20] If the latter is used, then apologetics should be placed "as the culminating department of systematic theology," and viewed as "the intellectualistic side of practical theology, or as an independent discipline between the two."[21] Warfield identifies Kuyper and Francis Landey Patton as being among those configuring apologetics in this latter sense and "artificially" separating it "from polemic theology and other similar disciplines."[22]

Warfield maintains that differing views regarding what apologetics is supposed to "establish" also play a significant role in creating different conceptions of the discipline.[23] Some consider "the truth of the Christian religion, or the validity of that knowledge of God which theology presents in systematized form," to be the object that apologetics attempts to establish.[24] Furthermore, people's conception of the "nature and subject-matter of that theology" was by no means uniform.[25] Then again, if theology is "the science of faith," and apologetics is to establish this understanding, then it should be regarded as a "branch of psychology."[26] This would make the subject matter of apologetics, first, "the subjective experiences of the human heart," and, second, the establishment of the "objective validity" of "these subjective experiences."[27] If theology is "the 'science of religion,'" or the "science of the Christian religion," then apologetics should be regarded as "a branch of history." This would

18. Ibid.
19. Ibid.
20. Ibid.
21. Ibid.
22. Ibid., 5–6.
23. Ibid., 6.
24. Ibid.
25. Ibid.
26. Ibid.
27. Ibid., 6–7.

mean apologetics is a historical inquiry into "what those who are called Christians believe."[28]

If theology is defined "as the 'science of God,'" then apologetics should be thought of "as a branch of science," and should address "a body of objective facts."[29] Moreover, "it is absurd to say that these facts must be assumed and developed unto their utmost implications before we stop to ask whether they are facts."[30] Warfield, of course, as has already been seen, considered theology to be the science of God, and states, "so as it is agreed that theology is a scientific discipline and has as its subject-matter the knowledge of God, we must recognize that it must begin by establishing the reality as objective facts of the data upon which it is based."[31]

Names for Apologetics

Warfield believed that as soon as theology is regarded as a scientific discipline, there are various names that could be used to refer to "the discipline by which the validity of the knowledge of God" is established.[32] "Apologetics is the name that most naturally suggests itself," but he also acknowledged that "'general theology,' or 'fundamental theology,' or 'principal theology,' or 'philosophical theology,' or 'rational theology' or 'natural theology,'" were legitimate names.[33] Far more important than the name one uses is the *conception* of this theology that one holds. Specifically, it is necessary to regard apologetics as belonging to "the complete theology of the Christian revelation" in order to protect against "the fatally dualistic conception which sets natural and revealed theology over against each other as separable entities, each with its own presuppositions requiring establishment."[34] If natural and revealed theology are viewed in this dualistic way, then "apologetics would be split into two quite diverse disciplines, given very different places in the theological encyclopedia."[35]

---

28. Ibid., 7.
29. Ibid.
30. Ibid.
31. Ibid.
32. Ibid., 7–8; quote from p. 8.
33. Ibid., 7. The use of the terms "natural" and "rational" to modify theology does not automatically mean Warfield conceived of those terms in philosophically naturalistic or rationalistic ways.
34. Ibid.
35. Ibid., 8.

Thus, as Warfield saw it, one's conception of theology determines one's understanding of the nature and role of apologetics. He believed that to prevent a split between the objective and subjective realms in knowledge claims, one has to operate with a view of theology that sees it as, first and foremost, grounded in objective realities. Those who regard theology in this way perceive the task of apologetics in a particular way, and this is what Warfield next addresses.

"The True Task of Apologetics"[36]

Warfield acknowledges that it is both accurate and customary to define apologetics as "'the science which establishes the truth of Christianity as the absolute religion.'"[37] The more pressing question, though, is exactly *how* this is accomplished. He rejects the claim that it is the "business of apologetics to take up each tenet of Christianity in turn and seek to establish its truth by a direct appeal to reason."[38] He maintains that to do so would be to engage "in the old vulgar rationalism" and fall prey to the requirement "for a direct rational demonstration of the truth of each Christian teaching in turn."[39] Warfield felt that instead the point is "to establish the truth of Christianity as the absolute religion directly only as a whole, and in its details only indirectly."[40] According to him, recognizing this focus rescues one from "perhaps the most distracting question which has vexed the whole history of the discipline," namely, whether to address all of Christianity's details or "the essence of Christianity."[41]

From Warfield's perspective, "the details of Christianity are all contained in Christianity: the minimum of Christianity is just Christianity itself."[42] That is, because he believed in the unity of truth, all truths are inherently and inevitably connected. Thus, apologetics is for the purpose of "establishing the truth of Christianity as a whole, and only then to proceed to explicate it into its details, each of which, if soundly explicated, has its truth guaranteed by its place as a detail in an entity already

---

36. Ibid.
37. Ibid.
38. Ibid.
39. Ibid., 8–9.
40. Ibid., 9.
41. Ibid. This would seem to address what Cornelius Van Til referred to as a "blockhouse" methodology. See Van Til, *Defense of the Faith*, 114–22.
42. Warfield, "Apologetics," *CW* 9:9.

established in its entirety."[43] Apologetics, then, lays "the foundations on which the temple of theology is built, and by which the whole structure of theology is determined."[44] In doing so, it:

> ... establishes the constitutive and regulative principles of theology as a science; and in establishing these it establishes all the details which are derived from them by the succeeding departments, in their sound explication and systematization.[45]

Misconceptions of the Place and Function of Apologetics

Having addressed the overarching function of apologetics, Warfield returns to a subject already addressed generally, namely, the specific place of apologetics within theology.

Section five of his essay is similar to section two in subject matter, but in section five he also discusses misconceptions by specific theologians regarding the place and function of apologetics within theology:

> Hermann Schultz . . . divides it [apologetics] into great sections with a third interposed between them: the first, "the apology of the religious conception of the world"; the last, "the apology of Christianity"; while between the two stands "the philosophy of religion, religion in its historical manifestation." . . . Henry B. Smith, viewing apologetics as "historico-philospophical dogmatics," charged with the defense of 'the whole contents and substance of the Christian faith,' divided the material to much the same effect into what he calls fundamental, historical, and philosophical apologetics. . . . Francis R. Beattie divided [it] into (1) fundamental or philosophical apologetics, which deals with the problem of God and religion; (2) Christian or historical apologetics, which deals with the problem of revelation and the Scriptures; and (3) applied or practical apologetics, which deals with the practical efficiency of Christianity in the world.[46]

Warfield states that these misconceptions testify to "some failure in unity of conception" that arose "apparently from a deficient grasp of the peculiarity of apologetics as a department of theological science, and a consequent inability to permit it as such to determine its own contents and the natural order of its constituent parts." Thus, Warfield again dem-

43. Ibid.
44. Ibid.
45. Ibid.
46. Ibid., 11.

onstrates a stress on the unitary character of truth and an attempt to be consistent with it. He critiques others based on his understanding of their failures to be faithful to this unitary character.[47]

"The Idea of Systematic Theology" Revisited

In section six of his "Apologetics" article, (the section titled "The Conception of Theology as a Science"), Warfield hits upon some of the salient points presented and elaborated upon in "The Idea of Systematic Theology"[48] (examined earlier). The reality of theology as a science presupposes: (1) "the reality of its subject-matter," (2) the human minds capacity to receive data on this subject matter and reason about it, and (3) some medium of communication that brings this subject to the mind.[49] What this means for a view that sees apologetics as laying a foundation is that three main topics have to be addressed: God, religion, and revelation.[50] These three topics are correlated with establishing: (1) "the existence of God," (2) "the capacity of the human mind to know Him," and (3) "the accessibility of knowledge concerning Him."[51] With the establishment of these three topics, theology as a science is possible, but this in turn presupposes the exhausting of "all the accessible sources and means of knowing God."[52] One cannot "arbitrarily limit the data lying within its sphere to which it will attend," and get away with calling such an endeavor "science."[53] As a specific example, Warfield uses the idea that theology needs to address "the presence of Christianity in the world making claim to present a revelation of God adapted to the condition and needs of sinners and documented in Scriptures."[54] If this claim is established, it "must form a part of the fundamental department of theology in which are laid the foundations for the systematization of

---

47. Ibid., 12.
48. IST, 49–90.
49. Ibid.
50. Ibid.
51. Warfield, "Apologetics," *CW* 9:11. When Warfield referred to "establishing God's existence," he did not mean that we create God. Rather, he had in mind helping a person accept the reality of God into his or her thinking. Warfield's conception of God included God's creation of all things out of nothing; God, thereby, being the source of all reality.
52. Ibid., 12.
53. Ibid.
54. Ibid.

the knowledge of God."⁵⁵ This in turn would necessitate apologetics addressing Christianity and the Bible.⁵⁶ Thinking of theology as a science, then, according to Warfield, means holding the view that apologetics establishes "the existence of a God who is capable of being known by man and who has made Himself known, not only in nature but in revelations of His grace to lost sinners, documented in the Christian Scriptures."⁵⁷ Warfield summarizes this section by stating that only with the "great facts" of "God, religion, revelation, Christianity, [and] the Bible" can we "go on and explicate the knowledge of God thus brought to us, trace the history of its workings in the world, systematize it, and propagate it in the world."⁵⁸

Parceling Out the Task

Next, Warfield takes up the topic of "The Five Subdivisions of Apologetics."⁵⁹ Although he is classifying apologetics into five divisions, Warfield acknowledges that the third subdivision that he lists could be subsumed "into its most closely related fellow," but he does not mention which "fellow" that would be, although it seems that it would be most closely related to historical apologetics.⁶⁰ Furthermore, though Warfield enumerates what each of the five subdivisions entail in terms of subject matter, he does not specifically state what characterizes the relationship between the five subdivisions.⁶¹ In addition, he gives names (philosophical, psychological, historical, and bibliological) to four of the subdivisions, but leaves the third unnamed, the one that he stated could be combined with the one to which it is most closely related. Each of the subdivisions is named according to the topics most immediately taken up by them.⁶² Thus, Warfield *sub*divides apologetics according to different tasks that must be accomplished *within* apologetics:

> . . . (1)The first, which may perhaps be called philosophical apologetics, undertakes the establishment of the being of God, as

55. Ibid.
56. Ibid.
57. Ibid.
58. Ibid.
59. Ibid., 13.
60. Ibid.
61. Ibid.
62. Ibid.

> a personal spirit, the creator, preserver, and governor of all things . . . (2) The second, which may perhaps be called psychological apologetics, undertakes the establishment of the religious nature of man . . . (3) To the third falls the establishment of the reality of the supernatural factor in history . . . (4) The fourth, which may perhaps be called historical apologetics, undertakes to establish the divine origin of Christianity as the religion of revelation in the special sense of that word . . . (5) The fifth, which may be called bibliological apologetics, undertakes to establish the trustworthiness of the Christian Scriptures as the documentation of the revelation of God for the redemption of sinners.[63]

This methodology demonstrates Warfield's stress on apologetics as fulfilling a particular practical end, which led to Warfield next addressing "The Value of Apologetics."[64]

Apologetics in the Wake of Mysticism and Rationalism

According to Warfield, the value that scholars see for apologetics varies according to their understanding of its nature and function.[65] As he analyzed it, the theological scholarly world of his time period, generally adrift in either mysticism or rationalism, saw very little need for apologetics.[66] Warfield believed that many theologians, scholars, and pastors had followed Schleiermacher's lead and had embraced Kant's epistemology, either in part or in whole, knowingly or unknowingly. From this they had concluded that the "subjective experience of faith" was the "ultimate fact."[67] The result was that "the only legitimate apologetic" was "the self-justification of this faith itself."[68] Warfield emphasized the ubiquitous nature of this way of thinking:

> For faith, it seems, after Kant, can no longer be looked upon as a matter of reasoning and does not rest on rational grounds, but is an affair of the heart, and manifests itself most powerfully when it has no reason out of itself (Brunetiere). If repetition had probative force, it would long ago have been established that

---

63. Ibid.
64. Ibid., 14.
65. Ibid.
66. Ibid.
67. Ibid.
68. Ibid.

faith, religion, theology, lie wholly outside of the realm of reason, proof, and demonstration.[69]

Warfield's view of apologetics was diametrically opposed to this dualistic pattern of thought, which bifurcates the subjective and objective realms in people's thinking. This division does not consider the Christian's reasoning about space/time, empirically verifiable realities, as having epistemic validity for the reality and propagation of the Christian faith. Consequently, Warfield identified the rationalism and mysticism prevalent in his day as undermining, if not altogether denying the need for, apologetics. As he expresses it, where rationalism prevails "the validity of apologetic proofs has been in more or less of their extent questioned."[70] With mysticism, "the validity of apologetics has been with more or less emphasis doubted."[71] Furthermore, he identified Albrecht Ritschl's distinction between "theoretical and religious knowledge" as possibly exhibiting the "most active" "form" of rationalism.[72] With Ritschl: "[R]eligious knowledge is not the knowledge of fact, but a perception of utility; and therefore positive religion, while it may be historically conditioned, has no theoretical basis, and is accordingly not the object of rational proof."[73] Still, rationalism was not the only major opponent of apologetics. Mysticism was exerting a significant influence as well.

According to Warfield, the mysticism he was encountering had a "wide spread inclination to set aside apologetics in favor of the 'witness of the Spirit.'"[74] This was because its adherents did not see the Christian's convictions as "the product of reason addressed to the intellect, but the immediate creation of the Holy Spirit in the heart."[75] Indeed, reasons, according to Warfield, were evidently considered by some to be "positively noxious," because they amounted to the substituting of "a barren

---

69. Ibid. Although Warfield criticized many features of the liberal theology of the nineteenth century, he readily identified and lauded the things that it did well. See "Century's Progress in Biblical Knowledge," *SSW* 2:3–13. This essay is one among many where Warfield's belief in the organic character of history and truth is present. See also "New Testament Puritanism," in Warfield, *Faith and Life*, 243–58.

70. Warfield, "Apologetics," *CW* 9:14.

71. Ibid.

72. Ibid., 14–15.

73. Ibid., 15.

74. Ibid.

75. Ibid.

intellectualism for a vital faith."[76] Warfield, though, identified this way of thinking as not corresponding to the true nature of either saving faith or of human beings. So, as Warfield notes:

> It seems to be forgotten that though faith be a moral act and the gift of God, it is yet formally conviction passing into confidence; and that all forms of convictions must rest on evidence as their ground, and it is not faith but reason which investigates the nature and validity of this ground.[77]

"Right Reason": The Regenerate Person's Reason Corresponds to Reality

Warfield[78] quotes Aquinas to corroborate his point regarding the reasonableness of saving faith: "'He who believes would not believe unless he saw that what he believes is worthy of belief.'"[79] The point is that even though saving faith is a gift from God, such faith is not an "irrational faith," or "a faith without cognizable ground in right reason."[80] Warfield continues:

> We believe in Christ because it is rational to believe in him, not even though it be irrational. Of course, mere reasoning cannot make a Christian; but that is not because faith is not the result of evidence, but because a dead soul cannot respond to evidence. The action of the Holy Spirit in giving faith is not apart from evidence, but along with evidence; and in the first instance consists in preparing the soul for the reception of the evidence.[81]

It should be emphasized that Warfield used the term "right reason" to refer to the reasoning of the regenerate sinner in accordance with true Christianity, not the reasoning of the unregenerate.[82] According to Warfield, the Christian is given the capacity for right reason along with saving faith. It should be further noted that this corresponds to exactly

---

76. Ibid.
77. Ibid.
78. Warfield, "Essence of Christianity and the Cross of Christ," *CW* 3:395. This is one of the places the term "right reason" can be found.
79. Ibid.
80. Ibid.
81. Ibid.
82. Ibid.

what Francis Turretin taught regarding "right reason."[83] Warfield did not believe that the regenerate sinner automatically possesses correct reasoning about everything by virtue of having been regenerated by the Holy Spirit. Warfield believed that human reason is progressively brought into conformity with God's truth, as can be seen from the following:

> One of the most grievous of the effects of sin is the deformation of the image of God reflected in the human mind, and there can be no recovery from sin which does not bring with it the correction of this deformation and the reflection in the soul of man of the whole glory of the Lord God Almighty. Man is an intelligent being; his superiority over the brute is found, among other things, precisely in the direction of all his life by his intelligence; and his blessedness is rooted in the true knowledge of his God—for this is life eternal, that we should know the only true God and Him whom He has sent. Dealing with man as an intelligent being, God the Lord has saved him by means of a revelation, by which he has been brought into an ever more and more adequate knowledge of God, and been led ever more and more to do his part in working out his own salvation with fear and trembling as he perceived with ever more and more clearness how God is working it out for him through mighty deeds of grace.[84]

---

83. For the use of the term "right reason" in Turretin, see his *Institutes of Elenctic Theology* 1:24–26. See Riddlebarger, "Lion of Princeton," 291–314, for the Scottish Presbyterian roots of Warfield's view of apologetics and the ministerial and instrumental use of reason that concurred with Turretin, but was not a rationalistic understanding. For the use of the term "right reason" in Charles Hodge's theology, see Helseth, "Moral Character and Moral Certainty," 56–66. Regarding the continuity in Hodge, Warfield, and Machen on the necessity of the Holy Spirit's work for saving faith, see Calhoun, *Majestic Testimony*, 417–21. For how Old Princeton faculty members before and after Warfield held to the belief that the regenerating work of the Holy Spirit was necessary for saving faith, see Helseth, "Moral Character and Moral Certainty." See Warfield, "Westminster Doctrine of Holy Scripture," in *The Westminster Assembly and Its Work, CW* 6:199; see 224–28 for Warfield's belief that the Scriptures teach, and the WCF confirms, the *instrument* of human reason to receive *some* true knowledge of God that leaves humans inexcusable for their rejection of God, but that it is the work of the inward illumination of the Holy Spirit that gives God's people right reason by which they are enabled to deduce from Scripture particular things not "expressly set down in Scripture." For a more detailed analysis of saving faith, see Warfield "Faith in Its Psychological Aspects," *CW* 9:313–42.

84. Warfield, "Biblical Idea of Revelation," *CW* 1:13. In the latter part of the quote, Warfield is quoting from John 17:3 and Phil 2:12. Warfield expressed on a number of occasions that human sin damaged thinking, or reasoning. This was a standard Calvinistic belief stated in the WCF, both in its Shorter and Larger Catechism. We should remind ourselves that Warfield had the Shorter Catechism memorized by the age of six and the

Apologetics in Principle: Establishing the Biblical Gospel

Cornelius Van Til, therefore, was incorrect in his assessment of Warfield's teaching on this point. Moreover, whatever rationalistic tendencies one may think exist in Warfield's view of apologetics, it obviously cannot be substantiated from the idea that Warfield taught that "right reason" was the reasoning of the unregenerate and that the Christian made an appeal to the non-Christian based on such unregenerate reasoning.[85] Instead, Warfield's view was that the Christian's saving faith reflects "right reason," or accurate or correct reason, and that this reasoning can be shown to correspond to the empirical, time/space realities that the non-Christian also has accessible to him or her. The unregenerate might still reject the regenerate person's conclusions, but the mere denial of a line of reasoning does not automatically render the rejected reasoning either incoherent or divergent from empirical reality. Nor does it, by the very nature of the case, rubberstamp every instance of reasoning of every Christian as "right." Warfield believed that sanctification is progressive, a process "by which he [the Christian] has been brought into an ever more and more adequate knowledge of God."[86]

Thus, in an ultimate sense, the non-Christian has to deny reality at a particular point, or even at numerous points, in order to avoid the conclusions reached by the regenerate person's right reason. That this is Warfield's view can be seen not only from the fourth section of "The Conception of Theology as a Science," but also from his repeated criticisms of some of the biblical critics for failing to attend to "all the avail-

---

Larger by sixteen, along with the Scripture proofs. Consider the following from Warfield, "Calvin's Doctrine of the Knowledge of God," in *CW* 5:44–45: "[T]he structure and organization of the world, and the things that daily happen out of the ordinary course of nature, that is under the providential government of God, bear witness to God which the dullest ear cannot fail to hear (Calvin, I. v. 1, 3, 7 esp. II. vi. 1); and that the light that shines from creation, while it may be smothered, cannot be so extinguished but that some rays of it find their way into the most darkened soul (Calvin, I. V. 14). . . . The sole cause of the failure of the natural revelation is to be found, therefore, in the corruption of the human heart. Two results flow from this fact. First, it is not a question of the extinction of the knowledge of God, but of the corruption of the knowledge of God. And secondly, men are without excuse for their corruption of the knowledge of God. On both points Calvin is insistent."

85. Van Til, *Defense of the Faith*, 264; *Christian Theory of Knowledge*, 244; Bahnsen, *Van Til's Apologetic*, 597–98, 602–12. For additional examples of criticisms that reflect and are based on an erroneous analysis of Warfield, see Bratt, "The Dutch Schools," 122. Bratt believes the Rogers and McKim proposal, which is critical of the Princetonians for their scholastic rationalism and deductive, defensive apologetics, "showed considerable debts to Dutch-Calvinist sources" (13).

86. Warfield, "Biblical Idea of Revelation," *CW* 1:13.

able evidence."[87] Warfield even branded some of these biblical critics "Herodlike" because of their murdering "a host of innocent facts which stood in the way of their purposes."[88]

According to Warfield, then, when Christianity is reconceptualized along the lines of rationalism and mysticism, it not only fails to do justice to what Scripture teaches, but also fails to take into full account reality as humans experience it. The result is that both mistakes, dressed within Christian garb, find little or no place for apologetics. These mistakes were identified by Warfield as leading to scholarship that is not only unbiblical but unscientific. Neither rationalism nor mysticism, in Warfield's estimation, has a place for apologetics because both operate with an unbiblical view of saving faith, which means an unbiblical view of human beings in relation to the object of their faith—Jesus. Thus, he felt it necessary to clarify the role apologetics possesses within the Christian faith.

The "Relation of Apologetics to the Christian Faith"

Warfield[89] most certainly did not believe that men could be made Christians by apologetics.[90] What then was the point of apologetics? In Warfield's view, "apologetics supplies to Christian men the systematically organized basis on which the faith of Christian men must rest."[91] It is at this point that Warfield communicates an important distinction; the distinction between the beliefs/truths that are conscious for the individual believer in his or her expression of Christian belief, and what those beliefs in reality rest upon. In other words, there is a difference between what a Christian thinks he understands about his or her act of faith, and its full basis and explication. As Warfield puts it, "It is not necessary for his act of faith that all the grounds of this conviction should be drawn into

---

87. Warfield, "Rights of Criticism and of the Church," *SSW* 2:595–603. After surveying and analyzing the best the higher critics had to offer, Warfield, rendered the following judgment: "Modern negative criticism neither on internal nor on external grounds has been able to throw any doubt on the authenticity of a single book of our New Testament" (418). "Modern criticism has absolutely no valid argument to bring against the church doctrine of verbal inspiration, drawn from the phenomena of Scripture" (423). See also "Christian Evidences: How Affected by Recent Criticisms," *SSW* 2:124–31; "Inspiration and Criticism," *CW* 1:395–425; and "Dr. Briggs Critical Method."

88. Warfield, "Christian Evidences," *SSW* 2:130.

89. Warfield, "Apologetics," 16. The section title is taken from Warfield's section title on this page.

90. Ibid.

91. Ibid.

full consciousness and given explicit assent of his understanding, though it is necessary for his faith that sufficient ground for his conviction be actively present and working in his spirit."[92] Thus, Warfield distinguished between how the believer thought about his faith and what was fully true of his faith.

Put another way, Warfield distinguished between the Christian's subjective comprehension of saving faith and the objective truth about saving faith. In turn, this certainly means that, by the very nature of the case, anyone *not* operating with this distinction (not division) between the objective and subjective realms, as Warfield did, will either simply not understand his argument at this point, or will deny that it has any truthfulness.[93] His response to any thinking that fails to make this distinction, and thereby collapses the Christian faith into simply the subjective realm, was to call it absurd.[94] For Warfield, calling this failure to distinguish between an objective and subjective realm absurd was not simply an expression of his feelings or thoughts on the issue; rather, it was a genuine philosophical assessment. To function either by collapsing the objective into the subjective, or by divorcing the two realms from each other completely, in principle renders all claims to knowledge in any sphere literally meaningless, incoherent, or unintelligible. As Warfield saw it, it simply is not a viable intellectual option. The imbalance that existed in certain forms of biblical scholarship during Warfield's day is evident by the fact that saving faith was relegated to the subjective sphere of "faith" and compartmentalized away from the objective sphere of "reason" or "science." Warfield operated with the belief that the God of Scripture was the creator, sustainer, judge, and redeemer of all reality. This means that both the empirical realities accessible to human beings (and even those that are not) and their subjective experiences are forever united, correlative to one another, and indistinguishable apart from one another. True biblical Christianity is about a particular interpretation of the empirical realities of the past and present that is related to the future, but is only accessible to the sinner through the supernatural work of the Holy Spirit. Apologetics is necessary because the subjective experience from the Holy

---

92. Ibid.

93. The point is not to render a verdict on whether such a denial is valid. The point is simply to illuminate what the state of the case would be if in fact one did not accept Warfield's premise of two distinct realms in epistemology (objective and subjective) that are united, but not conflated into each other in such a way as to render them indistinguishable from one another.

94. Warfield, "Right of Systematic Theology," *SSW* 2:219–29.

Spirit is not disconnected from the empirically verifiable or objective realities of human existence.

Thus, for Warfield, it is necessary for the Christian's faith "to reason in the form of scientific judgment, that the grounds on which it rests be explicated and established."[95] According to Warfield, as a science, theology has a practical dimension that addresses "how that knowledge of God with which it [theology] deals objectively may best be made the subjective possession of man."[96] Still, before theology is able to do this it has to establish "its right to rank" as knowledge.[97] If theology does not establish "its right to rank" as knowledge, it will merely hang "in the air" and "present the odd spectacle among the sciences of claiming a place among a series of systems of knowledge for an elaboration of pure assumptions."[98]

Apologetics: Before and After Christ's Incarnation

Warfield concluded his essay by briefly addressing the history of the discipline of apologetics. Apologetics is not, and has never been, only a Christian endeavor. It was a field of study for Plato, and in turn, for any others who thought of "God and the supernatural order," or who probed the justification for *believing* in "God and the supernatural order."[99] It was with the advent of Christianity that the "contents of theology to be stated became richer," and "the efforts to substantiate it became more fertile in apologetical elements."[100] Still, according to Warfield, one should be careful not to confuse "the apologies of the early Christian ages with formal apologetics."[101] Warfield considered Augustine "the most profound of all the defenders of Christianity among the Fathers," Eusebius of Caesarea "the most learned," and together they were "the greatest apologists of the patristic age."[102] Along with the "City of God," Augustine's writings, shaped within the furnace of theological controversy, formed "a vast mass of apologetical material" that Warfield considered still relevant.[103] As a

---

95. Warfield, "Apologetics," *CW* 9:16.
96. Ibid.
97. Ibid.
98. Ibid.
99. Ibid., 17.
100. Ibid., 16.
101. Ibid., 17.
102. Ibid.
103. Ibid., 17–18.

Apologetics in Principle: Establishing the Biblical Gospel

"constructive science," though, apologetics did not come "to its rights" until the scholastic period. According to Warfield, the "primary effort" of "the whole theological activity of the Middle Ages" "was the justification of faith to reason."[104] He regarded Anselm and Aquinas as "types of the whole series" of theologians during this time.[105] The Renaissance's "re-pristination of heathenism" brought apologetics to center stage, while the Reformation era "drove apologetics out of sight," though the Reformation theologians' work contributed to the "apologetical material."[106]

As Warfield finishes this essay, it is possible to catch sight of his understanding of the flow of philosophical thought subversive to biblical Christianity stretching from the end of the seventeenth century to his day. As he saw it, "irreligion" and "indifferentism" spread among the people "in the exhaustion of the seventeenth century," and it was indifferentism that ripened "into naturalism among the leaders of thought."[107] He recognized Philippe De Mornay (1581) and Hugo Grotius (1627) as "typical apologists" of the beginning part of this time period, Pascal as holding sway during its middle portion, and Butler and Paley as bringing it to a close.[108] Warfield summarizes the development of apologetics from Paley to his day as follows:

> As the assault against Christianity shifted its basis from the English deism of the early half of the eighteenth century through the German rationalism of its later half, the idealism which dominated the first half of the nineteenth century, and thence to the materialism of its later years, period after period was marked in the history of apology, and the particular elements of apologetics which were especially cultivated changed with the changing thought. But no epoch was marked in the history of apologetics itself, until under the guidance of Schleiermacher's attempt to trace the organism of the departments of theology, K. H. Sack essayed to set forth a scientifically organized "Christian Apologetics" (Hamburg, 1829; ed. 2, 1841). Since then an unbroken series of scientific systems of apologetics has flowed from the press.[109]

---

104. Ibid., 18.
105. Ibid.
106. Ibid.
107. Ibid.
108. Ibid.

109. Ibid., 19. Notice that, from Warfield's perspective, Christianity was under "assault." Further, since he perceived apologetics as having a constructive purpose, his conception warrants thinking of Christian apologetics as a kind of counter offensive.

According to Warfield, these various systems differed "in almost every conceivable way."[110] They differed according to their understanding of:

> ... the nature, task, compass and encyclopedic place of the science; in their methods of dealing with the material; in their conception of Christianity itself; and of religion and of God and of the nature of the evidence on which belief in one or the other must rest.[111]

Still, there was agreement that apologetics should be "a special department of theological science, capable of and demanding separate treatment."[112] It was in this way, then, that "the last two-thirds of the nineteenth century" saw apologetics come "to its rights."[113]

Yet, as we have already seen, though there was a distinct place for the treatment of apologetics within many theologians' conception of theology, not all theologians agreed on exactly where that place was within the realm of theology. Though Warfield believed that apologetics functioned as prolegomena to theology, some of those even within the Reformed camp, of which Warfield was a member, still continued to see very little need for apologetics. In two of his very early twentieth-century works, Warfield addressed issues directly related to the conception and function of apologetics, as these topics were handled by Herman Bavinck and Francis R. Beattie. Some of what appeared in the *Schaff-Herzog* article was actually repetition of points made more specifically in the review of Bavinck's book and in the introduction to Beattie's.

Admonishing Bavinck and Kuyper

In both the review and the introduction, Warfield addressed what he saw as a deficiency in some Dutch Reformed circles regarding the conception and practice of apologetics.[114] This view (later called the Amsterdam view) heralded most prominently by Abraham Kuyper and Herman Bavinck, was considered by Warfield to be a misconception because of its failure to recognize the proper relationship between the Spirit's work of regeneration and the sinner's comprehension and apprehension of the grounds of

110. Ibid.
111. Ibid.
112. Ibid.
113. Ibid.
114. Ibid. For helpful introductions to Kuyper and Bavinck, see Bratt, "Dutch Schools."

conviction for his or her faith. Warfield believed the Amsterdam view capitulated to the mysticism rampant in certain liberal reconceptualizations of the Christian faith. Thus, he accuses Kuyper and Bavinck of having accepted in principle the metaphysical and epistemological presuppositions of Kant and Schleiermacher. Though Warfield believed that much of what Kuyper and Bavinck offered in the totality of their theological work was biblical, he nonetheless faulted them for their view of apologetics and indicated that this view revealed an incipient mysticism that placated more radical manifestations of mysticism inimical to a biblically accurate conception of the Christian faith.

Commending and Critiquing Bavinck

Warfield called Bavinck's *De Zekerheid des Geloofs* a "delightful booklet."[115] According to Warfield, it provided "a popular discussion of the whole matter of certitude with reference to Christianity."[116] Warfield goes on to say that the first part of the "booklet" addresses the practical nature of the subject matter and defines certitude as "the complete resting of the spirit in an object of knowledge."[117] The second part entails "a rapid but illuminating survey" of "the history of certitude of faith in the Church."[118] Warfield notes the graciousness and clarity in Bavinck's judgments against those perspectives within Christendom that had deviated in various ways from a biblically faithful handling of the certitude of faith. Both Roman Catholics and Protestants are warned regarding their particular pitfalls: either works righteousness or doctrinal righteousness. Bavinck cautions Protestants that the former at least results in acts that benefit others, while the latter only leads to "loveless pride."[119]

Though the laudable results among the Moravians and Methodists (work righteousness) are commended, the overly subjective tendencies within these movements are faulted. Both are criticized for failing to deal substantively with the doctrine of God as creator and for underestimating "the value and significance" of the "earthly spheres of art and science, of literature and politics, of domestic and social economy," which, as a result, "are consequently not reformed and regenerated by the Christian

---

115. Warfield, "R. *Zekerheid*," 106.
116. Ibid.
117. Ibid., 107.
118. Ibid.
119. Ibid., 108.

principle."[120] This more expansive and broad conception of the Christian faith and life, characteristic of the Dutch Reformed, was shared by Warfield and Old Princeton. Warfield even uses this opportunity to explain the inadequacy of the criticism often lobbied against the Reformed doctrine of predestination as it was understood by those antagonistic to it. The idea that the Reformed doctrine of predestination leads to our earthly life having little significance can only be sustained, said Warfield, based on "the extremest [sic] individualistic presuppositions."[121]

The third part of the booklet is an explanation of how Christian certitude is gained.[122] It is on this subject that Warfield criticizes Bavinck. According to Warfield, Bavinck explains that there are two *illegitimate* ways to achieve certitude: "the apologetical and experimental ways."[123] The former of these consists of establishing the existence of God through reasoning and then attaining, through reasoning as well, subsequent truths integral to biblical Christianity that then terminate in faith in Jesus for salvation.[124] The latter method is that which was endorsed by Schleiermacher and essentially deifies individual experience.[125] Bavinck, according to Warfield,[126] believed that certitude was "the fruit of faith itself."[127] Bavinck states: "certitude flows to us immediately and directly out of faith itself; certitude is an essential quality of faith, it is inseparable from it and belongs to our nature."[128] Warfield saw some problems with this conception.

For Warfield, it is a "debatable point" as to whether "'certitude of the truth of the Christian religion' and 'assurance of faith' imply one another, and neither is ever present without the other.'"[129] This debate revolves around one's definition of faith, and this, of course, is intimately related to one's conception of human knowledge and its acquisition. Warfield maintains that faith is "a specific form of persuasion or conviction, and

120. Ibid.
121. Ibid., 110.
122. Ibid.
123. Ibid.
124. Ibid.
125. Ibid.
126. Ibid., 112. Here he admits that he is not sure he has "done full justice" to Bavinck's exposition.
127. Ibid., 111.
128. Ibid., 112.
129. Ibid.

all persuasion or conviction is grounded in evidence."[130] It was not readily apparent to Warfield that the evidence in which the conviction of the truth of Christianity is grounded is identical to the evidence in which assurance of personal redemption is grounded.[131] While Warfield was willing to admit that at some point they do "coalesce," he saw problems with the way Bavinck conceived their relationship.

Warfield makes the point that "the direct act of saving faith" is not the basis upon which one's certainty of the truth of Christianity rests.[132] This would be to reverse the order of their relationship.[133] It would be a *non sequitur*, however, to then conclude that one has to be some type of scholar in order to become a Christian, for the simple reason that philosophical and historical evidences are not the only ones that are compelling for Christianity, and one need not stockpile all the evidence in all subject spheres or even in one of them in order to exercise a rational and justified Christian faith.[134] As it is, though, the conception that Bavinck presented revealed why he, and those who agreed with him, esteemed apologetics so lightly.[135]

Though Bavinck acknowledges that Christians should not disparage using argumentation in order to give a reason for their hope, he states that, nonetheless, the "'proofs' the Christian can marshal are nevertheless insufficient to place the truth of Christianity beyond doubt."[136] Further, according to Warfield, Bavinck gives apologetics a secondary role and presents it in a curious relationship to the whole Christian faith by stating that "Apologetics is the fruit, not the root of faith."[137] To Warfield, this seems to demonstrate some "slight confusion."[138] Warfield affirms that evidences cannot produce faith, but neither can "the presentation of Christ in the gospel produce 'faith,'" because "'faith' is the gift of God."[139] But the gracious character of faith does not then mean that saving faith is

---

130. Ibid.
131. Ibid., 2:112–13.
132. Ibid., 113.
133. Ibid.
134. Ibid.
135. Ibid., 114.
136. Ibid.
137. Ibid.
138. Ibid.
139. Ibid.

not "grounded in 'the evidences.'"[140] The more accurate assessment is that one of the things God gives in saving faith is the ability to see the validity of the grounds of faith that are already present in the realities with which saving faith is joined. As Warfield states:

> But this faith that the prepared heart yields—is it yielded blindly and without reason, or is it yielded rationally and on the ground of sufficient reason? Does God the Holy Spirit work a blind and ungrounded faith in the heart? What is supplied by the Holy Spirit in working faith in the heart surely is not a ready-made faith, rooted in nothing and clinging without reason to its object; nor yet new grounds of belief in the object presented; but just a new power to the heart to respond to the grounds of faith, sufficient in themselves, already present to the mind.[141]

Moreover, the grounds upon which saving faith is rooted can and do, at times, produce a particular effect even in those polemicizing against Christianity.[142] According to Warfield, Bavinck's acknowledgement that the arguments for the truth of Christianity can and do, at times, silence "gainsayers" is an affirmation that the "'grounds'" for saving faith can produce a *type* of conviction in some minds, but they will still not possess salvation.[143] Warfield concludes that, thus, reasoning with non-Christians does "ground a genuine exercise of faith,"[144] even apart from the saving work of the Holy Spirit. According to him, recognition of this helps gain a better understanding of the nature of saving faith, its relationship to rational argumentation, and the work of the Holy Spirit. Central to an understanding of these matters is an understanding of sin's damage to a person's ability to trust in God, or depend upon him. This matter, in turn, was intimately joined to the Old Princeton understanding of the psychology of human faculties, which correlates with the belief that saving faith consists of factual knowledge (*notitia*), intellectual assent (*assensus*), and trust (*fiducia*).[145]

140. Ibid.
141. Ibid., 115.
142. Ibid.
143. Ibid. Bavinck evidently referred to it as "historical faith" and Warfield concurred that this is what it ought to be called.
144. Ibid., 115.
145. Ibid., 116. See also C. Hodge, *ST* 2:99–102 and 3:41–10; Stelten, *Dictionary of Ecclesiastical Latin*. For more intricate analyses regarding the character of saving faith by Warfield, see "Biblical Doctrine of Saving Faith," *CW* 2:467–508, where Warfield notes that Adolf Schlatter's "Der Glaube im NT" is "the most comprehensive work on the

Apologetics in Principle: Establishing the Biblical Gospel

According to Warfield, sin instituted a new relationship between God and human beings so that they were no longer able to exercise faith in a fiducial sense, while yet still capable of faith in an intellectual sense.[146] This "intellectual" faith consists of Man's innate sense of dependence on God, something that is integral to Man's self-consciousness.[147] Although this "intellectual" faith in relation to dependence on God remained part of the human makeup, sin caused faith in a fiducial sense to become "unfaith" or "distrust."[148] There is still present in fallen sinners a type of faith in God that "takes the 'form' of fear and despair."[149] The change of our faith from fear and despair to loving trust is not our work, but the work of the Holy Spirit.[150] Still, it is true of both types of faith that they are grounded in an understanding of the evidence that is inherent in the consciousness of each person.[151] Though the evidence for saving faith does not possess the ability to *produce* saving faith in an unregenerate sinner, it does not follow that rational argumentation regarding the evidence for saving faith is irrelevant to the work of the Spirit.[152] Herein rests one of the substantive points of disagreement that Warfield had with Kuyper and Bavinck on the subject of apologetics.

Two "Kinds" of Men and the Disparaging of Apologetics

Warfield faulted the Amsterdam theologians for making too little of apologetics, and saw Kuyper's depiction of "'two kinds of science'" from "'two kinds of men'" as a contrast being applied in an overly absolute sense.[153] Warfield expanded on his point by analyzing the doctrine of sin and what precisely sin has done to humans. Sin, he states, "has not destroyed or altered in its essential nature any one of man's faculties, although (since

---

biblical idea of faith" (507). See also "Faith In Its Psychological Aspects," *CW* 9:313–42.

146. Warfield, "R. *Zekerheid*," 116.

147. Ibid. I am calling this "innate" because Warfield states that "so long as he remains human he cannot escape the consciousness of dependence on God."

148. Ibid.

149. Ibid.

150. Ibid.

151. Ibid., 116–17.

152. Ibid.

153. Ibid., 117. "Beattie's *Apologetics*," 100–101, covers these same matters. Some might think that Warfield made too much over the choice of the word "kind" in Kuyper's construal. For Warfield the issue could be seen through this term because of the place that Kuyper gave to apologetics within Christian theology.

it has affected *homo totus et omnis*) it has affected the operation of them all."[154] This means that "man neither reasons, nor feels, nor wills as he ought," and therefore all of our scientific work is stained by this corruption, though such work is "affected in different degrees and through different channels" "in accordance with the nature of their object."[155] Up to this point, Warfield completely agreed with Kuyper. Where Warfield disagreed with him, and others siding with the Amsterdam theologian, was in how to conceive of the relationship between the scientific work of unregenerate and regenerate sinners.[156]

The difference between the two, according to Warfield, is one of "perfection" rather than "kind of performance."[157] Thus, Warfield argues there are not two different *kinds* of science. Instead, there is one science with varying degrees of perfection to it that mark the work of both unregenerate and regenerate sinners.[158] The unregenerate sinner is bound to engage in an "imperfect science—falling away from the ideal, here, there, and elsewhere, on account of all sorts of deflecting influences, entering it at all points of the process."[159] From Warfield's perspective, the unregenerate sinner is obviously engaged in an imperfect science precisely because the unregenerate sinner is not pressing the knowledge issues in relation to the Triune God of Scripture. Warfield's view does not consider the unregenerate sinner's every thought, at every single point, false. He does, however, maintain that the *regenerate* sinner, who presses the same knowledge issues but in relation to the God of Scripture, will invariably be engaged in a "fuller and truer"[160] science. Warfield reasons that regenerate and unregenerate sinners occupy the same material realm, and are marked by realities that are what they are regardless of one's perceptions of them. Both the regenerate and unregenerate remain human sinners, although

---

154. Warfield, "R. *Zekerheid*," 117; "Beattie's *Apologetics*," 100.

155. Warfield, "R. *Zekerheid*," 117. In "Beattie's *Apologetics*," 100, Warfield states that "The depraved man neither thinks, nor feels, nor wills as he ought; and the products of his action as a scientific thinker cannot possibly escape the influence of this everywhere operative destructive power."

156. Though it is certainly a worthy pursuit to discern to what degree, if any, Warfield accurately understood Kuyper and others on this point of two different *kinds* of men, this is not my primary concern. My primary concern is to discern Warfield's understanding of Kuyper and his response to Kuyper on this point, and others related to it.

157. Warfield, "R. *Zekerheid*," 117.

158. Ibid.

159. Ibid.

160. Ibid., 118.

Apologetics in Principle: Establishing the Biblical Gospel

in the midst of very different conditions.¹⁶¹ For Warfield, it certainly is true that the perceptions, analyses, argumentation, and conclusions of regenerate and unregenerate sinners cannot be classified as identical. Still, God created only one reality, and it does not become something else other than what God created and providentially governs simply because people do not perceive it correctly. From Warfield's perspective, his debate with Kuyper could be construed as a disagreement over the exact nature of the relationship between the objective and subjective elements in epistemology. In particular, it hinged on their differing conceptions of the noetic effects of sin and what is and is not accomplished through regeneration.

For Warfield, because "regenerated man remains a sinner," the contrast between the unregenerate sinner and the regenerate can only possibly be conceived of as absolute when the Christian's sanctification is complete.¹⁶² As Warfield saw it, "the perfected ectypal science" will exist only "in the mind of perfected humanity."¹⁶³ Although regeneration begins the sanctification process, which has an intellectual component that increases "intensively and extensively" throughout his life here, it does not allow for an absolute contrast between the intellect of the regenerate and unregenerate in *this* lifetime.¹⁶⁴ While they both remain in this world, the regenerated person has the same faculties as the unregenerate. The difference between the two is that the regenerated sinner has had his or her faculties, in some measure, restored to their proper functioning.¹⁶⁵ Still, for Warfield, the regenerated sinner has not ceased being a sinner, and therefore, the regenerate will continue to operate under the noetic affects of sin.¹⁶⁶ Thus, the regenerate sinner, strictly speaking, does not possess, during this lifetime, the ability to produce a different *kind* of science than that of the unregenerate.¹⁶⁷ Warfield considered the science produced by the regenerate to be the "best part" of the science produced by humanity and, by so doing, he granted that there was a sense in which the Christian has a type of privileged epistemic position.¹⁶⁸ Yet any "ideal

161. Ibid; see also "Beattie's *Apologetics*," 101.
162. Warfield, "R. *Zekerheid*," 118; "Beattie's *Apologetics*," 101.
163. Warfield, "R. *Zekerheid*," 119; "Beattie's *Apologetics*," 102.
164. Warfield, "R. *Zekerheid*," 118; "Beattie's *Apologetics*," 101.
165. Warfield, "R. *Zekerheid*," 118; "Beattie's *Apologetics*," 101.
166. Warfield, "R. *Zekerheid*," 118; "Beattie's *Apologetics*," 101.
167. Warfield, "R. *Zekerheid*," 118; "Beattie's *Apologetics*," 101.
168. Warfield, "R. *Zekerheid*," 118. For Warfield, though, precisely because he gave a

science" produced by human beings can only rightly consist of the work of both the regenerate and unregenerate.[169] The two types of people carry out the work together.

Furthermore, according to Warfield, it might be doubtful even after the sinner's sanctification is complete that the contrast of "the science of the two classes of men could be absolute."[170] After all, even the fully sanctified human remains human. Or, as Warfield wrote, "Even sinful men and sinless men are alike fundamentally men; and being both men, they know fundamentally alike."[171] It is precisely at this point that a significant part of the nature of Warfield's epistemology can be seen, for he writes, "There is ideally but one science, the subject of which is the human spirit, and the object, all that is."[172] This is significant because Warfield is affirming that the knowing subject is not the human mind or reasoning but the human *spirit*. Human knowing, for Warfield, is comprehensively and fundamentally religious or spiritual, which is to say moral, with the intellect conceived of as a constituent aspect of, and subordinated to, the religious or spiritual element. This reflects Warfield's most basic commitment to the belief that human beings are creatures created in the image of God.[173]

Despite these disagreements, Warfield still saw commonality between himself and Kuyper. He lauded Kuyper for recognizing that, in disagreements over knowledge among human beings, the one who ultimately wins is the one who has the "strongest energy and clearest thought."[174] Warfield questioned, however, why Kuyper did not then recognize that it is regeneration that prepares the sinner for having this stronger and clearer thought.[175] The regenerate sinner has the capacity to produce a

---

prominent place to an objective realm that did not change because of human perceptions or misperceptions of it, this privileged epistemic position would not be rightly construed as working contrary to the objective realm.

169. Ibid, 118–19. See also "Beattie's *Apologetics*," 101.

170. Warfield, "R. *Zekerheid*, 118.

171. Ibid.

172. Ibid. See also "Beattie's *Apologetics*," 101. This helps us to see that Warfield's conception of epistemology and theology resists in significant ways the label of rationalistic. When stating the true subject of human knowledge he did not say it was the human mind or intellect or reasoning capacities. He wrote that it was the human *spirit*.

173. This reflects Warfield's commitment to the Scriptures and the WCF. This corroborates Helseth's thesis. See Helseth's works listed in the bibliography.

174. Warfield, "R. *Zekerheid*," 118; "Beattie's *Apologetics*," 102.

175. Warfield, "R. *Zekerheid*," 118. Warfield's exact question was: "Why is not the

"better scientific outlook, and the better scientific product," while, to be sure, still working in conjunction with unregenerate sinners in the one "edifice of truth," of human knowledge.[176] This "edifice of truth" does rise through the work of unregenerate sinners, but it rises more quickly as the result of God's regenerating work upon his people, and their work following this regeneration.[177] Warfield then clarified how he understood God's knowledge in relation to Man's, both in its regenerate and unregenerate forms, and why it is a danger to misconstrue the relationship.

The Communal and Historical Character of Human Knowledge

Warfield's belief was that perfect science is only possible within the mind of God, and this consists of "perfect comprehension of all that is, in its organic completeness."[178] It is only "in the mind of perfected humanity" that "the perfected ectypal science" could exist.[179] In humanity's fallen state, both with the regenerate and unregenerate, human science or knowledge (these were synonymous terms for Warfield) is "only a broken reflection of the object," more accurately assessed as a "deflection."[180] The fundamental work of science is to complete "the edifice" and correct "the deflection."[181] Such work, then, is properly understood along both communal and historical lines. That is, the edifice of truth or knowledge is the work of the human race collectively throughout its entire history. It is regenerate sinners who possess the capacity to work more effectively on this project, and it is their work that Warfield believed would "increase intensively and extensively" through the progression of time.[182] Thus, Warfield understood human knowledge from the perspective that human faculties are comprehensively moral and are simultaneously bound to a

---

palingenesis to be conceived simply as preparing those stronger and clearer *spirits* (italics mine), whose thoughts shall finally prevail?" The almost verbatim quote appears in "Beattie's *Apologetics*," 102.

176. Warfield, "R. *Zekerheid*," 118–19; "Beattie's *Apologetics*," 102.

177. Warfield, "Beattie's *Apologetics*," 102. In "R. *Zekerheid*," 118, he refers to it as humanity's "common edifice."

178. Warfield, "R. *Zekerheid*," 119; "Beattie's *Apologetics*," 102.

179. Warfield, "R. *Zekerheid*," 119; "Beattie's *Apologetics*," 102. This was a rather standard way of thinking of the matter during the post-Reformation era, and that pattern of thought, as we have already seen, possessed significant continuity with reformation and medieval thought. See Muller, *PRRD* 1:225–38.

180. Warfield, "R. *Zekerheid*," 119; "Beattie's *Apologetics*," 102.

181. Warfield, "R. *Zekerheid*," 119; "Beattie's *Apologetics*," 102.

182. Warfield, "R. *Zekerheid*," 119; "Beattie's *Apologetics*," 102.

historical process. Eventually, as Warfield puts it, "the end comes" and then "the regenerated universe" will be "the well-comprehended object of the science of the regenerated race."[183] This being the case, it is more than a minor mistake to bifurcate the knowledge of regenerate and unregenerate humans into two fundamentally different kinds of knowledge, so that one actually construes them, not as possessing a radical union with one another and having something to say to each other, but as possessing a disunion and having virtually no means by which they can dialogue with each other in any meaningful way. Warfield believed that this is what Kuyper and Bavinck had done, and this can be seen even more clearly from where they placed apologetics within the theological taxonomy.

The Regenerate's Knowledge: Winning the "Way to Ultimate Recognition"

According to Warfield, "the vindication of Apologetics" will be seen when the science of regenerate sinners eventually achieves "recognition."[184] As Warfield puts it: "the task of the Christian is surely to continue hopefully to urge 'his stronger and purer thought' in all its details on the attention of men."[185] There are three things that Warfield maintains are simply not true: (1) that the Christian "cannot soundly prove his position," (2) "that the arguments he [the Christian] urges are not sufficient to validate the Christian religion," and (3) that the evidences for the Christian religion are "inaccessible" to the minds of the unregenerate.[186] In his introduction to Beattie's *Apologetics*, he states that "it is not true that the Christian view of the world is subjective merely, and is incapable of validation in the form of pure reason."[187] Thus, the only recourse for a Christian is to repeatedly

---

183. Warfield, "R. *Zekerheid*," 119; "Beattie's *Apologetics*," 102. Here again we see that Warfield interpreted humans as integrated with the entire creation and he viewed the redemption of God's people as inextricably knitted to God's redemption of the entire creation. This is distinctively a Westminsterian view that was also held by Calvin, who understood the doctrine of God as Redeemer within the context of the doctrine of God as Creator. Cf. the WCF and Calvin's *Institutes*. See also Warfield, "Doctrine of the Knowledge of God," *CW* 5:29–130.

184. Warfield, "R. *Zekerheid*," 118; "Beattie's *Apologetics*," 103.

185. Warfield, "R. *Zekerheid*," 118; "Beattie's *Apologetics*," 103.

186. Warfield, "R. *Zekerheid*," 119. Here Warfield uses the term "sinful" in contradistinction to "Christian." We should not lose sight of his already well-established point that the Christian is, in this lifetime, still a sinner. He used the phrase "sinful men" as a synonym for "unregenerate" men.

187. Warfield, "Beattie's *Apologetics*," 103.

urge and demonstrate how the Christian's epistemic work will be part of "the slowly rising fabric of truth."[188] This action will serve not only "his own generation" but also "all the generations of men."[189] It is also true, however, that what such a Christian would *not* be doing with apologetics is making people Christians. But that does not mean that apologetics is of little to no consequence and should be relegated to a small, or even insignificant, part within Christian theology and evangelism.

Understanding the Proper Place and Function of Apologetics: Offensive Not Defensive

Warfield, as he would later repeat in the *Schaff-Herzog* article, admitted that it is absurd to argue "that Apologetics will of itself make a man a Christian."[190] However, it is not the "proclaimed gospel" that makes people Christians either, because "only the Spirit of life can communicate life to a dead soul."[191] For Warfield, it was simply axiomatic that God, through the Holy Spirit, regenerates sinners and makes them Christians. Still, Warfield declared that affirming this did not give people warrant to think that reasoning with non-Christians is a waste of time or inherently offensive. God can and does, at times, work apart from secondary means, but he also can and does use secondary means to accomplish his purposes (cf. WCF III, 1–2).[192] Warfield's conception was that apologetics has a "primary" and "conquering part" in the Christianization of the world.[193] This was because, for Warfield, apologetics gives the Christian "the systematically organized basis on which the faith of Christian men must rest."[194] As a result, from Warfield's perspective, it is foolish to profess that unregenerate science is of a fundamentally different kind than regenerate, because this leads to relinquishing the very fight that the regenerate should be glad to enjoin and which he is fully capable, by the Holy Spirit, of winning. Moreover, unregenerate science is not wholly without merit and, as such, is part of the entire "edifice of truth" that will eventually

---

188. Warfield, "R. *Zekerheid*," 120.

189. Ibid. It would seem that we see here a glimpse of at least part of the way Warfield viewed his own work.

190. Warfield, "R. *Zekerheid*," 120; "Apologetics," *CW* 9:16.

191. Warfield, "Apologetics," *CW* 9:16.

192. Warfield, "Predestination," *CW* 2:3–67.

193. Warfield, "R. *Zekerheid*," 120; "Beattie's *Apologetic*s," 103; "Apologetics," *CW* 9:3–4.

194. Warfield, "Apologetics," *CW* 9:16.

be completed by the redeemed.[195] Yet, a necessary part of this "edifice of truth" is the conflict between the regenerate and unregenerate that Kuyper's scheme, in principle, would prevent from even taking place. Still further, part of ensuring that Christians do not avoid the conflict is ensuring that they have a correct understanding of what is and is not accomplished through apologetics.

Warfield did not think of apologetics as simply "defensive," but believed deeply that it is integral to establishing Christianity in the world; but he also did not think one needed to become deeply knowledgeable about apologetics and the arguments for Christianity before one could become a Christian.[196] Warfield believed that "ordinarily" it is not necessary for "the whole 'body of evidences'" in support of Christianity to be presented to a non-Christian in order for him or her to be convinced of Christianity's truthfulness.[197] Thus, it is not necessary to attain expert status in apologetics before engaging in fruitful Christian reasoning. Nonetheless, it is still true that the faith of every Christian is "a conviction of truth . . . founded upon evidence," and that "this kind and amount of evidence constitutes 'Apologetics.'"[198]

Warfield believed that the world confronts Christianity with plenty of "energy of thought" and an "incredible fertility in attack and defense," and that this requires a corresponding response by Christians, one that results in not merely a defense, but an "assault" against unbelief.[199] Thus, it is necessary for Christians to attack with higher-quality reasoning over and against the reasoning of the unregenerate, and in this way, Christianity could "*reason* its way to the dominion of the world."[200] Warfield also warns, though, that one should not confuse "the certainty of faith" with the "certainty of knowledge."[201]

---

195. Warfield, "Beattie's *Apologetics*," 103.

196. Ibid. See also "Apologetics," *CW* 9:4, for the point that apologetics is not primarily defensive.

197. Warfield, "Beattie's *Apologetics*," 103.

198. Warfield, "R. *Zekerheid*," 120.

199. Ibid.

200. Ibid., 121. As has already been established, Warfield believed that the work of the Holy Spirit was integral to this.

201. Ibid.

Distinguishing Faith from Knowledge

Although faith and knowledge are intimately united, they should also be distinguished from each other. The difference between the two is not that faith lacks evidence upon which to rest, while knowledge possesses it. Nor is the difference that the evidence upon which faith rests is insufficient, while that of knowledge is sufficient. Neither is it that knowledge alone possesses objectively or universally valid grounds.[202] Rather, the difference is that the evidence upon which knowledge rests is accurately labeled "sight," and that for faith, "testimony."[203] Warfield uses these terms, "sight" and "testimony," representatively and in order to a) clarify the distinction between the nature of faith and the nature of knowledge, and b) to make the distinction between the grounds of conviction that are inherent in each. The grounds of conviction for knowledge are not identical with those of faith, but that does not mean that somehow knowledge has to do with evidence while faith is void of it. With respect to faith, the element of trust is "peculiarly prominent," and yet it is also true that all knowledge "rests on trust."[204] So to configure the relationship between faith and knowledge, and the grounds of conviction for each, in such a way that one of them is entirely subjective and the other entirely objective is to misconceive both. Though it is true that the certainty of faith can be considered as retaining a "'more subjective' character," this should not be perceived as placing the certainty of faith into a fundamentally different and opposing category from the certainty of knowledge. In the end, if the validity of the testimony on which one's faith is grounded actually establishes a fact, it becomes apparent that the grounds for that faith impart a certainty or conviction that "is as valid as any knowledge founded on 'sight' can be."[205]

Warfield concludes his review by acknowledging that his criticisms of Bavinck's presentation on the intricacies of faith, knowledge, conviction, certainty, and their foundations should not be interpreted as his disagreeing with Bavinck on the entire substance of Bavinck's theology. Indeed, Warfield was not even precisely certain that Bavinck would disagree with him on the matters accentuated in the review. Warfield's last few comments revolve around Bavinck's "apparent assumption of the

---

202. Ibid. Warfield gave a more detailed analysis of faith in general and saving faith in particular in "Faith in Its Psychological Aspects," *CW* 9:313–42.

203. Warfield, " R. *Zekerheid*," 121.

204. Ibid.

205. Ibid., 122.

invariable or normal implication of 'assurance of salvation' in the direct act of faith."[206] This subject is a rather old one in the history of Christian theology and revolves around one's conception of faith's ultimate object. If faith terminates on a proposition, then it would appear that assurance would be of the very essence of faith. However, if faith terminates on a person, then it is not apparent how assurance would be of the very essence of faith, and, in fact, a way would be open to think of assurance as "a reflex of faith which may or may not manifest itself."[207]

Summarizing Thoughts on the De Zekerheid Review

While Warfield affirms the objective and subjective elements within biblical saving faith, he also warns against conceiving of saving faith in a way that confuses the exact relationship between the objective and subjective elements. Because saving faith consists of a person placing his or her faith in another person, indeed the divine person, the analysis between the objective and subjective elements cannot be facilely reduced to simply saying that the person who exercises faith places his or her faith in something objective. Nor can it simply be reduced to the subjective and be explained in terms of feelings, emotions, or intuitions. After all, the "object" in whom one is placing faith is actually another subject, who is in fact the Lord of Glory, the Second Person of the Trinity, who is the infinite and eternal creator of reality. Thus, the objective element in biblical saving faith is contained within the subjective, and this is not only true of biblical saving faith, but also knowledge. So, for Warfield, the subject/object question within epistemology and saving faith was not a matter of regarding the subjective elements simply from the standpoint of the individual person's apprehension and comprehension of knowledge. God is Triune, the object of saving faith, and is both what we know and the ultimate means by which we know. Thus, both the subjective and objective elements are forever joined in both knowledge and saving faith. Conceptions of Christianity that place too much weight upon either the objective or the subjective, or even conflate the two into one, are conceptions that are not faithful to what the Scriptures teach, nor able

---

206. Ibid.

207. Ibid., 122–23. Warfield believed the latter, and addressed this issue more specifically in "Faith In Its Psychological Aspects," *CW* 9:313–42. Warfield concluded his review with high praise for Bavinck's work. Warfield's views of faith and the matter of assurance related to saving faith demonstrate his commitment to the WCF. See WCF, XVIII.

to faithfully account for reality as humans experience it.[208] This means, among other things, that anyone reading Warfield from the perspective that he thought of science and truth from an Enlightenment paradigm that conceives of human beings as the knowing subject analyzing and investigating objects to be known has completely misconstrued his view of knowledge, truth, science, and human beings.

Some of the distinctive emphases in Warfield's review of Bavinck's booklet are present in his introduction to Beattie's *Apologetics* as well. In fact, some of the wording in the two writings is identical. In the introduction, though, Warfield enters into greater detail in analyzing and assessing Kuyper's work, as well as using the occasion for stating more about the precise character of apologetics, although some of the latter is clearer in his *Schaff-Herzog* article.

Accepting the Conflict

Warfield was pleased with Beattie's book, and in particular he was pleased with its comprehensiveness.[209] Despite the wealth of apologetical literature, the subject had been treated, according to Warfield, "like a step-child in the theological household."[210] The problem centers on the varying conceptions regarding the nature of apologetics. The result was that even though theologians acknowledged apologetics, it was "thrust away into some odd corner, where it could hide its diminished head behind the skirts of some of its more esteemed sisters."[211] Warfield saw this mistreatment as energized by two putative opposites—"Mysticism and Rationalism"[212]—that might be more accurately appraised as kissing

---

208. Warfield, "Authority, Intellect and the Heart," *SSW* 2:668–71. Warfield considered authority, intellect, and the heart as the three sides of the "triangle of truth." They were the three media by which truth is communicated to humans. Too much of an emphasis on authority results in traditionalism; on intellect, rationalism; and on the heart, mysticism.

209. Warfield, "Beattie's *Apologetics*," 93.

210. Ibid.

211. Ibid.

212. Ibid., 93–94. Warfield's criticisms of mysticism and rationalism are well expressed in a number of essays. In addition to what we have detailed in previous chapters, see "Mysticism and Christianity," *CW* 9:649–66; and "Latest Phase of Historical Rationalism," *CW* 9:585–645. The latter work is compiled from several essays that were originally published separately in different periodicals. See also "Ritschlian School," *SSW* 2:448–51, wherein Warfield details what J. Gresham Machen would later adopt as his approach to arguing against Protestant liberalism, namely, a historical approach that revealed the connection between the events of history, Jesus, and the life and writings of the apostles.

cousins. Furthermore, he felt it was necessary to mention that the *influence* exerted by mysticism and rationalism did not merely extend to those who heartily embraced these ideologies, but also to those who were in principle opposed to them.[213]

As Warfield would later stress in the *Schaff-Herzog* article, rationalism leads to questioning the validity of apologetics, while mysticism leads to distrusting its usefulness.[214] Warfield believed that at the time of his writing (1903 was the date of publishing) "the rationalistic tendency," due largely to Albrecht Ritschl, was "perhaps most active in the churches."[215] Such rationalism was known by its distinction between religious and theoretical knowledge, a distinction that struck "at the very roots of Apologetics."[216] In this rationalistic scheme, religion was relegated to "value-judgments" that were "the subjective product of the human soul in its struggle after personal freedom," and this was juxtaposed with "theoretical knowledge" that was the domain of reason.[217] This, of course, left no place for reason to give a justifiable account for faith, since the two realities had been placed in two different metaphysical domains.

While rationalism endorses the bifurcation of the subjective and objective in its division between religious and theoretical knowledge, mysticism condenses religious knowledge claims into the subjective realm and thus renders apologetics completely unnecessary. According to Warfield, some adherents of mysticism in his time were erroneously arguing that since the Holy Spirit works directly upon the Christian and thus cre-

---

Warfield believed this was necessary because "the fundamental evil of the Ritschlian movement lies in its attitude towards the authority of the teaching of the apostles. On the authority of the apostolic teaching, along with that of Jesus preserved by them, rests all that is really distinctive of Christianity. If that be cast away from us, Christianity in all its distinctive features goes with it". He also stated that apart from "the authority of the apostolic teaching, Socialism is inevitable; on that authority it is impossible" (ibid., 451). Warfield's fuller and more extended criticism of Rischlianism, see *CW* vol. 7. See also "Century's Progress in Biblical Knowledge," *SSW* 2:3–13; "Christian Evidences: How Affected by Recent Criticisms," *SSW* 2:124–31; "Recent Reconstructions of Theology," *SSW* 2:289–99; "Review of *Studies in Theology*" *SSW* 2:300–307; "Authority, Intellect, Heart," *SSW* 2:668–71. It is this latter article in which Warfield defines rationalism as "the exaggeration of the principle of intellect to the discrediting of the others" (authority and heart), and mysticism as "the exaggeration of the principle of the heart to the discrediting of the others" (authority and intellect).

213. Warfield, "Beattie's *Apologetics*," 93–94.
214. Ibid., 94.
215. Ibid.
216. Ibid.
217. Ibid.

ates the believer's convictions, quite apart from "reasons addressed to the intellect," then these convictions must be credited to the "*testimonium Spiritus Sancti*."[218] Thus, apologetics became, for them, nothing but "an impertinence."[219] Such a perspective was present with some, according to Warfield, who had determined that saving faith was irrational and had, therefore, fled for refuge to a mysticism that would allow such irrationalism to exist without challenge.[220] What is needed in these instances, said Warfield, is not less apologetics but more. More apologetics is certainly needed with "heroes of the faith," who have misconceived the relationship between the monergistic work of the Spirit in regeneration and the grounds of conviction on which a vital faith rests.[221] In Warfield's estimation, Kuyper et al., who rightly exalted the sovereign work of the Spirit, had unwittingly joined with those of their time who did not believe the gospel, were antagonistic to it, and, thereby, disparaged apologetics.[222]

Kuyper's "Great Assumption"

According to Warfield, Kuyper had given apologetics a subordinate place within theology by assigning it "the narrow task of defending developed Christianity against philosophy, falsely so called."[223] Because Kuyper conceived of apologetics as defending an already developed Christianity against philosophy, Warfield criticized him for operating with Christianity as "the great assumption."[224] As Warfield puts it:

> The work of the exegete, the historian, the systematist, has all hung, so to speak in the air; not until all their labor is accomplished do they pause to wipe their streaming brows and ask whether they have been dealing with realities, or perchance with fancies only.[225]

Working in this way, according to Warfield, amounts to possessing an unjustified faith that renders the work of the exegete, historian, and

---

218. Ibid.
219. Ibid.
220. Ibid., 94–95.
221. Ibid., 95.
222. Ibid.
223. Ibid.
224. Ibid., 96.
225. Ibid.

"systematist" as "unjustified, if not, unjustifiable."²²⁶ Warfield notes that Kuyper himself admitted that something seemed to be missing from his own schema, something that could justify the work of the exegete.²²⁷ Sensing a need for justifying such work, Kuyper did it on the grounds of the "*sensus divinitatis*" or "*semen religionis*" in each person.²²⁸ This sense of the divine is what leads each person to seek after God, and this is then "renewed and quickened by the palingenesis, through which the subject is opened for the reception of the special revelation of God made first by deed, culminating in the Incarnation and then by word, centering in the Scriptures."²²⁹ According to Warfield, crediting the testimony of the Holy Spirit for placing God's revelation—the Scriptures—in the Christian's possession, amounted to Kuyper actually giving the "outline of" a "very considerable" apologetic that had to "precede and prepare the way for the 'Bibliological Group.'"²³⁰ Though not specifying how the following could or should be done, Warfield states that Kuyper's scheme requires the following:

> We must, it seems, vindicate the existence of a *sensus divinitatis* in man capable of producing a natural theology independently of special revelation; and then the reality of a special revelation in deed and word; and, as well, the reality of a supernatural preparation of the heart of man to receive it; before we can proceed to the study of theology at all, as Dr. Kuyper has outlined it.²³¹

Kuyper, it seemed, was unaware of the questions that he was begging, and yet that was not the only mistake Warfield saw in Kuyper's configuration and theological content.²³²

---

226. Ibid.

227. Ibid. Kuyper divided theology into four groups, which he labeled Bibliological, Ecclesiological, Dogmatological, and Diaconological. These corresponded to the normal structure of exegetical, historical, systematic, and practical theology.

228. Ibid., 97.

229. Ibid., 96–97.

230. Ibid., 97.

231. Warfield, "Beattie's *Apologetics*," 97.

232. It is at this point in Warfield's criticism that one can see his stress on the historical character of human knowledge. Humans, from Warfield's perspective, simply have no other recourse to access God than the historical and empirically verifiable realm of the creation. God truly could and did, according to Warfield, reveal himself through direct intervention in a moment, but even such revelation was part of a historical process that was comprehensively governed by God. Warfield, then, did not simply view apologetics and the truth of the Bible from an ultimate perspective, but emphasized the historical

The Character of Scripture and the Character of Apologetics

Since the Scriptures are the source and not the object of theology, Warfield thought it a mistake for Kuyper to derive the *principium divisionis* from the Scriptures.[233] Since it is the "ectypal knowledge of God" that is the object of theology, Warfield believed that this ought to direct, and indeed had directed, the Church's organization of its theological work down through the ages.[234] As Warfield saw it, the ectypal knowledge of God is in Scripture, but has to "be drawn out of them" through exegesis.[235] Such knowledge has been assimilated over time into the life of the church, with particular "effects in the life of the Christian world," and so historical theology is necessary.[236] Furthermore, such knowledge is "capable of statement in a systematized thetical form" and is "made available for life," and so systematic and practical theology are necessary. Yet, all of this work actually presupposes a prior work. As Warfield declares:

> But certainly, before we draw it from the Scriptures, we must assure ourselves that there is a knowledge of God in the Scriptures. And, before we do that, we must assure ourselves that there is a knowledge of God in the world. And, before we do that, we must assure ourselves that a knowledge of God is possible for man. And, before we do that, we must assure ourselves that there is a God to know. Thus, we inevitably work back to first principles. And, in working thus back to first principles, we exhibit the indispensability of an "Apologetical Theology," which of necessity holds the place of the first among the five essential theological disciplines.[237]

It should be noted that since for Warfield theology is a human endeavor for a practical purpose and is unavoidably performed within a historical process, it ought to be organized with this historical progression and practical purpose in view, not simply according to the reality of God's primacy for the Christian. This view displays the practical and historical realities by which humans acquired a progressive knowledge of God and truth, and explained the Bible, and the truthfulness of Christianity, to some degree in accordance with that historical process.

233. Warfield, "Beattie's *Apologetics*," 97.

234. Ibid. Warfield, thus, operated with a distinction regarding knowledge of God as archetypal and ectypal that was present in the medieval, reformation and post-reformation time periods. See Muller, *PRRD* 1:225–45.

235. Warfield, "Beattie's *Apologetics*," 97.

236. Ibid.

237. Ibid., 98.

character of Warfield's thinking, both about human beings and theology. This in turn helps demonstrate the stress he placed on human beings as creatures created in the image of God, who gain access to God through the space/time realm of a creation that originates in, and is providentially governed and redeemed by God.[238]

Warfield was quick to acknowledge that it certainly is true that the Christian must take his "standpoint *in* the Scriptures," and "not *above*" them, but in order to do this the Christian "must first *have* the Scriptures, authenticated to him as such, before he can take his standpoint in them."[239] Warfield considered it a confusion of realities and categories to think that the necessity of regeneration for the making of a Christian means that Christians are to remain essentially idle with respect to establishing the knowledge of God in those who have yet to believe in Christ for salvation.[240] As Warfield saw it, just because the ultimate source of saving faith is God does not then mean that Christians should think that apologetics, which is correlative to the nature of what God gives in regeneration, is unnecessary. Therefore, because saving faith correlates with Man's rational, epistemic, and historical character, apologetics is necessary. As Warfield phrases it:

> Faith is the gift of God; but it does not in the least follow that the faith that God gives is an irrational faith, that is, a faith without grounds in right reason. It is beyond all question only the prepared heart that can fitly respond to the "reasons"; but how can even a prepared heart respond, when there are no "reasons" to draw out its actions? One might as well say that photography is independent of light, because no light can make an impression unless the plate is prepared to receive it. The Holy Spirit does not work a blind, an ungrounded faith in the heart. What is supplied by his creative energy in working faith is not a ready-made faith, rooted in nothing and clinging without reason to its object; nor yet new grounds of belief in the object presented; but just a new

---

238. For other essays that demonstrate Warfield's beliefs on these points, see "God's Providence over All," *SSW* 1:110–15; "Divine and Human in the Bible," *SSW* 2:542–48; "Predestination in the Reformed Confessions," *CW* 9:117–231; "Some Thoughts on Predestination," *SSW* 1:103–9; "Christian Supernaturalism," *CW* 9:25–46; "Biblical Idea of Revelation," *CW* 1:3–34; "Idea of Revelation and Theories of Revelation," *CW* 1:37–48; "Divine Origin of the Bible," *CW* 1:429–47; "Predestination," *CW* 2:3–67; "Christless Christianity," *CW* 3:313–67; "Essence of Christianity and the Cross of Christ," *CW* 3:393–444.

239. Warfield, "Beattie's *Apologetics*," 98.

240. Ibid.

ability of the heart to respond to the grounds of faith, sufficient in themselves, already present to the understanding. We believe in Christ because it is rational to believe in him, not though it be irrational.[241]

Apologetics and Right Reason Revisited

The introduction to Beattie's *Apologetics* is another instance of Warfield using the term "right reason" to refer to the reasoning of the regenerate person, which is the grounds upon which his or her faith conviction rests. It is not that Warfield believed that the object of the regenerate person's faith is his or her reasoning. The sole and ultimate object of faith for the Christian is Jesus Christ. Yet, according to Warfield, there are reasons for Jesus' being worthy of the sinner's faith. As these reasons become clearer to the conscience of a sinner, the conviction that it is right to place one's faith in Jesus grows stronger. Thus, he called this reasoning "right," the reasoning that is organically related to the Christian's faith. In a word, it is correct or truthful reasoning. It is reasoning that has been "righted" by the Holy Spirit.

Central, then, to Warfield's stress on the necessity for apologetics within Christian theology and the life of the church, were his beliefs regarding the nature of saving faith and how God accomplishes the regeneration and renewal of sinners. Viewed through another lens, this stress on apologetics was the result of recognizing the true differences between the Christian and non-Christian with respect to knowledge claims and the rational support for such claims. Warfield considered it absurd to think that apologetics, within itself, has the power to make someone a Christian.[242] According to him, though, this does not mean that evidence has little or no "part to play in the conversion of the soul," or "that the systematically organized evidence which we call Apologetics" does not have "its part to play in the Christianizing of the world."[243] Instead, apologetics has "a primary" and "conquering" part to play in the Christianizing of the world.[244] This is because, according to Warfield, Christianity came "into the world clothed with the mission to *reason* its

---

241. Ibid., 98–99. Some of these emphases are in Warfield, "Apologetics," *CW* 9:15; Helseth, *"Right Reason" and the Princeton Mind.*

242. Warfield, "Beattie's *Apologetics*," 99; "Apologetics," *CW* 9:15.

243. Warfield, "Beattie's *Apologetics*," 99; "Apologetics," *CW* 9:16.

244. Warfield, "Beattie's *Apologetics*," 99; "Apologetics," *CW* 9:3–4.

way to its dominion."²⁴⁵ As a result, "Christianity makes its appeal to right reason, and stands out among all the religions, therefore, distinctively as 'the Apologetic religion.'"²⁴⁶ Possessed with right reason, the Christian has a weapon to use in the war to conquer the "incredible fertility in assault" displayed in "anti-Christian" uses of reason.²⁴⁷ Though Warfield did not reduce Christianity to the intellect, he certainly did place a strong emphasis on the intellect, and the offensive nature of apologetics in the use of the intellect. This can be seen in his assessment that "Christianity finds its task in thinking itself thoroughly through, and in organizing, not its defense only, but also its attack."²⁴⁸

It was difficult for Warfield to see how Kuyper was "tempted to make little of Apologetics."²⁴⁹ After all, from Warfield's perspective, it is the regenerated person's reason that will "ultimately conquer to itself the whole race and all its products."²⁵⁰ Moreover, "we may equally assure ourselves that its gradually increasing power will show itself only as the result of conflict in the free intercourse of men."²⁵¹ For Warfield, then, apologetics is central to what the biblical gospel is and, therefore, what it does. This in turn, helps explain why he considered it erroneous to say that apologetics addresses "the *minimum* of Christianity."²⁵²

According to Warfield, Christian apologetics has to do with "just Christianity itself, whatever that may prove to be."²⁵³ The role of apologetics is not to "vindicate for us the least that we can get along with, and yet manage to call ourselves Christians; but to validate the Christian 'view of the world,' with all that is contained in the Christian 'view of the world,' for the science of men."²⁵⁴ Thus, as Warfield states, his conception of apologetics was not simply satisfied with apologies that might be "nothing more than 'a couple of starved and hunger-bitten dogmas'" that "we may choose to identify with 'the essence of Christianity.'"²⁵⁵ Instead,

245. Warfield, "Beattie's *Apologetics*," 99.
246. Ibid., 100.
247. Ibid.
248. Ibid.
249. Ibid.
250. Ibid., 104.
251. Ibid.
252. Ibid.
253. Ibid.
254. Ibid.
255. Ibid.

his perspective of apologetics considered it "a much more fundamental, a much more comprehensive, and a much more objective thing."[256] Warfield denied that apologetics is for the purpose of figuring out how to address any particular individual in order to persuade them to Christianity, or how any particular "age" might be persuaded "to give a hearing to the Christian conception of the world."[257] So, even though Warfield affirmed that apologetics has a conquering part to play in the Christianizing of the world, his conception of how this is to be accomplished was determined, first and foremost, by considering apologetics as it is in itself, that is, in principle. Thus, there was a primacy for Warfield on a decidedly non-Kantian view of reality and knowledge that led him not to reduce apologetics to a pragmatic end dictated by the subjective experience of an individual or a particular culture's idiosyncratic character. Warfield's approach was to affirm that an accurate, though not exhaustive, knowledge of God, Man, Christ, and the gospel is attainable, and the subjective experience of people in the world at any given time and place should be interpreted and approached from the light of former realities and not vice versa. Thus, as Warfield concludes, biblical apologetics:

> . . . concerns itself with the solid objective establishment, after a fashion valid for all normally working minds and for all ages of the world in its developing thought, of those great basal facts which constitute the Christian religion; or, better, which embody in the concrete the entire knowledge of God accessible to men, and which, therefore, need only explication by means of the further theological disciplines in order to lay openly before the eyes of men the entirety of the knowledge of God within their reach.[258]

Summarizing Thoughts on Warfield's View of Apologetics

Warfield viewed human knowledge from the perspective of the doctrine of God as creator and redeemer, with God's role as redeemer understood in light of his role as creator. Human beings are creatures who were created in the image of God with knowledge, righteousness, and holiness. This view of human beings and their knowledge was, in turn, subordinated to his understanding of God as creator and redeemer. Human beings

---

256. Ibid., 105.
257. Ibid.
258. Ibid.

are historically conditioned, time/space-bound creatures, whose means and purpose for knowing are inextricably conditioned by this creaturely historical condition, a condition that is inherently and comprehensively moral and subjective. Warfield also viewed human knowledge of God as progressing in space and time, or through human history, and providentially governed by God. In the course of human history, an "edifice of truth" is being built, and all people, regenerate and unregenerate, participate in the building. The regenerate are to give a reason for the faith they have in Jesus, and in order to do this they need to understand how the constituent parts of their objects of knowledge relate to saving faith in Christ. Since all human knowledge is part of one interrelated whole, because God is the source, means, and ultimate object of human knowledge, the project is not futile.

Apologetics within Christian theology ought to be thought of in terms of prolegomena and integral to the entire system of Christian theology. In Warfield's conception, apologetics can be thought of as the DNA of the Christian theological system. The main thrust of his arguments against various manifestations of what he deemed unbiblical perspectives on the Christian faith was that these perspectives operate with, or are the manifestation of, systems that are unable to accurately account for all the empirical evidence available to human beings regarding reality, which, of course, includes the Bible, along with the entire history of the church.[259] Warfield, in general, criticized either the presentations of their systems or their handling of the empirical evidence from which they built their case for their conclusions about the Christian faith.

Warfield believed that when thinking about or engaging in apologetics, the primacy of God should not be used in such a way that Man's creaturely condition is ignored, violated, or inadequately considered. Thus, the primacy of both God and Scripture for the Christian does not mean that we should think about the acquisition of knowledge of God as unconditioned by what characterizes the creation as a whole, and human beings as creatures created in the image of God, in particular. For Warfield, human knowledge of God is, by the very nature of the case, characterized by creational realities originating in, sustained, and redeemed by God. If one is to think rightly about human knowledge of

---

259. This is not to say one has to know everything in order to defend biblical Christianity or render a verdict regarding it. Warfield affirmed that "the logical capacity can scarcely be made the condition of our salvation," and that "it would surely be unfortunate if weakness of intellect were more fatal than wickedness of heart" ("Supernatural Birth of Jesus," *CW* 3:458).

God, then, one has to think of it from the perspective of the variety of relationships that are inherent in the multitude of variables that comprise it. God did not do violation to his people's creaturely status in giving them saving knowledge of him, and unredeemed humans remain creatures created in the image of God with some accurate knowledge of God, since they are indeed human creatures. Thus, Warfield's whole view is thoroughly Calvinistic and an exposition of the cardinal doctrines of the WCF regarding God and human beings.

With respect to metaphysics, Warfield viewed the relationship between the knowing subject and the object known as an unavoidably unified one, and this is rooted in his belief in God as creator and redeemer. All human knowledge is theological in that God is the ultimate object of our knowledge of anything, because God created all things, i.e., all things are what they are because God made them, or allowed them to be. Knowledge of everything that is known rightly is ultimately pushed back to God. Moreover, apart from a divine fiat in which God acts by himself immediately upon the knower, human beings know through the secondary means that God has provided. Either way, God is not simply the object of knowledge, but also the means to it. Thus, there is a radical union between the knowing subject and the object known, making it unintelligible for human knowledge to be either compartmentalized, or fragmented, into two categories comprehensively and fundamentally disconnected from each other as in rationalism. Neither is it comprehensible to think of the knowing subject and object known as submerged into each other so that we can no longer know or speak of any distinctions between the knower and the known, as in mysticism. With respect to knowledge of God specifically, the regenerate or unregenerate status of the human knower is of fundamental importance.

Human beings are morally culpable for their sin, and this sin results in a corruption in human beings that produces a "deflection" that causes them to not know or reason rightly. This failure to know or reason rightly is not absolute, because sin does not annihilate Man as Man; it does not cause human beings to stop being human. Instead, the unregenerate remain human and this, by the very nature of the case, means the unregenerate and regenerate sinner have their metaphysical status as human beings still in common. Regeneration then does not render the Christian something other than human, and the unregenerate do not stop being human. The difference between the regenerate and unregenerate does not have to do with a strict either/or regarding their status as humans or sinners, but rather how precisely their humanness is related to sin. The very nature of faith in Jesus that saves from sin, then, corresponds to who or what humans are, and because the unregenerate is still human and the regenerate still a sinner, the character of saving faith is not a totally, absolutely foreign reality to the unregenerate. This can be seen in the fact that God calls upon each regenerate person (not glorified) to "give a reason for the faith that is in him," and this reasoning is integral to the Christianizing of the world, though such Christianizing is not the only result or purpose for bringing this reasoning out into the consciousness of the Christian.[260]

For Warfield, apologetics is integral to the knowledge of God, which is, in turn, integral to what it means to be human. Warfield viewed human beings as the WCF describes them. Some knowledge of God is endemic to being human.[261] Since humans do not stop being human while in their sinful, unregenerate state, Warfield regarded unregenerate humans as genuine possessors of, and capable of further, knowledge of God, though such knowledge will not reach the point of salvation unless the Holy Spirit brings regeneration.[262] In this, Warfield's conception explicates the grounds upon which true communication can take place between the regenerate and unregenerate, and it also accounts for the role that the unregenerate have within the kingdom of God, albeit a reluctant one, under the providence of God. It also demonstrates that he viewed epistemology from what we could call a moral paradigm. Warfield believed that a

---

260. Warfield, "Apologetics," *CW* 9:4.

261. Calvin made the same point. See his *Institutes*, I.3.i. The chapter is titled "The Knowledge of God Has Been Naturally Implanted in the Minds of Men."

262. Calvin makes the same point in *Institutes*, II.3.iii–iv. Calvin's language and explanations in II.3.i–ii are at times so absolute that he seems to warrant the conclusion that the unregenerate have absolutely no knowledge of God within them at all and possess no virtue of any kind (this is, of course, how some have read him), and yet that is exactly what he denies in II.3.iii–iv. I think the most fundamental point to understand regarding Calvin's explanations in II.3.i–ii is that he is addressing what humans can rightly claim as only produced by them. Whatever knowledge of God or virtue of any kind that we have, it is present by God's act. Thus, this would include all of what it means to be human as God originally designed us, and that is seen in Adam and Eve in their original states of righteousness. The preservation of humans as humans would then constitute one of God's acts, require the presence of some knowledge of God, and virtuous thinking and living; but this would still have to be credited to God and not humans, because none of it originates with us, but with God. Thus, Calvin and Warfield are identical on this point, as they are on the necessity of the regenerating work of the Holy Spirit to create new life in the deadened sinner, and the renewing work of the Holy Spirit to sustain that work. See Warfield, *Plan of Salvation*.

necessary part of the advancement of the knowledge of God on earth is the conflict between the regenerate and unregenerate regarding human knowledge. From Warfield's perspective, Kuyper, Bavinck et al. were declining the whole conflict, or teaching that there were few, if any, means for the regenerate to engage the unregenerate. Though Warfield acknowledged that there was much to be praised in the Amsterdam theologians, he believed that their view of apologetics was formulated upon erroneous conceptions of human beings, knowledge, and theology, which Warfield was not altogether certain they meant to endorse. According to Warfield, the Amsterdam erroneous conceptions found a welcome correlate in the twin faults of rationalism and mysticism popular at the time.

While Warfield believed that the conflict between the regenerate and unregenerate is an important aspect of building the "edifice of God's truth," it is not opposition to the gospel that determines the character and purpose of apologetics. Instead, it is the "fundamental needs of the human spirit." According to Warfield, since humans are what they are based on what God has made them to be, and allows them to become, the character and purpose of apologetics is only rightly understood in relation to the larger, more foundational subjects of God, creation, and redemption. It is this perspective from which Warfield not only thought about apologetics, but also engaged in it.

The regenerate sinner possesses a soul capable of intellectual work of which the unregenerate sinner is not capable; so God's regenerate people are able to engage in acquiring and systematizing knowledge that is beyond the capacity of unregenerate people to accomplish. The best science that is a part of the edifice of God's truth, and that leads to further construction of God's truth, will have some overlap with the science of the unregenerate, but it will take unregenerate science and move it further than the unregenerate are capable of taking it. In the end, then, the primary criticisms that can be lobbied against the work of the unregenerate in their pursuit of knowledge is that it is not scientific enough (or at all) and that it is not constructive, but destructive. Both of these criticisms lead to the conclusion that the work of the unregenerate is simply not critical enough. It is these kinds of criticisms that Warfield lobbied time and again against the biblical and theological scholarship of his day, which he believed did not correspond to Scripture.

8

Apologetics in Practice: Biblical Doctrines, Morality, Subjectivity, and the Supernatural

It has been popular to claim that Warfield's epistemology, which is in the Old Princeton tradition, does not account for the subjective experience of the knower and the noetic effects of sin, and that it is generally ahistorical as well as rationalistic. This judgment cannot be sustained, though, by appealing to what he wrote. Nor can it be sustained by appealing to the fact that the Old Princeton tradition used Turretin's *Institutes of Elenctic Theology* and then Charles Hodge's *Systematic Theology*. Both Turretin and Hodge make it clear that although human reason has an instrumental use in humans receiving revelation, it is subordinate to revelation. Anything else would result in divine revelation being determined by human reason.[1] But one cannot receive a revelation that is utterly ineffable. There must be some level of understanding in order for a revelation to even be called "revelation."[2] It is in this sense that the Princetonians considered reason to be the judge of revelation. That is, "reason is necessarily presupposed in every revelation."[3] Nevertheless, the

---

1. Turretin, *Institutes of Elenctic Theology* 1:23–31; 2:561–66. According to Turretin, on pp. 25–26, the origin of the Christian faith is God, not nature, and, because God speaks to us in the Scriptures, we are to believe things based solely on the authority of Scripture. Scripture does not explicitly address all the specific details of life, so Turretin affirmed that it was the role of "right reason" that "apprehends the truth of conclusions, and of itself determines what may be inferred from some other thing." Yet, just because reason can be used in this way does not mean that it is "the principle and rule by which doctrines of faith should be measured." See Hodge, *ST* 1:34–60.

2. As we will see below, this is one of Warfield's dominant points in "The Biblical Idea of Revelation," *CW* 1:3–34.

3. Hodge, *ST* 1:49. Still further, according to Hodge, "Revelation is the communication of truth to the mind."

first and foremost requirement God places upon human beings, according to both Turretin and Hodge, is to believe God.

Humans, because they are created in the image of God, even though that image is marred by sin, still possess some true or accurate knowledge of God. The fall into sin did not make human beings something other than human.[4] Since possession of some accurate knowledge of God is intrinsic to being human, and sin did not obliterate our metaphysical status as humans, it is erroneous to conclude that unregenerate sinners are void of all understanding of God. Belief in God that results in salvation does not begin with a "blind leap of faith," nor does it consist of blind ignorance void of all understanding.[5] Furthermore, the command to believe God is always accompanied by a particular revelation of God, either in the past or present, which is to be believed. Human beings cannot gain access to God apart from his revelation in all its varied forms, and one's failure to believe in God is not only sin, it also sets one's thinking in a direction that cannot produce genuine "science," or knowledge of truth. Thus, in the Old Princeton theology, knowledge and faith are correlates that cannot be separated from each other, and yet they are still genuinely distinct; they are not the same thing, and both are integral to producing true science. As Warfield expresses it:

> No one, of course, would think of denying that the two terms "knowledge," and "faith," "belief" are frequently employed as wholly equivalent—each designating simply a conviction, without respect to the nature of its grounds. Augustine already recognized this broad use of both terms to cover the whole ground of convictions. But neither can it be denied that they are often brought into contrast with one another. The distinction indicated, no doubt, is often a distinction not in the nature of the evidence on which the several classes of conviction rest but in—shall we say the firmness, the clearness, the force of the conviction? The difficulty of finding the exact word to employ here may perhaps be instructive . . . There is an element of trust lying at the bottom of all our convictions, even those which we designate "knowledge," because, as we say they are of the order of "theoretic certitude," or "rational assurance.". . . To say that an element of trust underlies all our knowledge is therefore equivalent to saying that our knowledge rests on belief.[6]

---

4. See chapter 7 in this book, on "Apologetics in Principle."
5. Hodge, *ST* 1:49, wrote "Knowledge is essential to faith."
6. Warfield, "Faith in Its Psychological Aspects," *CW* 9:328, 329.

Throughout Warfield's treatment of various biblical doctrines, as well as in his essays on Augustine's and Calvin's views on the subject, one is confronted with abundantly detailed analyses of the precise features of a biblical epistemology.[7] From Warfield's perspective, Christianity will conquer the world to itself through truth.[8] Warfield believed that since Christianity is the truth, then it is its own defense—*and* offense. This phrase reflects his belief that "the details of Christianity are all contained in Christianity: the minimum of Christianity is just Christianity itself."[9] Apologetics "establishes the constitutive and regulative principles of theology as a science; and in establishing these it establishes all the details which are derived from them [the constitutive and regulative principles] by the succeeding departments, in their sound explication and systematization."[10] Thus, apologetics is about explaining the details of Christianity in order to establish Christianity.[11] Warfield, therefore, repeatedly correlates whatever his primary subject matter is to the various doctrines of the Christian faith. He is like a scientist who is dissecting an organism, observing and identifying the various relationships inherent in all its aspects.

Integrated Doctrines

Central to Warfield's view of knowledge are the doctrines of God as Creator and Redeemer; correlative to these are the doctrines of Man and salvation; and integral to all of them are the doctrines of revelation and inspiration. Warfield believed that all creation is revelation, that human beings are creatures created in the image of God, who not only are revelation in themselves, but also receive revelation. The creation is, thereby, thoroughly supernatural in character because it originates in, is sustained by, and is brought to its fulfillment by God. Thus, there is a sense in which that which is referred to as "natural" is actually "supernatural." Yet, rather than conflating the supernatural completely into the category of the natural like the pantheists, Warfield maintained that the natural has a supernatural character to it—but the natural and supernatural are still two distinct metaphysical realms.

---

7. Warfield, *CW* 4 and 5.
8. Warfield, "Introduction to Beattie's *Apologetics*," *SSW* 2:99–100.
9. Warfield, "Apologetics," *CW* 9:9.
10. Ibid., 9.
11. Ibid., 4.

Furthermore, God's revelation, precisely because it is just that—*revelation*—produces knowledge in all human beings that renders them accountable for their sin. Yet, God not only provided a revelation that results in all people being rightly declared guilty for sin, but also one that reveals and results in salvation. The latter does not merely make salvation possible, but actually saves sinners, again, precisely because it is a particular kind of revelation—a saving revelation. For Warfield to state that people "knew" salvation, he was not merely stating that they were cognitively aware of some facts, but rather that they experienced, albeit in a partial way in this lifetime, in the entirety of their being, the realities of saving revelation. Or, as Warfield expresses it, that revelation is "soteriological," not merely "natural."[12] Since this saving revelation is given by inspiration of God through the Holy Spirit to God's prophets and apostles, matters of canonicity and the biblical doctrine of inspiration are inseparable from the doctrine of God as creator and redeemer, as well as the doctrine of revelation.

Fundamental to these doctrinal features in Warfield's thought are metaphysical beliefs that run contrary to Kantian and neo-Kantian lines of thought. Warfield believed that God is the source of all reality, and as such, both God and the reality he created are not dependent upon human subjective apprehension and comprehension for their existence. This tenet does not mean that human beings cannot have some true, though not exhaustive, knowledge of God and many creational realities; but, because of sin, they are unable to know, either cognitively or experientially, some *particular* realities. Apart from the regenerating work of the Holy Spirit, human beings simply are unable to understand God's soteriological revelation. Even further, since all knowledge is knowledge of realities God has created, Warfield concluded that knowledge of all reality is ultimately theological, as well as subjective. Thus, the palingenesis gives a sinner the capacity to do superior work in the acquisition of knowledge. The point that should not be missed here is that Warfield's view of knowledge is unitary, theological, and organic. This fact is seen not only in his precise articulation of apologetics as prolegomena related to the entire system of Christian doctrine, but also in his explications of various Christian doctrines and their correlations to each other. Thus, the Christian system of doctrine is like a plant with all of its organic properties contained in a

---

12. Warfield, "Biblical Idea of Revelation," *CW* 1:3–34 (hereafter BIR).

seed that, as it grows, matures into something far greater than the seed. In other words, Warfield had a view of the Christian faith as living truth.[13]

Yet, the standard interpretation of Warfield by many scholars has been to deny that he recognized the noetic effects of sin and the subjective element in epistemology and failed to condition his thinking according to these realities. Given these rather severe inaccuracies, and the popularity of the narrative beholden to these inaccuracies, it is essential to explore what Warfield actually wrote concerning the noetic effects of sin, the subjective element in knowledge, and the historical character of truth, as well as how he relates these topics to the various doctrines within biblical Christianity.[14] If this is done, then these concepts can be seen throughout his treatments of the biblical doctrines of revelation and salvation, as well as in his analyses and criticisms of liberal theologians when they apply biblical criticism. Warfield also repeatedly correlates the doctrines of revelation and salvation to the doctrines of God as creator and redeemer. In doing so, he is expounding the contents of the WCF, which he deemed "a consensus of Reformed theology" at the time of its writing.[15]

---

13. A. A. Hodge and Warfield observed that some people's misunderstanding of the doctrine of inspiration is due to "extremely mechanical conceptions"(Hodge and Warfield, "Inspiration," 233).

14. Patton, "Benjamin Breckinridge Warfield," 378, makes it clear that it was a central feature of who Warfield was that he understood and heralded the biblical doctrine of sin. "To those who say, 'Change the circumstances of people and their character will improve,' he would in all probability have replied, 'Change the character of men and their circumstances will take care of themselves.' Character is an endogenous plant and grows from within. He was well acquainted with the types of current of thought that contradict this Augustinian doctrine. . . . But Dr. Warfield believed in the universal birth-stain of sin, and with his vast erudition could find, I venture to say, no better definition of it than that of the Westminster Divines given in our Shorter Catechism: 'Sin is any want of conformity unto or transgression of the law of God.'"

15. Warfield, "Westminster Doctrine of Holy Scripture," *CW* 6:159. This was contra Briggs, who, like many today, argued that the Confession was a form of Scholastic rationalism, as can be seen from the following quotation by Briggs: "Dogmatic Theology in Great Britain and America has been too long in the bondage of the seventeenth century Scholasticism and the eighteenth century Apologetics. The time has come for it to burst these bonds and march forward. It ought to run with all its might and march at the head of the column of modern learning. Christ is the king of a kingdom of truth, and his followers ought to be ashamed to drag His banner in the rear. The battle against science, philosophy, exegesis, and history must come to an end. All truth should be welcomed, from whatever source, and built into the structure of Christian doctrine. The attitude of *Traditional Orthodoxy* should be abandoned as real heterodoxy, and the attitude of *Advancing Orthodoxy* assumed as the *true* orthodoxy." Briggs, *Whither?*, 18–19; emphasis original. For a rather thorough negation of the thesis that the WCF is the product of

The Standard Misconception of Warfield's Beliefs on Knowledge and Truth

As previously mentioned, George Marsden, following Sydney Ahlstrom, and in concert with a multitude of other scholars, argues that the Old Princeton theological views were indebted to Scottish Common Sense Realism, and, as a result, held to a generally ahistorical notion of truth and, thus, failed to account for the human element in epistemology.[16] Furthermore, Marsden, consistent with Van Til, maintains that Warfield's use of "right reason" demonstrates a confidence in the unregenerate sinner's ability to reason rightly about empirical evidence apart from the illuminating work of the Holy Spirit.[17] It has already been shown, though, that Warfield did *not* use "right reason" to refer to the reasoning of unregenerate, or "unaided reason." Rather, "right reason" is the reasoning of a Christian, when that Christian is reasoning in accordance with what Scripture reveals as truth.[18] Keep in mind what Warfield wrote regarding "right reason" when he addressed it specifically and formally in his essay on apologetics:

> We believe in Christ because it is rational to believe in him, not even though it be irrational. Of course, mere reasoning cannot make a Christian; but that is not because faith is not the result of evidence, but because a dead soul cannot respond to evidence. The action of the Holy Spirit in giving faith is not apart from evi-

---

Scholastic rationalism see Muller, *PRRD*. With respect to the emphasis on the glory of God in the first question/answer of the Shorter Catechism, Warfield wrote: "The Shorter Catechism owes this elevated standpoint, of course, to the purity of its reflection of the Reformed consciousness" ("First Question of the Westminster Shorter Catechism," *CW* 6:379). Warfield believed that this was a superior starting point to the Heidelberg Catechism, which accentuated the believer's longing for comfort in life and death. The Heidelberg Catechism, said Warfield, catered to a "spiritual utilitarianism" that "claims the attention of the pupil from the beginning for his own state, his own present unhappiness, his own possibilities of bliss." Thus, it represented "some danger that the pupil should acquire the impression that God exists for his benefit." There was, therefore, according to Warfield a type of anthropocentricity within the Heidelberg Catechism that was avoided by the theocentric Shorter Catechism.

16. Marsden, *Fundamentalism and American Culture*, 110–15.

17. Ibid., 115.

18. Marsden et al. who wish to identify the Princetonians as operating rationalistically or operating with an Enlightenment view of science, because they could actually know some truth regarding external realities, are caught on the horns of a dilemma. Does believing that you know truth that is true for all people, for all times and places mean one is automatically a rationalist? If so, then none of us can escape that charge.

dence, but along with evidence; and in the first instance consists in preparing the soul for the reception of the evidence.[19]

Remember also that Warfield states clearly in his essay on apologetics that there is a difference between what is true about the Christian's faith in and of itself and that same Christian's understanding of that faith. In other words, Warfield made a distinction between saving faith objectively and subjectively considered.[20] Again, for Warfield, neither category, objectivity or subjectivity, makes sense, or is intelligible, without the other. Not only, then, did Warfield, contra Marsden, state specifically that the Holy Spirit must give faith, but Warfield also stated it within his analysis of saving faith in which he related the objective element to the subjective element and saw the two as intertwined, with neither one able to be addressed apart from the other. The very beliefs that Marsden attributed to Warfield are clearly and emphatically denied by Warfield in a comprehensive way.

The idea that Warfield's view of apologetics did not incorporate the doctrine of human sinfulness is, to put it mildly, also incorrect. Warfield not only analyzed apologetics with a clear eye to the reality of human sin, as well as the ways in which the reasoning of the regenerate can be used by the Holy Spirit to bring the unregenerate to saving faith, but he also made continual references to the reality of human sin and its effects on sinners throughout numerous writings on a variety of doctrinal matters. He not only affirmed the reality of human sin, but also emphasized God's autonomous vanquishing of it in his people—and he explicated all of this in relation to a number of Christian doctrines.

Warfield's correlations between the doctrine of human sin and so many other doctrines make it very difficult to understand how anyone could miss Warfield's emphasis upon the noetic effects of sin, the subjective element in epistemology, and the historically conditioned character of human knowledge. The failure of historians to understand Warfield accurately on these points means they have had to not merely miss a statement or two in a few essays, but have had to misunderstand, in a rather comprehensive way, everything he wrote on the doctrines of God, inspiration, revelation, and salvation, as well as the ways in which he saw these in relation to apologetics. In short, they would have to miss the substance of his entire theology.

19. Warfield, "Apologetics," *CW* 9:15. For further elaboration of Warfield's understanding of the doctrine of salvation see his *Plan of Salvation*.

20. See chapter 7 in this book.

Apologetics in Practice

Correlating Human Subjectivity, Sin, Saving Faith, and Revelation

In Warfield's essay "On Faith in Its Psychological Aspects,"[21] there is an explanation of faith and its relationship to knowledge that denies that either religious faith or its object finds its purest form in a proposition:

> It is the nature of trust to seek a personal object on which to repose, and it is only natural, therefore, that what we call religious faith does not reach its height in assent to propositions of whatever religious content and however well fitted to call out religious trust, but comes to its rights only when it rests with adoring trust on a person.[22]

In "Authority, Intellect and Heart,"[23] after writing, "Man is a unit; and the religious truth which impinges upon him must affect him in all his activities or none,"[24] Warfield asserts:

> The revelations of the Scriptures do not terminate upon the intellect. They were not given merely to enlighten the mind. They were given through the intellect to beautify the life. They terminate on the heart. Again, they do not, in affecting the heart, leave the intellect untouched. They cannot be fully understood by the intellect, acting alone. The natural man cannot receive the things of the Spirit of God. They must first convert the soul before they are fully comprehended by the intellect. Only as they are lived are they understood. Hence, the phrase, "Believe that you may understand," has its fullest validity. No man can intellectually grasp the full meaning of the revelations of authority, save as the result of an experience of their power in life. Hence, that the truths concerning divine things may be so comprehended that they may unite with a true system of divine truth, they must be: first, revealed in an authoritative word; second, experienced in a holy heart; and third, formulated by a sanctified intellect. Only as these three unite, then, can we have a true theology. And equally, that these same truths may be so received that they beget in us a living religion, they must be: first, revealed in an authoritative word; second, apprehended by a sound intellect; and third, expe-

---

21. Warfield, "Faith in Its Psychological Aspects," *CW* 9:313–42.
22. Ibid., 331.
23. Warfield, "Authority, Intellect, Heart," *SSW* 2:668–71.
24. Ibid., 668.

rienced in an instructed heart. Only as the three unite, then, can we have a vital religion.[25]

"Inspiration and Criticism": Addressing Fundamental Issues

Early in his career, upon inauguration to the Chair of New Testament Literature and Exegesis at Western Seminary in 1880, Warfield spoke on "Inspiration and Criticism."[26] In this address he clarified where he stood in relation to the Confession and how his allegiance to it related to his view of the Bible. He went on to discuss how his commitment to the Bible and the Confession related to the application of biblical criticism by those who sought to undermine the church's confidence in the biblical doctrine of inspiration. This address exhibits some of the lines of thought already mentioned, lines of thought that characterize his scholarship through the remainder of his career.

Warfield began by announcing that he signed the seminary standards, pledging his loyalty to the WCF not because he was committed to a humanly derived system and trying to make the Bible conform to it, but because he was committed to the Bible and could not make the Scriptures "teach anything else" but the system set forth in the Confession.[27] Thus, for Warfield, the system that had been indelibly imprinted upon him throughout his childhood years was identical to the teaching of Scripture. To be faithful to one was to be faithful to the other. Of course, as has been seen, throughout the nineteenth century the character, treatment, and teachings of the Bible, as they had been traditionally understood by faithful Christians, had been called into question. The result was that the idea that the Bible is supernatural revelation from the triune God for the purpose of revealing his Son in order to save his people, and the creation, was also called into question. Or, as Warfield notes, the doctrine of the inspiration of the Bible had been "attacked."[28] In this address, Warfield chooses to answer the question: "What seems the result of the attack?"[29] In his typically precise and methodical way he begins by defining the doctrine of verbal inspiration and then he more than hints at what he sees as a part, if not the whole, of the main problem.

25. Ibid., 671.
26. Reprinted in *CW* 1:395–425, and hereafter referred to as IC.
27. Warfield, IC, 396.
28. Ibid.
29. Ibid.

> At the very outset, that our inquiry may not be a mere beating of the air, we must briefly, indeed, but clearly, state what we mean by the Church Doctrine. For, unhappily, there are almost as many theories of inspiration held by individuals as there are possible stages imaginable between the slightest and the greatest influence God could exercise on man.[30]

It seems that there was rank confusion regarding the matter. Warfield, therefore, sets his hand to clearing up the uncertainty. He begins with a definition of the Reformed doctrine of verbal inspiration in order to demonstrate that the arguments lobbied against it not only failed to overthrow it, but actually strengthened it.[31] As Warfield states, "Inspiration is that extraordinary, supernatural influence (or, passively, the result of it,) exerted by the Holy Ghost on the writers of our Sacred Books, by which their words were rendered also the words of God, and, therefore, perfectly infallible."[32]

Warfield next expands on the definition. The influence of the Holy Ghost, he says, was "a supernatural one—something different from the inspiration of the poet or man of genius."[33] The accuracy of Luke as a historian, argues Warfield, is not merely to be equated with "'the diligent and accurate Suetonius.'"[34] Moreover, this influence of the Holy Spirit was not only something different from the inspiration of a poet or genius, but also different from the supernatural operations of "the Spirit in the conversion and sanctifying guidance of believers."[35] This means that the biblical writers in the employment of their task as biblical writers were protected against falsehoods in a way that the greatest theologians in the history of the church were not.[36] Finally, this also means that "an absolute infallibility" characterizes the divine words, "so that every part of Holy Writ is thus held alike infallibly true in all its statements, of whatever kind."[37] Warfield then proceeds to qualify what precisely is meant, or not meant, by this affirmation.

---

30. Ibid.
31. Ibid., 424.
32. Ibid.
33. Ibid., 396–97.
34. Ibid., 397.
35. Ibid.
36. Ibid.
37. Ibid.

First, this doctrine says nothing about the "mode of inspiration," which, according to Warfield, the Reformed churches confessed was "inscrutable."[38] Second, the doctrine is "framed as to distinguish it from revelation—seeing that it has to do with *communication* of truth not its acquirement."[39] Thirdly, it does not communicate a "mechanical theory of inspiration," despite the fact that "dishonest, careless, ignorant or over-eager controverters of its doctrine have often brought the charge."[40] This was to say, that the doctrine affirms the presence of the human element in the divine task of inspiration so "that every word of Scripture, without exception, is the word of God; but alongside of that, they [the Reformed churches] hold equally that every word is the word of man."[41] Finally, it means that the doctrine is not mysterious, "except, indeed, in the sense in which everything supernatural is mysterious."[42] Warfield states that there is an:

> . . . analogy here with all that we know of the Spirit's action in other spheres! Just as the first act of loving faith by which the regenerated soul flows out of itself to its Saviour [*sic*], is at once the consciously-chosen act of the soul and the direct work of the Holy Ghost; so, every word indited [*sic*] under the analogous influence of inspiration was at one and the same time the consciously self-chosen word of the writer and the divinely-inspired word of the Spirit.[43]

Having an understanding of the reality of this divine and human union and of the impossibility of separating the two in the production of the Bible is at the heart of recognizing the true biblical doctrine of verbal inspiration. Yet it is possible to understand the meaning of this union incorrectly. Warfield later had occasion to deny definitively that the divine-human union in the incarnation is a proper analogy at all points for the divine-human union in production of the Bible.[44] The incarnation is a

---

38. Ibid.

39. Ibid.

40. Ibid.

41. Ibid., 397–98. For a more detailed explanation of this, see Warfield, "Divine and Human in the Bible," *SSW* 2:542–48.

42. Warfield, IC, 398.

43. Ibid.

44. Warfield never deviated from this position. In "Inspiration," *CW* 1:108, he states: "The Scriptures are merely the product of Divine and human forces working together to produce a product in the production of which the human forces work under the initiation and prevalent direction of the Divine."

hypostatic union that is *not* part of the relationship between the Holy Spirit and the human authors of Scripture. So, even though there is a divine-human union in both the incarnation and the "'inscripturation' of the Holy Spirit," the analogy can clearly be pressed too far. Indeed, according to Warfield, it is actually quite a "remote analogy" that is based solely on the fact that there is a divine-human union in both cases.[45]

In the remainder of this address, Warfield chose not to endeavor to prove the doctrine of inspiration as he had stated it, but, "assuming it to have been accepted by the Church," decided instead to respond to the question of whether the conclusions of modern biblical criticism undermined the church's confidence in the doctrine.[46] According to Warfield, in order to genuinely shake the church's confidence in the doctrine, biblical critics would, in fact, have to attack "the proof which is relied on to establish" the doctrine.[47] That proof is bound up with the sacred writers' claims.[48] This is not to argue in a "vicious circle" so as to "assume inspiration in order to prove inspiration," but rather to assume "honesty and sobriety. If a sober and honest writer claims to be inspired by God, then here, at least, is a phenomenon to be accounted for."[49] In other words, Warfield's procedure presupposes a reality of which all men are a part, which makes a particular epistemic claim upon them. Furthermore, these epistemic claims are unavoidably united to the subjective character and orientation of the knower. The moral character of the investigator is also operative in the matter, for it calls for "honesty and sobriety." What exactly, though, does it mean to be honest and sober with respect to biblical criticism?

---

45. Ibid. The fundamental difference is that in the incarnation the divine-human union constitutes a person, while in the divine-human union of the inscripturation of the Holy Spirit one had a work. Thus, we have an example of Warfield analyzing a matter according to what it *is*, his belief that he has true knowledge of what the things *are*, distinguishing between them in accordance with this knowledge of metaphysical reality, and then drawing conclusions based on this true knowledge. His source for this true knowledge is the Bible. For a further treatment of some of these points as they relate to some current controversies in biblical scholarship, see Johnson, *B. B. Warfield*, 229–32. Johnson is addressing Peter Enns, *Inspiration and Incarnation: Evangelicals and the Problem of the Old Testament*.

46. Warfield, IC, 399.

47. Ibid.

48. Ibid.

49. Ibid., 399–400.

By criticism, Warfield is referring to "an investigation with three essential characteristics."[50] First, one needs to exercise "a fearless, honest mental abandonment, apart from presuppositions, to the facts of the case."[51] Second, "a most careful, complete and unprejudiced collection and examination of the facts" is required.[52] Third, "the most cautious care in founding inferences upon them" is mandated.[53] According to Warfield, the failure to exercise any one of these three attributes of an investigation calls the results of the criticism into question.[54] When all three characteristics are absent, they are replaced by "bondage to preconceived opinion," "careless, incomplete or prejudiced collection and examination of the facts," "and rashness of inferences."[55] Warfield, therefore, is clarifying what is and is not true criticism.

At first glance, Warfield *may* seem to have some significant empiricist leanings, if not a particular naïveté, that fails to account for the noetic effects of sin, or the subjective experience of the knower. Yet Warfield's conception of biblical criticism entailed a keen awareness of the dynamic relationship between the biblical exegete and the evidence handled while exegeting. At this point in the address, he is affirming the vital role of the moral character of the knower in investigating and drawing conclusions. Warfield was far from calling for a presuppositionless exegesis, or for giving short shrift to the noetic effects of sin. Instead, he was calling for a willingness to refuse to let *particular* presuppositions prejudice the whole course of one's work and thus its conclusions. He set forth three positive activities for biblical critics and offset these with three corresponding negatives. Opposite the endorsement of a "fearless, honest mental abandonment, apart from presuppositions, to the facts of the case," he set what it looks like not to do this—"*bondage* to preconceived opinion." Warfield was not declaring that one should not have any preconceived opinion. Rather, he was saying that one should not let oneself be enslaved by preconceived opinions that then dictate one's conclusions, or the course of one's conclusions before one even looks at the evidence. To do otherwise is simply to exalt one's opinions over any and all reality.

Warfield went on to ask the following question:

50. Ibid., 409.
51. Ibid.
52. Ibid.
53. Ibid.
54. Ibid.
55. Ibid.

> Now, it may well be asked, is that true criticism which starts with the presupposition that the supernatural is impossible, proceeds by a sustained effort to do violence to the facts, and ends by erecting a gigantic historical chimera—overturning all established history—on the appropriate basis of airy nothing?[56]

Moreover, Warfield stated, "the history of modern negative criticism is blotted all over and every page stained black with the proofs of work undertaken with its conclusion already foregone and prosecuted in a spirit that was blind to all adverse evidence."[57] Put another way, the subjective personal bias, or moral disposition, that prejudices the negative critic leads him to reject any evidence that calls his bias and moral disposition into question. Such an analysis is predicated on two interrelated realities that are part of the total knowing process: 1) the metaphysical status of objects outside of the human knower, which are not dependent on the human knower for their existence, and 2) the human knower's subjective apprehension and comprehension of the object, which is, by the very nature of the case, a moral issue.

One might raise the question, though, as to whether this awareness does not simply demonstrate that the whole matter is impossibly subjective. Warfield addresses this concern to some degree in a footnote in the printed version of his address:

> We hear much of "apologists" undertaking critical study with such preconceived theories as render the conclusion foregone. Perhaps this is sometimes true, but it is not so necessarily. A Theist, believing that there is a personal God, is open to the proof as to whether any particular message claiming to be a revelation is really from him or not, and according to the proof, he decides. A Pantheist or Materialist begins by denying the existence of a personal God, and hence the possibility of the supernatural. If he begins the study of an asserted revelation, his conclusion is necessarily foregone. An honest Theist, thus, is open to evidence either way; an honest Pantheist or Materialist is not open to any evidence for the supernatural.[58]

56. Ibid. Warfield made this same point in "'It Says,' 'God Says,' 'Scripture Says,'" *CW* 1:298, 300. The conceptual point is that presuppositions are not allowing the reality of the data, or the reality that inheres in the data, to condition how one thinks about that data. To deny that the reality of the object could or should direct or inform one's presuppositions is simply to beg the question and to presuppose that the only metaphysical status operative in the knowing process inheres in the knower.

57. Warfield, IC, 409–10.

58. Ibid., 410.

Thus, it *is* possible, according to Warfield, to operate with an openness that does not prejudice the results of one's exegetical work from the outset. His point has to do with one's attitude from the very beginning, from before the actual work has even begun. He does not claim that humans are capable of total objectivity or neutrality, but he does claim that *at a particular point* and *in particular ways* people are capable of a *certain measure* of objectivity.

Throughout the rest of the address, Warfield demonstrates how the work of negative critics had failed to overthrow the conclusions of "sober criticism."[59] He does this by addressing a series of arguments from the negative critics that he saw as not only demonstrating the invalidity of their own conclusions, but also as evidence that the church's doctrine of inspiration is actually in accordance with truth.[60] In the end, Warfield concludes that "modern criticism has absolutely no valid argument to bring against the church doctrine of verbal inspiration, drawn from the phenomena of Scripture."[61] In addition, Warfield insists that there is no middle ground upon which to stand between the confession of a fully, verbally inspired Bible and "no inspiration at all," and that it is "by a divinely permitted inconsistency" that the negative critics can "stand at all."[62] The summation of it all was that "modern biblical criticism has nothing valid to urge against the church doctrine of verbal inspiration, but that on the contrary it puts that doctrine on a new and firmer basis and secures to the church Scriptures which are truly divine."[63]

---

59. Ibid., 411.

60. Ibid., 417.

61. Ibid., 423. It would seem that by including the last clause: "drawn from the phenomena of Scripture," which was a repetition of something he had previously stated, Warfield is highlighting that whatever validity may inhere in their arguments it is not a validity that is supported by the character of the phenomena that they are investigating. Thus, whatever validity is present is based on the presuppositions that they brought to the handling of the evidence. The question then was not: Could the negative critics weave together a coherent argument? Instead, it was: Do the arguments made by the negative critics handle and credibly account for all the available evidence? Put another way: Can the presuppositions that the negative critics use to handle the evidence account for all the evidence?

62. Ibid. Warfield did not shy away from rather stiff language at this point. He called the negative critics "enemies of Christianity."

63. Ibid., 424. One might ask in what sense was this a "new" and "firmer basis." Though Warfield, does not address the question specifically at this point, I think the lines of his argumentation validate the conclusion that it was new and firmer in that the negative critics presented arguments that the church had not had to address previously, and thus it gave opportunity for the articulation of more detailed argumentation that

In this inaugural address, the lines along which Warfield would continue to argue against biblical and theological scholarship that he considered contrary to Scripture are already apparent. Central to his outlook is a particular view of human knowledge in relation to the Scriptures themselves, and therefore, to God, and this view is forever united with the church's doctrine of verbal inspiration. This can be seen in the way Warfield closed this address: "Revelation is but half revelation unless it be infallibly communicated; it is but half communicated unless it be infallibly recorded. The heathen in their blindness are our witnesses of what becomes of an unrecorded revelation."[64] Thus, one's views on inspiration are intimately joined to one's views of God and his relationship not only to humans, but also to the rest of creation. The way Warfield relates these various doctrines to each other and shows how they are also implicated or inherent in each other reveals the systemic character of his thought. These same lines of thought (stressing morality, subjectivity, the supernatural, and their correlation to other doctrines of the Christian faith) can be clearly seen in many of Warfield's other writings.

Human Sin and the Need for Regeneration by the Spirit in Order to Know Saving Truth

In his review of James Denny's *Studies in Theology,* Warfield criticizes Denny's perception of how the apostles understood the relationship between the Scriptures' authority and the ministry of the Holy Spirit in the Christian's heart.

---

helped at least some Christians to understand in a new way the validity of the church's doctrine. I believe this corresponds to Warfield's view of the nature of saving faith and its relation to evidence and conviction. For the latter topics see Warfield, "Faith in Its Psychological Aspects," *CW* 9:313–42. Warfield's conclusion regarding the result of the negative biblical criticism in "Inspiration and Criticism" was stated again in 1888 in "Christian Evidences: How Affected by Recent Criticisms," *SSW* 2:124–31. There he states: "Criticism has proved the best friend to apologetics a science ever had. It is as if it had walked with her around her battlements and, lending her its keen eyes, pointed out an insufficient guarded place here and an unbuttressed approach there; and then, taking playfully the part of the aggressor, made feint after feint towards capturing the citadel, and thus both persuaded and enabled and even compelled her to develop her resources, throw up new defenses, abandon all indefensible positions, and refurbish her weapons, until she now stands armed *cap-a pie*, impregnable to every enemy. The case is briefly this: recent criticism has had a very deep effect upon the Christian evidences in modernizing them and so developing and perfecting them that they stand now easily victor against all modern assaults" (131).

64. Warfield, IC, 424–25.

> It is surely not necessary to point out that such was not the way the apostles understood the matter. With them [the apostles] the authority of Scripture was the test rather of the professed deliverances of the Spirit in the heart (1 Cor. xiv. 37). Nor ought it to be necessary to say that such was not the way the Reformers understood the matter. With them the formal ground of Christian knowledge was the written Word of God, and the testimony of the Spirit was his creative act upon the heart quickening it to the perception and acceptance of this truth.[65]

Similar emphases are seen in "Christianity and Revelation":

> According to the Scriptures, therefore, special revelation is a *historic process, an organic system*, a *continuous divine activity* directed to destroying the power of sin, to the building up of the Kingdom of God, to the restoration of the Cosmos, to the summing up of all things in Christ. In this *historic process*, God makes himself known as the God of Grace: and *every element that enters into it is a substantial constituent of this special revelation*. Properly taken, therefore, special revelation is the redemptive process itself conceived as a manifestation of God's nature and character.[66]

Thus, for Warfield, the whole doctrine of revelation can be expressed as a historic process and a continuous divine activity. Special revelation is for the purpose of destroying sin, and all of revelation is the "manifestation of God's nature and character." Indeed, to properly understand the biblical doctrine of revelation, says Warfield, it must be recognized that special revelation is integral to the reality of God as the Gracious One who overcomes sin in fallen human beings. He continues:

> Its [revelation's] purpose in no case and in none of its applications can be summed up as merely to inform men's understandings (which would be intellectualism); or merely to correct their conduct (which would be ethicism [*sic*]); or merely to quicken within them religious emotions (which would be mysticism). It is always to be understood as taking its place in the great organic process by which God is rescuing mankind, the world, from the power of sin and making his name glorious. And as such it takes its place also, of course, with the totality of this process in the still broader process of revelation in general, into which it works to cure the faults of man induced by sin, and so to carry the revelatory pro-

---

65. Warfield, "Review of *Studies in Theology*," *SSW* 2:307.
66. Warfield, "Christianity and Revelation," *SSW* 1:29.

cess forward to its originally destined end of making known to the intelligent universe all the glory of divine nature.[67]

In "God and Human Religion and Morals,"[68] Warfield states that proclamation of "the elements of a true religion and morality"[69] were not enough to overcome the noetic effects of sin. God had to do something more:

> Sinful man, fearing God because guilty, and hating him because corrupt, would inevitably reject this revelation or distort it to his own mind. It was necessary to cure man's sin, which had "held down the truth in unrighteousness," and that, by delivering him from both its penalties, causing fear of God, and its corruption, causing dislike of God. Only thus could a hospitable reception in the human mind and heart be secured for the elements of true religion and morality published in God's intervening revelation.[70]

Warfield proceeds to explain the way in which God has overcome the sin-damaged mind and heart:

> But it has pleased him [God] to accomplish it only in the course of a process which extends through ages. He has first, in a progressive revelation, running through many generations, published the elements of a true religion and morality on his own authority, and embodied them in an authoritative record, which should stand for all time as the source and norm of the truth. He has then, in the fullness of the times, sent his own Son to be the propitiation for the sins of the world. And he has then sent his Spirit into the world to work upon the hearts of men, framing in them faith in the sacrifice of the Son of God through which they might receive forgiveness of their sins; and cleansing their hearts, that they might understand and obey the truth as it had been delivered to them. This, too, he does. However, not all at once, but in a process extending through ages. Thus it comes about that true religion and morality is only slowly made the possession of man. Objectively in the world in an authoritative revelation, it is subjectively assimilated by the world only as the Kingdom of God is built up, step by step, slowly to the end.[71]

---

67. Ibid., 30.
68. Warfield, "God and Human Religion and Morals," *SSW* 1:41–45.
69. Ibid., 43.
70. Ibid.
71. Ibid.

The correlated nature of Warfield's understanding of these matters can also be seen in other essays. He states that the attacks against the idea of a supernatural revelation from God had shifted during the nineteenth century from a "one-sided" emphasis on God's transcendence by deists to a "one-sided" emphasis on God's immanence by pantheists. He then goes on to depict what should actually be stressed in the relationship between reason and revelation.

> In order to defend the idea of distinctively supernatural revelation against this insidious undermining, it has become necessary, in defining it in its highest and strictest sense, to emphasize the supernatural in the mode of knowledge and not merely in its source. When stress is laid upon the source only without taking into account the mode of knowledge, the way lies open to those who postulate immanent deity in all human thought to confound the categories of reason and revelation, and so practically to do away with the latter altogether. Even when the data on which our faculties work belong to a distinctively supernatural order, yet so long as the mode of acquisition of knowledge from them is conceived as purely human, the resultant knowledge remains natural knowledge; and, since intuition is a purely human mode of knowledge, so-called intuitions of divine truth would form no exception to this classification. Only such knowledge as is immediately communicated by God is, in the highest and strictest sense, supernaturally revealed. The differentia of revelation in its narrowest and strictest sense, therefore, is not merely that the knowledge so designated has God for its source, nor merely that it becomes the property of men by a supernatural agency, but further that it does not emerge into human consciousness as an acquisition of the human faculties, pure and simple.[72]

He later states, speaking a bit more directly, "In the process of the new creation God, however, works also inwardly by his regenerating grace, creating new hearts in men and illuminating their minds for apprehending divine things."[73] Thus, according to Warfield, the doctrines of revelation and salvation are only correctly understood when they are correlated with each other so that the source and mode of the knowledge of God that is synonymous with salvation are both acknowledged as supernatural. Failure to understand Warfield on these points is, by the very nature of the case, to miss his avowal of the noetic effects of sin and how

---

72. Warfield, "Revelation and Inspiration," *CW* 1:40.
73. Ibid., 46.

God overcomes them. To genuinely read Warfield on these matters, then, leads to seeing him affirming the very thing that Marsden et al. deny that he affirmed or emphasized.

"The Biblical Idea of Revelation": Dissecting and Analyzing Revelation

It is not only in his works on systematic theology that Warfield explicates human knowledge and what characterizes the relationship between its objective and subjective elements, but also in his works on the biblical doctrine of revelation. According to him, revelation can be classified according to two categories and expressed in three different ways: 1) natural/supernatural, 2) general/special, or 3) natural/soteriological.[74] The first of each pair is "communicated through the media of natural phenomena occurring in the course of Nature or of history; the other implies an intervention in the natural course of things and is not merely in source but in mode supernatural."[75] The revelation that comes through the media of natural phenomena is "addressed generally to all intelligent creatures, and is therefore accessible to all men; the other is addressed to a special class of sinners, to whom God would make known His salvation."[76] It is this second "species" of revelation that "has in view" "to rescue broken and deformed sinners from their sin and its consequences."[77] The explicitly expressed character of the revelation that can be called "special," "supernatural," or "soteriological" is that it overcomes the effects of sin in particular sinners because it gives them a particular kind of knowledge that is supernaturally given and mediated through supernatural means. Still further, these two "species" of revelation are integrally related so that we do not rightly understand them apart from each other.

God's creation, in other words, forms the context, so to speak, of redemption; natural revelation is the context of soteriological or supernatural revelation. As Warfield phrases it:

> In its most general idea, revelation is rooted in creation and the relations with His intelligent creatures into which God has brought Himself by giving them being. Its object is to realize the end of man's creation, to be attained only through knowledge of

---

74. Warfield, BIR, 1:6.
75. Ibid.
76. Ibid.
77. Ibid.

> God and perfect and unbroken communion with Him. On the entrance of sin into the world, destroying this communion with God and obscuring the knowledge of Him derived from Nature, another mode of revelation was necessitated, having also another content, adapted to the new relation to God and the new conditions of intellect, heart and will brought about by sin.[78]

Warfield also believed it is necessary to recognize what characterizes this mutual dependence in order to better understand how, through their "cooperation," the effect intended in revelation is produced:

> Without special revelation, general revelation would be for sinful men incomplete and ineffective, and could issue, as in point of fact it has issued wherever it alone has been accessible, only in leaving them without excuse (Rom. i. 20). Without general revelation, special revelation would lack that basis in the fundamental knowledge of God as the mighty and wise, righteous and good, maker and ruler of all things, apart from which the further revelation of this great God's interventions in the world for the salvation of sinners could not be either intelligible, credible, or operative.[79]

Warfield then contrasts human knowledge of God prior to and after the fall into sin, and how overcoming human sin required a special or soteriological revelation from God:

> And not being a sinner, man in Eden, as he contemplated the works of God, saw God in the unclouded mirror of his mind with a clarity of vision, and lived with Him in the untroubled depths of his heart with a trustful intimacy of association, inconceivable to sinners. Nevertheless, the revelation of God in Eden was not merely "natural." Not only does the prohibition of the forbidden fruit involve a positive commandment (Gen. ii. 16), but the whole history implies an immediacy of intercourse with God which cannot easily be set to the credit of the picturesque art of the narrative, or be fully accounted for by the vividness of the perception of God in His works proper to sinless creatures.[80]

Thus, "It is not then the supernaturalness of special revelation which is rooted in sin, but, if we may be allowed the expression, the specialness

---

78. Ibid., 7.
79. Ibid., 8.
80. Ibid.

of supernatural revelation."[81] In other words, the soteriological revelation that overcame the effects of sin was not the only supernatural revelation. Instead, *all* of God's revelation, even prior to sin, is supernatural because the creation is the product of, and is providentially governed by, God. Before sin, man experienced "immediate intercourse" with God,[82] which was intimately bound up in God's providential presence in the creation and this tie was not fully eradicated when sin entered the created order. Furthermore, since these matters are not only related to the space God created, but also the realm of time, Warfield included temporality as a part of the correlation of these doctrines.

God, History, Revelation, and Sin

According to Warfield, after God banished Man from the Garden, his "general revelation ceased to be, in the strict sense, supernatural."[83] This does not mean, however, that God abandoned his creation. God's "providence still ruled over all, leading steadily onward to the goal for which man had been created."[84] Furthermore:

> . . . His [God's] Spirit still everywhere wrought upon the hearts of men, stirring up all their powers (though created in the image of God, marred and impaired by sin) to their best activities, and to such splendid effect in every department of human achievement as to command the admiration of all ages, and in the highest region of all, that of conduct, to call out from an apostle the encomium that though they had no law they did by nature (observe the word "nature") the things of the law.[85]

So, for Warfield, all creation is subject to God's governance, and no aspect of creation is rightly understood until it is understood in such terms, and conditioned by its relation to God. Thus, even the unregenerate can accomplish significant thoughts and deeds that conform to varying degrees to God's truth, and this "illustrates merely the heights to which the powers of man may attain under the guidance of providence and the influences of what we have learned to call God's "common grace."[86]

81. Ibid.
82. Ibid.
83. Ibid.
84. Ibid., 9.
85. Ibid.
86. Ibid.

To be certain, though, such attainments did not amount to knowledge of God's "'saving truth' or "special revelation,'"[87] Yet, throughout history, God's supernatural or soteriological revelation, which results in salvation, has been and is intimately bound to the general revelation of God to Man. They have an unbroken and intimate relationship with each other, although all of the details that characterize that relationship are not necessarily known.[88]

Warfield then embarks on an explanation of God's revelation as "The Process of Revelation."[89]

> In contrast with His general, natural revelation, in which all men by virtue of their very nature as men share, this special, supernatural revelation was granted at first only to individuals, then progressively to a family, a tribe, a nation, a race, until when the fullness of time was come it was made the possession of the whole world. It may be difficult to obtain from Scripture a clear account of why God chose thus *to give this revelation of His grace only progressively*; or, to be more explicit, *through the process of a historical development*. Such is, however, the ordinary mode of the Divine working.[90]

Further, the same historical, progressive development that characterizes God's special revelation can also be seen in the Scriptures "in their own growth."[91] According to Warfield, God's saving revelation is so wedded to historical events, and thereby the historical process, that, in Warfield's time, it had become the custom of some to relegate and reduce saving revelation to simply God's deeds or acts. Although God's acts in history *are* properly termed revelation, they do not constitute all of God's revelation. God's *written* word is revelation as well. It is in understanding Warfield's conception of some of what distinguishes the relationship between God's deeds and his written revelation that Warfield's emphasis on God overcoming the noetic effects of sin can be seen. Throughout this, the theological basis of Warfield's beliefs regarding human knowledge become clear:

> But revelation, after all, is the correlate of understanding and has as its proximate end just the *production of knowledge*, though not

87. Ibid.
88. Ibid., 10.
89. Ibid., 11.
90. Ibid; emphasis added.
91. Ibid., 11.

of course, knowledge for its own sake, but for the sake of salvation. The series of the redemptive acts of God, accordingly, can properly be designated "revelation" only when and so far as they are contemplated as adapted and designed to produce knowledge of God and His purpose and methods of grace. *No bare series of unexplained acts can be thought, however, adapted to produce knowledge,* especially if these acts be, as in this case, of a highly transcendental character. Nor can this particular series of acts be thought to have as its main design the production of knowledge; its main design is rather to save man.[92]

In Warfield's thinking, God's revelation gives a particular kind of knowledge and understanding. Moreover, when Warfield modifies the term "revelation" with "soteriological," he is claiming that there is a knowledge of God that is able to save people when it is received. Thus, to deny that Warfield failed to account for the subjective element in epistemology and the noetic effects of sin is to miss a fundamental and significant part of what he wrote regarding the character and administration of God's revelation, as well as the way in which he correlated this to the doctrines of man and salvation.

To accomplish salvation God not only had to perform particular acts, but also, at times, precede those acts with his preparatory word and then follow them with his explanatory word. Moreover, Warfield maintains that these ideas are contained in Scripture. He states:

> No doubt the production of knowledge of the Divine grace is one of the means by which this main design of the redemptive acts of God is attained. But this only renders it the more necessary that the proximate result of producing knowledge should not fail; and it is doubtless for this reason that the series of redemptive acts of God has not been left to explain itself, but the explanatory word has been added to it. Revelation thus appears, however, not as the mere reflection of the redeeming acts of God in the minds of men, but as a factor in the redeeming work of God, a component part of the series of His redeeming acts, without which that series would be incomplete and so far inoperative for its main end. Thus *the Scriptures* represent it, not confounding revelation with the series of the redemptive acts of God, but placing it among the redemptive acts of God and giving it a function as a substantive element in the operations by which the merciful God saves sinful men.[93]

---

92. Ibid., 12.
93. Ibid.; emphasis added. Warfield's view of revelation then is that God's revelation is

Warfield stresses the point that one is not thinking biblically about the doctrine of revelation unless one understands it in relation to the noetic effects of sin. This is apparent not only in his analysis of the biblical idea of revelation, as seen above, but also in the following:

> One of the most grievous of the effects of sin is the deformation of the image of God reflected in the human mind, and there can be no recovery from sin which does not bring with it the correction of this deformation and the reflection in the soul of man of the whole glory of the Lord God Almighty. Man is an intelligent being; his superiority over the brute is found, among other things, precisely in the direction of all his life by his intelligence; and his blessedness is rooted in the true knowledge of his God—for this is life eternal, that we should know the only true God and Him whom He has sent. Dealing with man as an intelligent being, God the Lord has saved him by means of a revelation, by which he has been brought into an ever more adequate knowledge of God, and been led ever more and more to do his part in working out his own salvation with fear and trembling as he perceived with ever more and more clearness how God is working it out for him through mighty deeds of grace.[94]

---

an integral part of God's redemption. That is virtually identical to that found in Ridderbos, *Redemptive History and the New Testament Scriptures*. See also Warfield, "Formation of the Canon of the New Testament," *CW* 1:451–56; and "Inspiration," *CW* 1:107. This was the standard Old Princeton view of the relationship between holiness and truth, or piety and learning. Consider the following from Archibald Alexander's preface to *Memoirs of the Rev. Thomas Halyburton*, as quoted in Calhoun, *Princeton Seminary* 1:130: "'. . . he who trifles with the truth, trifles with his own life.' 'Truth is so vital, and so necessary to the existence and perfection of a pious character…that we cannot be too solicitous to acquire correct knowledge.' "This 'pursuit of truth' does not depend solely on one's mind; it depends on 'the love of truth' which lays aside 'pride, prejudice, and partiality.' 'Honesty and deep humility' are its 'essential prerequisites.'"

94. Warfield, BIR, 13. In the latter part of the quote Warfield is quoting from John 17:3 and Phil 2:12. Or consider the following from Warfield, "Calvin's Doctrine of the Knowledge of God," in *CW* 5:44–45: "[T]he structure and organization of the world, and the things that daily happen out of the ordinary course of nature, that is under the providential government of God, bear witness to God which the dullest ear cannot fail to hear (I. v. 1, 3, 7 esp. II. vi. 1); and that the light that shines from creation, while it may be smothered, cannot be so extinguished but that some rays of it find their way into the most darkened soul (I. V. 14). . . . The sole cause of the failure of the natural revelation is to be found, therefore, in the corruption of the human heart. Two results flow from this fact. First, it is not a question of the extinction of the knowledge of God, but of the corruption of the knowledge of God. And secondly, men are without excuse for their corruption of the knowledge of God. On both points Calvin is insistent."

Here Warfield not only specifically and directly testifies to the reality and effects of the noetic effects of sin, but also explains how they are overcome. This includes the idea that an integral part of the Christian's salvation is a progression in right thinking regarding God and how this salvation is being accomplished in the Christian's life—another way of talking about the concept of "right reason" as the possession of those whom God has made the objects of his mercy by overcoming the noetic effects of sin.

Still further, claiming that Warfield viewed truth as a "stable entity" and not "historically relative" raises a question as to just what Marsden means by those terms.[95] As has been shown, Warfield goes into significant detail regarding the historical character of God's revelation, in terms of both God's deeds and his written revelation as given to the prophets and apostles. Warfield quite explicitly discusses a variety of ways in which God's revelation is conditioned by and integrated into the historical process, explaining these matters within the context of God's providential governing of that process. Still further, it is not simply God's written revelation, Scripture, that was given through and wedded to a historical process, but also the understanding of this revelation by God's people as they have grown in the knowledge of biblical doctrine.[96] According

---

95. It would seem that Marsden considers them to be the equivalent of believing that there is a truth that can be communicated to, and known by, people in all times and places, since he states in *Fundamentalism and American Culture*, 110: "In either case truth was a stable entity, not historically relative, best expressed in written language that, at least potentially, would convey one message in all times and places." One is left wondering if Marsden believes that there are truths that can be expressed in written language and can communicate one message in all times and places. If not, then it would be important for him to articulate what he thinks the church throughout the centuries has confessed to believe. If it is possible to convey one message for all times and places through written language, then one wonders why Warfield and other Princetonians are criticized for such views, and identified as relying upon Scottish Common Sense Realism for holding to them. Presumably, Marsden and many others, who criticize the Princetonians for the latter's belief that they could know truth that was true for all people for all times and places—what we might call transcendental truth—also believe that they can know what is true for all people for all time and places, or they would not seek to claim to tell others what was true about the Princetonians. In other words, by faulting the Princetonians for making "absolute" truth claims, they in turn have to make their own "absolute" truth claim.

96. Warfield, "Century's Progress in Biblical Knowledge," *SSW* 2:3–14. The whole point of this essay is to identify how the nineteenth century ought to be thought of in terms of its place within mankind's historical progress in biblical knowledge. Warfield acknowledged that there were different perspectives or approaches from which to think about the progress of biblical knowledge in history. See chapter 4 in this book.

to Warfield, historical process, or progress, is and has been an integral part of the life of the church and the advancement of God's kingdom on earth. Warfield, however, could not sit idle while liberal theologians, who were at work reconceptualizing the Christian faith, imposed their definitions of "historical process" or "progress" on to the doctrinal conceptions that the church is to believe.[97] Arthur C. McGiffert's inaugural address when he assumed the Chair of Church History at Union Seminary in New York brought this response from Warfield:

> This "formal principle" of Protestantism, of course, does not deny that there has been such a thing as a "development of doctrine." It does not make its appeal to the early Church as the norm of Christian truth; and it does not imagine that the first generation of Christians had already sounded all the depths of revelation, It [sic] makes its appeal to the Scriptures of God, which embody in written form the teaching of Christ through His apostles upon which the earliest as well as the latest Church was builded [sic]. Protestantism expects to find, and does find, a progressive understanding and realization of this teaching of Christ in the Church. The Reformers knew, as well as the end of the nineteenth century knows, that there is a sense in which the Nicene Christology, the Augustinian Anthropology, the Anselmic Soteriology, their own doctrine of Justification by Faith alone, were new in the Church. They thought of nothing so little as discarding these doctrines because they were "new," in the sense in which they were new. They rather held them to constitute the very essence of Christian truth. They believed in "the development of true Christian doctrine," and looked upon themselves as raised up by God to be the instruments of a new step in this development.[98]

This belief in the historical character of God's revelation and the work of the church in formulating ever more and more correct expressions of what the faithful are to believe is intimately joined to Warfield's belief that the Scriptures are "living words still speaking to us."[99]

Marsden's assertions, then, simply do not match the actual content of Warfield's writings on these issues. Of course, if one defines "historical" in a way that automatically rules out the ability of human beings, as historically, time/space-bound creatures, to apprehend and comprehend truths that are true for *all* times and places, then you have a view of "his-

---

97. See chapter 6 in this book.
98. Warfield, "Latest Phase of Historical Rationalism," *CW* 9:602.
99. Warfield, "'It Says:' 'Scripture Says:' 'God Says:'" *CW* 1:300.

torical" that does not fit with Warfield's beliefs. The irony at this point is that Warfield claimed that this was exactly what was being done by a number of liberal scholars of his day. Rather than truly investigating a particular historical phenomenon, these scholars were prone to substitute their own reactions to any such phenomena under investigation, or whatever they desired the outcome of an investigation to be, for the actual answers to historical questions. For instance, Warfield faulted Douglas Clyde Macintosh for answering the question "What is Christianity?" with "What is Christianity *for* me?"[100] Thus he saw Macintosh et al. as guilty of the following:

> Out of the general Pragmatic doctrine that "reality must be defined in terms of experience"—or, as even more sharply expressed, that "reality is experience"—these thinkers have evolved the notion that the "essence" of anything is not what it is, but what it is, not merely to but for me; not that which makes the thing precisely the thing it is, but that in the thing, whatever it may be, which I find needful for the realization of a purpose of my own. "The essence of a thing," says William James, "is that one of its properties which is so *important for my interests* that, in comparison with it, I may neglect the rest." Applying this astonishing doctrine to historical entities, and especially to Christianity, which is the historical entity in which at the moment he is interested, Professor Macintosh feels able to argue that the essence of Christianity is not that in Christianity which makes it the particular thing which we call Christianity, but that in Christianity which he finds it desirable to preserve in constructing what he considers the ideal religion.[101]

These scholars rejected the idea that human beings can have true knowledge of what something is. They could only speak about their perceptions of the thing, and they based their identification of what something is on whatever they wanted it to be, or what they wanted out of it. Or, they accepted a Kantian or neo-Kantian epistemology as determinative for their pronouncements regarding what they "knew."[102] It should be noted that Warfield made the point that asking the ques-

---

100. Warfield, "Essence of Christianity and the Cross of Christ," *CW* 3:397.

101. Ibid., 397–98.

102. Macintosh's and James' approach is Kantian in that it follows the following principle of Kant's: "'objects must be viewed as conforming to human thought, not human thought to the independently real.'" See Yarbrough, *Salvation Historical Fallacy*, 75.

tion "What is Christianity?" was no different than asking "what is an old Hellenic doctrine or what Ritschlism really teaches."[103] Warfield summarized the matter: "In the very nature of the case such questions are purely historical and are purely objective in their character, and the answers to them are not in the least advanced by any judgments we may pass upon the rationality or morality of the several doctrines or systems which come under our survey."[104] It should also be stressed that Warfield did not claim that *answering* the question was a purely objective enterprise, rather, his statement addressed the character of the *question* itself. Indeed, his whole point recognized a distinction between one's subjective response to a particular objective reality, and the vital importance of not confusing the two.

Warfield, therefore, did have an explicitly stated historical view of truth and human knowledge that incorporated the subjective element and he also accounted for the noetic effects of sin. He did not, however, operate with a view of history and truth that corresponded to the liberal theology that he criticized. To state it differently, Warfield did not operate with a view of history or human knowledge that fit with a Kantian or neo-Kantian metaphysics or epistemology. Still further, he argued that his account of, or his reasoning about, history and truth was not only biblical, but also corresponded to the reality that human beings experience and the historical record. In other words, it handled all the evidence available to humans on these issues and, therefore, it was worthy of the label "scientific," while that of his opponents did not merit that label. Finally, because Warfield believed that his account of these ideas, which are inherently related to all Christian doctrine, were truly scientific, they were, ipso facto, "constructive," because they built upon previous work by people both in and outside of the church that contributed to the ongoing, i.e., historical, advancement of God's truth in God's creation.[105]

Warfield and the Historical Character of Truth

As discussed earlier, in his essay "The Biblical Idea of Revelation" Warfield emphasized the historical process through which God made his revelation, and how that revelation is even comprehended progressively by an individual possessing salvation. Thus, Warfield not only stressed

---

103. Warfield, "Essence of Christianity and the Cross of Christ," *CW* 3:397.

104. Ibid.

105. Warfield, IC, 395–425; "Christian Evidences: How Affected by Recent Criticism, *SSW* 2:124–31; and "Rights of Criticism and of the Church, *SSW* 2:595–603.

the fact that God's revelation, or truth, has a historical character on a macro scale—within the creation and its whole history—but also on a micro scale—within the individual saved by God's soteriological, or special, revelation. These emphases, however, are not simply relegated to *one* of Warfield's essays; instead we find them throughout numerous essays. Moreover, it is not a mystery as to why Warfield emphasized the macro and micro historical character of God's truth. He was responding to a reconstruction or reconceptualization of Christianity by liberal theologians that led to a view of God's revelation based on either rationalism or mysticism. These theologians also employed the historical-critical method of biblical interpretation based on a naturalistic view of history.[106] That is, this view either found no correlate for the Bible and its claims outside of the metaphysical plane of the material realm, and fell prey to rationalism; or it embraced a spiritual contact point between God and Man that had no connection to anything else in the material realm, and thus fell prey to mysticism. Both errors are ahistorical conceptions of God, his revelation, and truth, because they either reduce the definition of revelation and truth to only that which is empirically verifiable or they refuse to accept that revelation and truth can be present in empirically verifiable realities, finding correlates only through mystical and virtually ineffable experience. Both cases have a conception of God that differs radically from the God of Scripture, who exists both inside and outside of the metaphysical realm of time and space that human beings experience, and providentially guides that realm.

Thus, Warfield went to great lengths to emphasize that the biblically Christian view of reality does not reduce reality to the physical, material, and empirically verifiable realm of human existence, nor does it postulate a view of the spiritual that completely splits it from those same empirically verifiable realities of human existence. The God spoken of in Scripture is neither wholly immanent nor wholly transcendent, but transcendent and immanent simultaneously. In part, this means that human beings can neither fully comprehend God nor fully resist him.[107] Warfield, therefore,

---

106. Warfield, IC, 395–425; "Rights of Criticism and of the Church," *SSW* 2:595–603; "Christian Evidences: How Affected by Recent Criticism," *SSW* 2:124–31; "Heresy and Concession," *SSW* 2:672–79; "Evading the Supernatural," *SSW* 2:680–84; and "Latest Phase of Historical Rationalism," *CW* 9:585–645.

107. That is not to say that people could not resist God to the point of being damned for eternity. They surely could and did. Yet even this damnation was proof that God had not been exhaustively resisted, because the just penalty that he had brought and would bring had not been, nor could be, resisted.

highlights the radical union between the divine and human, spiritual and physical, and argues against Kantian and neo-Kantian conceptions of metaphysics, knowledge, and history.

"God's Providence over All"

Warfield's view of God's providence is integral to all his aforementioned beliefs. In "God's Providence over All,"[108] Warfield places his emphasis on the practical consequences of knowing that the time and space realm of human existence is not governed by God from a distance, but with God himself present. After attributing the title of the essay to Thomas Carlyle, Warfield begins by proclaiming that knowledge of God's providence over all things is the root of the Christian's comfort in life.[109] Reminiscent of Calvin's treatment of the same subject in *The Institutes*, Warfield discusses the significance of the doctrine of God's providence for the Christian, in its personal and devotional functions, as well as its cognitive theological applications:

> A firm faith in the universal providence of God is the solution of all earthly troubles. It is almost equally true that a clear and full apprehension of the universal providence of God is the solution of most theological problems. Most of the religious difficulties with which men disturb their minds, rest on the subtle intrusion into our thinking of what we may call Deistic postulates, and would vanish could but the full meaning of God's universal providence enter and condition all our thinking. It is because we forget this great truth that we vex and puzzle ourselves over difficulties which seem to be insoluble, but which cease to be difficulties at all so soon as we remember that God's providence extends over all.[110]

Warfield's first example of this is the relationship between the divine and human aspects of the Bible; the second deals with the administration of God's saving grace. There is no reason, states Warfield, to play the divine and human aspects of the Bible against each other, since God has been and is providentially present within his creation guiding all things.

---

108. Reprinted in *SSW* 1:110–15 (the table of contents in *SSW* 1 incorrectly lists this as beginning on page 111), and hereafter referred to as GPOA. See also "Divine and Human in the Bible," *SSW* 2:542–48; and "Authority and Inspiration of the Scriptures," *SSW* 2:537–41 for identical lines of argumentation and further elaboration upon these themes.

109. Warfield, GPOA, 110.

110. Ibid., 111.

Since some liberal reconstructions of Christian theology result in, and are dependent upon, exactly that juxtaposition, Warfield declares that such views conceive of the divine and human "as contradictory forces infringing upon one another, and the Bible is the resultant of the two."[111] He, however, challenges the idea that somehow the nature of the Bible itself necessitates a bifurcation of the divine and human in its production. Fundamental to a true understanding of the nature of the Bible is a recognition that it distinctly teaches God's providential presence within all creation. As Warfield states:

> We are not to conceive the matter as if God had simply found the Chronicler, say, with his historical bias; of the Psalmist with his emotional nature already hardened in a purely earthly mould; or Paul with his habits of thought already developed and fixed: and has been compelled, by the pure force of his inspirational impact, to force his word with difficulty through their resisting tissue. Were this so, it might well be that God's Word would come out stained and discolored by the "personal equations" of the human authors, and would no longer be the pure Word of God, but, at best only the mixed word of God and man. But there was, in fact, no Chronicler save as God had himself made him by the providence which is over all.[112]

All that has taken and will take place within the creation is governed by God. The only way the divine and human can be played against each other in the production of the Bible is to fail to affirm God's providential presence and direction within all creation. Of course, Warfield is here affirming exactly what the WCF expresses.[113] Not only what has been labeled the "divine" element is from God, but the human element as well.[114] A genuine understanding of God's providence in the production of the Bible enriches people's "conception of the ways in which God was active in producing" it.[115] Integral to this view are Warfield's doctrines of God as Creator and Redeemer, as previously seen in "The Biblical Idea of Revelation."

111. Ibid., 112.
112. Ibid.
113. WCF, V, SC Q. & A. 11.
114. Warfield, GPOA, 112. This meant, according to Warfield, that in the production of the Bible the real contrast was not between the divine and the human, "but between the inspirational and providential factors which entered into the divine making of the Bible" (113).
115. Ibid., 113.

The second example of a problem resolved by holding the correct belief of God's providence over all things is related to "the distribution of God's saving grace."[116] Some of those around Warfield were having grave difficulties with the idea that the salvation of the lost is dependent in some way upon their hearing the gospel message. If this is true but there are none to bring that message to them, this would mean that they have no chance to escape dying in sin. They did not want to believe that these would die "without hope, because of the mere accident that the gospel has not been carried to them?"[117] Again, Warfield answers these concerns by strongly emphasizing God's providence. God's providence and grace are no more to be set against each other than the divine and human elements in the production of the Bible. "It is only, then, when we forget that God's providence is over all that we are tempted to fancy that need may arise for him to save his people by some exceptional method, outside or beyond his announced method of salvation through faith in Jesus Christ."[118] Here Warfield correlates the doctrine of God with the doctrine of salvation and revelation by accentuating God's providence over and in human history. In Warfield's view, it was simply a matter of detailing what was present in the WCF, which he had been steeped in as a child and which held his allegiance throughout his life.[119]

---

116. Ibid.

117. Ibid., 114.

118. Ibid., 115.

119. For a reaffirmation of his commitment to the WCF at approximately the midpoint of his academic career, see Warfield, "Brief and Untechnical Statement of the Reformed Faith," *SSW* 1:407–10. In response to the 1900 General Assembly that appointed a "'Committee of Fifteen'" to write a "nontechnical statement of the Reformed faith," Warfield wrote his own, as well as a number of responses to the General Assembly's call for this that appeared in *The Presbyterian Banner* and *The Presbyterian*. One can get a sense of Warfield's displeasure in some of his responses to the actions of the General Assembly. For example: "What is seriously wrong with them (these propositions)? We are compelled to conclude that the only thing the matter with them is that they are Calvinistic: uncompromisingly Calvinistic; irredeemably Calvinistic. To a convinced and resolute Calvinist, that surely ought to be no objection. But to the anti-Calvinist it is an objection that outweighs all other objections. And unfortunately there are many Calvinists who have listened to the ravings of the anti-Calvinists until there seems to be a permanent roar left in their ears that accompanies, as an undertone of objection, every purely Calvinistic tone that reaches them. Under the influence of this pressure from without they talk of revising the Confession. But do they really imagine they can so phrase or adjust a faithfully guarded Calvinism that it will no longer be unacceptable to the anti-Calvinistic objector? No, the opposition between Calvinism and anti-Calvinism is incredible." See Warfield, "Revision and the Third Chapter."

Apologetics in Practice

For Warfield, the question of the inspiration of Scripture not only includes the question of whether God has revealed himself to particular men, but also whether God is able to cause others to accept that same revelation. Since this revelation is about particular things, it has an objective character to it, but since it must be comprehended and apprehended by human beings, it also has a subjective character. From Warfield's perspective, since the Bible teaches that God created all reality, then God is Lord of *both* those objective realities that can be known and the subjective apprehension and comprehension of those realities by human beings. Thus, he viewed epistemology as being simultaneously anthropological, theological, and historical. This view compels recognition of the importance of preaching and teaching God's word to his people so they will not only be gathered in but also sanctified. God's work in perfecting his people in holiness, according to Warfield, is something that ministers of the gospel can participate in as they faithfully proclaim biblical doctrine. Although sin caused some fragmentation in the relationship inherent between thinking, willing, and feeling, nonetheless, Warfield, standing in the Old Princeton tradition, believed that there is an integral relationship between right doctrine and thinking on one hand, and right affections and action on the other. In other words, the subjective state of one's soul and the subjective element in human knowledge are inseparable from the objective character of what one is seeking to understand. In order to bring one's thinking, willing, and feeling into harmony with the realities of God's creations, one must align one's thinking with what God has revealed in the Scriptures.

Warfield's scholarly essays reveal that he not only *believed* that knowledge claims can and should be analyzed from both an objective and subjective perspective, but they also demonstrate that he *applied* that approach to his own analyses. This union between the objective and subjective in Warfield's thought can also be seen in some of the sermons he preached at the Sabbath Afternoon Conferences[120] that were a regular part of Princeton Seminary life throughout Warfield's years, both as a student and as a professor. An emphasis on the subjective aspect of knowing, and an analysis of it in relation to the objective realm of knowing, are also evident in two addresses that he gave on the religious life of seminarians near the beginning and end of his teaching career. Through some of these sermons and addresses it is also quite apparent that Warfield had a clearly

---

120. For historical details regarding the origin of the Sabbath Afternoon Conference see Calhoun, *Princeton Seminary* 1:131–36.

articulated view of the subjective nature of truth and the obstacle that sin is in the comprehension and apprehension of truth by human beings.

The Sabbath Afternoon Conference: The Subjective and Moral Character of Knowing

The Sabbath Afternoon Conference was a time set aside by the seminary community for professors and students to come together to encourage and teach one another as well as to support each other in their commitment to, and expression of, Christian virtues.[121] A number of sermons that Warfield gave at some of these meetings are preserved in the book *Faith and Life*.[122] These sermons provide a glimpse of Warfield the exegete working in a pastoral way for the Christian edification of his listeners. While these are devotional in character, it does not mean that they are void of scholarship. Rather, they are the pastoral fruits of a biblical scholar.

In "The Spirit of Faith," Warfield expounds 2 Corinthians 4:13. He begins by noting that this verse is Paul's testimony concerning "the grounds of his courage and faithfulness in preaching the glorious Gospel of Christ."[123] These words of Paul are actually from a time when he was "pressed, perplexed, pursued, smitten down."[124] This gives the reader "a vivid picture of the defeated warrior, who is . . . at his wits ends."[125] Warfield describes the relationship between Paul's work as a minister of the gospel and Christ's work.

> . . . there is thus a marvellous [sic] co-existence of experiences the most desperate and of deliverances the most remarkable. It is as if destruction had continually befallen him; yet ever out of destruction he rises afresh to the continuance of his work. In this remarkable contrast of his experiences the Apostle sees a dramatic reenactment of Christ's saving work, who died that he might live and might bring life to the world. In it he sees himself, he says, ever re-enacting the putting to death of Jesus, that the life also of Jesus may be manifested in his body. As Jesus died and rose again, so he daily dies in the service of Christ and comes to life again; and so, abiding in life, he is ever delivered to death for Jesus' sake

121. Ibid.
122. Warfield, *Faith and Life*.
123. Ibid., 231.
124. Ibid.
125. Ibid.

that the life also of Jesus might be manifested in his mortal flesh. Oh, marvellous [sic] destiny of the followers of Christ, in the very nature and circumstances of their service to placard before the world the great lesson of the redemption of Christ—the great lesson of life by death . . .[126]

Warfield goes on to say, "Thus the very life circumstances of Paul become a preached Gospel."[127] Whereas some theologians might be nervous about using this experiential language identifying the life of a Christian as a "preached Gospel," even if it is the Apostle Paul's life, Warfield seems completely at ease using the expression to depict the Christian life that Paul is describing. It is a "preached Gospel" because, "[T]hey ["Paul's life circumstances" and "the followers of Christ"] manifest Christ and his work for souls."[128] For Warfield to say that they manifest Christ is equal to him saying that they reveal Christ; the Christian, in other words, can properly be called revelation, revelation from God and of God.

Warfield reminds the students and faculty that Paul's account states that the "purpose of God" dictated the circumstances in which he preached the gospel.[129] "The great treasure of the glorious Gospel has been put into such earthen vessels for the very purpose of more fully manifesting its divine glory"[130] Moreover, the ability to endure the weight of this experience was also from God, since:

> Paul attributes it to God's upholding power, operating through faith. That in the midst of such trials he is enabled to endure; that though smitten down continuously he is not destroyed; that though dying daily he still lives with a living Gospel still on his lips; it is all due to his firm conviction and faith.[131]

The Christian's experience, in other words, is to be interpreted through the knowledge that God governs the circumstances of life, and also gives and nurtures the faith that gives the Christian the power to persevere through those circumstances. Furthermore, it is in possessing this interpretive framework that the Christian is empowered to live as a follower of Christ. The Christian life, in other words, is a thoroughly theocentric

---

126. Ibid., 232.
127. Ibid.
128. Ibid., 233.
129. Ibid.
130. Ibid.
131. Ibid.

matter that enlivens the Christian.[132] Warfield continues by quoting the Apostle Paul's words from 2 Corinthians 4:13–14: "So, then, it is death that worketh in us, but life in you, and having the same Spirit of faith, according as it is written, I believed and, therefore, did I speak, since we know that He that raised up Jesus shall raise us up also with Jesus, and shall present us with you." This is where, said Warfield, the apostle acquired his strength and courage.[133] "It is only because of his firm faith in the Gospel he preaches that he can endure through the trials into which its service has immersed him."[134] Warfield elaborates:

> With a less clear conviction and less firm faith in it, he would long ago have succumbed to the evils of his life and his lips have long ago become dumb. But he believed; and, therefore, though earth and hell combined to destroy him, he could not but speak. Let earthly trials multiply; beyond the daily deaths of earth there was an eternal life in store for him; and the more he could rescue from that death to that life, the more multiplied grace would redound to increased thanksgiving and abound to God's glory. In the power of this faith the Apostle can face and overcome the trials of life.[135]

There are a number of lessons to be drawn from these truths. First, Paul acquired the "norm of his faith in the Old Testament saints."[136] Though this might seem strange to some, Warfield points out that, though the word "faith" is not littered throughout the Old Testament, and Christians are likely to associate Old Testament "religion" with "awe" and "fear" and the New Testament with "faith," this conception is definitely less than accurate.[137] Recognizing this inaccuracy is dependent on understanding that one is wrestling with *concepts*, not simply words, and the concepts of awe, fear, faith, and trust are not "antagonistic," but

---

132. We should be reminded of Sydney Ahlstrom's conclusion that with the Old Princeton theology expressed by Charles Hodge, "doctrine became less a living language of piety than a complex burden to be borne," that there was a departure from the "fervent theocentricity of Calvin which Edwards had striven to reinstate," and "that Reformed theology was "emptied of its most dynamic element" and "[A] kind of rationalistic *rigor mortis* set in" that "made traditional doctrines so lifeless and static that a new theological turn was virtually inevitable." See chapter 1 in this book.

133. Warfield, *Faith and Life*, 234.
134. Ibid.
135. Ibid.
136. Ibid.
137. Ibid., 234–35.

"correlative."¹³⁸ The Old Testament "heroes of the faith lived in the twilight of knowledge."¹³⁹ Abraham is the primary example, presented by both Paul and James "both in the subjective and objective" sense "as the Father of the Faithful."¹⁴⁰ Thus, according to Warfield, "knowledge and faith stand in relation to one another, but are not the measure of one another."¹⁴¹ While it is true that faith cannot be present where there is *no* knowledge, "dim knowledge" can result in "strong faith."¹⁴² Consequently, Warfield specifically characterizes the saving faith of the Christian in a non-rationalistic way, and, by implication, the whole Christian life in a decidedly non-rationalistic manner.¹⁴³

138. Ibid., 235.
139. Ibid., 235–36.
140. Ibid., 235.
141. Ibid., 236.
142. Ibid.

143. For an identical view, see Turretin, *Institutes of Elenctic Theology* 1:23–39, 565–66. Turretin states, "faith includes knowledge in its conception, not that faith is absolutely the same as knowledge, or that to believe is the same as to understand (as Bellarmine falsely states our opinion); but that since knowledge is the genus of all habits, while faith by his own confession is an intellectual habit, faith also ought necessarily to embrace knowledge that it may be true" (565). He then follows this by quoting Bellarmine and Calvin to show that the former did not understand the latter, and that Calvin repudiated the idea of implicit faith. Each believer had to possess a particular knowledge of the gospel in order to embrace the promises in it by faith and be saved (565–66), and Charles Hodge, *ST* 1:49, affirms the same things with respect to the relationship of saving faith to knowledge: ". . . reason is necessarily presupposed in every revelation. Revelation is the communication of truth to the mind. But the communication of truth supposes the capacity to receive it. Revelations cannot be made to brutes or idiots. Truths, to be received as objects of faith, must be intellectually apprehended. A proposition, to which we attach no meaning, however important the truth it may contain, cannot be an object of faith . . . unless we know the meaning of the words nothing is communicated to the mind, and the mind can affirm or deny nothing on the subject. In other words knowledge is essential to faith. In believing we affirm the truth of the proposition believed. But we can affirm nothing of that of which we know nothing. The first and indispensable office of reason, therefore, in matters of faith, is the cognition, or intelligent apprehension of the truths proposed for our reception." In *ST* 3:34 we find Hodge stating the following on regeneration, saving faith, and knowledge: "This new life, therefore, manifests itself in new views of God, of Christ, of sin, of holiness, of the world, of the gospel, and of the life to come; in short, of all those truths which God has revealed as necessary for salvation. This spiritual illumination is so important

Something else that Paul reveals is that the origin of saving faith is the Holy Ghost.[144] To those who would think of the Holy Spirit as primarily, if not exclusively, the possession of Christians in the New Testament era, Warfield asked the following question, which reveals the dominant conception in his thinking regarding the central role of the Spirit in the Christian's life. "Or shall we say that only in New Testament times men are dead in sin, and only in these days of the completed Gospel and of the New Covenant do men need the almighty power of God to raise them from their spiritual death?"[145] In other words, Warfield clarifies that it is the Spirit of God that must overcome the effects of sin in order for *any* sinner to become a Christian.[146] Warfield has already made it clear that this saving faith that the Spirit of God gives is joined to and correlated with knowledge. It is certainly not to be *equated* with knowledge, but it certainly does affect the intellect, while resurrecting the deadened sinner. The primary point or focus in the passage, however, is to emphasize that the Spirit of God is called "the Spirit of faith."

"Faith is, therefore, conceived of by the Apostle as absolutely not the product of our own powers but of the Spirit of God, and it is inconceiv-

---

and so necessary and such an immediate effect of regeneration (Colossians 3:10; 1 Timothy 2:4), that the whole of conversion (which is the effect of regeneration) is summed up in knowledge. . . . Inseparably connected with this knowledge and included in it, is faith, in all the forms and exercises in which spiritual truths are its objects."

144. Warfield, *Faith and Life*, 236. Warfield uses the terms "Holy Ghost" and "Holy Spirit" interchangeably.

145. Ibid., 237.

146. Given that Warfield had the Shorter catechism (SC) memorized by the age of six, then memorized the Scripture proofs and the Larger catechism by the age of sixteen it is not surprising that he would have this perspective. SC Q. & A. 29–31 specifically address these matters: "Q. 29) How are we [Christians] made partakers of the redemption purchased by Christ? A. We are made partakers of the redemption purchased by Christ, by the effectual application to us by his Holy Spirit." "Q. 30) How doth the Spirit apply to us the redemption purchased by Christ? A. The Spirit applieth to us the redemption purchased by Christ, by working faith in us, and thereby uniting us to Christ in our effectual calling." "Q. 31) What is effectual calling? A. Effectual calling is the work of God's Spirit, whereby, convincing us of our sin and misery, enlightening our minds in the knowledge of Christ, and renewing our wills, he doth persuade and enable us to embrace Jesus Christ, freely offered to us in the gospel." We should note that the catechism makes clear that the Spirit of God operates on the person so as to overcome the noetic effects of sin and "renewing" the will. Thus, it does not teach that new faculties are given but that the already created faculties are given a new capacity. This is one of the primary points Warfield made in his response to Herman Bavinck and Abraham Kuyper in Warfield, "Review of *De Zekerheid des Geloofs*," *SSW* 2:106–23.

able to him that it can exist apart from His gift."[147] This means that "faith is the gift of God in its innermost essence."[148] This is further stressed in 1 Corinthians 12:7, where it is listed as one of the gifts given by the Spirit to men. Warfield states that it is here "used as a characterizing description of the Spirit,"[149] which means "all faith comes from Him."[150]

This led Warfield to elaborate on a third lesson for the Christian's life; one that he applied particularly to those that would be entrusted with preaching the gospel. Warfield exhorted these budding pastors with Paul's own mainstay—that "faithfulness and steadfastness" in gospel work is the result of "a Spirit-wrought faith in the Gospel which he preached."[151] As Warfield writes:

> The secret, he tells us, of his ability to continue throughout his dreadful trials in the work to which he had been called; the secret of his power to faint not, that is not to play the coward, but to renounce the hidden things of shame and refuse to walk in craftiness or handle the Word of God deceitfully; the secret of his power to preach a simple Gospel in honest faithfulness in the face of all temptations to please men, and to preach the saving Gospel in the face of all persecution—was simply that he had a hearty and unfeigned faith in it.[152]

Warfield concludes his sermon by cautioning that God does not send his gospel preachers "to say the most plausible things," or "to teach men what they already believe."[153] He then characterizes the truths that are to be preached as "unpalatable," "apparently absurd," and "mysterious."[154] Yet, as Warfield reflects, "What care we if it be unpalatable, if it be true? For if it be true, it is urgent."[155]

On another occasion Warfield spoke to the students regarding "Spiritual Strengthening," from Ephesians 3:14–19.[156] This brief exposition stresses the mystical nature of the Christian's strengthening for the

---

147. Warfield, *Faith and Life*, 239.
148. Ibid.
149. Ibid.
150. Ibid., 240.
151. Ibid.
152. Ibid., 240–41.
153. Ibid., 242.
154. Ibid.
155. Ibid.
156. Ibid., 267–78.

purpose of "apprehending the incomparable mysteries of our faith."[157] This passage is Paul's prayer for God's people to experience great and wondrous blessings. Warfield notes that though it enumerates a succession of topics, the prayer forms a united whole so that its several parts are only properly understood when related to one another.[158]

The main thing for which Paul prayed is "spiritual strengthening," and this can be taken in two senses.[159] Warfield tells his audience that this can be understood to refer to "spiritual" as opposed to "physical" strengthening. Or, it can be understood to refer to the power that performs the strengthening, that is, the Spirit of God, over and against an earthly power. Paul's prayer includes both notions.[160] Indeed, both concepts capture, according to Warfield, "the substance of his [Paul's] prayer," which is "that we may be strengthened with respect to the inner man by the Spirit of God.[161] This, in turn, is the same as Christ dwelling "by faith in our hearts."[162] It is at this point that Warfield steers his listeners through an understanding of the relationship that the series of clauses in vv. 14–17 have to each other. If taken one way, they communicate "what the spiritual strengthening consists in," and "in the other, what it eventuates in."[163] Still, regardless of which way one chooses, the emphasis is upon Christ's abiding and thus leads to two important points.[164]

First, this emphasis on Christ's abiding reveals that Paul's audience were Christians since he does not speak of Christ coming to them, but rather of Christ already abiding with them.[165] Second, "the spiritual strengthening . . . is dependent on the abiding presence of Christ in their hearts."[166] Paul was not discounting the role or presence of the Holy Spirit, said Warfield, because Paul, as well as the rest of the New Testament, taught that Jesus and the Spirit were united, working together to strengthen the believer in order to form Christ within him or her.[167]

---

157. Ibid., 274.
158. Ibid., 267.
159. Ibid., 268.
160. Ibid.
161. Ibid.
162. Ibid.
163. Ibid., 269.
164. Ibid.
165. Ibid.
166. Ibid., 270.
167. Ibid.

Yet, as Warfield phrases it, "the Apostle is one of the most fecund writers,"[168] so he elaborates on this reality of which he wrote. Warfield states that there is both an objective fact—Christ dwelling within the believer—and a subjective fact—the faith of the Christian by which Christ dwells in the believer.[169] Paul's emphasis was on the continuing presence of Christ abiding with the Christian, but this relationship was conceived of as taking place through the believer's faith, and to the degree that faith fails, "so do the signs of His presence within: the strengthening of the Spirit and the steady burning of the flame of faith are correlative."[170]

It is only as the Spirit keeps the Christian's faith "firm and clear" that Christ abides in "the inner man" and gives strength.[171] The result of such strengthening is love and knowledge, and thus the goal of the prayer is "expansion of spiritual apprehension."[172] Paul's emphasis, at this point, is seen through his use of three distinct words that communicate the single thought of elevation by the Holy Spirit to "the capacity of spiritual apprehension indicated."[173] The "proximate" end of the prayer was the "expansion of the heart for the apprehension of spiritual things."[174] As Warfield expresses it, "These things to be apprehended are too great for man's natural powers. He must have new strength from on high given him to compass them. He may by the Spirit be raised to a higher potency of apprehension for them. God grant it to you!"[175] Next, Warfield asks, "[W]hat are these things?" and then begins to set forth the answer from the text.[176]

Warfield first observes that Paul wrote in generalities about these matters that are apprehended through increased strength by the Holy Spirit.[177] The significant point made, though, is "on the bigness of the thing" apprehended.[178] "It is because the thing is so big that they need strengthening in the inner man before they have full strength to appre-

168. Ibid.
169. Ibid., 270–71.
170. Ibid., 271.
171. Ibid., 272.
172. Ibid.
173. Ibid., 272–73.
174. Ibid., 273.
175. Ibid.
176. Ibid.
177. Warfield, *Faith and Life*, 273.
178. Ibid.

hend it."[179] Furthermore, this is not only for all Christians to experience, but is also a prayer for the Christians' spiritual expansion, building them up to the level of those things apprehended, and not by spiritual apprehension of "great ideas."[180] In other words, the spiritual expansion takes place neither exclusively, nor even primarily, by the mere intellectual grasping of thoughts. Put yet another way, the stress here is on a mystical experience, not a rationalistic one, which is governed by Jesus through the Holy Spirit in union with the Christian. Though it is properly termed *knowledge*, it is a knowledge "too high for us" and, therefore, the Christian needs spiritual strengthening in order to receive it, and only those in whom Christ abides have this strengthening.[181] There is, however, according to Warfield, an "intermediate step in the attainment of this large spiritual apprehension."

Warfield notes that Paul did not move from God's spiritual strengthening to the result of an increased spiritual apprehension, but rather, between these two was a "proximate effect of the Spirit's work—love.[182] The result was that:

> The proximate effect of the Spirit's work in empowering the inner man with might is not knowledge but love; and the proximate cause of our enlarged spiritual apprehension is not the strengthening of our inner man, but love. The Spirit does not immediately work this enlargement of mind in us; He immediately works love, and only through working this love, enlarges our apprehension. The Holy Ghost "sheds love abroad in our hearts." Love is the great enlarger. It is love which stretches the intellect. He who is not filled with love is necessarily small, withered, shriveled in his outlook on life and things. And conversely he who is filled with love is large and copious in his apprehensions. Only he can apprehend with all saints what is the breadth and length and height and depth of things.[183]

The ultimate goal of this spiritual apprehension, though, has not yet been addressed. There is still one more aspect to be understood. The Christian is not strengthened to know just for the sake of knowing, but rather the aim is that the Christian might be "filled unto the whole full-

179. Ibid.
180. Ibid., 273–74.
181. Ibid., 274.
182. Ibid., 275.
183. Ibid., 275–76.

ness of God."[184] Warfield then explains that this phrase might mean either "the fullness which God possesses" or "the fullness which God provides."[185] It does not matter which it means, because it is "enough in either meaning for any Christian's hope," because "there is no reason to doubt that it does mean the greatest thing," namely, to "be like" God.[186] Warfield called it "a giddy height to which our eyes are raised."[187] He is careful, however, to mention what this does *not* mean. It does not mean either that "we are to be transmuted into God," so that we can claim parity with him, nor that God is "transfused into us, so that we shall be God, part of His very essence."[188] To be like God was to be "holy as He is holy, pure as He is pure," to the end that God's people and God would "belong to one class, the class of holy beings."[189] In a point reminiscent of the one made to Kuyper and Bavinck regarding the differences between the regenerate and unregenerate, Warfield states that the moral difference between the Christian's once sinful state and the one to which he or she shall attain in holiness is "a difference so great that we are almost tempted to call it a difference of kind and not merely degree."[190] It seems to be "but barely begun for most of us [Christians] in this life," and yet it has, and will be accomplished, "and it shall never cease."[191]

In this address Warfield's exposition of Scripture accentuates the mystical experience of the Christian in knowing and loving God, as well as in reaching the goal to which God has appointed the sinner through the work of Jesus by way of the Holy Spirit. There are several subjects interwoven in this sermon. Union with Christ, the role of the Holy Spirit, the reality and presence of Christ with the Christian, knowledge of God, spiritual strengthening, and ethical purity are all seen as part of one great whole. While it is true that Warfield stresses that this knowledge or apprehension spoken of by the Apostle Paul in Ephesians 3:14–19 concerns the "great and incomparable mysteries of our faith," it is also true that for Warfield knowledge of God is central to knowledge of all things. Thus, there is significant insight here as to the character of his epistemology

184. Ibid., 276.
185. Ibid., 277.
186. Ibid.
187. Ibid.
188. Ibid.
189. Ibid., 278.
190. Ibid. See also Warfield, "Review of *De Zekerheid Geloofs*," *SSW* 2:106–23.
191. Warfield, *Faith and Life*, 278.

regarding all things, not simply the specific matters which he addressed from this passage of Ephesians.

In his sermon "The Heritage of the Saints in Light,"[192] Warfield discusses the noetic effects of sin, the need for regeneration by God, and the response that should follow from the Christian.

> Now he [Paul] tells us further that it is God and God alone who can introduce men into this glorious region of "the light." It is God who is light and all the light that is in the world streams from Him. We, on our part, are under the dominion of "darkness," and darkness has filled our hearts. How can we be rescued from the rule of darkness and translated into the kingdom of the Son of God's love? *Obviously it is only by an act of God, the Light, Himself shining into our darkened heart.* And so the Apostle tells us, declaring that it is God who has made us meet for a share in the heritage of the saints. Our idea of the English word "meet" probably only brokenly represents the Greek word which he employs. In the Greek word the idea of sufficiency, adequacy, ability, is more prominent than that of worthiness, suitability. The notion conveyed is, perhaps, not so much that God has made us fit, worthy to be in the Kingdom of light—though that in any event it included, and as to the thing itself is not inharmonious with the Apostle's main intention; but that He has made us able to enter into this state. Immersed in the kingdom of darkness, or worse than that, with the kingdom of darkness within ourselves, we were incapable of entering the kingdom of light. We needed to be made "sufficient," "competent," "adequate," "capable," to be "qualified," "capacitated," for entering into our portion in the allotment of the saints. There was no power in us for entering these light-sown regions; our natural home was elsewhere. Only by a creative act of God were we able to enter upon their sacred precincts."[193]

Warfield continues to hammer home the point:

> You see the idea is not that we had the power to enter but not the fitness to abide there; it is that we had no power to enter—the light striking us in the face drove us away because we were of the darkness and incapable of the light. It was God and God alone who made us able to receive a portion in the inheritance of the saints in light; He alone who delivered us from the authority (we were under its authority) of darkness and translated us into the

---

192. Ibid., 340–49.
193. Ibid., 347–48; emphasis added.

kingdom of the Son of His love. And we utterly fail to catch Paul's real meaning unless we feel profoundly how entirely he ascribes the totality of the transaction by which we are vested with a heritage among the saints "in the light" to God and God alone. It is to God and not to ourselves—not to our fellow-men, nor yet to angels,—to God and God alone, that we owe it that our part is with the saints in the light. It is He that has qualified, capacitated, compentized [sic], sufficientized [sic] us, for our part in the lot of the saints.[194]

Warfield closes by linking the monergistic work of God in saving his people to the motivation for Christian living. It is on the "basis" of God's solitary work in bringing his people out of darkness that God's people are to live "in one long thanksgiving to God."[195] As Warfield summarizes it, "thanksgiving presupposes indebtedness."[196] He finishes by clarifying that God's people:

> ... were under the curse of sin; we have received in Him redemption, even the forgiveness of sins. In this great rescue we have been made sufficient for both things. There is obviously an objective and a subjective side to it; an ideal and an actual possession involved. But the upshot of it all is—that God has taken us out of darkness with all that that involves and placed us in the light, with all that that involves. And as children of the light we must rejoice in the light—which light God is.[197]

These sermons demonstrate that Warfield proclaimed and explained the noetic effects of sin and the subjective element within the individual Christian's relationship to Jesus, relating these to a variety of doctrines within the Christian faith. Furthermore, he did this in a way that was fully consistent with the doctrines expressed in the WCF. It is quite doubtful that Warfield's listeners would ever have mistaken him for one who skirted the importance of the noetic effects of sin or the subjective element in religious epistemology. Indeed, stressing these matters was one of the constant refrains of Warfield's teaching career as can be further seen in his addresses "The Religious Element in the Preparation for the Ministry" and "The Religious Life of Theological Students."[198] In

---

194. Ibid., 348–49.
195. Ibid., 349.
196. Ibid.
197. Ibid.
198. Warfield, "Religious Element in the Preparation for the Ministry," in *The*

these two addresses, given twenty-six years apart, yet handling the same fundamental topic, Warfield's consistency in stressing the subjective and moral side not only of knowing in the Christian faith but also of fitness in Christian ministry becomes very apparent.

Seminary Studies, Spiritual Disposition, and Maturation

For Warfield, theological learning and religious affections and actions are not inimical to one another, though they have been set against each other by theological liberalism rooted in Schleiermacher and mediated through various liberal pastors and scholars of the nineteenth century. This theology and epistemology, which subordinates doctrine to affections, or fuses knowledge claims with the individual's subjective experience, was gaining increasing control within American culture in the nineteenth century. Theology was being assigned to a subjective realm completely divorced from any ability to make knowledge claims that had objective validity for all people, for all times and places. This, of course, did not stop some who operated according to the presuppositions of Schleiermacher and Kant from *making* claims that they thought had objective validity for all people, for all times and places. What it does mean is that they were making such claims in contradiction to the presuppositions or principles that they claimed to believe, or affirmed to be true. It also meant that what they accepted as "science" could only be identified with the hard, empirical sciences. Among other things, this approach resulted in people becoming more and more unaware of what Scripture teaches regarding the relationship between the objective and subjective elements not only in religious epistemology, narrowly defined, but also in knowledge claims in virtually every sphere of human learning. Thus, Warfield made it a point to address some of the issues within this debate. The liberal theologians of Warfield's day regarded religious affections and doctrine as adversaries and responded by making doctrine subservient to feelings. Warfield, though, believed this was inconsistent with the nature of Man, the teachings of Scripture, and a correct view of science. This was not to say, however, that Warfield taught that the person's affections, feelings, intuitions (or whatever term one wishes to use to refer to the subjective element in human beings) are inoperative or non-existent in the knowing process regarding *any* subject discipline, and that, of course, includes theology. As Warfield states:

Presbyterian Observer; "The Religious Life of Theological Students," *SSW* 1:411–25.

"To know God" in the deeper sense is not the act of the mere understanding, nor can theology fulfill its function of making man "to know God" simply by framing propositions for the logical intellect. As Aesthetics or Ethics cannot fulfill its calling without calling into action something much deeper than the mere understanding, no more can Theology. For Ethics there is requisite a moral nature and that not merely in possession, but in use; Aesthetics does not consist in a series of propositions about beauty; and similarly Theology does not exist when only the intellect is busy with the apprehension of logical propositions about God, but can come into existence only in beings that possess religious natures and through the actions of the religious faculty. The knowledge of God, accordingly, which it is the end of Theology to produce, is that vital knowledge of God which engages the whole man; it can terminate only in distinctively *religious* knowledge— and this adjective must needs describe the quantity of knowledge as well as its sphere. As well say that a being without a moral nature can produce a scientific ethic, or a being without a sense of beauty can produce a scientific aesthetic, as to say that a being without a religious nature, or without his religious nature stirred and in action, can produce a Scientific Theology. "Science" in no one of these cases consists of a bare series of intellectual propositions, however logically constructed. [199]

When addressing the students and faculty at Western Seminary in Alleghany, Pennsylvania, on October 15, 1885, Warfield invited them to join him in thinking about "preparation for the ministry" and to give "attention to one single side of this great subject and consider a little the religious element in the preparation for the ministry."[200] This address exhibits some of the characteristic elements of Warfield's understanding of the correlation between intellectual study and religious affections/actions in preparation for gospel ministry. Warfield wasted little time in making clear where he stood on the role of the intellect in preparation for gospel ministry:

---

199. Warfield, "Theology a Science," *SSW* 2:207–12. This was in response to Andrew Dickson White's *History of the Warfare of Science with Theology*, in which White set science against theology and defined science in an empiricist way. In Warfield's estimation it was "as absurd to talk of warfare between Science and Theology as of warfare between Science and Astronomy" (207–8). He argues that to set science against theology is to have too low a view of either science or theology, or even both. His argument is predicated upon, and the expression of, his unitary or systemic view of knowledge.

200. Warfield, "Religious Element in the Preparation for the Ministry," 48.

> I should be sorry were I to leave the impression that the intellectual outfit that is needed for our ministry had been overestimated by the Church in the provision made for the training of its clergy. Justly does Dr. Duryea declare that "it is high time that the question whether culture and learning do not unfit preachers for the preaching ef [sic] the Gospel to ordinary men and women were referred back without response to the stupidity that inspires it."[201]

Warfield continues by highlighting a topic that he would return to twenty-six years later in an address to Princeton Seminary students—the necessity of intellectual work for gospel ministry. As Warfield phrases it:

> "Without study," says an experienced bishop of the Church of England "we shall not only fail to bring to our people all the blessings which God intends for them, but we shall gradually become feeble and perfunctory in our ministrations. Our life may apparently be a busy one, and our time incessantly occupied, but our work will be comparatively fruitless, and we shall be fighting as one that beateth [sic] the air."[202]

Warfield believed that in order for students to have an accurate conception of their ministerial preparation, they need to understand the nature of human beings and how this specifically relates to the intellectual work of learning. Warfield states that there are, generally speaking, two kinds of students who profit little from their time in seminary, and that they exhibit two fundamental mistakes in their approach to seminary studies:[203]

> Now and then at the head of our classes we find a student or two who rapidly assimilates and makes thoroughly his own all the mental pabulum that is placed within his reach; who becomes a thorough linguist, a learned exegete, an acute theologian, a thorough historian and an unmatched Church lawyer, and yet who with perfectly finished sermons makes no converts, with deeply reasoned arguments wins no souls. Out of sympathy with the common practical life of mankind he passes his life on the cold heights of "thought" and "science" and "culture." In a word he has learned to *know* but not to *feel*, and through his case *we* learn that the most thorough teaching, the most elaborate and pefect [sic] appliances conveying and testing knowledge will not of themselves secure the spiritual application of that knowledge

---

201. Ibid.
202. Ibid., 49.
203. Ibid., 49–50.

Apologetics in Practice

to the heart and conscience. They may make the scholar, but will not alone make the preacher, who must be the man who has himself eaten the prophetic roll the contents of which he is to communicate to others.[204]

There is another class of men who make a mistake in the other direction. These students are more than a little reluctant to study, and it seems that nothing can move them to do what they are supposed to do.[205] The problem with these students is that they have a "cold and barren" intellect.[206] Such a student, said Warfield, leaves school "intellectually unimproved," and "morally injured perhaps by the discovery that he can with apparent success neglect his opportunities if I should not even say violate his pledges."[207] The result is that "not only is the truth not applied to the heart but it is not grasped by the mind. The whole system of instruction inaugurated by the Church and supported at so great a cost has been to these students a complete and abject failure."[208] So what can be done? A prescription for a remedy obviously depends on a correct diagnosis of the actual problem.

Warfield then acknowledges that there probably were students who thought that the training of ministers is overly intellectual, but he then asserts his doubt that this is actually the case.[209] He bases this assessment on the fact that the demands placed upon ministers warrant an emphasis on the intellect, and the requirements placed upon students simply are not beyond their capacities.[210] No, the problem lies elsewhere, and the solution depends on a recognition that the issue is actually one of proportionality. If the problem is not due to an over-emphasis on the intellect, it must be from an under-emphasis somewhere else. The problem with such students is "not that their head has received too much but that their heart has received too little."[211] The problem with those who do not avail themselves of what the seminary offers is not that their "intellectual training" was "pitched on too high a key, but that their consciences" were

204. Ibid.
205. Ibid., 50.
206. Ibid.
207. Ibid.
208. Ibid.
209. Ibid.
210. Ibid.
211. Ibid.

"pitched on too low a key."[212] Warfield also acknowledges that there are those who cannot profitably pursue seminary course work and yet may indeed "be so baptized by the Holy Spirit that the Church may profitably, and ought, in humble obedience to God's call, induct them into the ministry."[213] Still, he knew these were "very exceptional cases," and the seminary curriculum should not be built around exceptional cases.[214] The remedy, Warfield maintains, lies in recognizing the need to "heighten our demand on the other elements of man's nature."[215]

Next, Warfield reminds his listeners that the New Testament sets forth requirements for a minister that stress the "religious," "moral," and "spiritual" qualities.[216] Is Warfield contradicting himself? His point is that because Man is a unit there is an unbreakable union between the intellect, the affections, and actions; stressing the intellect does not necessarily mean that a corresponding affective goal will be reached. Yet, Jesus did not merely ordain a message, but that the message should come "warm from a heart that had personally appropriated it and drank from it all its blessings and experienced all its joys," and that that message, delivered by one transformed by it, "should conquer the world."[217] Or, as Warfield reiterates, the minister who is transformed by the gospel will be "the hammer to drive the message home into other hearts."[218] The point that Warfield wants to make sure they understand, though, is that the sanctification, or changing, of their character is not ultimately their own doing. As he puts it, "it is God's ordinance what the Christian personality of the speaker should be."[219] Thus, it is "easy to see . . . that the most fundamental requirement for the outfit of a preacher is that he must himself be an example of the power of grace in the saving of man; that he must himself be Christ's own man."[220] It is not biblical, however, to construe the matter as a choice between the "devotional," "practical," and

212. Ibid., 51.
213. Ibid.
214. Ibid.
215. Ibid.

216. Ibid., 52. Warfield mentioned that the New Testament listed fifteen qualities and only one was concerned "an intellectual fitting." Warfield also stated, "It is easy to say which is the most fundamental: a personal knowledge of Christ, personal piety and sanctification, lie at the base of all preaching of the Gospel."

217. Ibid.
218. Ibid.
219. Ibid.
220. Warfield, "Religious Element in the Preparation for the Ministry," 52.

"intellectual."[221] The three elements are not to be considered as a "rope of three cords which because twisted together become capable of bearing a greater weight than any one alone could support; they rather require to be all three twisted together before there is any cord at all."[222] To conceive of any one of them as sufficient in itself, or any two isolated from the other, is to fail to have the reality of what the three together constitute. In consistency with his illustration, Warfield states that if one does not have all three simultaneously, one simply has "fluffy patches of raw cotton."[223] The practical application of this is that students and professors are:

> not to ask whether we will cultivate this one of the three or that one; we are not to ask whether we are to give our chief attention to this one or to that. We must cultivate all and give our chief attention to all. They represent not three kinds of preparation between which we are to choose, but three lines of approach along which we must simultaneously push our [f]orces if we are to capture the stronghold of a successful ministry. Their interaction is so complete, indeed, that each is the best means of securing the others.[224]

For Warfield, then, the intellect is automatically moral. It is moral precisely because human beings are a unit; a composite whole. Ever the systematician, Warfield maintains that actions are intellectual in nature, and that intellectual endeavors are ipso facto practical and spiritual (or devotional). The idea of intellectual work being impractical in any way or lacking in any way a moral character was not only foreign to him, but considered by him to be completely out of sync with what Scripture and human existence reveal. These very same lines of thought were expressed by Warfield many years later near the twilight of his career.

On October 4, 1911, Warfield delivered an address at the Autumn Conference at Princeton entitled "The Religious Life of a Theological Student."[225] In this address Warfield expressed the union that he believed is present between thinking, theology, doctrine, and intellectual study on one hand, and feeling, willing, prayer, and religious zeal, on the other. He began by announcing that he considered the religious life of the theological student as the "most important subject which can

---

221. Ibid.
222. Ibid.
223. Ibid.
224. Ibid.
225. Warfield, "Religious Life of a Theological Student," *SSW* 1:411–29.

engage our thought."²²⁶ The very existence of theological seminaries is predicated upon the significance of the intellectual preparation for ministry.²²⁷ Learning is indispensable for the ministry, Warfield states, but it "is not the most indispensable thing for a minister."²²⁸ It is true that the Apostle Paul said that the minister must be apt to teach, and this means the minister must possess knowledge. Still, aptness to teach is not the only requirement and is not even the "primary qualification."²²⁹ There are several other qualifications besides aptness to teach given by Paul and they all have to do with "spiritual fitness."²³⁰ Above all things, however, including learning, "a minister must be godly."²³¹

Warfield quickly cautions his listeners, though, that it is "fatal" to set learning and godliness against each other.²³² After mentioning an adage that was evidently prevalent at the time—that ten minutes on one's knees was worthier than ten hours over one's books—he counters by asking: "Why should you turn from God when you turn to your books, or feel that you must turn from your books in order to turn to God?"²³³ Such an antithetical separation between religious devotion and theological learning, in Warfield's beliefs, is "absurd."²³⁴ God's call is for minister's to be men of *both* learning and religious devotion; both are required for godliness and for ministerial success.²³⁵ The real danger is not that students will think of the two as contradictory pursuits, but as existing "too much apart," so that students will tend to approach their studies and religious life in a way that reflects a belief that what "is given to the one is taken from the other."²³⁶ Warfield said, "No mistake could be more gross."²³⁷ Religion does not "take a man away from his work," but sends "him

226. Ibid., 411.
227. Ibid.
228. Ibid.
229. Ibid.
230. Ibid.
231. Ibid., 412.
232. Ibid.
233. Ibid.
234. Ibid.
235. Ibid. It may be necessary to state that the Presbyterian Church of which Warfield was a part did not ordain women to the office of teaching elder.
236. Ibid.
237. Ibid.

to his work with an added quality of devotion."[238] This truth regarding the intimate relationship between one's religious devotion and work, or everyday labors, "is the doctrine, the fundamental doctrine, of Protestant morality, from which the whole system of Christian ethics unfolds."[239] It was characteristic of the Middle Ages that it operated with a division between one's religious life and the "congeries of occupations," but it was Luther, and even to a more consistent degree, Calvin, who proclaimed "the great idea of 'vocation.'"[240]

Warfield then calls upon the young men present to recognize that their vocation is to "diligently . . . study theology."[241] To illustrate this, Warfield tells a story from his days as a student under Charles Hodge. Hodge told his students that when he was a student under Philip Lindsay, the latter would tell his students that they "'would find that one of the best preparations for death was a thorough knowledge of the Greek grammar.'"[242] This was, according to Warfield, Hodge's "quaint" way of teaching them that they should do their duty.[243] The link between religious life and doing one's daily tasks is so tight that if one's daily task is studying, then one's religious life depends on studying.[244] Warfield, therefore, reiterates that regardless of what students think or feel about their studies, it is imperative that they understand that in doing them they are engaging in a religious act, and their whole religious life revolves around this fulfillment of their duty.[245]

Warfield continues, though, by cautioning against another fallacy. Just because the religious life of a theological student is dependent upon studying, this does not mean that *all* study is automatically religiously beneficial; it is "possible to study—even study theology—in an entirely secular spirit."[246] Warfield clarifies that when he referred to engaging in one's studies as an act of devotion, he meant for devotion "to be taken in both its senses," as "'zealous application'" and "'a religious exercise.'"[247]

238. Ibid.
239. Ibid., 413.
240. Ibid.
241. Ibid., 414.
242. Ibid.
243. Ibid.
244. Ibid.
245. Ibid., 415.
246. Ibid.
247. Ibid.

There are works that do not tend "to feed the religious life . . . directly," but this is not so with theological studies, because "in all its branches" it "has as its unique end to make God known."[248] This led Warfield to ask: "Can a religious man stand in the presence of God, and not worship?"[249] Though it is possible to study theology "in a purely secular spirit," this is only "possible for an irreligious man, or at least for an unreligious" one.[250] Warfield's point is not that there are some people who do not worship in the broad sense, or have, again, broadly speaking, thoughts about God. For Warfield, the term "religion" refers to the practical devotional life, while "theology" refers to one's thoughts.[251] Instead, his point is that it is possible to study theology and not be brought into a state of humble devotion and worship to God, and so Warfield asks a question that he feels is a "touchstone" that will enable his audience to "discern" their "religious state, and be an instrument for the quickening of their "religious life."[252] He asks: "Do you prosecute your daily tasks as students of theology as 'religious exercises?'"[253] Shortly thereafter he exhorts these students:

> Whatever you may have done in the past, for the future make all your theological studies "religious exercises." This is the great rule for a rich and wholesome religious life in a theological student. Put your heart into your studies; do not merely occupy your mind with them, but put your heart into them. They bring you daily and hourly into the very presence of God; his ways, his dealing with men, the infinite majesty of his Being form their very subject-matter. Put the shoes from off your feet in this holy presence![254]

Warfield then adds a caution that over-familiarity with the very things of God through daily studies could lead them to become numb to their significance.[255] Still, he explains, this "great danger" is "only because it is your great privilege. Think of what your privilege is when your great-

---

248. Ibid.
249. Ibid.
250. Ibid.
251. Warfield, "Authority, Intellect, Heart," *SSW* 2:668.
252. Warfield, "Religious Life of a Theological Student," *SSW* 1:416.
253. Ibid.
254. Ibid.
255. Ibid.

est danger is that the great things of religion may become common to you!"[256] The exhortation also includes this rather sober warning:

> Are you, by this constant contact with divine things, growing in holiness, becoming every day more and more men of God? If not, you are hardening! And I am here today to warn you to take seriously your theological study, not merely as a duty, done for God's sake and therefore made divine, but as a religious exercise, itself charged with religious blessing to you; as fitted by its very nature to fill all your mind and heart and soul and life with divine thoughts and feelings and aspirations and achievement.[257]

In this sermon, Warfield also wants to make it clear that he is not encouraging neglect of other duties, but is providing a basis to remain faithful to them, such as "the formal religious meeting of the Seminary."[258] Warfield warns them that regular absence from corporate worship with the seminary community would prove injurious to their religious development.[259] In fact, Warfield advocated morning and evening corporate gatherings for prayer, as well as worship twice every "Sabbath."[260] There were, evidently, standard excuses used by students as to why they were not present at such gatherings. He hoped that students would not offer the explanation that the "religious exercises" were "too numerous, or are wearying."[261] These excuses simply betrayed "the low ebb of" their "religious vitality."[262] Warfield then goes through a litany of other excuses and states: "Such things I seem to have heard before; and yours will be an exceptional pastorate, if you do not hear something very like them, before you have been in a pastorate six months."[263] Warfield adds to his counsel by calling the students to be careful not to blame their religious dullness on their leaders, but to examine themselves and look to the example of Jesus, who made it "his habitual practice to be found in his place on the Sabbath day at the stated place of worship to which he belonged."[264] Even though Jesus was consistent in his public attendance, such attendance

256. Ibid., 417.
257. Ibid.
258. Ibid., 418.
259. Ibid.
260. Ibid., 419.
261. Ibid.
262. Ibid.
263. Ibid., 420.
264. Ibid., 421.

was not merely to set "a good example."[265] Instead, there were deeper matters connected to his observance of public worship, and this leads Warfield to move on from public to private religious devotion.

He begins by saying that it is of central importance to nurture one's inner life by contemplating "the immensity" of one's task and the "infinitude of the resources" at one's disposal,[266] since such contemplations drive men to their knees in prayer continuously.[267] The great danger to be avoided is an approach to ministerial tasks that is bereft of the seriousness mandated by the task, and to substitute ministerial and "restless activity" for "depth of Christian affections." He concludes by telling his audience that the latter of these can only be acquired through the public and private religious tasks of consecrated study of those things the professors require, heartfelt and constant prayer, and faithful participation in corporate worship.[268]

Conclusion

As has been shown, Warfield believed that all branches of human knowledge should be viewed from a theological perspective. He wrote the following in one of his more formal scholarly treatments of systematic theology and its relationship to all the branches of human science or knowledge:

> There is no one of them all which is not, in some measure, touched by it [theology], or which is not in some measure included in it. As all nature, whether mental or material, may be conceived of as only the mode in which God manifests Himself, every science which investigates nature and ascertains its laws is occupied with the discovery of the modes of the divine action and as such might be considered a branch of theology. And, on the other hand, as all nature, whether mental or material, owes its existence to God, every science which investigates nature and ascertains its laws, depends for its foundation upon that science which could make known what God is and what the relations are in which He stands to the work of His hands and in which they stand to Him; and must borrow from it those conceptions through which alone the material with which it deals can find its explanation or receive its proper significance. . . . The science of Him [God] and His rela-

---

265. Ibid., 422.
266. Ibid.
267. Ibid.
268. Ibid., 424.

tions is the necessary ground of all science. All speculation takes us back to Him; all inquiry presupposes Him; and every phase of science consciously or unconsciously rests at every step on the science that makes Him known. Theology, thus, as the science which treats of God, lies at the root of all sciences.[269]

Warfield conceived of reality in an organic, unitary, and systematic way, because he believed God was the creator and sustainer of all reality. Hence, reality not only has to be thought of as a systematic whole, but, in real sense, as living. Warfield's view of theology in all its branches was to think of it as an "organism." This is true not only of theology, but all aspects of human knowledge, because of what reality is, namely, God's creation. He, therefore, thought of human knowledge as involving the whole person. Of course, because humans are sinners, sin affects their knowing, and this influence, in turn, affects knowledge not simply of Scripture, but also of all aspects of reality. Still, because human beings possess knowledge just by virtue of being human, and they remain human even though corrupted by sin, it is therefore true that unregenerate sinners continue to know some truth.

The epistemic apparatus of a sinner is acted upon by God because God has to overcome the noetic effects of sin in order for a sinner to know God in a saving way. This act by God is not only a particular kind of revelation; it also corresponds to the nature that Man has by virtue of being part of creation. One cannot think rightly or in a biblically Christian way about saving revelation unless one understands it as corresponding in particular ways to the rest of human activity, as well as to knowledge claims in other subject spheres. This is because God has only created one reality, of which the Bible is a constituent part, and the Bible is therefore unavoidably related to all aspects of this reality. This is not to say, however, that people automatically understand *all* of what characterizes the relationship between the Bible and other aspects of reality.

Since all reality is unified, knowledge claims are, by the very nature of the case, all spiritual or moral issues, while simultaneously being intellectual and practical. One can arrive at knowledge of some of the particulars of reality in a number of ways. As Warfield saw it, the biblical truth regarding the unitary nature of reality means that any knowledge claim that is false will fail to conform to reality's unitary nature. This in turn means that one of the ways of demonstrating the truthfulness of biblical Christianity is to demonstrate the correlation of the various doc-

---

269. Warfield, "Idea of Systematic Theology," *CW* 9:69, 71.

trines to each other, as well as to correlate these doctrines to other aspects of reality. In other words, the biblical doctrines are not only a coherent whole within themselves, but they are also part of a larger coherent whole to which they correspond. Doctrinal claims that are false cannot be correlated to biblical doctrines, nor can they be shown to actually correspond to other aspects of reality. Thus, Warfield's response to what he considered the doctrinal falsehoods of his day was an explanation of how such false claims cannot be correlated to the teachings of Scripture, and how particular evidences outside of the biblical text cannot be correlated with these false claims either. In short, such false doctrinal claims are contradictory. Put another way, Warfield worked at showing how the line of reasoning of liberal theologians ultimately fails to cohere by showing how it fails to correspond to all the available evidence for which it has to account.

While Warfield's epistemology is certainly explicated in his essays on systematic theology and apologetics, it is not confined to these essays. Instead, Warfield's epistemology in all its unitary character is seen through numerous expositions of biblical doctrine. Warfield's approach was to constantly correlate epistemology to other biblical doctrines—God the creator and redeemer, saving faith, revelation, inspiration of Scripture, human beings as created in the image of God—and then to compare these doctrines to what he considered false teachings. In doing so he was consistent with his view of the unitary, systematic, and organic view of reality and truth.

His theological affirmations show no discontinuity between his scholarly writings and his sermons at the Sabbath Afternoon Conference. When he declared what he believed regarding the biblical doctrines of salvation as they related to the doctrine of God, his thoughts were substantively the same, whether those declarations were in a journal article, a book, or a Sabbath Afternoon Conference sermon. He emphasized God's work in bringing a particular understanding of his revelation to a sinner to overcome the effects of sin, and this, in turn, is correlated with God's role as creator and as providential director of all creation, who through the Holy Spirit enlivens God's people to persevere through faith in Jesus. By doing so, Warfield not only expounded what he believed Scripture teaches, but also what is expressed in the WCF. Warfield, then, not only correlated his epistemology with theology, but also demonstrated his commitment to what he believed was a faithfully Calvinistic position on these subjects.[270] He put into practice what he believed was true of apologetics in principle. He states that it is the "function of apologetics to investigate, explicate and establish the grounds on which a theology—a science, or systematized knowledge of God—is possible."[271] In doing so, he not only expounded what he believed was God's truth, revealed in Scripture and faithful to the WCF, but also what was "right reasoning," all the while believing that this "logic will always work itself ultimately out into history."[272]

---

270. This view corroborates Paul Helseth's conclusions regarding Warfield and the moral and affective dimensions of epistemology. See Helseth's works listed in the bibliography. For how Warfield saw these emphases corresponding to Calvin's beliefs, see Warfield, *Calvin and Calvinism*, *CW* 5. Especially see "Calvin's Doctrine of the Knowledge of God," *CW* 5:29–130; "Calvin's Doctrine of God," *CW* 5:133–85; "Calvin's Doctrine of the Trinity," *CW* 5:189–284; and "Calvin's Doctrine of the Creation," *CW* 5:287–349. For Warfield's awareness of the diversity within the Calvinistic tradition see "Calvinism," *CW* 5:353–69.

271. Warfield, "Apologetics," *CW* 9:4.

272. Warfield, "Dogmatic Spirit," *SSW* 2:666.

Conclusion

Throughout his career as a seminary professor, first at Western and then at Princeton, B. B. Warfield sought to faithfully uphold the doctrines expressed in the Westminster Confession of Faith. He gave a great amount of attention to countering the theological conceptions represented in the Protestant liberal theology of his day. He attempted to demonstrate that this latter theology was not only unfaithful to Scripture, but also failed to give a credible account of all the available data for which the theologian was accountable. Warfield believed that this liberal theology was indebted to Schleiermacher and Kant, and sought to reconstruct Christianity upon an anthropocentric foundation that manifested itself in either rationalism or mysticism. In the nineteenth and early portion of the twentieth century both mistakes were prevalent, and not merely among advocates of modern Protestant liberalism.[1]

Since Warfield believed that "the details of Christianity are all contained in Christianity: the minimum of Christianity is just Christianity itself," his defense of Christianity was his exposition of the doctrinal system warranted by Scripture, and expressed in the WCF.[2] Apologetics in Warfield's conception functions as the prolegomena intimately related to the entire system of doctrine that the Christian should confess.[3] Thus, Warfield's idea was that every individual doctrine in the Christian system is implicated in any one affirmation of Christian belief, although the Christian does not have to *understand* all of what characterizes the relationships between the doctrines in order for there to be a relationship. Ultimately, the believer's faith "reposes" in the person of the Lord Jesus,

1. See Warfield, *CW* 7: *Perfectionism, Volume I*; *CW* 8: *Perfectionism, Volume II*.
2. Warfield, "Apologetics," *CW* 9:9.
3. Ibid., 4.

who is the source, means, and object of saving faith.[4] Because Warfield believed that the doctrines articulated in the WCF are the most accurate representation of what the Bible teaches, he repeatedly explained these doctrines in the face of liberal attempts to reconstruct the Christian faith along other doctrinal lines. Because he believed that the fullest manifestation of the truth is a person—the Lord Jesus—he spoke of truth in organic or living terms, and thought of it as constructive and productive of life. Moreover, this view was correlated with the doctrine of God as creator and redeemer, providentially operative in the creation. Warfield's epistemology, then, was wedded to not only theology, but also a particular view of history and all branches of knowledge. Warfield's apologetic, in other words, was comprehensive and unitary in nature, addressed objectivity and subjectivity simultaneously, because they cannot be isolated from each other, and he required that his theological opponents be able to match his ubiquitous explanations if they were going to assail his position. Perhaps the best illustration of Warfield's view of biblically Christian apologetics is that it is the DNA of biblically Christian doctrine.

Rather than matching the ubiquity of his explanations, though, scholars have instead misrepresented his views and thereby undercut the force of his arguments. To clarify Warfield's true positions, I have employed extensive quotes from Warfield's own writing. The Scottish Philosophy thesis made popular by Sydney Ahsltrom's 1955 article, "The Scottish Philosophy and American Theology," should be seen as significantly responsible for such misrepresentations, and holds little actual value for understanding the true character of Warfield's scholarship, or even the Old Princeton School in general. Those who have followed Ahlstrom in his thesis, have, like Ahlstrom, failed to wrestle substantively with what Warfield actually stated in his writings. They have perpetuated reasoning that fails to make the fundamental distinction between a relationship of correlation and one of dependence, that fails to demonstrate a relation of dependence between what Warfield actually stated and what is expressed in the various manifestations of Scottish philosophy, and that fails to take seriously the chronology of the history of ideas and the history of Warfield's life. Of course, this claim raises serious questions regarding the historiography that is indebted to Ahlstrom. Moreover, if Warfield was correct in what he affirmed—a question not driving this work, in order to better address the question of what Warfield actually affirmed—then there is significant reason to believe that some of the explanations for

---

4. Warfield, "Faith in Its Psychological Aspects," *CW* 9:313–42.

the existence and character of Ahlstrom's thesis, and the historiography embracing it, may be contained in what Warfield affirmed. After all, if theology is intimately related to one's views of knowledge (science) and history, then those who reject Warfield's theology will oppose his views of knowledge and history to whatever degree they are consistent in their thinking. What appears to be the case, in other words, is that there is a significant historiography that is acting as theological polemic.

Seeman's analysis regarding evangelical historians who acquiesce to philosophically naturalistic methods of argumentation, and who will not allow for particular kinds of evidence and lines of argumentation that challenge philosophical naturalism, sounds very similar to not only some of what Warfield was addressing within Protestant liberalism, but also may provide helpful insights as to why Warfield seems to have been "silenced" or "ignored."[5] At the core of Warfield's conflict with the Protestant liberal reconstructions was their fact/value split. Obviously this split existed in the minds of those who postulated it, but the question remains as to whether their thinking actually corresponds to reality.[6] Warfield believed that it does not because it cannot give a sufficient account of reality. Warfield's perspective is that every aspect of the created order can only be rightly interpreted through the doctrinal system found in Scripture. He affirmed this because he believed that God was truly present in, and revealed through, all creation, and thus everything takes us back to God, everything presupposes him.[7] Only God interprets himself and this means, by the very nature of the case, that he also interprets the created realities through which human beings know him.[8] Just as Scripture inter-

---

5. Seeman, "Evangelical Historiography beyond the 'Outward Clash,'" 95–124. See the discussion on Seeman in ch. 4, n32 and 119.

6. Nancy Pearcey, in "Evangelicals' Two-Story Truth,"ch. 11 of her *Total Truth*, completely embraces the Ahlstrom-Noll-Marsden historiographical line that is welcomed in the mainstream academy, and thus fails to recognize that the very foil that she is arguing against is actually committed by such people, as Seeman cogently demonstrated. Furthermore, Seeman, "Evangelical Historiography," 113, rightly analyzes the matters when he presses the point that Noll, Marsden, Stout and others adopting their thinking and historiographical practices, that allow for the telling of two significantly different stories, leave the allegedly Christian historian with the following questions: " . . . which of the two incommensurable stories is *his* story? Which does he take to be true, representing how things actually are in reality? The fact we actually believe things to be true betrays the alternation approach at its very core."

7. Warfield, "Theology as a Science," *SSW* 2:210; "Idea of Systematic Theology," *CW* 9:68–69; "Task and Method of Systematic Theology," *CW* 9:97.

8. Warfield, "Right of Systematic Theology," *SSW* 2:219–79.

prets Scripture, Scripture is the fundamental basis by which everything else is interpreted. From Warfield's view, one certainly cannot label as "Christian" an interpretation of any aspect of reality that denies that the biblical doctrine of God is able to provide the explanatory account of that reality.[9] Historians who are trying to hold on to the name "Christian" and yet remain within an academy that will not allow for truly biblical or Christian presuppositions to function as the substance of their work have a vested interest in distorting the truth about Warfield. Warfield tolerated no compromise with non-Christian thinking, because he did not think that one could bifurcate either reality or one's self by pretending that one can think and act like a Christian in one setting in creation (the church), and then think and act like a non-Christian in a different setting within creation (the academy). Those who claim to follow Kuyper regarding the antithesis between regenerate and unregenerate thinking, and then construe this division as giving them license to acquiesce to the fundamental presuppositions of the academy that are contrary to Scripture, appear to give credence to the argument that Warfield was correct about Kuyper making the antithesis too absolute. If the antithesis between the Christian and non-Christian is to such a degree that one believes that "theological affirmations about the transcendent and social scientific statements about observed behavior operate within 'strictly discrepant frames of reference,'"[10] then one has either ruled human knowledge of God out of existence, or relegated it to a privatized sphere that correlates quite well with the affirmations of Protestant liberalism. Ironically, it was Kuyper who claimed to believe that there is not one square inch of the creation of which Christ did not claim ownership; yet it is Kuyper whom Marsden and others have hailed as one to follow.[11] Given that the historiography on Warfield is filled with such misleading and errant analyses, one wonders what sort of reassessment may need to take place regarding Kuyper's thought.

If indeed Marsden and Noll and others are faithful to Kuyper in stressing the antithesis between Christian and non-Christian thinking so that non-Christian presuppositions are placated in allegedly Christian scholarship, then it is difficult to see how Kuyper's thought, at least on that point, can be of much help to the Christian proclaiming truth,

---

9. Warfield, "Predestination," *CW* 2:3–67.

10. Seeman, "Evangelical Historiography beyond the 'Outward Clash,'" 103. Seeman was quoting Mark Noll.

11. Marsden, "Collapse of American Evangelical Academia."

within the public arena, that calls into question such non-Christian thinking. To operate with a fact/value split that concedes the fact realm to the non-Christian within historiography is to affirm that God is not known in the existential realities of time and space that humans occupy. How exactly that can correspond in any meaningful way with the notion that God created all realities, fills them with his presence, sustains them, interprets them, and makes himself known is not exactly clear. The "alternation" approach that Marsden, Noll, Stout and others have adopted only allows for a view of knowledge of God that is gnostic, and matches the emphases of Schleiermacher and Kant. Warfield demonstrated how such thinking was unbiblical and incoherent.

When historians operate with a fact/value split, they are likely to be prone to making factually incorrect statements about Warfield. First, by the very nature of the case, if they truly believe that Christian scholars can and must operate with a fact/value split, because there are, in reality, multiple logical realms that simply do not intersect, then they have already admitted that they are de facto *incapable* of understanding Warfield's points, which are predicated on the unitary nature of truth. That hardly constitutes a polemic against Warfield, though. Indeed, it actually provides evidence for one of Warfield's primary points regarding the inability of some to perceive truth.[12] Secondly, factual inaccuracy is also likely to occur among historians who operate with a fact/value split because that split allows them to use their own chosen value structure to interpret the facts that they have chosen, or to choose to focus on facts that fit most readily into the narrative that they have chosen. The fact/value split makes this all the more likely to occur simply because that split is the affirmation that the factual data of history offers the historian no morally compelling force or signification regarding its interpretation. The result is that such historians believe they have to provide (remember the facts don't compel any value explanation) some explanatory narrative to the facts. When the facts themselves do not compel a particular explanatory narrative, it means the historian gets to select whatever explanatory narrative seems amenable to him or her. Such historians are hardly going to choose an explanatory narrative that calls into question that fact/value split. It is also not surprising, then, that such historians juxtapose "scientific" with "religious" and believe that a "nonreligious" view of history can exist.[13] Historians who have embraced a particular theology no doubt

---

12. Warfield, "Right of Systematic Theology," *SSW* 2:230–38.
13. Marsden, *Outrageous Idea of Christian Scholarship*, 45, 57. According to Genesis

have a vested interest in protecting the theology they have embraced. It is not being argued here that historians ought not do that. On the contrary, *historians cannot help but do that.* What is called for is for historians to come clean and admit what they are doing and not cloak their work in an air of objectivity and value neutrality, when, in point of fact, their choice to operate with a fact/value split is itself a value judgment, and a choice that is filled with significant metaphysical, theological, and epistemological beliefs.[14] It is all the more problematic when these same historians claim to be knowledgeable about the noetic effects of sin.

Evangelicals who want to truly challenge and engage the non-Christian academy with arguments against the fact/value split that is a hallmark feature of the Kantian or neo-Kantian worldview of that academy, would do well to read Warfield. The lack of factual precision regarding Warfield by many of that academy's historians suggests that they have no reputable arguments against his positions. Moreover, this suggests that Warfield's view of apologetics in relation to theology in general and systematic theology in particular would likely be of great help to the project of integration that many Christian scholars attempt to fulfill in their various subject disciplines. Warfield's thought provides a rich storehouse regarding the basis and legitimacy of that project, along with how it might be understood in relation to theology and Christian discipleship.[15]

Though the primary concern here has not been to compare Warfield's thought to Van Til's, stress on the presuppositional nature of human thought is not at all out of accord with Warfield's beliefs. Indeed, one could make the argument, I believe quite easily, that what we have in Warfield's writings is a demonstration that one cannot get to the presuppositional nature of human thought without demonstrating how one is handling the available evidence. Indeed, it seems that if one focuses too

---

1 and Romans 1, humans do all of what they do either in obedience to or in rebellion against God. There is no "neutrality" or "non-religious" way of thinking and living. Marsden's analysis is muddled and strained throughout because he is trying to operate based on the rules of engagement established by the academy that endorses this fact/value split. According to Warfield, when one adopts the fact/value split, one is unable to do full justice to all reality.

14. Seeman, "Evangelical Historiography beyond the 'Outward Clash,'" 120. This gives credence to the thesis that there is not much, if any, substantive difference between Cartesian "modernism" and Kantian or neo-Kantian "postmodernism." In both, the individual knower becomes the primary arbiter of what passes for knowledge and truth.

15. For a discussion on these matters see Hart, "Christian Scholars, Secular Universities"; Davis, "Contra Hart." The best place to start would be Zaspel, *Theology of B. B. Warfield.*

much just on the presuppositional nature of human thinking, one can too easily lose sight of the very point that Richard Evans makes quite well, namely, that "the past does impose its reality through the sources in a basic way,"[16] Or, as Seeman, utilizing Charles Peirce, phrases it, there is "the physical encounter with traces that all historians must face when they give their accounts of history."[17] This was also stressed by Warfield in his highlighting of the reality of empirical data. It seems that one of the effects of an overemphasis on the presuppositional nature of human thought would be losing sight of the judgments that can be rendered against particular presuppositions or explanatory schemes. Warfield was constantly drawing his reader's attention to such judgments by showing how only the doctrines of the Bible, as articulated in the WCF, give sufficient explanation for all the available data. Thus, concentrating too much on the presuppositional nature of human thought may lead to a failure to recognize that some presuppositions are mandated and others nullified by empirically verifiable data. In this sense, Warfield took much more seriously, and was conditioned much more thoroughly by history, than it appears was Van Til. Warfield's stress on creation, and therefore the doctrine of God as creator and redeemer, and his polemic for an epistemology wedded to the biblical view of human beings as creatures whose redemption is part of creation, should be mastered by those with a concern for apologetics and evangelism in the evangelical tradition.

All of this suggests that a healthy amount of the evangelical historiography popularized at least over the past forty years likely stands in need of serious modifications. The storyline of Van Til, Marsden et al. that establishes Kuyper and some of the Dutch Reformed as faithfully upholding the Calvinist and biblical distinctives over and against the rationalistic tendencies of Warfield and the Old Princetonians is tendentiously skewed.[18] While it may be true that Van Til's *fullest* assessment was to recognize more of what Warfield got correct than Marsden allows for, it seems that those seeking faithfulness to Van Til are generally critical of Warfield, with John Frame remaining perhaps the most prominent exception.[19] If Warfield was correct in his analysis of Kuyper and Bavinck

---

16. Evans, *In Defense of History*, 99.

17. Seeman, "Evangelical Historiography beyond the 'Outward Clash,'" 116.

18. Van Til, *Defense of the Faith*, 264.

19. Logan, "Theological Decline in Christian Institutions," and Bahnsen, *Van Til's Apologetic*, took a much more critical view of the Princeton legacy as a whole and, therefore, Warfield (see chapter one of this book). Frame does not seem to give a strong

in their notion of two kinds of men that allow for two kinds of science, it would seem that we have a scenario in which this Kuyperian distinctive may be embraced precisely because it corresponds perfectly with the alternation approach that Seeman trenchantly exposed as an illegitimate option for those seeking to do Christian scholarship. Thus, Noll's and Marsden's endorsement of the alternation approach that allows for a fact/value split gives permission for the historian to be less than faithful to primary sources and appears to lead to a bias against Warfield. That is not to argue that Marsden and Noll have necessarily been conscious that this was the direction they were moving or had moved. Nevertheless, the fact remains that Marsden and Noll, along with Van Til, missed what Warfield actually affirmed on a number of important points. Certainly Marsden and Noll have repeatedly attempted to justify that a Christian scholar can engage in Christian scholarship while acquiescing to the non-Christian academy's most basic presuppositions, which are antithetical to Warfield's understanding of the Christian faith. One would do well to understand that the essence of the Marsden, Noll, and Stout position was alive and well in Warfield's day, for there were:

> men still professing historical Christianity, who reason themselves into the conclusion that 'in the nature of the case, no external authority can possibly be absolute in regard to spiritual truth'; just as men have been known to reason themselves into the conclusion that the external world has no objective reality and is naught but the projection of their own faculties.[20]

The view of Warfield as a rationalist who did not account for the noetic effects of sin not only flies full in the face of documentary evidence to the contrary, but also presents a most implausible picture of Warfield. Are we to imagine that after having memorized the Westminster Shorter Catechism by age six the Larger Catechism and Scripture proofs by sixteen, and having studied the theology of the church and the history of philosophy—as he had to have done to write such detailed analyses and critiques of various theological and exegetical positions during his academic career—Warfield forgot to condition his views of human knowledge with the basic doctrine of sin? Warfield not only accounted for the

---

hearty endorsement of Warfield, but he seems to more readily acknowledge what Warfield gets correct, and where Van Til may have mis-analyzed others. See Frame, *Cornelius Van Til*.

20. Warfield, "Inspiration of the Bible," *CW* 1:69. Warfield identified this as stemming from naturalism.

noetic effects of sin, but also regularly related that doctrine to multiple biblical doctrines. In an age, though, in which knowledge claims are quite easily mistaken, along Kantian or neo-Kantian lines, as only private perceptions of reality, Warfield's stress on a true or accurate knowledge of reality that holds to an objective element within epistemology may seem rationalistic, and may be difficult to accept. For those, however, who take the time to wrestle with what he actually wrote, and how he analyzed the objective and subjective elements in epistemology, there will likely come the recognition that Warfield not only accounted for the influence of sin on the mind, but also, in detailed fashion, related this influence to a variety of other doctrines.

Warfield's view of apologetics places it as integral to Christian discipleship and a companion of evangelism. For Warfield, apologetics is central to Christianity and the individual Christian's identity. In his conception, evangelism is one of the fruits of apologetics, so apologetics is not governed by evangelism, or enslaved to the practical goal of trying to bring people into God's kingdom. For Warfield, apologetics is endemic to everything God created human beings to be and do. The Christian, in other words, should engage in apologetics—exploring and explaining the biblical gospel—and in doing so may, through the Holy Spirit, see it established in others. Still, though no conversions be seen, there is still the fruit of the gospel's establishment in the one who explores and explains it. Those seeking to establish practical theology goals grounded in a rather comprehensive biblical and systematic theology would do well to read Warfield.

Studies within Warfield's writings alone could and should be numerous. Because of his belief in the unitary nature of truth, and his view of apologetics, there are many intersecting lines of relationships that mark Warfield's expositions and analyses of various doctrines. Fascinating historical studies could be done in comparing Warfield's views on a number of doctrines to the views of others in the Reformed tradition. In this regard, some of Muller's work in post-Reformation Reformed dogmatics is suggestive.

For those interested in the character of Christian apologetics, Warfield is a gold mine. Warfield's intellectual capabilities, academic prowess, and skills in biblical exegesis and systematic and historical theology leave the serious reader in awe. His constant articulation of the multiform relationships between various biblical doctrines and philosophical concepts helps the reader to see the place of apologetics not only within systematic theology, but also within Christian discipleship and God's eschatological purpose. This, of course, is also one reason why Warfield may not find a ready audience among some today. His ability to make fine distinctions, and explain deeply and broadly the intricacies of the relationships between doctrines and ideas and creational realities, are likely to lose some readers. Still, to those who persevere, Warfield will repay rich benefits. Such benefits will be garnered by those who have a concern for establishing the biblical gospel in the lives of others, as Warfield did. For it is in Warfield's explanations of various biblical doctrines that one not only discovers in detail what the gospel entails, but how the exploration of those doctrines will aid one in explaining them, so that, by the power of the Holy Spirit, the gospel is established.

Warfield's theological scholarship is rightly characterized as "scientific" and "constructive" because he correlated his various theological positions to each other and explained their relationship to human knowledge, with the latter recognized as a theologically conditioned reality. In doing this, he believed that he was building upon the edifice of truth that he had received, and was providing further construction upon which the building of that edifice could continue.

Bibliography

Ahlstrom, Sydney E. "The Scottish Philosophy and American Theology." *Church History* 24 (1955) 257–72.
Aiken, Charles A. "The Variable and the Constant in Christian Apology." *PQ/PRev* 1 (January 1872) 9–29.
Alexander, Archibald. "Nature and Evidence of Truth." In *The Princeton Theology, 1812–1921: Scripture, Science, and Theological Method from Archibald Alexander to Benjamin Breckenridge Warfield*, edited by Mark A. Noll, 61–71. Grand Rapids: Baker Academic, 2001.
———. *Thoughts on Religious Experience*. 3rd ed. 1844. Carlisle, PA: Banner of Truth Trust, 1998.
Alexander, James Waddell. "Institutio Theologiae Elencticae." *PRev* (July 1848) 452–63.
Alston, William P. "Thomas Reid on Epistemic Principles." Lectures on Thomas Reid, Wheaton Philosophy Conference, July 1983.
Anderson, Owen. *Benjamin B. Warfield and Right Reason: The Clarity of General Revelation and Function of Apologetics*. Lanham, MD: University Press of America, 2005.
Appleby, Joyce Oldham, Lynn Hunt, and Margaret Jacob. *Telling the Truth about History*. New York: Norton, 1994.
Armstrong, Brian G. *Calvinism and the Amyraut Heresy: Protestant Scholasticism and Humanism in Seventeenth-Century France*. Madison: University of Wisconsin Press, 1969.
Ashworth, William B., Jr. "Christianity and the Mechanistic Universe." In *When Science & Christianity Meet*, edited by David C. Lindberg and Ronald L. Numbers, 61–84. Chicago: University of Chicago Press, 2003.
Asselt, Willem J. van, and Eef Dekker. "Introduction." In *Reformation and Scholasticism: An Ecumenical Enterprise*, 11–43. Grand Rapids: Baker Academic, 2001.
Averill, Lloyd J. *American Theology in the Liberal Tradition*. Philadelphia: Westminster, 1967.
Bahnsen, Greg L. *Van Til's Apologetic: Readings and Analysis*. Phillipsburg, NJ: P&R, 1998.
Baird, William. "Biblical Criticism: New Testament Criticism." In *The Anchor Bible Dictionary*, edited by David Noel Freedman, 1:730–36. New York: Doubleday, 1992.
———. *History of New Testament Research*. 2 vols. Minneapolis: Fortress, 1992, 2003.
Barth, Karl. *Protestant Theology in the Nineteenth Century: Its Background and History*. Translated by Brian Cozens and John Bowden. Grand Rapids: Eerdmans, 2002.

Bibliography

Barzun, Jacques. *From Dawn to Decadence: 500 Years of Western Cultural Life, 1500 to the Present.* New York: HarperCollins, 2000.

Bratt, James. "The Dutch Schools." In *Reformed Theology in America: A History of Its Modern Development*, edited by David F. Wells, 115–32. Grand Rapids: Baker, 1997.

Briggs, Charles Augustus. *The Authority of Holy Scripture: An Inaugural Address.* 2nd ed. New York: Scribner, 1891.

———. *Whither?: A Theological Question for the Times.* New York: Scribner, 1889.

Broadie, Alexander. *A History of Scottish Philosophy.* Edinburgh: Edinburgh University Press, 2009.

Brown, Colin. *Christianity & Western Thought: A History of Philosophers, Ideas & Movements*, vol. 1: *From the Ancient World to the Age of Enlightenment.* Downers Grove, IL: InterVarsity, 1990.

———. *Jesus in European Protestant Thought, 1778–1860.* Studies in Historical Theology 1. Durham, NC: Labyrinth, 1985.

Brown, Jerry Wayne. *The Rise of Biblical Criticism in America, 1800–1870: The New England Scholars.* Middletown, CT: Wesleyan University Press, 1969.

Calhoun, David B. *Princeton Seminary.* 2 vols. Carlisle, PA: Banner of Truth Trust, 1994, 1996.

Calvin, John. *Institutes of the Christian Religion.* 2 vols. Edited by John T. McNeill, translated by Ford Lewis Battles. Library of Christian Classics 20, 21. Philadelphia: Westminster, 1960.

Carson, D. A. "The Dangers and Delights of Postmodernism." *Modern Reformation* (July/August 2003) 11–17.

———. *The Gagging of God: Christianity Confronts Pluralism.* Grand Rapids: Zondervan, 1996.

Cassirer, Ernst. *The Platonic Renaissance in England.* Translated by James P. Pettegrove. New York: T. Nelson, 1953.

Cauthen, Kenneth. *The Impact of American Religious Liberalism.* New York: Harper & Row, 1962.

Chrisope, Terry A. "J. Gresham Machen and the Modern Intellectual Crisis." *Presbyterion* 24.2 (Fall 1998) 92–109.

———. *Toward a Sure Faith: J. Gresham Machen and the Dilemma of Biblical Criticism, 1881–1915.* Ross-Shire, England: Mentor, 2000.

Cohen, L. Jonathan. "Rationality." In *A Companion to Epistemology*, edited by Jonathan Dancy and Ernest Sosa, 415–20. Blackwell Companions to Philosophy 4. Cambridge, MA: Blackwell, 1992.

Colie, Rosalie. *Light and Enlightenment: A Study of the Cambridge Platonists and the Dutch Arminians.* Cambridge: Cambridge University Press, 1957.

———. "Spinoza and the Early English Deists." *Journal of the History of Ideas* 20 (January 1959) 23–46.

Copleston, Fredrick Charles. *A History of Philosophy*, vol. 5: *Hobbes to Hume*; vol. 6: *Wolff to Kant.* New York: Doubleday, 1985.

Cragg, Gerald R. *The Church and the Age of Reason, 1648–1789.* New York: Penguin, 1976.

———. *Freedom and Authority: A Study of English Thought in the Early Seventeenth Century.* Philadelphia: Westminster, 1975.

Curley, Edwin. "Rationalism" in *A Companion to Epistemology*, edited by Jonathan Dancy and Ernest Sosa, 411–15. Blackwell Companions to Philosophy 4. Cambridge: Blackwell, 1992.

Bibliography

Davis, D. Clair. "Princeton and Inerrancy: The Nineteenth Century Philosophical Background of Contemporary Concerns." In *Inerrancy and the Church*, edited by John D. Hannah, 359–78. Chicago: Moody, 1984.
Davis, William C. "Contra Hart: Christian Scholars Should Not Throw in the Towel." *Christian Scholar's Review* 34.2 (2005) 187–200.
Diamond, Peter J. "Witherspoon, William Smith, and the Scottish Philosophy in Revolutionary America." In *Scotland and America in the Age of the Enlightenment*, edited by Richard B. Sher and Jeffrey R. Smitten, 115–32. Edinburgh: Edinburgh University Press, 1990.
Dorrien, Gary. *The Making of American Liberal Theology: Imagining Progressive Religion, 1805–1900*. Louisville: Westminster John Knox, 2001.
———. *The Remaking of Evangelical Theology*. Louisville: Westminster John Knox, 1998.
Emerson, Roger L. "Science and Moral Philosophy in the Scottish Enlightenment." In *Studies in the Philosophy of the Scottish Enlightenment*, edited by M. A. Stewart, 11–36. Oxford: Clarendon, 1990.
Evans, C. Stephen. "Critical Historical Judgment and Biblical Faith." In *History and the Christian Historian*, edited by Ronald A. Wells, 41–67. Grand Rapids: Eerdmans, 1998.
———. "Empiricism, Rationalism, and the Possibility of Historical Religious Knowledge." In *Christian Perspectives on Religious Knowledge*, edited by C. Stephen Evans and Merold Westphal, 134–60. Grand Rapids: Eerdmans, 1993.
Evans, Richard J. *In Defense of History*. New York: Norton, 1999.
Frame, John M. *Cornelius Van Til: An Analysis of His Thought*. Phillipsburg, NJ: P&R, 1995.
———. "In Defense of Something Close to Biblicism: Reflections on *Sola Scriptura* and History in Theological Method." *WTJ* 59 (1997) 269–91.
———. *The Doctrine of God*. Phillipsburg, NJ: P&R, 2002.
———. *The Doctrine of the Knowledge of God*. Phillipsburg, NJ: P&R, 1987.
Frei, Hans W. *The Eclipse of the Biblical Narrative: A Study in Eighteenth and Nineteenth Century Hermeneutics*. New Haven, CT: Yale University Press, 1974.
Fuller, Donald, and Ronald Gardiner. "Reformed Theology at Princeton and Amsterdam in the Late Nineteenth Century: A Reappraisal." *Presbyterion* 21.2 (Fall 1995) 89–117.
Gabbey, Alan. "Cudworth, More, and the Mechanical Analogy." In *Philosophy, Science, and Religion in England, 1640–1700*, edited by Richard Kroll, Richard Ashcraft, and Perez Zagorin, 109–27. Cambridge: Cambridge University Press, 1992.
Galloway, George. "The Theology of Albrecht Ritschl." *The Presbyterian Review* 10.38 (1889) 192–209.
Garretson, James M. *Princeton and Preaching: Archibald Alexander and the Christian Ministry*. Carlisle, PA: Banner of Truth Trust, 2005.
Gay, Peter. *The Enlightenment: An Interpretation: The Rise of Modern Paganism*. New York: Norton, 1995.
Gerrish, B. A. "Natural and Revealed Religion." In *The Cambridge History of Eighteenth-Century Philosophy*, edited by Knud Haakonssen, 2:662. Cambridge: Cambridge University Press, 2006.
———. *A Prince of the Church : Schleiermacher and the Beginnings of Modern Theology*. Philadelphia: Fortress, 1984

Bibliography

Giltner, John H. *Moses Stuart : The Father of Biblical Science in America*. Atlanta: Scholars, 1988.
González, Justo L. *The Story of Christianity*. 2 vols. San Francisco: Harper & Row, 1984, 1985.
Grave, S. A. "Common Sense." *The Encyclopedia of Philosophy*, edited by Donald M. Borchert et al., 2:354–61. 2nd ed. New York: Macmillan, 2006.
———. *The Scottish Philosophy of Common Sense*. Westport, CT: Greenwood, 1973.
Greaves, Richard L. "Puritanism and Science: The Anatomy of a Controversy." *Journal of the History of Ideas* 30 (1969) 345–68.
Grenz, Stanley J. *Revisioning Evangelical Theology: A Fresh Agenda for the 21st Century*. Downers Grove, IL: InterVarsity, 1993.
Gundlach, Bradley J. "B Is for Breckinridge: Benjamin B. Warfield, His Maternal Kin, and Princeton Seminary." In *B. B. Warfield: Essays on His Life and Thought*, edited by Gary L. W. Johnson, 13–53. Phillipsburg, NJ: P&R, 2007.
———. "The Evolution Question at Princeton, 1845–1929." PhD diss., University of Rochester, 1995.
———. "'Wicked Caste': Warfield, Biblical Authority, and Jim Crow." In *B. B. Warfield: Essays on His Life and Thought*, edited by Gary L. W. Johnson, 136–68. Phillipsburg, NJ: P&R, 2007.
Gunton, Colin E. *The One, the Three, and the Many: God, Creation, and the Culture of Modernity*. Cambridge: Cambridge University Press, 1993.
Harkness, N. W. "B. B. Warfield Systematic Theology Lecture Notes, 1898–1901." Unpublished. Box 49, Princeton Theological Seminary archives.
Harrisville, Roy A., and Walter Sundberg. *The Bible in Modern Culture: Theology and Historical-Critical Method from Spinoza to Käsemann*. Grand Rapids: Eerdmans, 1995.
Hart, D. G. "Christian Scholars, Secular Universities, and the Problem of the Antithesis." *Christian Scholar's Review* 30.4 (2001) 383–402.
———. *Defending the Faith: J. Gresham Machen and the Crisis of Conservative Protestantism in Modern America*. Baltimore: Johns Hopkins University Press, 1991.
Hart, D. G., Sean Michael Lucas, and Stephen J. Nichols, editors. *The Legacy of Jonathan Edwards: American Religion and the Evangelical Tradition*. Publication of the Reformed Bible Conference, October 26–28, 2001, Lancaster, PA. Grand Rapids: Baker Academic, 2003.
Harvey, Van Austin. *The Historian and the Believer: The Morality of Historical Knowledge and Christian Belief*. Urbana: University of Illinois Press, 1996.
Hazard, Paul. *The European Mind, 1680–1715*. Translated by J. Lewis May. Cleveland: World Pub., 1967.
Helm, Paul. "Reid and 'Reformed' Epistemology." In *Thomas Reid: Context, Influence and Significance*, 103–22. Edinburgh: Dunedin Academic, 2004.
———. "Scottish Realism." In *Dictionary of Scottish Church History & Theology*, edited by Nigel M. de. S. Cameron et al., 759. Edinburgh: T. & T. Clark, 1993.
Helseth, Paul Kjoss. "B. B. Warfield on the Apologetical Nature of Christian Scholarship: An Analysis of His Solution to the Problem of the Relationship between Christianity and Culture." *WTJ* 62.1 (Spring 2000) 89–111.
———. "B. B. Warfield's Apologetical Appeal to 'Right Reason': Evidence of a Rather Bald Rationalism'?" *Scottish Bulletin of Evangelical Theology* 16.2 (Autumn 1998) 156–77.

―――. "Moral Character and Moral Certainty: The Subjective State of the Soul and J. G. Machen's Critique of Theological Liberalism." PhD diss., Marquette University, 1996.

―――. "'Re-Imagining' the Princeton Mind: Postconservative Evangelicalism, Old Princeton, and the Rise of Neo-Fundamentalism." *Journal of the Evangelical Theological Society* 45.3 (September 2002) 427–50.

―――. "Right Reason" and the Princeton Mind: An Unorthodox Proposal. Phillipsburg, NJ: P&R, 2010.

Henry, Carl F. H. *The Uneasy Conscience of Modern Fundamentalism.* Grand Rapids: Eerdmans, 1947; reprint, 2003.

Herrera, R. A. *Reasons for Our Rhymes: An Inquiry into the Philosophy of History.* Grand Rapids: Eerdmans, 2001.

Hicks, Peter. *The Philosophy of Charles Hodge: A 19th Century Evangelical Approach to Reason, Knowledge and Truth.* Studies in American Religion 65. Lewiston, NY: E. Mellen, 1997.

Hirst, R. J. "Realism," *The Encyclopedia of Philosophy*, edited by Donald M. Borchert et al., 8:260–69. 2nd ed. New York: Macmillan, 2006.

Hodge, A. A., and B. B. Warfield. "Inspiration." *The Presbyterian Review* 2.6 (April 1881) 225–60.

Hodge, Charles. "Retrospect of the History of the *Princeton Review*." *BRep/PRev, Index Volume*, 1:11.

―――. *Systematic Theology.* 3 vols. Peabody, MA: Hendrickson, 1999.

―――. "What Is Christianity?" *BRep/PRev* 32 (1860) 118–61.

―――. *BRep/PRev* 17 (1845) 190.

Hoffecker, W. Andrew, Jr. *Piety and the Princeton Theologians: Archibald Alexander, Charles Hodge, Benjamin Warfield.* Phillipsburg, NJ: P&R, 1981.

―――. "The Relation Between the Objective and Subjective Aspects in Christian Religious Experience: A Study in the Systematic and Devotional Writings of Archibald Alexander, Charles Hodge and Benjamin B. Warfield." PhD diss., Brown University, 1970.

Holifield, E. Brooks. *Theology in America: Christian Thought from the Age of the Puritans to the Civil War.* New Haven, CT: Yale University Press, 2003.

Hope, Nicholas. *German and Scandinavian Protestantism: 1700–1918.* Oxford History of the Christian Church. Oxford: Clarendon, 1995.

Hutchison, William R. *The Modernist Impulse in American Protestantism.* Durham, NC: Duke University Press, 1992.

Johnson, Gary L. W., editor. *B. B. Warfield: Essays on His Life and Thought.* Phillipsburg, NJ: P &R, 2007.

Jordan, W. K. *The Development of Religious Toleration in England: From the Accession of James I to the Convention of the Long Parliament (1603–1640).* Cambridge, MA: Harvard University Press, 1936; reprint, Gloucester, MA: Peter Smith, 1965.

Kelly, Douglas F. "Witherspoon, John." In *Dictionary of Scottish Church History & Theology*, edited by Nigel M. de. S. Cameron et al., 880. Edinburgh: T. & T. Clark, 1993.

Kelly, J. N. D. *Early Christian Doctrines.* Rev. ed. San Francisco: Harper & Row, 1978.

Kerr, Hugh Thompson. "Warfield: The Person behind the Theology." Edited by William O. Harris. *Princeton Seminary Bulletin* 25(2004) 92.

Kuklick, Bruce "On Critical History." In *Religious Advocacy and American History*, edited by Bruce Kuklick and D. G. Hart, 54–64. Grand Rapids: Eerdmans, 1997.

Bibliography

Lee, Sang Hyun, and Allen C. Guelzo, editors. *Edwards in Our Time: Jonathan Edwards and the Shaping of American Religion*. Grand Rapids: Eerdmans, 1999.
Leff, Gordon. *Medieval Thought: St. Augustine to Ockham*. Baltimore: Penguin, 1962.
Lehrer, Keith. "Reid, Thomas." In *A Companion to Epistemology*, edited by Jonathan Dancy and Ernest Sosa, 427–28. Blackwell Companions to Philosophy 4. Cambridge, MA: Blackwell, 1992.
Lemos, Noah. "Commonsensism and Critical Cognitivism." In *A Companion to Epistemology*, edited by Jonathan Dancy and Ernest Sosa, 71–74. Blackwell Companions to Philosophy 4. Cambridge, MA: Blackwell, 1992.
Letis, Theodore P. "B. B. Warfield, Common-Sense Philosophy and Biblical Criticism." *American Presbyterians* 69 (Fall 1991) 175–90.
Levine, Joseph M. "Latitudinarians, Neoplatonists and the Ancient Wisdom." In *Philosophy, Science, and Religion in England, 1640–1700*, edited by Richard Kroll, Richard Ashcraft, and Perez Zagorin, 85–108. Cambridge: Cambridge University Press, 1992.
Lindberg, David C., and Ronald L. Numbers, editors. *When Science & Christianity Meet*. Chicago: University of Chicago Press, 2003.
Linnemann, Eta. *Biblical Criticism on Trial: How Scientific Is "Scientific Theology"?* Translated by Robert W. Yarbrough. Grand Rapids: Kregel, 2001.
———. *Historical Criticism of the Bible: Methodology or Ideology?* Translated by Robert W. Yarbrough. Grand Rapids: Baker, 1990.
———. *Is There a Synoptic Problem?: Rethinking the Literary Dependence of the First Three Gospels*. Translated by Robert W. Yarbrough. Grand Rapids: Baker, 1992.
Livingstone, William D. "The Princeton Apologetic as Exemplified by the Work of Benjamin B. Warfield and J. Gresham Machen: A Study in American Theology 1880–1930." PhD diss., Yale University, 1948.
Lloyd Jones, D. M. "Defender of the Faith." *The Banner of Truth* 89 (Fall 1971) 16–18.
Loetscher, Lefferts A. *The Broadening Church: A Study of Theological Issues in the Presbyterian Church since 1869*. Philadelphia: University of Pennsylvania Press, 1954.
———. *Facing the Enlightenment and Pietism: Archibald Alexander the Founding of Princeton Theological Seminary*. Contributions to the Study of Religion 8. Westport, CT: Greenwood, 1983.
Logan, Samuel T. Jr. "Theological Decline in Christian Institutions and the Value of Van Til's Epistemology." *WTJ* 57.1 (1995) 145–63.
Longfield, Bradley J. *The Presbyterian Controversy: Fundamentalists, Modernists, and Moderates*. Religion in America. New York: Oxford University Press, 1991.
Lloyd-Jones, Martyn. "Defender of the Faith," *Banner of Truth* 89 (Fall 1971) 16–18.
Macgregor, James. *The Apology of the Christian Religion: Historically Regarded with Reference to Supernatural Revelation and Redemption*. Edinburgh: T. & T. Clark, 1891.
Machen, J. Gresham. *Christianity and Liberalism*. New York: Macmillan, 1923.
———. *The Origin of Paul's Religion*. New York: Macmillan, 1921.
———. *The Virgin Birth of Christ*. New York: Harper, 1930.
———. *What Is Christianity? and Other Addresses*. Edited by Ned Bernard Stonehouse. Grand Rapids: Eerdmans, 1951.
Mackintosh, H. R. *Types of Modern Theology: Schleiermacher to Barth*. New York: Scribner, 1937.
Maier, Gerhard. *Biblical Hermeneutics*. Translated by Robert W. Yarbrough. Wheaton, IL: Crossway, 1994.

Bibliography

Marsden, George. "The Collapse of American Evangelical Academia." In *Faith and Rationality: Reason and Belief in God*, edited by Alvin Plantinga and Nicholas Wolterstorff, 219–64. Notre Dame: University of Notre Dame Press, 1983.

———. *Fundamentalism and American Culture:* . 2nd ed. New York: Oxford University Press, 2006.

———. *The Outrageous Idea of Christian Scholarship*. New York: Oxford University Press, 1997.

———. *The Soul of the American University: From Protestant Establishment to Established Nonbelief*. New York: Oxford University Press, 1994.

———. *Understanding Fundamentalism and Evangelicalism*. Grand Rapids: Eerdmans, 1991.

May, Henry F. *The Enlightenment in America*. New York: Oxford University Press, 1976.

McClanahan, James Samuel. "Benjamin B. Warfield: Historian of Doctrine In Defense of Orthodoxy, 1881–1921." PhD diss., Union Theological Seminary in Virginia, 1988.

McConnel, Tim. "The Old Princeton Apologetic: Common Sense or Reformed?" *Journal of the Evangelical Theological Society* 46.4 (December 2003) 647–72.

McCosh, James. "Recent Works on Kant." *The Presbyterian and Reformed Review* 1.3 (1890) 425–440.

McGrath, Alistair E. *The Genesis of Doctrine: A Study in the Foundation of Doctrinal Criticism*. Grand Rapids: Eerdmans, 1990.

———. *The Making of Modern German Christology, 1750–1990*. 2nd ed. Grand Rapids: Zondervan, 1994.

———. *Reformation Thought: An Introduction*. 2nd ed. Cambridge, MA: Blackwell, 1993.

Meeter, John E., and Roger Nicole, *A Bibliography of Benjamin Breckinridge Warfield, 1851–1921*. Phillipsburg, NJ: P&R, 1974.

Ménégoz, "The Theology of Auguste Sabatier of Paris." Translated by J. Dick Fleming. *Expository Times* 15 (1903–4) 30–34.

Muller, Richard A. "Calvin and the 'Calvinists': Assessing Continuities and Discontinuities between the Reformation and Orthodoxy, Part I." *Calvin Theological Journal* 30 (1995) 345–75.

———. "Calvin and the 'Calvinists': Assessing Continuities and Discontinuities between the Reformation and Orthodoxy, Part II." *Calvin Theological Journal* 31 (1996) 125–60.

———. "Historiography in the Service of Theology and Worship: Toward Dialogue with John Frame." *WTJ* 59 (1997) 301–10.

———. *Post-Reformation Reformed Dogmatics: The Rise and Development of Reformed Orthodoxy, ca. 1520 to ca. 1725*. 4 vols. 2nd ed. Grand Rapids: Baker Academic, 2003.

———. "The Problem of Protestant Scholasticism—A Review and Definition." In *Reformation and Scholasticism: An Ecumenical Enterprise*, edited by Willem J. van Asselt and Eef Dekker, 45–64. Grand Rapids: Baker Academic, 2001.

Murphey, Nancey C. *Beyond Liberalism and Fundamentalism: How Modern and Postmodern Philosophy Set the Theological Agenda*. Valley Forge, PA: Trinity, 1996.

Nash, Ronald H. *Faith and Reason: Searching for a Rational Faith*. Grand Rapids: Zondervan, 1988.

Naugle, David K. *Worldview: The History of a Concept*. Grand Rapids: Eerdmans, 2002.

Bibliography

Neur, Werner, *Adolf Schlatter: A Biography of Germany's Premier Biblical Theologian.* Translated Robert W. Yarbrough. Grand Rapids: Baker, 1995.

Noll, Mark A. *America's God: From Jonathan Edwards to Abraham Lincoln.* New York: Oxford University Press, 2002.

———. "Common Sense Traditions and American Evangelical Thought." *American Quarterly* 37.2 (1985) 216–38.

———. *Princeton and the Republic, 1768–1822: The Search for a Christian Enlightenment in the Era of Samuel Stanhope Smith.* Princeton: Princeton University Press, 1989.

———. "The *Princeton Review.*" *WTJ* 50 (1988) 283–304.

———, editor. *The Princeton Theology 1812–1921: Scripture, Science, and Theological Method from Archibald Alexander to Benjamin Breckenridge Warfield.* Grand Rapids: Baker, 2001.

———. *The Scandal of the Evangelical Mind.* Grand Rapids: Eerdmans, 1994.

Oberman, Heiko A. *Forerunners of the Reformation: The Shape of Late Medieval Thought.* Philadelphia: Fortress, 1981.

———. *The Harvest of Medieval Theology: Gabriel Biel and Late Medieval Nominalism.* Cambridge, MA: Harvard University Press, 1963.

Orr, James. "Criticism of the Bible." In *The International Standard Bible Encyclopaedia* edited by James Orr, 2:748–53. Chicago: Howard-Severance, 1930.

Ozment, Steven. *The Age of Reform (1250–1550): An Intellectual and Religious History of Late Medieval and Reformation Europe.* New Haven, CT: Yale University Press, 1981.

Patton, Francis Landey. "Benjamin Breckinridge Warfield, D.D., LL.D., Litt.D.: A Memorial Address." *Princeton Theological Review* 29 (July 1921) 369–91.

Pearcey, Nancy. *Total Truth: Liberating Christianity from Its Cultural Captivity.* Wheaton, IL: Crossway, 2004.

Pelikan, Jaroslav. *The Christian Tradition: A History of the Development of Doctrine.* 5 vols. Chicago: University of Chicago Press, 1971–1989.

Penelhum, Terence. "Thomas Reid and Contemporary Apologetic." *Reid Studies: An International Review of Scottish Philosophy* 2.1 (Autumn 1998) 3–14.

Plantinga, Alvin. "Reason and Belief in God." In *Faith and Rationality: Reason and Belief in God*, edited by Alvin Plantinga and Nicholas Wolterstorff, 16–93. Notre Dame: University of Notre Dame Press, 1983.

Popkin, Richard. *The History of Skepticism from Erasmus to Descartes.* Rev. ed. New York: Harper & Row, 1968.

Princeton versus the New Divinity: The Meaning of Sin, Grace, Salvation, Revival. Carlisle, PA: Banner of Truth Trust, 2001.

Rayburn, Robert S. "The Presbyterian Doctrines of Covenant Children, Covenant Nurture, and Covenant Succession." *Presbyterion* 22. 2 (Fall, 1996) 76–109.

Reid, Thomas. *Essays on the Intellectual Powers of Man.* Cambridge, MA: MIT Press, 1969.

Rian, Edwin H. *The Presbyterian Conflict.* Grand Rapids: Eerdmans, 1940; reprint, Philadelphia: Committee for the Historian of the Orthodox Presbyterian Church, 1992.

Ridderbos, Herman N. *Redemptive History and the New Testament Scriptures.* 2nd rev. ed. Translated by H. De Jongste, revised by Richard B. Gaffin Jr. Phillipsburg, NJ: P&R, 1988.

Riddlebarger, Kim. "The Lion of Princeton: Benjamin Breckinridge Warfield on Apologetics, Theological Method and Polemics." PhD diss., Fuller Seminary, 1997.

Rogers, Jack, and Donald K. McKim. *The Authority and Interpretation of the Bible: An Historical Approach*. New York: Harper & Row, 1979.

Sabatier, Auguste. *Outlines of a Philosophy of Religion Based on Psychology and History*. London: Hodder & Stoughton, 1897.

Sandeen, Ernest R. *The Roots of Fundamentalism: British and American Millenarianism, 1800–1930*. Chicago: Chicago University Press, 1970.

Schlatter, Adolf. "The Theology of the New Testament and Dogmatics." In *The Nature of New Testament Theology*, edited by Robert Morgan, 117–66. London: SCM, 1973.

Schleiermacher, Friedrich. *On Religion: Speeches to Its Cultured Despisers*. Translated by John Oman. New York: Harper, 1958.

Scholder, Klaus. *The Birth of Modern Critical Theology: Origins and Problems of Biblical Criticism in the Seventeenth Century*. London: SCM, 1990.

Schreiner, Susan E. *The Theater of His Glory: Nature and the Natural Order in the Thought of John Calvin*. Studies in Historical Theology 3. Durham, NC: Labyrinth, 1991.

Seeman, Bradley N. "Evangelical Historiography beyond the 'Outward Clash': A Case Study on the Alternation Approach." *Christian Scholar's Review* 33.1 (Fall 2003) 95–124.

Silva, Moises. "Old Princeton, Westminster and Inerrancy." *WTJ* 50 (1988) 65–80.

Sloan, Douglas. *Faith and Knowledge: Mainline Protestantism and American Higher Education*. Louisville: Westminster John Knox, 1994.

Smith, Christian. *American Evangelicalism: Embattled and Thriving*. Chicago: University of Chicago Press, 1998.

———. "Introduction: Rethinking the Secularization of American Public Life." In *The Secular Revolution: Power, Interests and Conflict in the Secularization of American Public Life*, 1–90. Berkeley: University of California Press, 2002.

Smith, David P. "The Scientifically Constructive Scholarship of B. B. Warfield." *Mid-America Journal of Theology* 15 (2004) 87–123.

Spinoza, Benedict de. *A Theologico-Political Treatise and A Political Treatise*. Translated by R. H. M. Elwes. New York: Dover, 1951.

Sprunger, Keith L. *The Learned Doctor William Ames: Dutch Backgrounds of English and American Puritanism*. Urbana: University of Illinois Press, 1972.

Stackhouse, John. *Humble Apologetics: Defending the Faith Today*. New York: Oxford University Press, 2002.

Stelten, Leo F. *Dictionary of Ecclesiastical Latin*. Peabody, MA: Hendrickson, 1995.

Stevens, G. B. "Auguste Sabatier and the Paris School of Theology." *Hibbert Journal* 1.3 (1903) 553–68.

Stewart, John William. "The Tethered Theology: Biblical Criticism, Common Sense Philosophy, and the Princeton Theologians, 1812–1860." PhD diss., University of Michigan, 1990.

Stonehouse, Ned B. *J. Gresham Machen: A Biographical Memoir*. 3rd ed. Carlisle, PA: Banner of Truth Trust, 1987.

Stout, Harry S. and Robert M. Taylor Jr. "Studies of Religion in American Society: The State of the Art." In *New Directions in American Religious History*, edited by D. G. Hart and Harry S. Stout, 15–47. New York: Oxford University Press, 1997.

Stumpf, Samuel Enoch. *Socrates to Sartre: A History of Philosophy*. 5th ed. New York: McGraw-Hill, 1993.

Sundberg, Walter. "Princeton School." In *Dictionary for Theological Interpretation of the Bible*, edited by Kevin J. Vanhoozer et al., 621–22. Grand Rapids: Baker Academic, 2005.

Bibliography

Sweeney, Douglas A. *The American Evangelical Story: A History of the Movement.* Grand Rapids: Baker Academic, 2005.

———. *Nathaniel Taylor, New Haven Theology, and the Legacy of Jonathan Edwards.* Religion in America. New York: Oxford University Press, 2003.

Sweeney, Douglas A., and Allen C. Guelzo, editors. *The New England Theology: From Jonathan Edwards to Edward Amasa Park.* Grand Rapids: Baker Academic, 2006.

Taylor, Marion Ann. *The Old Testament in the Old Princeton School (1812–1929).* San Francisco: Mellen Research University Press, 1992.

Tillich, Paul. *A History of Christian Thought: From Its Judaic and Hellenistic Origins to Existentialism.* Edited by Carl E. Braaten. New York: Simon and Schuster.

"Translation of Beckii Monogrammata Hermeneutices N. T." *BRep* 1.1 (1825) 1–122.

"Translation of Tittmann on Historical Interpretation." *BRep* 1.1 (1825) 123–53.

"Translation of an Extract from Staeudlin's *Geschicte der Theologischen Wissenchaften.*" *BRep* 1.2 (1825) 199–235.

Tulloch, John. *Rational Theology and Christian Philosophy in England in the 17th Century.* 2 vols. 1874; reprint, Hildesheim: Georg Olms Verlagsbuchhandlung, 1966.

Turretin, Francis. *Institutes of Elenctic Theology.* 3 vols. Translated by George Musgrave Geiger, edited by James T. Dennison Jr. Phillipsburg, NJ: P&R, 1992–1997.

Van Cleve, James. "Reid, Thomas." In *Encyclopedia of Philosophy*, edited by Donald M. Borchert et al., 8:322–30. 2nd ed. New York: Macmillan, 2006.

Van Til, Cornelius. *A Christian Theory of Knowledge.* Phillipsburg, NJ: P&R, 1969.

———. *The Defense of the Faith.* Grand Rapids: Baker, 1972.

Vander Stelt, John C. *Philosophy and Scripture: A Study in Old Princeton and Westminster Theology.* Marlton, NJ: Mack, 1978.

Vanhoozer, Kevin J. *Is There a Meaning in This Text?: The Bible, the Reader, and the Morality of Literary Knowledge.* Grand Rapids: Zondervan, 1998.

Wallace, Peter J. "The Foundations of Reformed Biblical Theology: The Development of Old Testament Theology at Old Princeton, 1812–1932." *WTJ* 59 (1997) 41–69.

Warfield, Benjamin Breckinridge. "Dr. Briggs' Critical Method." *The Interior* 14 (February 4, 1883). Warfield Papers, box 53, Princeton Theological Seminary archives.

———. "Dr. Duffield's Proposition to the Presbytery." *The Presbyterian*, September 12, 1900. Warfield Papers, box 53, Princeton Theological Seminary archives.

———. *Faith and Life.* 1916; reprint, Carlisle, PA: Banner of Truth Trust, 1990.

———. *An Introduction to the Textual Criticism of the New Testament.* London: Hodder & Stoughton, 1886.

———. *The Lord of Glory: A Study of the Designations of Our Lord in the New Testament with Especial Reference to His Deity.* New York: American Tract Society, 1907.

———. *The Plan of Salvation.* 5 lectures delivered at the Princeton Summer School of Theology, June 1914. 1915; reprint, Boonton, NJ: Simpson, 1989.

———. "The Religious Element in the Preparation for the Ministry." *The Presbyterian Observer.* Baltimore, October 15, 1885. Warfield Papers, box 53, Princeton Theological Seminary archives.

———. "Review of Dr. Wildeboer's treatise on *The Literature of the Old Testament in Its Chronological Sequence.*" *The Presbyterian and Reformed Review* 6.23 (1895) 537.

———. "Revision and the Third Chapter." *The Presbyterian Banner.* August 30, 1900. Warfield MSS Scrapbooks, vol. 1 (1900–11), box 53, Princeton Theological Seminary archives.

———. "Revision and the Third Chapter." *The Presbyterian Banner.* September 6, 1900. Warfield MSS Scrapbooks, vol. 1(1900–11), box 53, Princeton Theological Seminary archives.

———. Select Correspondence, 1876–1883. Warfield Papers, box 13, Princeton Theological Seminary archives.

———. *Selected Shorter Writings of Benjamin B. Warfield*. Edited by John E. Meeter. 2 vols. Phillipsburg, NJ: P&R, 1970, 1973; reprint, 2001.

———. *The Works of Benjamin B. Warfield*. 10 vols. New York: Oxford University Press, 1927–1932; reprint, Grand Rapids: Baker, 1991.

Warfield, Ethelbert D. "Biographical Sketch of Benjamin Breckinridge Warfield." In *The Works of Benjamin B. Warfield*, 1:v–ix. New York: Oxford University Press, 1927.

Wells, David F. *Above All Earthly Pow'rs: Christ in a Postmodern World*. Grand Rapids: Eerdmans, 2005.

———. *The Courage to Be Protestant: Truth-Lovers, Marketers, and Emergents in the Postmodern World*. Grand Rapids: Eerdmans, 2008.

———. *God in the Wasteland: The Reality of Truth in a World of Fading Dreams*. Grand Rapids: Eerdmans, 1994.

———. *Losing Our Virtue: Why the Church Must Recover Its Moral Vision*. Grand Rapids: Eerdmans, 1998.

———. *No Place for Truth, or, Whatever Happened to Evangelical Theology?* Grand Rapids: Eerdmans, 1993.

———. "On Being Framed." *WTJ* 59 (1997) 293–300.

———, editor. *Reformed Theology in America: A History of Its Modern Development*. Grand Rapids: Baker, 1997.

———. "The Theologian's Craft." In *Doing Theology in Today's World: Essays in Honor of Kenneth S. Kantzer*, edited by John D. Woodbridge and Thomas McComiskey, 171–94. Grand Rapids: Zondervan, 1991.

Wilkens, Steve, and Alan G. Padgett. *Christianity & Western Thought*, vol. 2: *Faith and Reason in the 19th Century*. Downers Grove, IL: InterVarsity, 2000.

Wiley, Basil. *The Seventeenth Century Background: Studies in the Thought of the Age in Relation to Poetry and Religion*. New York: Columbia University Press, 1977.

Williams, Daniel H. *Evangelicals and Tradition: The Formative Influence of the Early Church*. Grand Rapids: Baker Academic, 2005.

———. *Retrieving the Tradition and Renewing Evangelicalism: A Primer for Suspicious Protestants*. Grand Rapids: Eerdmans, 1999.

Willis-Watkins, E. Davis. "*Systematic Theology* by Charles Hodge." *American Presbyterians* 66 (1988) 269–72.

Wolterstorff, Nicholas. "Can Belief in God Be Rational If It Has No Foundations?" *Faith and Rationality: Reason and Belief in God*, edited by Alvin Plantinga and Nicholas Wolterstorff, 135–86. Notre Dame: University of Notre Dame Press, 1983.

———. "Thomas Reid and Rationality." In *Rationality in the Calvinian Tradition*, edited by Hendrik Hart, Johan van der Hoeven, and Nicholas Wolterstorff, 43–70. Christian Studies Today. Lanham, MD: University Press of America, 1983.

———. *Thomas Reid and the Story of Epistemology*. New York: Cambridge University Press, 2001.

Woodbridge, John D. *Biblical Authority: A Critique of the Rogers/McKim Proposal*. Grand Rapids: Zondervan, 1982.

Yarbrough, Robert W. *The Salvation-Historical Fallacy?: Reassessing the History of New Testament Theology*. History of Biblical Interpretation 2. Leiden: Deo, 2004.

Zaspel, Fred G. *The Theology of B. B. Warfield: A Systematic Summary*. Wheaton, IL: Crossway, 2010.

www.ingramcontent.com/pod-product-compliance
Lightning Source LLC
Chambersburg PA
CBHW070013010526
44117CB00011B/1551